To Anthony

with congratulations
on the occasion of your
Graduation
12th July 2013.

Bill (+Kathy)

Unity and Diversity in Christ: Interpreting Paul in Context

Unity and Diversity in Christ: Interpreting Paul in Context

Collected Essays

WILLIAM S. CAMPBELL

CASCADE *Books* · Eugene, Oregon

Cascade Books
An Imprint of Wipf and Stock Publishers
199 W. 8th Ave., Suite 3
Eugene, OR 97401

www.wipfandstock.com

ISBN 13: 978-1-62032-293-2

Cataloguing-in-Publication data:

Campbell, William S.

Unity and diversity in Christ : interpreting Paul in context : collected essays / William S. Campbell.

xii + 256 pp. ; 23 cm. Includes bibliographical references and indexes.

ISBN 13: 978-1-62032-293-2

1. Paul, the Apostle, Saint. 2. Bible. Epistles of Paul—Criticism, interpretation, etc. 3. Gentiles in the New Testament. 4. Jews in the New Testament. I. Title.

BS2655.J4 C34 2013

Manufactured in the U.S.A.

Permissions

I wish to thank the following publishers for permission to include the essays in this volume:

"The Contribution of Traditions to Paul's Theology: A Response to Calvin Roetzel." In *Pauline Theology Vol. II: 1 and 2 Corinthians*, edited by David M. Hay, 234–54. Atlanta: Society of Biblical Literature, 2002 (originally published by Fortress Press, 1993).

"The Rule of Faith in Romans 12:1—15:13: The Obligation of Obedience to Christ as the Only Adequate Response to the Mercies of God." In *Pauline Theology Vol.III: Romans*, edited by David M. Hay and E. Elizabeth Johnson, 259–86. Atlanta: Society of Biblical Literature, 2002 (originally published by Fortress Press, 1995).

"Divergent Images of Paul and His Mission." In *Reading Israel in Romans: Legitimacy and Plausibility of Divergent Interpretations*, edited by Cristina Grenholm and Daniel Patte, 187–211. Romans through History and Cultures Series vol. 1. London: T. & T. Clark, 2000.

"'All God's Beloved in Rome': Jewish Roots and Christian Identity." In *Celebrating Romans: Template for Pauline Theology. Essays in Honor of Robert Jewett*, edited by Sheila McGinn, 67–82. Grand Rapids: Eerdmans 2004.

"Unity and Diversity in the Church: Transformed Identities and the Peace of Christ in Ephesians." *Transformation* 25.1 (2008) 15–30. SAGE Publishing.

"The Addressees of Paul's Letter to the Romans: Assemblies of God in House Churches and Synagogues." In *Between Gospel and Election: Explorations in the Interpretation of Romans 9–11*, edited by Florian Wilk and J Ross Wagner, 171–96. Tübingen: Mohr Siebeck, 2010.

"'Let Us Maintain Peace' (Rom. 5:2): Reconciliation and Social Responsibility." In *The Bible in Academy, Church, and Culture: Essays in Honour of John T. Williams*, edited by Alan P. F. Sell, 58–80. Eugene, OR: Pickwick, 2011.

"Universality and Particularity in Paul's Understanding and Strategy of Mission." In *Paul as Missionary*, edited by Trevor J. Burke and Brian S. Rosner, 195–208. London: T. & T. Clark, 2011.

"'I Rate All Things as Loss': Paul's Puzzling Accounting System: Judaism as Loss or the Re-Evaluation of All Things in Christ?" In *Celebrating Paul: Festschrift in Honour of J. A.Fitzmyer and J. Murphy-O'Connor*, edited by Peter Spitaler, 39–61. CBQ Supplements Series 48. Washington, DC: Catholic Biblical Association of America, 2012.

To Daniel Patte
a valued friend
who acknowledges plausibility within diversity of interpretation

Contents

Abbreviations

Bib	*Biblica*
BibInt	*Biblical Interpretation*
BJRL	*Bulletin of the John Rylands University Library Manchester*
BR	*Biblical Research*
BTB	*Biblical Theology Bulletin*
BZ	*Biblische Zeitschrift*
CBQ	*Catholic Biblical Quarterly*
CBQMS	*Catholic Biblical Quarterly Monograph Series*
EvTheol	*Evangelische Theologie*
HTR	*Harvard Theological Review*
IBS	*Irish Biblical Studies*
ICC	*International Critical Commentary*
INT	*Interpretation*
JAC	*Jahrbuch für Antike und Christentum*
JBL	*Journal of Biblical Literature*
JBV	*Journal of Beliefs and Values*
JES	*Journal of Ecumenical Studies*
JR	*Journal of Religion*
JSJ	*Journal for the Study of Judaism*
JSNT	*Journal for the Study of the New Testament*

Abbreviations

JSNTSup	Journal for the Study of the New Testament Supplement Series
JSOT	Journal for the Study of the Old Testament
JSP	Journal for the Study of the Pseudepigrapha
JSR	Journal for Scriptural Reasoning
JTS	Journal of Theological Studies
NovT	Novum Testamentum
NRSV	New Revised Standard Version
NTS	New Testament Studies
RB	Revue Biblique
RSR	Recherches de science religieuse
SBL	Society of Biblical Literature
SBLASP	SBL Abstracts and Seminar Papers
SBLDS	SBL Dissertations Series
SBLMS	Society of Biblical Literature Monograph Series
SBLSP	SBL Seminar Papers
SBLSS	SBL Semeia Studies
SJT	Scottish Journal of Theology
SNTSMS	Society of New Testament Studies Monograph Series
SR	Studies in Religion/Sciences religieuses
ST	Studia Theologica
TR	Theologische Rundschau
TynBul	Tyndale Bulletin
TZ	Theologische Zeitschrift
WBC	Word Biblical Commentary
WMANT	Wissenschaftliche Monographien zum Alten und Neuen Testament
WUNT	Wissenschaftliche Untersuchungen zum Neuen Testament
WW	Word and World

ZNW   *Zeitschrift für die neutestamentliche Wissenschaft*

ZTK   *Zeitschrift für Theologie und Kirche*

Trajectories of Conversations with Paul and Others

T HE FOLLOWING ESSAYS ARE the product of almost twenty years of research, and represent my continuing focus on several topics that may
be grouped under the following themes: Paul's Jewish roots, diversity within
the Christ-movement, and the formation of identity in the Pauline communities.[1] All of these are investigated in conjunction with my long-term
interest in the letter to the Romans, especially its historical context, and on
the particularity of Paul's statements in his letters as made in, and directed
to, a specific set of circumstances. These statements are virtually unique
and non-recurring and must not be generalized and universalized.[2] To read
Romans in light of the Galatians context, or vice versa, is to create an artificial and unwarranted "Paulinism" that is a product of scholarly invention
rather than of historical existence. Similarly it is my contention that we must
oppose the tendency to harmonize and correlate Paul's particular statements into some system of theology to which the apostle neither adhered
nor even aspired.[3] When we join what Paul kept separate, or when we divide

---

1. Thus, in this introduction to the content of the essays, I will consider them thematically rather than simply individually in their numerical sequence.

2. As I will demonstrate in chapters 6 and 11, even when Paul repeats the same words
in differing letter contexts, the meaning of his statements must be sought separately in
relation to their place in the argument and within the context of each letter, rather than
attempting to harmonize these into something that Paul did not actually say.

3. As may be recognized from this emphasis, there are echoes of Krister Stendahl's
Paul among Jews and Gentiles and, whilst benefitting from Stendahl's revised perspec-
tive on Paul, I point out that my 1972 doctoral research on "The Purpose of Paul in the
Letter to the Romans: A Survey of Romans I–XI with Particular Reference to Chapters
IX–XI," was completed prior to the publication of this volume, and that I was one of the
first in the last century to stress in a sustained interpretation the significance of Romans

what Paul put together, we produce a different outcome and may develop a hermeneutic alien to Paul's purposes. Paul both held, and was held by, theological convictions that can be recognized and explored to produce a meaningful description of his thought,[4] but this can only be achieved when his statements are read in coherence with the context in which these were expressed.

One of the most significant aspects of a thoroughly contextual reading of Paul's letters is the fact that they are all addressed to gentiles. Of course, almost all of the first generation of leaders in the Pauline communities were Jewish, and there is no suggestion that Jewish Christ-followers would not have been welcome in such communities had they so wished, but the incontrovertible fact is that Paul's mission was to the gentiles, and his letters are specifically addressed to these. In chapter 8 of this volume, "The Addressees of Paul's Letter to the Romans: Assemblies of God in House Churches and Synagogues," I argue this with particular reference to Romans. As gentiles, the Pauline communities represent only one section of the early Christ-movement, and thus only one way of following Christ. Such phrases as "the churches of the gentiles" (Rom 16:3–5) alongside the inclusive "all the churches of Christ" (Rom 16:16) should remind us of this. If, despite disagreements as in all human families, the early Christ-followers did acknowledge and accept as legitimate two specific and differing ways of following Christ, the missions to the circumcision and to the gentiles respectively, it is quite clear that neither Peter nor Paul were attempting to compete with each other's mission, nor working towards a monochrome Christ-movement in which Jewish and gentile members were no longer visible as such.[5] To read this perspective into Paul's letters is grossly anachronistic, as likewise is the reading of Paul in the light of the Gospels or in light of later New Testament and early Christian literature. My specific vision of Paul's activity and thought emerges mainly as a result of a combination of a contextual reading and an emphasis upon a conscious awareness in Paul of diversity in Christ. This is not to deny that there may not have been differing perceptions of Paul's mission in circulation even in his own day, a possibility that I consider in chapter 4, "Divergent Images of Paul and His

9–11 as the climax of Paul's argument in Romans.

4. As T. R. Donaldson has demonstrated in his *Paul and the Gentiles* and *Paul, Judaism and the Gentiles*. I prefer to regard convictions not as fixed beliefs held by a person as if they can freely select which items they wish to affirm, but rather as Daniel Patte (*Paul's Faith and the Power of the Gospel*, 11–17) has noted, "faith is nothing other than being held by a system of convictions."

5. As J. Christiaan Beker (*Paul, the Apostle,* 126) recognizes, "because Paul is convinced that the apostolic college is in agreement on the core of the gospel, the authority of the other apostles is as weighty in the churches as Paul's own."

Mission." As will be evident in the course of reading these essays, my thinking, whilst remaining reasonably consistent throughout the period of their composition, has inevitably developed in certain respects. Certain nuances have become more emphasized and certain details elaborated and clarified. I hope, therefore, that those who share the development of thought on this journey may find my conclusions easier to understand in the light of this.

As is indicated by the second essay in this collection, "The Contribution of Traditions to Paul's Theology," I have maintained a strong interest in how Paul theologizes, particularly in which elements of his thought are original, and which he shares with contemporary Jews and others. I recognize that whatever the extent of this commonality, it must have been deeply affected by the Apostle's understanding of the Christ-event. Yet I also recognize that we must not too readily presume a complete disjuncture between Saul the Pharisee and Paul the apostle. Even when the Damascus road experience of Paul is emphasized, the closest parallel to his own thought world cannot be the psychologically slanted experiences of the last century, but rather the call of the great prophets Isaiah, Jeremiah, and Ezekiel. And even with this terminology, it has to be acknowledged that Paul, in contrast to the prophets, is called not to address the people of Israel, but rather the nations who did not share in her inheritance. He thus unavoidably opened up new issues not merely such as were internal to Israel but, more seriously, those concerning Israel's relation to the nations.[6] Here we must clearly distinguish which effects or outcomes were intended or possibly foreseen by Paul, and which emerged incidentally or only partially as a result of his activities. It is entirely unwarranted to blame Paul for what happened in the years following his death or even in subsequent centuries. As the historical leader of the gentile mission, he bears a certain responsibility, but none for what he could not have foreseen or possibly would have supported. In any case, what is important is not the description of Paul's experience, whatever that may be, but the outcome that he would view himself as henceforth living "in Christ," and working with Christ, in a task for which he believed himself chosen and called. And as will also become evident in chapter 2, "The Contribution of Traditions to Paul's Theology," if Paul had not already possessed an adequate

---

6. But even this new factor has to be viewed from the perspective that the story of the patriarchs in Gen 12–50 is set within the primordial accounts of the creation of the world and the origins of human culture in Gen 1–11, so that "the God who eventually calls Abraham to be the progenitor of a special nation is first encountered as the creator of the cosmos and the providential overseer of every nation. . . . Israel's story is thus set within the universal story of God's dealings with the whole human race, rather than over against it" (Donaldson, *Judaism and the Gentiles*, 477).

framework of understanding,[7] acquired specifically as a result of his Jewish faith, he would have had no way of comprehending the meaning of Christ or what response this required of him. As I have noted elsewhere,[8] imported knowledge requires a plausibility structure if it is not to be meaningless, and if the Christ-movement as a whole is not to be portrayed as "a metaphysical miracle without concrete relationship to the Jewish community."[9] For the meaningful integration of something new with what is already within one's grasp, there has to be the possibility to relate what is new to previous experience and to prior existing categories and paradigms.

The Scriptures of Israel were the most probable source of Paul's understanding of the Christ-event as "the kerygmatic story of God's action through Jesus Christ."[10] These constituted the record of how God's actions in relation to Israel in the past had been interpreted, and as such could be related afresh to contemporary events as a means of illumination and explanation,[11] and as providing dominant motifs for Paul's gospel. Like many Jews of his time, Paul was an interpreter and re-interpreter of the Scriptures. Thus in Rom 9:24, Paul reinterpreted the Hosea text concerning the "not my people," to give grounds for the future restoration of Israel (and not merely as indicating the incoming of the gentiles, as many commentators have failed to recognize).[12] It was in interaction with these Scriptures that Paul was able to slowly conceive a theological explanation of how and why God had acted in the Christ-event, and thus to interpret the gospel.[13] Hence his understanding of the new events that had recently taken place was unlikely to be one that rejected or depreciated God's prior revelation to Israel. As Harink has argued, "God in his

---

7. On how Paul's theologizing operated in the space between Jewish and gentile cultures, thus negotiating the meaning of the Christ-event in relation to, and in appreciation of, both Jewish and gentile identity, see Ehrensperger, *Paul at the Crossroads*.

8. Imported knowledge requires a social base—a plausibility structure—otherwise the knowledge becomes meaningless because it has been separated from the authenticating community. Cf. my *Paul and the Creation of Christian Identity*, 143. Similarly, H. C. Kee (*Knowing the Truth*, 6) notes, "knowledge throughout the range of human inquiry is social in nature and oriented within a community sharing convictions and assumptions."

9. As Beker (somewhat harshly in my view) describes the view of Jesus in John's Gospel, *Paul the Apostle*, 328.

10. Cf. Hays, "Crucified with Christ," 231–32.

11. On this see Schueler, "Theology as Wintess," 263–67.

12. I propose a new alternative interpretation of Rom 9:24 in this regard in chapter 4, "Divergent Images of Paul and His Mission," 78–81.

13. Cf. Beker's (*Paul the Apostle*, 94) description of Paul, "Paul is not a dogmatic theologian but an interpreter of the gospel who is engaged in a hermeneutic that fits the occasion."

apocalyptic action cannot be unfaithful to his creative and elective action."[14] If otherwise, it would be hard to explain how the Scriptures of Israel could be used as a means to denigrate Israel. But, despite its basis in the Scriptures, it must be asserted that Paul's theologizing was radical and tended to transform everything that came within its orbit through his experience of Christ. Beker regards Jewish apocalyptic as the "substratum and master symbolism of Paul's thought because it constituted the linguistic world of Paul the Pharisee and therefore formed the indispensable filter, context, and grammar by which he appropriated and interpreted the Christ-event."[15]

Whilst the Christ-event is something radically new, it is not so new that this action of God is entirely without precedent in divine actions in the exodus or at Sinai. It is significant, for example, that Paul, after referring in Rom 9:24 to the call of people into the Christ-movement "not from the Jews only but also from the gentiles," can proceed in Rom 11:29 to use the same term "call of God" without any qualification, and with reference only to the people of Israel.[16] Few scholars would totally deny any element of continuity between God's actions in relation to Israel and in the Christ-event, but it is in the interpretation of the extent and significance of this continuity that readings diverge. Even E. P. Sanders, despite all his excellent rebuttal of biased and unwarranted claims concerning Judaism as a legalistic religion, can still assert that Paul did not affirm the twin pillars of election and covenant in his revision of the religion of Israel.[17] In my view this indicates that Sanders did not go far enough in rehabilitating Paul in his Jewish context.

In contrast to Sanders, more recent research indicates that covenantal renewal conceptions and terminology make better sense of Paul's

14. Harink, *Paul among the Postliberals*, 179 n.34.

15. "Recasting Pauline Theology: The Coherence-Contingency Scheme as Interpretive Model," 17. Jouette Bassler ("Pauline Theology: Whence and Whither?," 11) uses the image of a lens to demonstrate how everything Paul touches is creatively transformed but concludes that it is "necessary to think in terms of a more complex series of activities, *all of which* contribute to Paul's theology and none of which in isolation is Paul's theology."

16. Yet despite his use of common calling terminology in relation to both Israel and those in Christ, Paul never calls gentiles "Israelites" or includes them within the term Israel, a view now increasingly accepted, which I have consistently maintained throughout my academic career, Cf. my article "Israel" (first published in the *Dictionary of Paul and His Letters*, edited by Gerald Hawthorn et al., 441–46. Downers Grove, IL: InterVarsity, 1993, and republished in *The IVP Dictionary of the New Testament: A One Volume Compendium of Biblical Scholarship*, edited by Dan Red, 523–29. Downers Grove, IL, InterVarsity, 2004) My stance on the place of gentiles is that they have been "brought near" to, but are not fully incorporated into, Israel (cf. Eph 2:13).

17. E. P. Sanders, *Paul and Palestinian Judaism*, 514. Similarly, E. P. Sanders, *Paul, the Law and the Jewish People*, 46–47.

argumentation in 2 Cor 3 in particular. The re-ratification of the covenant does not imply an entirely new covenant but rather the renewal and confirmation of the covenant relationship in a new context.[18] Sanders failed to view participation in Christ as coherent with some form of covenantal theology, as Morna Hooker famously observed.[19] But if and when we acknowledge the importance of renewal terminology, this also means giving adequate recognition of the fact, and the significance, of this renewal in our representation of Judaism,[20] and likewise in the lives of those Jews who chose to become Christ-followers, issues that I must now consider.

In my dissertation research on Romans, completed in 1972, I had come to the conclusion that Paul sought, amongst other goals in this letter, to defend a Jewish lifestyle as permissible for those in Christ of Jewish descent.[21] If these were not to be discriminated against, they too must be permitted to retain all those elements of their way of life that were not found to be in conflict with the claims of Christ. This was in the 1970s when identity research had not yet influenced New Testament scholarship.[22] Some twenty years later in my SBL essay on Rom 12:1—15:13 ("The Rule of Faith," chapter 3 of this volume), instead of interpreting Paul as allowing individuals, whether of Jewish or gentile background, to choose which lifestyle they would follow, I concluded—despite an interesting proposal by Paul Sampley[23]—that it was

18. Cf. Blanton ,"Paul's Covenantal Theology in 2 Corinthians 2:14–7:4," 61–71.

19. Hooker, "Paul and 'Covenantal Nomism,'" 47. On this see my "Covenantal Theology and Participation in Christ," 41–60.

20. Thus I consider J. Louis Martyn's stark contrast between flesh and spirit in apocalyptic opposition (as, for example, in his "Apocalyptic Antinomies in Paul's Letter to the Galatians," 410–24, and "Events in Galatia," 160–79), to be an inadequate representation of Paul's thought, which follows a "how much more" pattern rather than one of stark opposition between the Testaments. Flesh and Spirit in Paul relate to an ethical, not an ontological dualism. See McGinn, "Feminists and Paul in Romans 8:18–23," 29. Cf. also Nanos, "Inter-Christian Approaches," 255–69.

21. That Jewishness was an issue in Rome at the time Paul wrote his letter is indicated by the reference to "calling yourself a Jew" in 2:19. Whatever the precise historical reference here, two things are clear: either someone who is not by birth a Jew adopts this identity (which is my view) or, alternatively, someone who is a Jew is reminded of the essential characteristics of living Jewishly. In either case Jewish identity or living Jewishly is the main issue. Cf. my *Paul and the Creation of Christian Identity*, 105–7.

22. The interest in the social aspects of early Christianity began properly in the mid-seventies as, for example, in the SNTS Annual Meeting in Paris, and in A. Malherbe's 1975 Rockwall Lectures, *Social Aspects of Early Christianity*. John Gager ("Social Description and Sociological Explanation in Early Christianity," 428–40) stated in 1979, "As recently as five years ago, scarcely anyone would have ventured to predict a revival of interest in the social history of early Christianity. As things stand now, however, the case for the legitimacy and viability of the enterprise is clearly established and accepted."

23. Sampley, "The Weak and the Strong," 40–52.

not individuals who would determine which form of lifestyle they would follow,[24] but rather groups and leaders of such groups. Hence Jewishness, or as I came to understand, Jewish identity,[25] was both legitimate and relevant for Jews and should be retained in Christ.[26] If Christ as the promised one of Israel apparently lived life as a Jew, there should be no contradiction in his followers, even after the outpouring of the Holy Spirit upon the gentiles, continuing to live the same way (as did innumerable Christ-followers for several centuries later).

Romans 14–15 is the key passage for establishing the legitimacy of Christ-followers living "Jewishly." Of course, by the same argument these chapters also confirm the right of gentile Christ-followers, despite substantial difference, likewise to retain their identity as gentiles in Christ. The basis of this argument lies in Paul's understanding of being in Christ as involving a transformation of Christ-followers and of their social and communal life, rather than a complete rejection of all past cultural patterns. Everything must be judged and brought into conformity with the values of Christ, and if found to be in conflict with the kingdom of God, only then must such be rejected and left behind. This demonstrates that transformation in Christ involves retention and renewal of the same person in their social and cultural context rather than a displacement or replacement of everything in their life in a utopian fashion.

Paul's teaching in 1 Cor 7:17–24 was that everyone whether circumcised or uncircumcised should remain in the status (κλῆσις) in which they were at the point of call. Each was called in one of only two categories, circumcised or uncircumcised, and Paul's teaching was that they should

---

24. See chapter 3, "The Rule of Faith in Romans 12:1—15:13," for the discussion of this issue.

25. Already in my *Paul's Gospel in an Intercultural Context* (1991), I had concluded that "Paul is arguing concerning the *identity* of the new believing community . . . in such a way that positive links with its Jewish roots is retained, that a positive hope for Israel is shown to be still viable, and that the church is truly seen to be a unity of Jews and gentiles . . ." (203–4). Identity is not so much determined by affirming core doctrines as by affirming the core story, and it is this narrative that is identity forming. But the Pauline interpretation of the core messianic narrative has differing outcomes for Jews and gentiles.

26. This thesis is developed in my book, *Paul and the Creation of Christian Identity*. The first four of the essays in this volume were written prior to the publication of this book, but may reflect some aspects of my developing opinions. To avoid undue duplication and repetition, I have not included an essay outlining my most recent thinking on identity issues such as hybridity, etc. On this see my, "Gentile Identity and Transformation in Christ according to Paul," 23–55. For an excellent overview of very recent research on identity, particularly the theoretical discourse on this area, see Tucker, *"Remain in Your Calling."*

continue in whichever of these they were when called.[27] And if those of Jewish descent have the right to live "Jewishly" in the Christ-movement, this must mean something so fundamental to Jews as circumcision cannot be regarded simply as an indifferent thing that no longer has any significance. This I discuss in chapter 6 ("'As Having and as Not Having': Paul, Circumcision, and Indifferent Things") and to some extent also in chapter 11 ("'I Rate All Things as Loss': Paul's Puzzling Accounting System: Judaism as Loss or the Re-evaluation of all Things in Christ?"). I maintain that though Paul may have been influenced by contemporary forms of thought such as Stoicism, he did not follow their emphasis upon regarding certain things as "indifferents," but for him circumcision and other aspects of Jewish life remained important. Viewed in this light, Paul is neither sectarian nor countercultural, but a reformer of his own people by the strange route of a mission to the nations.[28]

The role of Paul's mission and theology in cultural reform has been viewed in various ways, some of which we discuss in chapter 10, "Universality and Particularity in Paul's Understanding and Strategy of Mission." Does being "in Christ," according to Paul, involve the creation of a whole new cultural entity in which the past is regarded as dead, and in which a whole new group of people with the same "in Christ" identity together form a people that is neither Jewish nor gentile? In this perspective Paul, as the founder of Christianity (which this view would suggest), could be of great assistance in any imperialistic attempt to cause disparate peoples, especially minorities, to conform.[29] Thus Christianity could become a useful servant in the promo-

27. Thus Paul never refers to proselytes since in his view these are subsumed within the category of circumcision. This is why he so clearly stated in Gal 5:3 that he who receives circumcision is bound to keep the whole law.

28. As emphasized by Niebuhr, *Heidenapostel aus Israel,* 175–84.

29. Christopher D. Stanley has questioned whether Paul's handling of ethnic categories is not more complex and situational than is often recognized. He does recognize that the world in which Paul lived and operated was ethnically diverse, but notes that in Paul's letters this ethnic diversity is largely obscured since Paul consistently uses binary terms when referring to ethnic differences. Stanley does give a good overview of these issues, but the binary pattern Paul tends to prefer does not necessarily denote a tendency to eliminate or tone down ethnic difference—it still draws attention to ethnic differences in a very vivid fashion and ought to be read in relation to the rhetoric and function of the passages in which this is done. I cannot concur that Rom 1–2 can be used to indicate that Paul either depicts his identity in association with, or in the guise of, gentile identity or that he seems at certain points to regard gentiles as somehow superior to Israel. As Esler has shown, Rom 1:18–32 is largely based on the story of Sodom ("Sodom Tradition in Romans 1:18–32," 2–16)! The diatribe style of parts of Romans, especially Rom 2 must be given due weight so that Paul's rhetoric is not misinterpreted. On this also see n.21 above. I agree with Stanley that gentile identity is an imprecise description, and incorporates the particular identity of the nations grouped

tion of empire as, in the days of colonial expansion, it was often expected to be. In contrast to this perspective, the only conformity that Paul advocates is conformity with Christ, which in fact means transformation in Christ. Historically, being "in Christ" has been as much a cause of diversity as of uniformity. The stress upon reforming and renewal in the Christ-movement would appear to indicate that there can be no such entity as a common universal Christianity which is culture-free (i.e., free from the limits and traditions of particular nations or ethnic groups), but rather that being in Christ involves a diversity that continues in diverse ways to transform particular differentiated cultures. This seems to be becoming most explicit in the Letter to the Ephesians, in which those in the Pauline tradition intermingle with other early mission groups as well as Jews. We deal with this diversity in chapter 7 "Unity and Diversity in the Church: Transformed Identities and the Peace of Christ in Ephesians."

Such a view of Paul's mission as involving a theology that recognizes and underpins social and cultural diversity demands the correlative that since, according to Paul, difference is integral to the Christ-movement, the enmity that is almost universally associated with difference can have no place amongst those in Christ and simply cannot be tolerated. Thus reconciliation emerges as a fundamental Christian value.[30] Indeed, it cannot occur and is not strictly necessary if one merely cultivates indifference to differences.[31] Likewise a proper evaluation of both past and future is essential if the temporal reality of life in the here and now is to be seriously and christologically understood.[32] Christ's work in Pauline theology, as described by the author of Ephesians, means the breaking down, not of difference itself—the removal of diversity—but rather a call to peace in view of the fact that Christ has made possible the total removal of enmity between Jew and gentile. Reconciliation with God through Christ means reconciliation with one another however different.[33]

---

together; for that same reason I no longer use a capital when referring to gentiles. Cf. "Paul the Ethnic Hybrid?," esp. 117–22.

30. As this volume was being finalized, I was informed of the death of Ralph P. Martin, to whose work on the New Testament, and reconciliation in particular, and to whose generous friendship I am deeply indebted.

31. Fowl, "Badiou and Paul," 133.

32. See also " Expropriating Agamben on Paul," in which Griffiths draws attention to Agamben's reflection on Paul's use of the verb *katargeo* and of the theme of messianic time, the "as (if) not" of the *nun kairos* of the church (187–89).

33. Cf. R. N. Longenecker's (*Introducing Romans*, 341) claim concerning reconciliation, "he [Paul] made this relational and personal soteriological language central to his preaching to pagan Gentiles . . ."

This is the theme of chapter 9, "'Let Us Maintain Peace' (Rom 5:2): Reconciliation and Social Responsibility," in which I maintain that the theme of reconciliation is a central focus of Paul's letter to the Romans. Paul's gospel demands not the removal of difference in Christ, but rather the erasure of the enmity due to difference. There is a general scholarly consensus that Romans focuses, perhaps more than any other of Paul's letters, on the relationship of Jew and gentile in the purpose of God. But because this letter has often been regarded as an, or perhaps even *the,* example of Pauline theology, it has tended to be interpreted in an abstract decontextualized manner as if Paul's theology were static rather than dynamic, and as if it had no reference to the social and political realities of his time.[34] The older tendency was to stress the (doctrinal) content of Romans 1–8 and to treat the remainder of the letter as of secondary importance. But as I argued in my doctoral dissertation, chapters 9–11 are really the climax of the argument in this letter. In chapter 5 of this volume, "Jewish Roots and Christian Identity," I demonstrate that the structure of Romans supports such a claim concerning the significance and relevance of chapters 9–11 within the letter.

These chapters deal with a contemporary first-century issue, the question why many Jewish people were unwilling to join in the Christ-movement. In this respect Romans is an occasional letter and, like all others of his letters, addresses a particular exigency that Paul attempts to influence. And as in his other letters, theological statements, however abundant in this instance, are designed to motivate a change of attitude and conduct on the part of those addressed. Thus it is inadequate to claim Rom 9–11 as the climax of the letter (in the sense of conclusion) as if all that needed to be said has been completed at 11:32. Rather, my view is that *the content of these chapters has a backward reference as the climax to an ongoing argument in Rom 1–11, but that this climax also has a forward reference to the chapters that succeed.* If Rom 9–11 is regarded as the climax and conclusion of Paul's argument, then the ethical dimension so strong in chapters 12–16, is diminished in importance. However, in relation to the posited occasion of the letter, some would maintain that chapters 14–15 are sometimes given undue significance, as if these alone could account for all that has preceded them.[35] But this is not so when it is recognized that chapters 9–11 are the basis for

34. One of the areas where research in Romans has developed is in the emphasis upon the political context. I have updated my work in Romans in this area by increased emphasis on the recognition of the political pressure that Rome influenced upon the divergent groups in Judaism as well as upon emergent Christianity.

35. Thus Karris, "The Occasion of Romans: A Response to Professor Donfried," 65–84 and 125–27. Karris questioned that "even if Rom 14:1—15:13 is actual paraenesis to what concrete situation in the Roman church(e)s is it addressed?" (127). For further on this see chapter 8 ("The Addressees of Paul's Letter to the Romans") in this volume.

what is stated in 12:1—15:13, and that there are direct and specific links between these chapters. What is required is an interpretation of Romans that does not render certain sections of the letter redundant[36] or irrelevant, and my argument in chapter 5 ("Jewish Roots and Christian Identity") concerning the structure of the letter demonstrates the plausibility of such an interpretation.

In my understanding of the letter, as I will show in chapter 8, "The Addressees of Paul's Letter to the Romans: Assemblies of God in House Churches and Synagogues," Paul in Romans addresses an almost entirely gentile audience even though Jewish issues are very much part of the discussion. It should be noted that Jews in Romans are present only as a third party rather than in direct address, even though the diatribal style might at points appear to suggest otherwise.[37] Nevertheless, there were many Jews living in Rome when Paul wrote his letter, and some of these were certainly Christ-followers. It is also clear that the gentile addressees of Romans are in contact and discussion with Jews both inside and beyond the Christ-movement. The issue of a lack of positive response to the Christ-movement was not a purely theoretical matter, nor could it have been an issue arising only elsewhere or at a different period than when Paul writes to Rome.[38] It had to be an issue that immediately affects the situation of the Christ-followers at Rome whatever the ethnic composition of the Christ communities there.

36. I agree with Grieb's ("Paul's Theological Preoccupation in Romans 9–11," 301–400) comment, "I tend to prefer readings that make sense of the letter as a whole, assuming, until convinced otherwise, that Paul was a gifted rhetorician who knew exactly what he was doing." Käsemann (*Commentary on Romans*, 254–56) acknowledged the heroic attempt by F. C. Baur to give significance to chapters 9–11 in his claim that it is in these chapters, despite their neglect by the Reformation, that we should find the germ and center of the whole, but concluded that Baur's conception of Jewish Christians being dominant at Rome, and the agitated reception of his views by other interpreters prevented him from achieving a meaningful interpretation of the whole of the letter. Cf. also my essay, "Ernst Käsemann on Romans," 161–86.

37. Paul's rhetoric in the diatribe does not necessarily mean that when he apparently addresses a Jewish critic, the letter may be directed to an audience including Jews, Cf. Stowers, *The Diatribe and Paul's Letter to the Romans*, esp. 75–79. Also "Paul's Dialogue with a Fellow-Jew in Romans 3:1–9," 707–22. See also my discussion of diatribe style in chapter 3 in this volume. In his later (1994) commentary, *A Rereading of Romans*, Stowers makes a strong argument that "11:13 makes it transparently clear, that the letter addresses itself only to Gentile believers" (288).

38. Thus regarding Rom 9–11 as a discussion of the theme "The Church and Israel" can lead to these chapters being treated almost exclusively theologically without sufficient reference to historical actualities in terms of time and place. What Paul discusses is not a general topic such as the failure of Jews generally, or even universally to respond to the gospel of Christ, but rather some aspect of this theme that has a basis in recent history in Rome. For a useful recent discussion see Zoccali, *Whom God Has Called*.

My perception of this issue has continued to develop in that I had not earlier taken Paul's repeated direct address to gentiles sufficiently into account, as for example in chapter 3 ("The Rule of Faith") below. It is the hostility on the part of some gentile Christ-followers at Rome towards Christ-followers living a Jewish lifestyle, combined with an awareness of Jewish lack of response to the Christ-movement, that has caused Paul to react strongly and to write at length on God's purpose for Jew and gentile in Christ as this impinges on the relation of Jews and gentiles in Rome at this time.

I earlier interpreted this factor mainly (but not exclusively) as a theological problem. But as empire studies and Paul's political relevance have increasingly become very significant, I have sought to adjust to that influence. Neil Elliott has noted, "that the context of ideological claims made by the emperor and court propagandists, specifically regarding the inevitable supremacy of Rome and the destiny of the Roman people to rule inferiors, would have been sufficient to provoke the 'error' among Paul's non-Jewish hearers in Rome." In his view gentiles in Rome had come to boast over Israel not because of some theological reason such as the failure of the mission to Jews, but simply "as non Judeans living in Rome, they had been seduced by imperial explanations for the apparent downfall of the Judean people as 'the conquered (Seneca), a people born to servitude' (Cicero)."[39]

Thus somewhat surprisingly, despite its emphasis on the distinctiveness of Jew and gentile, Romans also implies common ground between conquered peoples both within and beyond the Christ-movement. When the political setting of Rome within the context of the Empire generally is fully taken into account, then it becomes apparent that Jews and the nations, with the exception of Rome (and to a lesser extent Greece) both share the status of conquered peoples.[40] Paul reminds the Romans that when Pharaoh's heart became hardened, the God of Israel was still able to rescue her, and he thus implies that the same God is able to rescue his people even though they may now appear to some at least somewhat similar to the Northern Kingdom, a "not my people."[41] Paul stresses that despite the all-encompassing power of Pharaoh or of Rome and despite the apparent weakness of the Jews as a subject people, the God of Israel through Jesus Christ has the power to determine the destiny of both Israel and the nations. Rome, like Pharaoh, was raised up in history for the very purpose of demonstrating the power of the

---

39. Elliott, "Paul's Political Christology: Examples from Romans," 40–41. I very much value Elliott's fine insight in this essay and similarly in his book, *The Arrogance of Nations.*

40. Here I am indebted to the work of Kahl, *Galatians Re-Imagined,* and Lopez, *Apostle to the Conquered.*

41. Further on this, see chapter 4, "Divergent Images of Paul and His Mission."

God of Israel (Rom 9:17).[42] The principal enemy of the Christ-movement, and mistakenly viewed as the main obstacle to its growth, was not the resistance of devout Jews but rather the power of Rome, which was able to determine the fate of both of these. Yet even this power is temporary, not eternal, and will continue only so long as the divine purpose is served.

Thus, Paul in Rom 11:13–32 reminds the gentile Christ-followers not to view the world from the "monopoly of power" perspective of Roman gentile arrogance[43] (v. 25) but to view it afresh from the perspective of the God of Israel whose purpose for Jew and gentile has not yet reached its consummation.[44] From this vantage point of faith, neither Jews nor a Jewish lifestyle should be rejected or abandoned by those in Christ, since these have not been rejected or abandoned by God. Contrary to the pattern of Roman domination, those who are powerful in the Christ communities at Rome must not determine the way of life of those less powerful, but must voluntarily, like Christ who did not please himself (Rom 15:3), give up their own freedom to facilitate fellowship with those whose convictions prevent them conforming to an imposed pattern.[45]

One of my persistent goals in these essays has been to view Paul, as far as humanly possible, from a pre-70 C.E. perspective. If, as is increasingly recognized, there was no immediate or widespread separation between Jewish and Christ-following communities even after the fall of Jerusalem, and that only after the reign of Nerva was the Christ-movement clearly identified in some regions as distinct from Judaism,[46] then it becomes all the more essential to try to view Paul in his pre-70 context.

This means that we must be careful in our use of the terms "Christian" and "Christianity" since both are anachronistic when applied to Paul.[47] Again

---

42. Ian E. Rock has demonstrated that Paul in Rom 9–11 is informed by the Song of Moses in Deut 32, and that it is on the basis of this passage of Scripture that Paul interprets the present state of the Jewish people vis-a-vis Rome. Though Rome may have been used by God to discipline his own people, those who oppose the divine purpose will soon meet their demise, *Paul's Letter to the Romans and Roman Imperialism,* esp. 288–326. See also Rock's essay, "Another Reason for Romans," 74–89. On strategies of resistance in Early Judaism see Portier-Young, *Apocalypse against Empire,* 390–95, and Elliott, "The Patience of the Jews," 32–41.

43. Cf. Strecker, "Fides-Pistis-Glaube," 236–37.

44. For my resistance to an over-realized eschatology in relation to this issue, see chapter 6 ("As Having and as Not Having: Paul, Circumcision, and Indifferent Things") in this volume.

45. On the centrality of suffering in the formation of Christian Identity, see Lim, *The Sufferings of Christ are Abundant in Us.*

46. Cf. Heemstra, *The Fiscus Judaicus,* 188–210.

47. Thus Magnus Zetterholm ("Jews, Christians and Gentiles," 242–54) maintains

we must attempt to view Paul on his own terms, and not presume that he conforms to what may be regarded as the ideals of a post-Enlightenment liberal Protestantism. If Paul helped to create a movement of gentile Christ-following communities that eventually, for social and political reasons as much as theological, became distinct from Judaism, we must not presume that what much later became a historical reality was conceived, planned, or even inaugurated as such by the Apostle. Post-Enlightenment Christian theology tends to perceive Paul as the emancipator of Christ-followers from legalistic morality, from a narrow Jewish tribalism and Jewish Christianity to the law-free gospel of freedom in Christ. One aspect of this perspective impinges heavily on our understanding of ethnicity and ethnic identity issues. This arises from the perception that Paul argued continuously for the erasure or obliteration of all ethnic distinction in Christ. The ideal if not the reality for him was supposedly that these were relegated to the pre-Christ past of each individual so that all could now be equal and the same in Christ. In theory this seems a plausible goal for the Christ-following communities. However, ethnic distinctions cannot and ought not to be so easily discarded. The experience of diverse communities and "ethnic cleansing" in Yugoslavia is often held up as a warning against the recognition of ethnic groupings. The opposite is in fact the case. It was precisely because ethnic realities were not recognized or permitted recognition over a long period of history that, when more freedom was granted, ethnic hostility emerged in its full force.[48]

But however we regard ethnic issues in recent European history, liberal Christian ideals, whatever these may be, ought not to be casually read back into Paul's period of history, and Paul should not be expected to conform to such. Paul is usually very even-handed in relation to the main ethnic grouping of Jews and gentiles with which he chiefly operated in his mission. Thus in 1 Cor 7:17ff. he commands "no circumcision for gentiles" and likewise "no *epispasmos* for Jews."[49] But this demonstrates his ongoing acknowledgment of ethnic difference rather than a mission for its removal, a stance further developed in the letter to the Ephesians, which I discuss in chapter 7. As Philip Esler has clearly recognized in relation to the sub-groups he identifies in Romans, such groups are more likely to live at peace with one another when their own specific ethnic groupings are acknowl-

---

that the label "Christianity" should be used strictly for the non-Jewish religion that emerged during the second century. On this see also p. 20, note 6.

48. We are referring here to Tito's rule in Yugoslavia, which by means of a totalitarian regime temporarily suppressed recognition of ethnic diversity.

49. Andreas Blanschke is one of the few interpreters to recognize this even-handedness in Paul, and that in this the apostle is not following Graeco-Roman cultural opinion, *Beschneidung*, 397–401.

edged rather than ignored.[50] Anachronistic readings of Paul can be avoided or at least reduced in frequency only when it is acknowledged that post-Enlightenment liberal ideals of equality and freedom owe much to Paul and his ideals, whereas the apostle himself owes nothing to these, and cannot by any stretch of the imagination be legitimately judged by this standard. Our task as interpreters is to ensure that we read Paul carefully in his own context[51] and then, as far as is possible, to relate his thinking to our times, rather than mold Paul's thought into our systems.

A popular reading of Rom 10:12 combined with Gal 3:28 suggests that "there is no distinction between Jew and Greek" was a dominant slogan in Pauline teaching, thus indicating his opposition to all ethnic differentiation. Dunn's explanation of what Paul found wrong with Judaism unfortunately contributed to the view that Paul opposed ethnic differentiation.[52] Dunn's emphasis has similarities with C. H. Dodd's use of a "no distinction hermeneutic" in Romans. When Galatians and parts of Romans are taken out of context these can be combined into a "Paulinism" that, though attractive and apparently convincing in its universalizing tendency, cannot integrate all of Paul's statements, particularly in Rom 9–16 and other passages such as 1 Cor 7:17–24, into a meaningful coherence without in some respect judging Paul as incapable of living up to the best of his own insights.[53] However, a careful reading of οὐ γάρ ἐστιν διαστολή in Rom 10:12 would suggest that another reading is both feasible and warranted by the emphasis on interethnic differentiation in Romans. The phrase is better

---

50. Cf. Esler, *Conflict and Identity in Romans*, e.g., 144–45. He states "the solution in the challenging context of interethnic conflict, seems to be to make a virtue out of necessity by establishing a common superordinate identity while simultaneously maintaining the salience of subgroup identities." Although not in agreement with Esler's view of superordinate identity, I support his emphasis on maintaining the salience of subgroup identities as the way to peace, and especially his view that "Paul does not seek to achieve the difficult task of erasing the two broad ethnic identities present in the Roman Christ-movement, Judean and Greek." Cf. ibid., 355–56, and 365. Esler is extremely perceptive in his understanding of ingroup identity and intergroup conflict, not least in how the latter may possibly be reduced, cf. ibid., 29–39.

51. Thus, particular care must be exercised in relating Pauline theology to that of, for example, 1 Peter. We can be reasonably confident about the date of Paul's writing most of his letters, but this historical precision is lost when Paul is closely associated without distinction with other letters of which the date is later than Paul and less certain.

52. Dunn's view on this has recently been criticized for emphasizing the form of expression of Paul's zeal language to the neglect of its substance and essence, "While he [Paul] casts his previously cherished qualifications in ethnic terms . . . it was his activity, not the ethnicity in which such activity took form . . . which he now considered σκύβαλα in light of knowing Christ." (Ortlund, *Zeal without Knowledge,* 164–65).

53. See Dodd, *The Epistle to the Romans,* 63; see also 43–44 and 182–83.

read as "for no distinction *is made* between Jew and Greek," or even "for there is no discrimination between Jew and Greek."[54] In Romans this policy is clearly based on Paul's understanding of divine impartiality towards Jew and Greek, but impartiality implies the recognition of diversity rather than the ignoring of it. Some scholars have become so immersed in the (former) consensus we label as Paulinism, that they view any opinion that suggests Paul's statements cannot be generalized, harmonized, or universalized as ill advised. But philosophers such as Emmanuel Levinas and Hannah Arendt suggest otherwise in specific relation to alterity. The attempt to assimilate minorities into the dominant culture in an imperialistic manner, and the resulting dangers of lost or confused identities, such as in the case of some Muslim youth recently in the UK, also indicates that peace and harmony arise from recognition of difference rather than advocating its demise. We are seeking to describe the peace of Christ, and it is not to be mistaken for the Roman conception of the Augustan peace. Harmony is something that cannot be imposed by force or even by ignoring the rights or the identity of the other who is different.

As is emphasized in chapter 11 ("'I Rate All Things as Loss': Paul's Puzzling Accounting System: Judaism as Loss or the Re-Evaluation of All Things in Christ?"), the Paul of the letters is radical in almost every respect. But this particular radical remains a Jew as well as being an apostle of Christ for the nations. He counsels remaining in the status in which one was called. He recognizes the "giftedness" of the spiritual gifts of his converts, and he likewise seeks to remain within the given confines in which his mission is legitimately operated. Despite the newness of life in Christ, a particular identity is given as are certain differing spiritual gifts, and a given sphere of mission is also a factor that limits and confines the work of Paul. Thus new and old are both aspects of this radical reformer who can still state that the gospel is "to the Jew first and also to the gentile" despite his claim that there can be no favoritism with the impartial God of Israel.[55] Paul is difficult to categorize in that at times he appears quite traditional, but everything he touches, he transforms in unexpected ways so that we must be extremely careful with our own understanding of Paul in order to mold (and formulate) it in accordance with his writings and reported activities, and not to

54. See my "Differentiation and Discrimination in Paul's Ethnic Discourse."

55. As Esler (*Conflict and Identity in Romans*, 364) notes, even in the image of unity in the one olive tree in Rom 11, the Judean parts have precedence." Cf. also Hultgren's (*Paul's Letter to the Romans*, 135) comment on Rom 3:1–8: "advantage can be understood as a privilege that one has by virtue of a status given; but on the other hand, it can be understood simply as a benefit or gain for which one should be grateful. . . . The Jews have some advantages even if no privileges."

allow it to be completely prescribed or subsumed by our recent or contemporary presuppositions or logic. Paul's voice needs to be heard afresh within the clamor of the competing voices of our time. I hope that these essays will contribute positively towards meeting this need.

I have been closely involved in the discussions and developments of Pauline studies over many years. It has been educational to look at how and when new developments have occurred, and to what extent they have realized their initial promise. An awareness of the course of biblical interpretation is an invaluable asset. My approach has always been deeply theological and appreciative of the insights of the Reformation and succeeding centuries. But, becoming more familiar with the divergent insights of earlier scholarship, and combining some of these with the exciting new approaches of the last half century in particular, has led me to become more open to readings of Paul that formerly I did not always find convincing. My stance is both theological and sociological, aiming to hold the two perspectives together, to offer a more comprehensive understanding of an apostle who was a theologian par excellence, but not in any contemporary meaning of this term since his theology emerged in and from practice rather than merely from a theoretical stance. Moreover, my stress on the contextual approach has made historical issues equally significant with the theological. Thus any approach that can better enable contemporary scholars to understand what the historical Paul was (and is) saying in his context deserves to be developed in order that misperceptions may not stand in the way of the gospel, and so that outdated modes of understanding may be laid to rest as soon as possible.

One of the advantages of participating in scholarly research, particularly in group ventures over a period of years, is that one's own deep convictions are gradually exposed and challenged. Thus I am deeply indebted to Daniel Patte, with whom I cooperated for over a decade in the Romans through History and Cultures Series, for convincing me that my reading of Romans, though not necessarily in error, was only one way of understanding this text! These essays are the result of participation in the scholarly debates of several decades and, as such, I trust that they may illustrate that the quest for a fuller and deeper understanding of Paul's activities, his faith, and his practice is an on-going and never-ending process since we are always bringing new and differing questions for illumination in the light of his apostolic guidance.

2

The Contribution
of Traditions to Paul's Theology

A Response to C. J. Roetzel

AT THE 1990 ANNUAL Meeting of the Society of Biblical Literature in New Orleans, I presented a response to a very innovative study by Professor Calvin J. Roetzel.[1] This essay is based on that paper and on subsequent reflections on Professor Roetzel's contribution. He stresses that Paul's cross symbolism differs markedly and develops throughout his letters, making it difficult, if not risky, to identify what is foundational in the apostle's theology.

While being in general agreement with this finding, I have given myself the task in this response of considering to what extent Paul's theology arises from, and is indebted to, earlier and contemporary traditions. I endeavor to show that, while Paul's theology develops creatively and contextually, it does so in a loose dialectic with existing traditions.

The Need for a Framework of Interpretation

Paul, like his contemporaries, was born into a community with its own traditions, representing the accumulated wisdom of earlier generations and their attempts to make sense out of their experience. Like any other human, Paul had mediated to him via the community an authoritative total vision of what the world is ultimately like and the place of the individual within it. He learned to participate in the symbolic universe of his Pharisaic

1. Roetzel, "The Grammar of Election in Four Pauline Letters," 211–33.

community—to perceive the world as that community perceived it, interpreting his experience from their perspective.

In making this particular point, we are simply stressing that the human being is not a *tabula rasa* covered little by little with new knowledge through new experiences. We are, on the contrary, affirming that all experience and all perception are deeply colored by existing theory.[2] So Paul learned the language of Pharisaism, and this process in itself prepared him to receive the world in a particular way in keeping with its tradition. Membership in this community provided Paul with a framework into which his experience as an individual could be integrated from the start. Within this system of shared meaning, Paul became familiar with the fundamental (Pharisaic) perceptions that had come so to ground and define the community's existence that they did not need to be debated or justified, let alone questioned. A tendency to adhere to or to develop a covenantal theology or a covenantal mode of thinking, if such there be, was probably one example of such perceptions.

As a young man, Paul had to relate and accommodate his own experience to these inherited values—most of this probably taking place unconsciously. Nevertheless, not all experiences can always be interpreted as fitting easily and harmoniously into the tradition, and at this point for Paul, as for others, a tension would emerge between tradition and experience. There are a number of specific examples in the New Testament in which we can see a group stressing their continuity with the past with, for example, the Old Testament Scriptures—and seeking to legitimate (new) elements of their practice by insisting that it is their interpretation rather than that of (other) older communities that upholds true continuity with the great values of the past.[3]

Thus far we have simply outlined the normal communal constraints on human thinking and development to which Paul, his contemporaries, and we ourselves are subject. Through this, we can explain how he related to his own and other groups in his society. But one significant aspect of Paul's life does not fit in quite so easily with this or other attempts to describe normal human religious development. Paul's "conversion"[4] implies a major watershed in his life and thought that has frequently, whether deliberately or inadvertently, caused Paul and his theological thought to be seen in terms of some immediate revelation rather than in any sense of continuity

2. See Räisänen, *Beyond New Testament Theology*, 129–31.

3. See Watson, *Paul, Judaism, and the Gentiles*, 49–50.

4. I put "conversion" in inverted commas here to indicate that Paul's "conversion" is not identical with the modern phenomenon of conversion.

with his previous religious upbringing. The point at issue here is, of course, what understanding is to be given to a revelation of God. Is it simply a new self-understanding, or does it involve an introduction to, or a discovery of, new theological concepts or propositions?[5] Is it not rather a new point of departure that impacts all existing presuppositions?

Whatever our particular understanding of Paul's revelation on the Damascus road, one thing is clear: only those things could have been revealed to Paul that he and his new Christian[6] community could understand. R. M. Hare points out that our conceptual language games, like group dances, assume intersubjective cooperation within a community. Proposals for conceptual renewal that deviate too far from the conceptual forms current within the community are not intelligible to others and thus make cooperation with them impossible.[7] For this reason, philosophers or theologians who make proposals for conceptual innovation must necessarily leave unchallenged and unchanged the greater part of the conceptual apparatus of the cultural community to which they are addressing themselves. Even Paul must be bound by this factor since he necessarily had both to understand and to communicate his message. Even the most revolutionary thinker must speak—and think—in the language of his day.[8]

A possible refuge from this kind of argument is to insist that Paul's religious experience on the Damascus road was self-authenticating and self-explanatory. This is not an adequate response. Paul's religious experience—and religious experience in general—is absolutely central to our discussion, and yet experience and its interpretation are closely connected and difficult to dissociate from each other.

Räisänen criticizes Johnson for talking of "resurrection experiences."

> Talk of Jesus' resurrection already implies a particular interpretation of the event in question. It would be correct to say that the disciples experienced something which they interpreted with the help of categories of resurrection belief. . . . Had they lacked the conceptual framework supplied by apocalyptic Jewish eschatology, they would have been bound to search for a different explanation of what they had seen. . . . Without this pre-existing

5. See Kim, *The Origin of Paul's Gospel*, 233–34.

6 Although I no longer continue to use the word "Christian" in relation to the period of Paul's lifetime, I have not changed this in the earlier essays reproduced in this volume where I used that terminology.

7. Hare, *Essays in Philosophical Method*, 33. I am indebted for this reference and a good discussion of this issue to Vincent Brummer's essay "Philosophy, Theology and the Reading of Texts," 451–62.

8. See Nineham, *The Use and Abuse of the Bible*, 13–14.

interpretative frame of reference, the Easter experiences would have remained mute.[9]

The frame that provided the Easter appearances with meaning consisted of both traditional elements (the eschatological thought world) and recent elements (the experiences with the earthly Jesus). So too in our search for Paul's thinking we must presuppose this pre-existing frame of reference, irrespective of how we evaluate his revelatory experience. Indeed, W. Van Orman Quine reminds us:

> The totality of our so-called knowledge or beliefs . . . is a man-made fabric which impinges on experience only along the edges. Or, to change the figure, total science is like a field of force whose boundary conditions are experience. A conflict with experience at the periphery occasions readjustments in the interior of the field. . . . Re-evaluation of some statements entails re-evaluation of others, because of their logical interconnections . . . But the total field is so underdetermined by its boundary conditions, experience, that there is much latitude of choice as to what statements to re-evaluate in the light of any single contrary experience.[10]

The Cultural Context that Informed Paul's Experience

Räisänen is convinced that "core experiences" of themselves are not sufficient to explain why Christianity emerged. Why did Paul draw different conclusions from his ecstatic vision than the Jerusalemites? He is of the opinion that, though we are certain that Paul's values were changed (Phil 3:1–16), it is hard to distinguish the immediate consequences of the experience for Paul's life and thought from what dawned on him later, under the influence of quite different experiences such as social conflict; for Räisänen the role of the latter—that is, of social conflict, seems much more important than "core experiences."[11]

The result of this inquiry leads us to consider afresh the inherited framework Paul had acquired prior to his Damascus road experience. Here the recent magisterial work of Alan Segal is most instructive. Although Segal believes that Paul's "conversion" and his mystical ascension form the basis of his theology, "his language shows the marks of a man

9. Räisänen, *Beyond New Testament Theology*, 127–28.

10. Quine, *From a Logical Point of View*, 42–43.

11. Räisänen, *Beyond New Testament Theology*, 125–26.

who has learned the contemporary vocabulary for expressing a theophany and then has received one."[12]

There is now considerable agreement among scholars that Paul, like most Christians in his day, was profoundly apocalyptic in his thinking. Paul's most characteristic topics are typical of apocalypticism. Segal sees the distinction between apocalypticism and mysticism as being an artificial theoretical one not warranted by the realities of first-century religious experience. Apocalypticism and mysticism were inextricably bound up in first-century Judaism and Paul himself is a prime example of the way in which the two were united phenomenologically.

In his writings to his new Christian communities among the gentiles, it is evident that the apostle's understanding is similar in some ways to that of the Qumran community. In both there is a rigorous distinction between the community and the outside world. Paul sees Christians as a congregation united by their absorption into Christ, the angelic vice-regent of God. Segal concludes that Paul's understanding of this issue is exclusively mystical and apocalyptic, with one proviso. The activity of the end-time has already begun. In this and in his abrogation of the special laws of Judaism for his gentile mission, Paul's view of community is unique.[13] But in the Pauline communities, high-group definition—as also in the extreme Torah-true apocalyptic groups—enforced the separation from the outside world. Both in Qumran and in early Christianity, the process of salvation was inaugurated by membership in a religious sect, which considered itself a new covenantal congregation.

Segal seeks to fill in the cultural context that informed Paul's experience. Ezekiel 1, though often ignored in this context, was one of the central scriptures that Paul and Luke used to understand Paul's "conversion."

> The vision of the throne-chariot, with its attendant description of Glory (*kavod*), God's Glory or form, for the human figure, is a central image of Jewish mysticism, which is closely related to the apocalyptic tradition. . . . Paul is an important witness to the kind of experience apocalyptic Jews were having and an important predecessor to merkabah mysticism.[14]

Stories of heavenly journeys, of angelic transformation, or even of the ascent of exemplary men to divinity by identification with, or transformation into, the enthroned figure abound in early apocalyptic texts. "The journeys here usually begin after a crisis of human confidence about God's

---

12. Segal, *Paul the Convert*, 69.

13. Ibid., 158–61.

14. Ibid., 39–40.

intention to bring justice to the world, and they result in the discovery that the universe is indeed following God's moral plan—the ancient scriptures about God's providence are proved true." The narration of exotic and amazing events is a pragmatic one—to explain the structure of heaven, thus providing an eschatological verification that God's plan will come to fruition and also a mechanism by which immortality is achieved.

Segal maintains that in this context Paul did not have to be a religious innovator to posit an identification between a vindicated hero and the image of the *kavod*, the manlike figure in heaven, although the identification of the figure with the risen Christ is obviously a uniquely Christian development.[15]

Segal comes to the conclusion that "the center of Paul's gospel is the identification of Christ as the Glory of God" and that "Paul's vocation is to make known the identification of Jesus Christ as the Glory of God."[16] This language of vision has informed his thought in a number of crucial respects. According to Segal, it allowed Paul to develop a concept of the divinity of Christ or the Messiah both as a unique development within the Jewish mystical tradition and as characteristically Christian. He uses Jewish mystical vocabulary to express the transformation experienced by believers, and he uses the language of transformation to discuss the ultimate salvation and fulfillment of the apocalypse, raising believers to immortality. Paul's vision also allows him to describe his teaching as an "apocalypse"—a revelation of hidden knowledge through the Holy Spirit, though it is mediated through the mind, not through the speaking of tongues.

Although it was possible to go from Pharisaic Judaism to Christianity without having a "conversion" experience such as Paul's, Paul is not one of those Jews whose faith in Christ only completed a previous belief in Judaism. His conversion caused him to *revalue* his Judaism, in turn creating a new understanding of Jesus' mission. In addition to this, in contrast to the Jerusalem church's conception of apostolate as deriving from Jesus' personal appointment, Paul develops a charismatic idea of apostleship dependent on a vision of the risen Christ—exactly what modern psychology and sociology would call a conversion (despite Paul's frequent use of the concept of prophetic commissioning, e.g., κλήτος in Gal 1 and Rom 1).[17]

We are deeply indebted to Segal's creative and convincing understanding of Paul and particularly for this useful description of the cultural context that informed the apostle's experience. The broad outlines of his study have elicited our support, though there may be some residual tension

---

15. Ibid., 51.
16. Ibid., 156–57.
17. Ibid., 69–71.

in regarding Paul's "conversion" and mystical ascension as the basis of his theology—while at the same time stressing the inheritance that provided the language to interpret this theophany.

The Influence of Scriptural Interpretation in the Formulation of Paul's Theological Statements

A crucial question in the development of Paul's theology must be the actual role played by the Scriptures both in his understanding of God's purpose and in his self-understanding. There is good reason to maintain that in the past scholars have not paid adequate attention either to Paul's explicit or implicit use of Scripture.[18] Segal is quite clear that Paul does not forget his Jewish past; rather he bends his Pharisaic exegesis to new ends.[19] Paul describes social groupings on the basis of Scripture and of his previously learned methodology, which he never abandoned. But we would wish to question Segal's conclusion that his conversion experience turns Scripture on its head and makes it come true in an ironic, unexpected way.[20]

One would not wish to argue against the thesis that Paul's perspective on the meaning of Scripture has changed, reflecting the change from one community to another. But how new are the new assumptions about the meaning of Scripture, which Paul does not so much argue as present? It is important not to exaggerate the new perspective that Paul brings to Scripture. We are, of course, aware that Paul cannot possibly be regarded as presenting a phenomenological description of Torah (rather Paul's statements are the result of cognitive changes in a man who has experienced dissonance in a sharper way than most Christians).[21]

Segal himself insists that Paul's doctrines are not to be understood merely as opposition to midrash or to the LXX—a more complicated and more subtle dynamic is operating. He points out that, although no other Jews in the first century distinguish faith and law in the way Paul does, it is in fact Paul's experience as a Christian that encourages the reformulation of biblical promises. However, he is not talking about Torah in general in these places; he talks only about the use of Torah to define the basic community.

---

18. An exception to this is the late Professor A. T. Hanson, my esteemed teacher and friend, who throughout his life devoted much of his work to this theme. See his *Studies in Paul's Technique and Theology* and *The Living Utterances of God: The New Testament Exegesis of the Old.*

19. Segal, *Paul the Convert*, 117.

20. Ibid., 122–23.

21. Ibid., 148; see also 120–22.

Faith, not Torah observance, defines the Christian community.[22] But we should not take this to mean that Paul concludes the Torah is wrong or completely irrelevant; it signifies rather a fresh understanding of the place of Torah in the divine purpose. He now realizes that there are specific limits to the Torah's scope and perhaps too that there are temporal limits now that the Messiah has come.

The earliest Christians understood the Scriptures both as Torah and, eschatologically, as prophecy of the fullness of time. In a striking example of *pesher* interpretation, Luke reports Jesus as saying in the synagogue at Nazareth, "this day is the Scripture fulfilled in your ears." For Paul, as for many of his contemporaries, the interpretation of the Scriptures becomes at the same time the medium of self-understanding and self-disclosure (not to say self-authorization). The earliest Christians could interpret only in the medium of their own day. Their self-understanding was not independent of history and tradition, as if by the invention of a new language, but within tradition and in the very language tradition made available in their texts. The Gospel texts (but Luke especially) picture Christ as an observant Jew who enters into tradition, and understands himself in it.

In a certain way he understands himself in front of the Scriptures, standing before them and answering to them and to a form of life that they project. The basic hermeneutical principle of *pesher* interpretation is that Scripture makes sense not by opening inwardly to an intention that lies behind the text but by laying open (in front of itself or into its future) a possibility which the community takes upon itself to actualize or fulfill in terms of action, that is, in its forms or way of life.[23]

There can be no doubt that Paul stands in this *pesher* tradition. The Scriptures open up to the immediate future and challenge Paul and his communities to live the life of the end-time, the coming aeon. If we exaggerate Paul's distance from Pharisaism or see him in continual opposition to it or to Torah in general, we fail to give adequate significance to the obvious fact that the apostle still lives very much in this world of *pesher* interpretation. It is not so much a world that he creates or one that is peculiar to him or his communities; it is rather part of a wider world that influences both him and other widely divergent groups.

Paul's interpretive activity is not purely an individual activity. However socially distinct from Judaism the Pauline communities may have been, it is quite clear that both the Qumran and the Pauline communities saw

---

22. Ibid., 128.

23. See Bruns, "Midrash and Allegory," 634–35.

themselves as new covenantal congregations.[24] Paul goes to great lengths to show that those who have faith can also count themselves part of the covenant relationship with Abraham. Granted that Paul's perspective on the meaning of Scripture has changed, reflecting the change from one community to another, it is no surprise that his emphasis as apostle to the gentiles is on the entry requirements for the new covenantal community, in which the performance of the special laws of Judaism are not binding. This emphasis for gentiles is necessarily different from that of Judaism, which naturally assumed a prior faith commitment and a prior act on God's part in justifying that never needs to be discussed.

But despite this radical difference, we must not lose sight of what was held in common. Paul's perspective is different; his communities are not synagogal communities. Nevertheless, the common goal of becoming God's covenantal congregation has real significance. There is an air of expectancy in Paul's converts; there is a new creation. But at least some of the framework of this expectation is taken over from and shared with Pharisaism. The fact that Paul and other Jews shared and took seriously the exegetical tradition of scriptural interpretation of their own day is a powerful and pervasive influence, the significance of which is difficult both to estimate and to exaggerate.

We may illustrate this with one example. Terence Donaldson, in a careful study of how Paul in Gal 3:13–14 argues for the inclusion of the gentiles, comes to the conclusion that in these two verses Paul sees the cross as the eschatological redemption of Israel that sets the stage for the inclusion of the gentiles. Donaldson suggests that there may be here a radical reinterpretation, in the light of the cross event, of a Jewish pattern of thought in which the inclusion of the gentiles is seen as a consequence of the eschatological redemption of Israel. The fact that the same eschatological model of the relationship between Jew and gentile in salvation history underlies both Gal 3:1–4:7 and Rom 11 raises the possibility that this aspect of Jewish tradition played a more important part in Paul's thought than has hitherto been recognized. As Donaldson notes, "while the revision is radical, it is nonetheless a revision."[25]

24. See Segal, *Paul the Convert*, 180.

25. Donaldson, "The 'Curse of the Law' and the Inclusion of the Gentiles," 94–112, 106.

The Interaction between Scriptural Interpretation and Events of Everyday Life

There is no need to argue that scriptural interpretation never takes place in a vacuum; there is an obvious dialectical relationship between ideas and their social context. In stressing that scriptural interpretive tradition influenced Paul and his communities, we need to be more explicit as to how this actually took place. Paul was certainly no "ivory-tower" academic, and we need to be careful lest we adopt a too academic model. In Qumran we can see that the disciplined study of Scripture did occupy a specific place in the life of the community. But one factor that was influential in Paul's interpretation may easily be overlooked—that is, the interaction between interpretation and events, whether internal or external to the community, that impinged in some way on their daily life.

We could argue that the Pauline communities, like other similar groups, saw what they expected to see and filtered out what did not suit their theoretical view of the world and its operation. But their own experience of events in the daily life of the community could not easily be ignored. The practice was here, to some extent at least, the mother of the theory, and interpretation had to provide an explanation of events in order to make sense of their experience. However, the fact that the Spirit was seen as leading and directing the life of the community underlined the need for this and ensured its recognition as a theological activity. In the tradition of the prophets, the events of political life also required interpretation to explain God's ways with his people.

We see this, then, as a two-way process. The interpretive framework of these communities helped them to make sense of contemporary events. But there was genuine interaction, especially in relation to events within the life of the community, and these events in turn were active in giving direction about the meaning of Scripture. It was not simply that one text directly influenced in a literary way the interpretation of another text somehow associated with it. It was rather that the texts themselves were interpreted by living communities, and what was happening to these people in their daily life was a powerful influence in their interaction with the text.

What we have here, then, is not a static formulation of accepted propositions. It is rather a living scriptural tradition that gives meaning to, and receives meaning from, events in the daily life of the community. Because the group perceives itself, as it were, in transit, traveling onward to its destined goal of transformation into the image of Christ, its interpretation can never remain static. The interpretation is not fixed by its past, but its real meaning is discovered in the living dynamic of the Spirit at work in an ever-new and ever-changing present.

If this argument carries conviction, it would help to explain why Paul, as Professor Roetzel has clearly indicated, feels little compulsion to repeat previously stated formulas in any coherent systematic way.[26]

New and Old in Paul's Theology

Depending on which aspects one emphasizes, it is possible to paint two contradictory pictures of Paul's theological statements. One can see him as a radical innovator who emphasizes the new creation, someone with little concern for the motifs or traditions of Judaism. On the other hand, there are sufficient Jewish elements in his writings for some to insist that he is a devout Jew for whom Jesus the Messiah is the completion of his faith.[27]

We will not resolve this issue simply by noting the frequency of certain motifs, however valuable this may be. Wider and more basic issues need to be considered. The first of these is how we should regard Paul's "conversion" experience. We have already outlined our views in this matter, but it will be instructive to look also at John Gager's contribution. He sees Paul's "conversion" as that type of conversion in which the fundamental system of values and commitments is preserved intact "but it is turned upside down, reversed, and transvalued." "For Paul, the religious target remains the same but whereas the law had been the chosen path to the goal, and Christ the rejected one, beforehand, their order is reversed after the event."[28]

This is a perfectly appropriate model and useful in some respects, but it also has certain limitations. I am concerned at the use that may be made of the stark "reversal of values." Thinking of this kind may tend to support the view that Christ stands in absolute opposition to Judaism (since *nomos* is the law of the Jewish people and not simply an abstract concept).[29]

26. Roetzel, "The Grammar of Election."

27. Davies speaks of "a covenantal nomism in Christ," which also incorporates gentile believers. See the new preface to the fourth edition of *Paul and Rabbinic Judaism*, 30–31, in which Davies responds to criticisms of his views by E. P. Sanders in *Paul and Palestinian Judaism*, 422, 478–79.

28. Gager, "Some Notes on Paul's Conversion," 697–704, 700. For a good discussion of the issues at stake here, see Gaventa, *From Darkness to Light*, 36–40. See also Räisänen, "Paul's Conversion and the Development of His View of the Law," 404–19; and Dunn, "'A Light to the Gentiles' or The End of the Law?," now in *Jesus, Paul and the Law*, 89–107.

29. Donaldson ("Curse of the Law," 102) points out that we all too readily see *nomos* as an abstract concept, hanging in the air and (especially) disconnected from the people who found their identity in it, whereas for Paul this was not possible—"a statement

I prefer a paradigm that suggests a reorganization in one's priorities rather than a stark reversal. The latter view is too blunt an instrument to describe the complexity of the apostle's thinking. The primacy of Paul's experience has recently been given more significance. Associated with this is the attempt to relate experience to basic convictions that are so powerful they may even lead their exponents into contradictory arguments in order to support them.[30]

Räisänen sees some merit in Patte's fundamental distinction between "convictions" and ideas. Räisänen believes that the crucial line of demarcation should be drawn not between "convictions" and "ideas" (which cannot be neatly separated) but between experiences and their interpretations. Interpretations resulting from experience include a whole spectrum of ad hoc ideas that never reappear in the person's writings. He continues: "instead of dividing Paul's thoughts into two different groups, one might wish to establish a hierarchy ranging from the all-important to the casual."[31]

It seems to me that Paul did experience a cognitive shift, but it meant a reordering of his ideas into a new hierarchy. This seems a much better model than that of reversal/inversion. What is also important is that the process of reordering can be seen as an ongoing one (to some extent), and this allows room for development in Paul's thought such as Professor Roetzel has indicated.[32] This model allows for sharing of traditions, for some commonality across group boundaries (though common motifs might not take on the same role in different communities). It allows for a much more fluid situation among religious groups impinging on one another.

---

about the law was at the same time a statement about *hoi hupo nomou or hoi en to nomo.*" See also Gaventa's ("The Singularity of the Gospel," 147–59, 158) comment "In Galatians, the historical locus of the Christ-event means that Christ is not some eternal aeon that exists in contrast to the realm of the flesh. Neither does Paul interpret Christ and the law as ontological opposites."

30. For the concept of a distinction between Paul's reasons (or fundamental convictions) and his arguments, and the idea that his arguments be seen as attempts to work out problems raised by conflicting convictions, see E. P. Sanders, *Paul, the Law, and the Jewish People,* 144–48.

31. Räisänen, *Beyond New Testament Theology,* 134–35, 198–99; and Patte, *Paul's Faith and the Power of the Gospel,* 268–69.

32. See Roetzel, "Grammar of Election," 219. In an appendix entitled "Psychological Study of Paul's Conversion," Alan Segal (*Paul the Convert,* 299) writes: "The most recent data on religious defection and disaffiliation shows how complex and individual the process of religious change can be. . . . The most important conclusion from these studies is to note all the kinds of interactions in values that an actively questing subject can provide. Thus, while Paul's conversion brought a high degree of commitment to his Christian group, and a disaffiliation from Pharisaism, he may still have valued his Jewish identity . . ."

Professor Roetzel's study of Paul's grammar of election found Paul's thinking in his letters to be very fluid indeed. In 1 Thessalonians, Roetzel notes that, in spite of Jewish apocalyptic and martyrological traditions, Paul nowhere in this letter seeks to associate either divine election or the status and behavior of the elect with God's election of the Jewish people. But Paul in this letter does tie election and holiness intimately together. In doing this, he not only uses Old Testament themes but also maintains the normal Old Testament link between the two. What is lacking, however, is any explicit connection between election and the Pauline gentile community.

In Philippians, even though "no explicit reference to election appears," Roetzel finds that a vocabulary of election does appear nevertheless in metaphors, synonyms, and symbolic language drawn from Jewish traditions.[33] In Corinthians, he observes, Paul uses the word καλέω ("call") no fewer than nine times in the space of eight verses. The divine choice is also shown to reverse the normal human hierarchical order, thus preventing believers from linking their identity to social or religious status. He concludes: "Paul secures the identity of the Corinthians in the call of God rather than in an order established by circumcision or uncircumcision, slavery or freedom, marriage or celibacy."[34] It is Paul's use of the cross in Galatians to support the inclusion in the elect of gentiles qua gentiles that Roetzel finds most instructive.

> By noticing how Paul's Galatian cross symbolism differs markedly at points from cross symbolism in 1 Corinthians, Philippians, and 1 Thessalonians, we can see how our attempt to find what is foundational in Paul's theology is risky. For if the cross is at the core of Paul's theology, as many argue, it is simply inadequate to say the cross is foundational without noting the way the interpretation of the cross is changed by its context and then bends back onto the context to shape that as well. This dialectical relationship of symbol and setting is fundamentally unstable and resists our tendency to find a resolution in Paul's theology that has a "totalizing impact."[35]

Roetzel concludes that "Paul did not come to his context culturally naked. Paul's grammar of election emerged in part from the language of the church about God, sin, Jesus Christ, . . . and in part from the venerable traditions of Israel."[36]

---

33. Roetzel, "Grammar of Election," 220–22.

34. Ibid., 232–33.

35. Ibid., 228.

36. Ibid., 233.

To describe Paul's grammar of election as a combination of church traditions and traditions concerning Israel is, we believe, a correct and useful assessment of the evidence. Professor Roetzel has clearly indicated the variability in Paul's theologizing and particularly how his theology develops en route. We acknowledge the validity of the latter conclusion, but feel that he underestimates the significance of Paul's inherited traditions.

The Shape of Paul's Theology

To describe all or part of the origins of Paul's language of discourse is not sufficient. It is in the end not so much origins as usage that is unique to Paul. It is the peculiar combinations and transformations of language that are typical of the apostle. In this respect Roetzel's emphasis on a grammar of election is most apt. But if the language usage is so fluid and flexible, what, if anything, is constant in Paul? What is it, in fact, that determines how Paul uses his language?

Two candidates present themselves; we might describe these as (1) the singularity of the gospel and (2) the unity and upbuilding of the community.[37] It would appear that all use of symbols, all theological constructions had for Paul no ultimacy or abiding significance as formulations in and of themselves.

Rather, the purpose they served was to ensure absolute obedience to the gospel and the ultimate unity and well-being of the believing community. What served these ends was useful and beneficial, and what hindered them was to be opposed or discarded. So Paul's language of discourse is as flexible as the varied situation of his communities demands; it is only an instrument of a greater good. As we have already noted, Paul believed himself to be living in the end-time, already begun with Jesus' resurrection. He did not expect things to remain static or constant; he expected new things. Thus, all our concern for creedal statements retaining their ancient meaning and constancy would have been lost on Paul. He lived at a time before Christian doctrines had had time to harden into fixed formulations, and he does not appear to share our concern that he should repeat again in identical form his earlier pronouncements.[38]

37. See Schütz, *Paul and the Anatomy of Apostolic Authority*, 154–55, 243–44, 281–82; and Gaventa, "The Singularity of the Gospel," 153–54.

38. See also Schütz's (*Paul and the Anatomy of Apostolic Authority*, 119) comment on the topic "another gospel" in Galatians: "The problem is all the more difficult when we remember that there is virtually no evidence that Paul regards 'gospel' as coterminous with a body of information or propositions."

From a sociological perspective, it is indeed a blessing that Paul repeats himself as little as he actually does. The appearance of apparently similar arguments about justification by faith in Galatians and in Romans has often obscured the particularity of both these letters and the fact that the repetition of the same doctrine in a different context does not warrant the view that its function is identical in each instance.[39]

On the other hand, Paul is, as Professor Beker has emphasized, essentially a hermeneutic theologian—an interpreter whose thought is delimited by the tradition in which he stands and which he interprets. Our study of the scriptural interpretive tradition that Paul inherited and shared supports this emphasis.[40] As we noted, there was an expectancy to discover new things in the vital interaction between Scripture and the everyday life of the community—the community lived in the Scriptures and the Scriptures lived in them! But their interpretation remains in some sense still bound to the (original) text, although "the occasion that prompts it may be external to it, some kind of crisis that is historical and theological."[41]

It is the Scriptures that provide such a powerful and meaningful link between Paul and his Jewish heritage.[42] But it is the apocalyptic worldview in which the Scriptures are interpreted that sustains and heightens the expectancy for new things.[43] As Räisänen notes, it is "the dialectical interaction between tradition (symbolic universe), experience and [its] interpretation that governs the way in which the world is perceived and

39. Dahl ("The Doctrine of Justification and its Implications," 115) notes that "Paul does not present the doctrine of justification as a dogmatic abstraction"; see also my study, *Paul's Gospel in an Intercultural Context*, 106–7; and Kee, *Knowing the Truth*, 24.

40. While being in general agreement with Beker's thesis that Paul is essentially an interpreter of the gospel ("Paul the Theologian: Major Motifs in Pauline Theology," 353), I would also stress that Paul is more than simply an interpreter of traditions: Paul interprets the gospel in the context of his daily mission work. That is, the subject matter of Paul's interpretive activity is not limited to traditions but includes the interpretation of divine activity in the course of his apostolic work.

41. See Sabin, "Reading Mark 4 as Midrash," 6. The failure of Israel to respond positively to the gospel, the success of the mission to the gentiles, and the fall of Jerusalem are obvious examples of such times of crisis.

42. Writing about Galatians, Gaventa ("The Singularity of the Gospel," 159) states, "Paul constantly uses biblical interpretation and imagery, not only in response to his opponents' claims about the law but in reference to his own apostolic role (1:15). This absorption in scripture indicates that the gospel's invasion does not negate the place of Israel."

43. There is some diversity still in the definition of "apocalyptic." We have concentrated here on the attitude of mind, rather than on the actual content of an apocalyptic outlook. On this, see Rowland, *The Open Heaven*, 20; see also Sturm, "Defining the Word 'Apocalyptic': A Problem in Biblical Criticism," 39–40. See also de Boer, "Paul and Jewish Apocalyptic Theology," in the same volume, 180–81.

interpreted by groups and individuals."[44] Thus, this relation to, and understanding of, the Scriptures interpreted in the light of the Christ-event operates in some respects at least as "a foundational story about what God has done to bring salvation to his elect people."[45] A further example of an underlying foundational story is identified by Jouette Bassler in a summary of the convictions that seem to undergird 1 Thessalonians: God through the Holy Spirit is working through Paul and in the church God has called. This call is not only a call of election, but also a call to community and holiness.[46] She rightly concludes that, however interesting the kerygmatic story is in and for itself, it became important to Paul and his churches because it was their story. "By God's election they had been grafted into it, and their sense of being a part of this story of God's presence with God's people is the only reason for remembering the story and writing to the churches."[47]

Professor Roetzel has not found it permissible to regard election and calling as key propositional statements or even as foundational expressions in Paul.[48] Nevertheless, the presence and use of election-calling convictions still carries some significance. Thus, one way to account for Paul's continuing use of Scripture, of election terminology, people of God motifs, and so on (however sparse this use may be in some instances) is to maintain that the apostle sees himself and his work as part of an ongoing activity of God in which the Spirit is ever leading into new paths and new experiences. For Paul it is presupposed that God is at work in Christian proclamation and witness and in the emerging communities of believers. The work inaugurated in the resurrection of Christ is being continually demonstrated and carried forward in the power of the Spirit.

To a great extent, this "story" is implicit in Paul; it does not need to be argued because the Spirit's presence is proof itself of God at work; but sometimes we get glimpses of it in elements of covenantal language. The issue remains as to how to evaluate the significance of those elements in Pauline statements that often have little or no explicit connection with the traditional language of first-century Judaism.

Richard Hays, in his study of five letters in the Pauline corpus, has drawn attention to the surprising frequency of the theme of God's calling.

44. Räisänen, *Beyond New Testament Theology*, 131.

45. See Hays, "Crucified with Christ: A Synthesis of the Theology of 1 and 2 Thessalonians, Philemon, Philippians, and Galatians," 231–32.

46. Bassler, "Paul's Theology: Whence and Whither?" 14.

47. Ibid., 16.

48. Roetzel, "Grammar of Election," 214, 233.

He suggests that the background of this imagery is to be found in Deutero-Isaiah, where there are repeated references to God's calling of the Servant/Israel. Hays argues:

> If one hears such echoes in Paul's use of καλεῖν, the close association of the "calling" imagery with the idea of Israel as a covenant people becomes more evident. Just as God called the Servant/Israel by gathering them from the corners of the earth so that they might be "a covenant to the people, a light to the nations," so God now calls the "Israel of God" (= the church) for a similar reason, so that the gospel might be proclaimed.[49]

What we find in Paul is that the apostle has creatively appropriated scriptural imagery in his understanding of believers in Christ. However vague the allusions, or however flexible the terminology, it is arguable that Paul sees the believing community as somehow a continuation of a covenantal people.[50] Just as God was working out his purpose in history through Israel, so now God is active in a special way in believers in Christ.

For Paul it would appear that God's activity through the Spirit is concentrated in the Christian community in that God is, at the moment,[51] working out his purpose in and through them. Perhaps this is because they especially represent the new thing that God is doing in the world: it is not that the rest of the world is outside the rule of God entirely; rather God has chosen to work in and through the believing community to bring the rest of creation back to his control.

The basis for this is probably to be found in Paul's understanding of the revelation of the divine righteousness. Paul saw the resurrection of Jesus as a source of power which is released through the gospel and thus activated among believers. He sometimes equates grace and power (e.g., 2 Cor 1:12;

49. Hays, "Crucified with Christ," 238. Hays is careful to note that Paul never speaks of the church as the "new Israel," as though the old one had been supplanted. "Rather, believers in Jesus simply are Israel" (238 n.25).

50. I use "covenantal" here in a very general sense. I do not mean to refer to a specific system of theology (we have already demonstrated Paul's "apocalyptic" freedom in creating new theological approaches). Paul's use of election and calling terminology is difficult to evaluate precisely, but the presence of this terminology in his letters is sufficient to merit the description "covenantal" in this limited sense. R. D. Kaylor (*Paul's Covenant Community*, 2–3) argues that "covenant as conviction rather than concept functions as a persistent presence and a dominant reality in Paul's life, work, and thought. . . . Covenant was one of the primary but unconsciously worn lenses through which Paul perceived himself and his world."

51. See Krentz, "Tracking the Elusive Center: On Integrating Paul's Theology," 23. On God's activity in the world, see Thomas, "Recent Thought on Divine Agency," and Foreman, "Double Agency and Identifying Reference to God," 35–50, 123–42.

12:10; 1 Cor 15:10). Since grace is the sphere in which all Christians exist (Gal 5:4), the territory of the divine deed's sway, any apostasy is a departure from power, a moving away from one's standing in the gospel.[52]

The gospel is the power of God that leads to salvation, and Paul himself has experienced that power in his own life. Yet he himself as apostle is subordinate to the gospel norm. The power is not Paul's power; he can only make it available since he himself does not provide or control it. It is nevertheless closely associated with the gospel. As Schütz observes, "all of this makes sense only where power and the gospel are thought of within the milieu of a history moving to fulfilment, where there is still a frontier to cross, a *telos* yet to arrive. The final judgement is the final and unmistakable manifestation of power."[53] Paul's ambition, therefore, despite his concentration on his believing communities, is not to subject others to his authority but to subject all, including himself, to the power which manifests itself in the gospel and which will be manifest in the eschaton.

It seems legitimate to conclude that Paul's theologizing takes place within the specific context of ongoing divine activity in relation to a people who are called. Within this context, which includes the scriptural imagery and traditions relating to Israel, Paul felt free to theologize as the Spirit led—apparently with a great degree of freedom. On the other hand, the outcome of the divine activity, which is his basic theme, is not entirely open-ended. Covenant faith saw God's purpose as having a destined goal. The divine purpose will lead to a final transformation and consummation. As Dunn writes (in a different context) "the outworking of God's saving power will be consistent with its initial expression."[54]

Within this purpose and in pursuit of this goal, Paul works with a great sense of freedom, but it is not an absolute freedom; and to some extent the content of his theology is also fixed. It is about the purpose of God revealed in Christ, about the people of God, and about the apostle's commission to work toward the achievement of that divine purpose in the lives of his converts.

Conclusion

In this paper I have sought to take Daniel Patte's advice not to interpret Paul from "a history of ideas" approach.[55] Hence I have sought to pay due regard to the interaction between tradition and experience of events in daily life—

52. See Schütz, *Paul and the Anatomy of Apostolic Authority*, 116–17.
53. Ibid., 285–86.
54. Dunn, "The Theology of Galatians," 242.
55. Patte, *Paul's Faith and the Power of the Gospel*, 11.

to show how the Scriptures and Paul's daily life interact with and recipro-cally interpret each other. I have sought to avoid a too-academic model lest Paul be portrayed simply as an interpreter of texts.

Attention has been focused also on Paul's apocalyptic outlook. Our thesis is that to view Paul as an apocalyptic is not to maintain that he ad-hered to a particular set of doctrines. It is rather a "mind-set," an expectancy that God is doing or is about to do new things. It is to view apocalyptic cat-egories as the justification for the innovative in Paul's mission as a whole.[56] Thus, the Spirit is always revealing new truths and thereby transforming the tradition of the past; so, in effect, the Scriptures themselves relate not to the ancient past but to the immediate present and its future. Paul, in contrast to his interpreters, is not interested in the past as such, nor even in a narrative of the past involving promise and election—nor even in a past Christ-event. For the apostle, continuity and consistency in God's relation with his people are presupposed, and in his earlier letters he does not even seem to be aware of any need to be explicit about this. We have concluded, therefore, that Professor Roetzel's study has correctly demonstrated Paul's freedom and flexibility of discourse in addressing his communities.

But we wish to insist that all of Paul's thinking takes place in the very specific context of God's purpose for his "called" people. Thus despite his radical theologizing, there are elements both old and new in his thought. We argued that Paul, the convert, was dependent on Jewish cultural traditions in which and with which to interpret himself and his experience. Following the thesis of Alan Segal, we came to see the apostle's life as a prime example of how mysticism and apocalypticism could be united phenomenologically.

The combination in one person of these influences requires us to deal seriously with the whole of Paul, his mystical experience, his mission activ-ity, his authority and pastoral care, not just his theological ideas. But the recognition of Paul's indebtedness to his cultural heritage also requires that it be not lightly dismissed or regarded merely as a foil for a contrary lifestyle. We refused to follow the route that seeks to explain all Paul's theology as emanating directly from his Damascus road experience.

We could have insisted that Paul received all his theology, implicitly at least, in his "conversion." But this would be to deny the influence of his Pharisaic past and of Antiochene Christianity. If we stress only the radical newness of Paul's experience, we make him too much a Melchizedek fig-ure without historical antecedent—and thereby render him inexplicable in

56. See Meeks, *The First Urban Christians*, 117, 175.

either social or historical terms by cutting him off from his cultural and religious past.[57]

We have also rejected explanations of Paul's thought that posit a strong antithesis between Paul's Jewish past—for example, his former view of the law—and his adherence to Christ. Instead of radical reversal, we preferred to think of his "conversion" in terms of a cognitive shift in which a new hierarchy of values was established. We sought thereby to avoid a hermeneutic of antithesis with Judaism.[58]

We also sought to stress the dynamic and dialectical nature of Paul's thought. Some otherwise excellent publications on Paul present a wooden image of the apostle that is only a pale reflection of the living dynamic person, one who could not possibly achieve the eminence we know he did.[59] We are very much aware of the complexity of the apostle's life and thought and how difficult it is to understand him without a certain degree of anachronism; we too readily make Paul one of us in anticipating that he will share our interest in carefully formulated propositions or abstract theoretical concepts.

Central to Paul's concern were obedience to the gospel and the unity of his communities. What promoted this concern determined the content of his pastoral writings. Because the apostle lived in a vital tradition of scriptural interpretation, he used the imagery of Scripture, especially that relating to God's call of Israel, as a central theme in his letters. Though he used this scriptural tradition freely and loosely, it did provide a framework for the apostle's diverse theological activity.

We have come to the conclusion, therefore, that if we look for firm propositions or for repetition in a fixed form of major doctrinal statements, we have the wrong presuppositions. Nor should we be disappointed that the "dialectical relationship of symbol and setting is fundamentally unstable and resists our tendency to find a resolution in Paul's theology that has a 'totalizing' impact."[60]

If we set out to find propositional or foundational statements and failed to do so, this factor ought not to cause us to undervalue what we have found just because it is rather different from what might have been

---

57. See Dunn, "A Light to the Gentiles," 105–6.

58. See Gaston, "Retrospect," 163–74, especially 163–64.

59. Perhaps it would be fairer to acknowledge here that most books concentrate only on certain aspects of Paul's work or thought. The result is that when scholars treat a topic such as "the law in Paul," one cannot escape the suspicion that this kind of abstract discussion inevitably distorts the image of the person under investigation. I am not sure that even Stephen Westerholm's useful study *Israel's Law and the Church's Faith* can be completely exonerated from this criticism.

60. Roetzel, "Grammar of Election," 228.

anticipated. Even the evaluation of Paul's theology as being in a formative state needs to be treated with a degree of suspicion. It is possible that if Paul had lived longer his theology would have continued to show this same quality; in fact, he might even have been proud of it. Accordingly, Beker insists that "the fluid boundaries between convictions and contingency belong to the essence of Paul's hermeneutic."[61]

Paul's theologizing takes place in a context of interaction with Scripture and the everyday life of his communities. It is an inner-scriptural, intertextual type of thinking,[62] a world full of images and metaphors that can be used and reused in differing settings. As already noted, it is not a world of propositional truths, of abstract theorizing, or even of precise concepts.

It was the peculiarity of Paul's cultural inheritance that contributed largely to this thought world. The twin elements of continuity of scriptural tradition, tending toward conserving the insights of the past, and of an apocalyptic-mystical outlook, tending toward creative and imaginative new perspectives, might actually be regarded as contradictory. But in Paul's creative mind, under the unifying impulse of his vision of Christ, a complex web of ideas was drawn together. This combination of apocalyptic and mystical in fact offered Paul the freedom to innovate. Moreover, the metaphorical imagery provided a creative and flexible language amenable to fresh combinations and associations ideal for the volatile early days of a new movement. For a group oriented to the present and future, this symbolic language was also essential in order for it to be able to develop its own vision.

What we wish to stress here is that it was Paul's cultural inheritance that provided him with a tradition in which creative freedom was valued and visibly present. His creative freedom was already inculcated in his religious upbringing. This tradition gave Paul the language for expressing a theophany, and his vision of Christ provided a new point of departure within a traditional web of ideas.

Those scholars who have insisted that Paul is no systematic theologian are perfectly correct. We misunderstand his theological method when we abstract his statements and lay them side by side to check for contradictions. It is also probably wrong to look for any one key or central element to elucidate Paul's theology. It is a body of tradition rather than a system of theology with which Paul interacts. But if the creative reformulating and transforming of inherited images and metaphors are what constitutes doing theology, then Paul is certainly a theologian par excellence.

61. Beker, "Paul the Theologian: Major Motifs in Pauline Theology," 353.

62. For Paul's indebtedness to Scripture generally and for the most recent discussion of this aspect of his thought, see Hays, *Echoes of Scripture in the Letters of Paul*, esp. 154–55.

3

The Rule of Faith
in Romans 12:1–15:13

*The Obligation of Humble Obedience to Christ as
the Only Adequate Response to the Mercies of God*

Introduction: Interpretive Tendencies in the
Understanding of the Letter

CHAPTERS 12–15 OF ROMANS have been allowed in some instances to be
determinative of the interpretation of the entire letter.[1] However, this
approach has not met with wide acclaim, and any interpretation of these
chapters must take into account the wider issues that affect the understanding of the letter as a whole.[2]

There has been in recent years a growing tendency to note the verbal
and argumentative connections between chapters 1–11 and chapters 12–
15/16.[3] Earlier emphasis on how little Paul could be expected to know about
the Roman Christians' situation had tended in the opposite direction, but
the increasing awareness of the contingency of many of Paul's statements in
his letters was bound eventually to force commentators to pay strict attention to the relation between argument and the context addressed. This was
complicated by another factor—namely, the dialogical style in which major
sections of the letter were formulated. Earlier discussions about whether

1. See Minear, *The Obedience of Faith*.

2. See Cranfield, *A Critical and Exegetical Commentary on the Epistle to the Romans*
2.820–22.

3. See Dunn, *Romans 1–8*; Dunn, *Romans 9–16*.

or not such a genre as the diatribe actually existed in ancient times have given way to a full-blown discussion of Paul's rhetoric generally and that of Romans in particular.[4]

But the crucial issue still requiring to be addressed is this: Having clarified, to some extent at least, the role played by certain elements in the rhetorical argumentation in Romans, how can we determine their relation to actual positions held by Christians in Rome? It is precisely at this point that interpretative presuppositions and tendencies come into play. Because of the stylistically necessary dissociation between the argumentative strategy and that to which it is addressed, scholarly subjectivity and selectivity once again have space in which to manoeuvre.

The dominant tendency of exegesis of Romans in this century has been the tendency to interpret its contents as Paul's critique of Judaism in contrast to his own law-free gospel. Since the Reformation, scholars have implicitly or explicitly interpreted Paul's arguments in the context of a debate with Judaism. However unsure a scholar may have been about Paul's knowledge of the Romans' context, one thing remained unquestioned: that Paul in Romans confronts Judaism polemically as the apostle to the gentiles.[5] Even in contemporary scholarship, wherever there is interpretative uncertainty this assumption tends to creep in.[6] In my own research, I found it most obviously emerging in scholars' interpretations of Paul's citation of biblical texts in chapters 9–11. Even the RSV in 9:27 adds a gratuitous "only" before the reference to a remnant being saved. Again in similar vein in 11:17 according to the RSV the wild olives are not grafted in among the remaining branches on the olive tree, but are situated "in their place." The NRSV remains unchanged at this point!

What is the significance of this for interpreting Rom 12–15? It is that since the approach to these chapters not only depends on but also reinforces one's view of the preceding chapters, then what one brings to the understanding of the section is vitally important because it is bound up with one's approach to the entire letter.[7] My own conclusion on Paul's attitude to Judaism in Romans, particularly in chapters 9–11, I will state clearly rather than

---

4. See Stowers, *The Diatribe and Paul's Letter to the Romans*, and Elliott, *The Rhetoric of Romans*.

5. The antithesis with Judaism is not integral to justification by faith (which can also serve an apologetic purpose); *contra* Käsemann, *Commentary on Romans*, 85. On Paul's critique of Judaism and of legalism in general, see Sanders, *Paul, the Law, and the Jewish People*, 154–60.

6. On this, see my *Paul's Gospel in an Intercultural Context*, esp. 136–40.

7. Francis Watson (*Paul, Judaism and the Gentiles*, 107) holds that Rom 1–11 is "the theoretical legitimation for the social reorientation called for in Rom 14:1—15:13."

attempt to argue in detail. Paul, because of nascent anti-Judaism among the Roman gentile Christians, finds himself cast in the role of defender of Israel against gentiles, probably for the first time in his apostolic career.[8] If it is true that Paul is here actually forced to defend Israel against gentile prejudice, then any residue of anti-Jewish interpretation is bound to distort the understanding of this letter more than any other.

The real issue at stake is to try to determine how Paul meant his arguments to be understood.[9] Is the apostle always equally fair and balanced to both Jew and gentile at each point in the letter? This may not be his strategy. For instance, James Dunn's generally well-balanced approach to Romans concludes the exposition of chapter 11 by stressing Paul's use of Job to maintain that God "owes no one anything." Dunn then goes on to state:

> The thought is particularly appropriate in the epilogue to an argument intended to confront and refute the assumption of most of Paul's Jewish contemporaries that God's mercy was their national prerogative, for such an assumption too easily becomes the presumption that God's mercy is Israel's right, something God owes to them, as some later rabbinic statements show.[10]

This particular statement seems to imply that it is mainly the Jews who need such a corrective. Whether or not Dunn is right to see this as directed mainly toward Jewish assumptions and presumptions, the gentile Christians recently addressed in 11:13 also needed to hear that God owes them nothing. This understanding would concur better with Paul's universal emphasis in Romans and the entire letter can be regarded not just as a warning against Jewish presumption but against all human presumption, which I understand the doctrine of justification essentially to preclude.[11]

Where we are not sure whether Paul addresses Jews or gentiles, it is only appropriate to apply the argument universally rather than selectively to Jews. Otherwise we risk dealing in generalizations or stereotypes rather than actualities.[12]

---

8. See Campbell, *Paul's Gospel*, 201.

9. See Martyn, "Listening to John and Paul on the Subject of Gospel and Scripture," 61–81, esp. 69–70.

10. Dunn, *Romans 9–16*, 703.

11. Which Dunn ("The Formal and Theological Coherence of Romans," 245–50, esp. 150) likewise stresses: "a consistent concern throughout the letter is to puncture presumption, wherever he finds it."

12. On this, see E. P. Sanders, *Paul, the Law*, 154–60. Markus Barth ("St. Paul—a Good Jew," 7–8) criticized Käsemann for the assertion that "the apostle's essential enemy is the pious Jew."

Thus, the crucial question in relation to the example cited above is whether Rom 11:33–36 is the conclusion to the immediately preceding section, which opposes gentile arrogance and presumption (which 12:2–3 would seem to imply), or whether, on the other hand, it is designed to serve as a conclusion for all of chapters 1–11, in which case it is legitimate to speak at this point of Jewish presumption as well as gentile, but certainly not the one without the other.

If Romans could simply be regarded as Paul's theology per se and not the contingent set of specifically targeted words that most scholars now recognize it to be, then we would not need to question Paul's stance or strategy in the epistle. But since this is not the case, how can we be sure about Paul's stance toward Judaism? Is Paul's dialogue with the Jew in 2:17ʾ–29 to be regarded as a polemical attack on contemporary Judaism, and is his "pro-Jewish" conclusion in 11:25–32 to be viewed as somehow at odds with it?[13] Paul does appear to oscillate somewhat: sometimes he seems critically anti-Jewish, but at other points so pro-Jewish that C. H. Dodd considered that here his Christian apostleship had been subsumed under a residual Jewish patriotism![14]

Only by finding some congruence between Paul's purpose in writing the letter, the argumentative style and strategy he employs in the text, and the theological arguments undergirding the whole, can we hope to reach any measure of agreement on the relative significance of the diverse statements Paul somehow fuses together in this document. One of the most complicating factors in all this is the question of the diatribe style, and it is to this that we must now turn.

The Diatribe Style as an Indirect Witness to What Paul is Not Saying: He Intends to Preclude an Anti-Jewish Interpretation of His Gospel

Amid all the intricacies of interpretation of the significance of the diatribe style, what may be missed is the obvious point, the fact that by mentioning a particular interpretation at all (even to refute or disown it), Paul indicates his awareness of theological stances and conclusions which he chooses not

13. On the possibility of contradictions in Paul's thought, see Watson, *Paul, Judaism and the Gentiles*, 170–73; and Räisänen, *Paul and the Law*. See also E. P. Sanders, *Paul, the Law*, 144–54; and Fitzmyer, *Romans*, 131–32.

14. On this, see Gaston, *Paul and the Torah*, 92 and 217 n.60; cf. Marxsen, *Introduction to the New Testament*, 103.

to follow or which he even explicitly disowns. The actual outcome of the uncertainty about how to interpret the diatribe style is a weakening of confidence about what Paul did intend to say or even to refute. It is in order to counteract this debilitating malaise that I wish to point to another aspect of dialogical style as such.

If one deals with issues directly or in a straightforward manner, it will be evident what one supports or promotes but not perhaps so clear *what one rejects*. The advantage of Paul's dialogical approach in Romans is that alongside the letter he actually wrote, we can to some extent at least, envisage the letter *he chose not to write*.

In my own work on Romans, I have tried to demonstrate that when one puts together Paul's ten rejected theses, one gets a kind of summary outline of the issues the apostle faced in writing the letter.[15] Paul's strategy appears to be to highlight his own stance by a categorical rejection of extreme positions adopted by, or available to, at least some of the Roman Christians. A crucial indicator of the interpreter's stance is usually presented in the approach to 2:1–29. Neither grammar nor rhetoric constrains us to presume that the Jew explicitly addressed in 2:17 is already presupposed in 2:1; yet this interpretation still dominates in the literature. Stowers's careful rhetorical analysis demonstrates that the admonitory apostrophe beginning in 2:1 clearly addresses the Greek. Only at 2:17 does Paul turn to an imaginary Jew, a pretentious teacher of the law. The fictitious persona and life situation depicted here—a well-known character type that appears as a gentile in 2:1–5 and as a Jew in 2:17–29—are used by Paul as an argument against pretension and boasting. By applying the type to both Greek and Jew, he reinforces the theme of equity. Despite its precise targeting of the pretentious Jewish teacher (who thinks he holds the cure to the moral and religious malaise of gentiles), even 2:17–29 criticizes "not Jews or Judaism as such but teachers who in Paul's view stand in antithesis to his own gospel concerning justification of the Gentile peoples."[16] We are forced to the conclusion here that while "an anti-Jewish interpretation of Romans has been a frequent phenomenon, it was certainly not the original historical meaning of Romans as a public text."[17]

---

15. See Campbell, *Paul's Gospel,* 178–84. See also Jewett, "Following the Argument of Romans," 265–77.

16. Stowers, *A Rereading of Romans,* 153.

17. Contra Cosgrove, "The Justification of the Other: An Interpretation of Romans 1:18—4:25," 613–34, esp. 631. Cosgrove thinks that Paul leaned in the direction of the privileged gentile majority. See also Meyer, "The Justification of God" (a paper read at the SBL Pauline Theology Group meeting in 1992 in response to Cosgrove's paper).

The Situation of Paul's Addressees in Romans 12–15

Recent research would appear to indicate that several factors were influential in producing the situation that Paul addressed in Romans.

Political Factors

A unique factor of the "Roman context" was that the emperor Claudius, during the period 41–49 C.E., was forced to intervene at least once in disputes among the Jews in Rome.[18] As a result, it seems that there may have been a prohibition of synagogal meetings, and there is evidence that a number of Jews were expelled from the city in 49 C.E. It would appear that at least the leaders of the Jewish Christians were temporarily absent from Rome. Some gentiles in close adherence to the synagogue may also have been expelled, since to the Romans they would appear to be living as Jews. Whether or not the expulsion led to a complete severance between house groups and synagogues, it probably did contribute to a splintering into the diverse groups that were typical of Roman Christianity several decades later. In any case, what is fundamental to the Roman situation is that political factors may have been instrumental in encouraging a rupture in relations between the gentile churches and the synagogues.

Peter Lampe maintains that by the time Romans was written the Christians were certainly separated from the synagogue. Recent proselytes and God-worshipers would also have been forced to reconsider their adherence to the Jewish community.[19] Some doubtless would conclude that it was politic to sever these links. The ejection of Jews from Rome may have encouraged feelings that God's purpose had now moved on from the Jews, bringing a status reversal that some welcomed (Jews were now the adherents and fringe members).[20]

We would not wish to claim a complete break between house groups and synagogues *prior* to Paul's writing to the Romans. It is true that Paul seems to openly acknowledge little positive response to the gospel from

18. See Smallwood, *The Jews under Roman Rule*, 251. See also Lüdemann, *Paul, Apostle to the* Gentiles, 164–65; and Brändle and Stegemann, "The Emergence of the First Christian Community in Rome in the Context of the Jewish Communities" (a paper read at the 1993 SNTS meeting in Chicago).

19. Peter Lampe (*Die stadtrömischen Christen in den ersten beiden Jahrhunderten*, 56–58) considers that the gentiles in Rome were predominantly "God-fearers," both because this was normal in many early Christian communities and also because of the "Jewish" context of Romans.

20. See Dunn, *Romans 9–16*, 662.

Jews (see Rom 9:30). It is also clear that those gentiles who boasted over the branches broken off (11:19) are unlikely to be part of a synagogue community. But, despite this, there is evidence throughout Romans, and especially in chapters 14–15, of a form of Christianity that is still attached to the synagogue. Romans, in our view, represents not the final divorce in the "marriage" between house groups and synagogues but only the beginnings of that separation—the marriage is in trouble but it's not yet clear that it is irreparably damaged.[21]

As it is unlikely that up to fifty thousand Jews were expelled from Rome, some form of Jewish community activities would probably continue. But the point we wish to stress here is that the political factors we have noted may have caused, or at least encouraged, a period of relative separation of gentile Christians from the synagogue.

Theological Factors

This period came to an end when expelled Christians such as Aquila and Priscilla returned to Rome after Nero came to power. Those Christians who previously had had close links with the synagogue may have found they were no longer welcome there lest future disturbances ensue. They may not have been able to return to the same area of the city, so that it may have been difficult to find ceremonially pure food, and a type of vegetarianism may have been temporarily practiced.[22] Neither were they necessarily welcomed by all the gentile Christians at Rome. Most Pauline Christians would doubtless have welcomed such people. But there seems to be some diversity in theology among the Roman Christians. Despite the clear evidence for gentile Christianity evinced by Paul's letter to Rome, there is good reason to believe that the earlier forms of Christianity that existed there, both Jewish and gentile, were strongly influenced by Jewish teaching and practice. There is a growing scholarly consensus that the earliest Christianity in Rome was an intra-Jewish phenomenon.[23] Alongside this there are signs of a radical Hellenist Christianity, also of early origin.[24] There is evidence of frequent

---

21. See Campbell, *Paul's Gospel,* 150–53.

22. See Watson, *Paul, Judaism and the Gentiles,* 95.

23. See Lampe, *Die Stadtrömischen Christen,* 10–35; and Walters, *Ethnic Issues in Paul's Letter to the Romans,* esp. chapter 2, which deals with Jewish socialization in ancient Rome (pp. 19–58).

24. See Brown, "Not Jewish Christianity and Gentile Christianity but Types of Jewish/ Gentile Christianity," 74–79. This essay is similar to Brown's introduction (with John P. Meier) *Antioch and Rome: New Testament Cradles of Catholic Christianity.*

journeys by Jews between Rome and Jerusalem, and it is quite likely that Hellenists like Pauline converts would migrate to the imperial city.[25]

The disturbances in 49 C.E. may not have been caused by the advent of Christianity in Rome, which probably should be dated some years earlier. The riots possibly resulted from radical Hellenists preaching a law-free gospel to gentiles and God-worshipers associated with the synagogue. With the expulsion of Jewish Christian leaders, it may be that more radical forms of gentile Christianity developed in the house-churches in the period prior to the succession of Nero.[26] An alternative scenario is that the radicals were internal to the Roman congregations and that the anti-Jewish bias developed out of disputes about the relevance of Torah to Christians (see 16:17).

Beyond the fact that we know for certain that Claudius moved against the Jews in Rome at least once, we have no real evidence concerning the precise significance of this political factor for understanding Romans. All we can claim with any degree of certainty is that the daily life and worship of both Roman Jews and Christians were *in all probability* strongly influenced in certain respects.

A heightened consciousness of ethnic differences in relation to Roman legal status would necessarily emerge, since the Jews were those officially targeted, despite a historic regard for their special status. Jews in Rome as a close-knit immigrant ethnic community would already have a very strong sense of identity, but the edict may well have accentuated this and also encouraged a comparable gentile response. Anti-Jewish sentiments common among the Romans may have become intensified. The outcome of all this would necessarily lead to divergent self-definitions by the different strands of Roman Christianity. James C. Walters has given a good rationale for the view that the intervention of Claudius led to *changing* self-definitions among the Roman groups.

> The turmoil that Jewish Christians and God-fearing Gentiles experienced was compounded in the aftermath of the edict; not only were they separated from their "ethnos," but they had at the same time to deal with the heightened dissonance caused by changes in the Roman communities. . . . The pressure that

---

25. See Brown and Meier, *Antioch and Rome*, 110; also Judge and Thomas, "The Origin of the Church at Rome: A New Solution," 81–93. Lampe estimates that two thirds of the names of the Christians mentioned in Rom 16 indicate Greek background, and hence immigrant status (*Die Stadtrömischen Christen*, 153).

26. See Jewett, "Tenement Churches and Communal Meals in the Early Church," 23–24. Jewett argues against the traditional dominance of the house church model (ibid., 29–30).

law-abiding Christians felt under these circumstances must have been enormous.[27]

We can reasonably assume, therefore, that the Edict of Claudius had a lasting divisive influence on the situation of the Roman Christians. As already noted, the growing consensus is that almost all of the Roman Christians had had contact with Judaism at some point in their lives.[28] So we can posit that when Paul wrote his letter there were probably some Christians of Jewish background or at least proselytes and former God-worshipers who by conviction still sought to follow the law and who, given the opportunity, would have preferred to keep their connection with synagogue worship.[29]

But there were probably other Christians who had never had this close contact with the synagogue. Among these we would expect to find converts from Paul's mission in the east. Others also may have found in Christianity freedom from the constraints of their previous adherence to Judaism. Yet others, caught up in the problems resulting from the expulsion, may have been rejected by Jews who blamed the advent of the Christian message for their punishment.[30]

Major studies such as those of James D. G. Dunn and Robert Jewett, among others, see the theme of the relation of Jew and gentile as a constituent element in the discussion in chapters 14–15.[31] With H. W Bartsch one can affirm the connection of 11:25 via 12:3 to chapters 14–15.[32] But from F. C. Baur to G. Bornkamm, Robert Karris, and others, the precise identification of specific groups has been deeply disputed.[33] If the thesis that the Roman Christians are essentially gentile (at least by birth) could be sustained—and it does have some substance—then where can we locate the (Jewish) Christians frequently identified as "the weak"? What is required to make sense of the content of Romans is not Jewish Christians as such but a context in which Judaism plays a role, even if that role is simply to provide a

---

27. See Walters, *Ethnic Issues*, 64.

28. In addition to the views noted above in n.23, see Wedderburn, *The Reasons for Romans*, 50–54; Fitzmyer, *Romans*, 33–34; and Brändle and Stegemann, "Emergence."

29. Watson (*Paul, Judaism and the Gentiles*, 93) suggests that Jewish success in attracting proselytes led to the expulsion of Jews in 19 C.E.

30. Ibid., 95.

31. See Jewett, "Following the Argument," esp. 43–67.

32. Bartsch, "Die antisemitischen Gegner des Paulus im Römerbrief," 27–43.

33. Bornkamm's essay "The Letter to the Romans as Paul's Last Will and Testament" and Karris's essay "The Occasion of Romans: A Response to Professor Donfried" are both included in *The Romans Debate* (rev. ed.), 16–28 and 65–84, respectively. Recent research has demonstrated the specificity in the application of Paul's parenesis within each letter, even though not all of the content may be unique to a particular letter.

foil for gentile Christian arrogance. It would make better sense, however, if there were lively social links between gentile Christian assemblies and local synagogues.

But even if the great majority of the Roman Christians were gentile (with only a few Jewish leaders such as Aquila and Priscilla), we are not obligated to accept the hypothesis that the weak were all Jewish by birth (and the resultant correlation of Jewishness with weakness). It is feasible that many of them were gentiles influenced in different degrees by Jewish practices. Thus, the debates may be mainly between gentile Christians about the degree of Jewishness (if any) obligatory on such Christians. The issue at stake must then be the legitimacy of the residual Judaism still prevailing in the lifestyle of certain gentile Christians and, issuing from that, the fundamental question of the relationship of the Pauline movement to Judaism and its ultimate identity.

Social Factors: The Weak and the Strong in First-Century Roman Society

Some recent studies suggest that the alienation between weak and strong in Rome may have been due to social factors as much as to political or theological ones. Mark Reasoner has recently drawn attention to the social connotations of the words for strong and weak which Paul uses in Rom 15:1: δυνατός ("strong") and ἀδυνατός ("weak") are nearly exact Greek counterparts of the Latin *potens, firmus*, and *vis*, on one hand, and *inferior, tenuus*, and *invalidus* on the other.[34] Roman society at this period had a very fixed social order; however, within the given social divisions there also operated a *potentior/inferior* distinction. Social strength consisted of some kind of prestige "from physical strength to financial wealth to *auctoritas*."[35]

Reasoner finds it instructive to consider the ideology of weakness in Roman society: "The *inferiores* appear in the literature of the late Republic and early Empire to be those who were vulnerable to exercises of social power from those above them on the social ladder."[36] In such a society, where people measured their worth by the people over whom they could

---

34. See Reasoner, "Potentes and Inferiores in Roman Society and the Roman Church" (a paper read at the 1992 SBL meeting in San Francisco). See also his "The 'Strong' and 'Weak' in Rome and in Paul's Theology" (Ph.D. dissertation, University of Chicago, 1990).

35. Reasoner, "Potentes," 12 . I am indebted also to Carolyn Osiek's paper read at the 1993 SNTS meeting in Chicago, "The Oral World of the First Christians at Rome."

36. See Reasoner, "Potentes," 12.

exercise social power, it is significant that Paul uniquely in Romans uses the terms δυνατός and ἀδύνατός and does not mention categories otherwise used to describe Roman society, as, for example, the imperial distinction in orders, categories related to status such as patron/client or citizen/peregrinus, or categories related to class such as rich/poor or free/servile.

If we were to attempt to determine which group in Rome was the more likely to be considered "weak" in social terms, it is quite likely that a Jewish Christian group would be a better candidate than a gentile one; however, Reasoner holds that the household of Aristobulus (if, as is likely, he belonged to the Herodian family and was a friend of Claudius) would count among the *potentes* of the Roman church.[37] The "strong" in terms of social significance would most naturally refer to Roman citizens or foreign-born who display a proclivity toward things Roman. Such persons would exercise their *auctoritas* over those whom Roman society placed below them in status. Freedmen who had risen in status, social influence, and property holdings above the freeborn within the lower population might form a significant proportion of the group.

Carolyn Osiek thinks that "if the language of weak and strong had such inescapably social connotations, then its use in Romans 14–15 must have referred not primarily to legal or moral differences, but to differences in social status."[38] She goes on to note that "a possible qualification for being assigned to the category of the weak is having foreign lower class connections, in this case the foreign religion of Judaism." Other factors such as the degree of romanization in language, customs, and so on, and the degree of literacy and Roman citizenship may also have been factors. Osiek holds that κρίνειν ("to judge") ἐξουθενεῖν ("to despise") in Rom 14 denote the language of power and that "the entire persuasive strategy of Paul's rhetoric is to convince the powerful that they are not to oppress the weak by exerting social pressure on them in the matter of diet."[39]

Paul ranks himself with the δυνατοί ("strong") on the basis of the criterion of conscience in regard to diet (14:14). But do his Roman citizenship and literacy also contribute to this social strength? It is exceedingly difficult to distinguish the relative significance of the social and theological factors. Perhaps it is the combination of them that is so powerful. Paul uses every theological weapon at his disposal to convince his fellow δυνατοί not only not to exploit the "weak" believers, nor simply to *tolerate*

---

37. Ibid. Lampe has identified Marsfield and Aventine as districts where Christians of higher social status lived (*Die Stadtrömischen Christen*, 46–52). See also Jewett, "Tenement Churches," 6–7.

38. Osiek, "Oral World,"

39. Ibid., 11.

them, but rather positively *to bear with*, to *support*, the powerless after the example of Christ.[40]

What emerges from this discussion is that it is unlikely that we can say with any confidence that either group, Jewish Christians or gentile Christians, as such was clearly identifiable as being socially weak or strong, though Jewish Christians for cultural and other reasons might be less likely to have been regarded as the strong.[41] The exhortation not to be high-minded but to associate with the lowly (12:16) would have much greater weight if "the weak" are identified as those of low social status.

Stanley Stowers also acknowledges that "the weak" and "weakness" were well-established concepts in Greco-Roman society. Stowers holds that Paul employed categories such as mature or immature, weak (or sick) and strong in his communities. These are not fixed roles but relative categories. Nor are they groups, parties, or theological positions; they are dispositions of character. Stowers reads Romans very much in the light of the current first-century interest in an ethic of self-mastery (though this is not its most important theme).[42] "Until recently scholars have not noted that the concept of "weakness, so prominent in Paul's letters, had its cultural home at the very heart of Greco-Roman discourse about the passions and self-mastery." Romans 14–15 can be "read as a hortatory distillation of Paul's advice to gentile converts who sought to learn mastery of their passions and desires through psychagogic practices within the community of Christ." This influence derived "either from popular moral philosophy or from the kind of Judaism we meet in Philo." Despite the fact that "the weak hold to false beliefs about things like food and special days"—which causes them to reject the strong—the latter are not to approach the weak like philosophers who subjected the foolish to "therapy of the passions with reason." "Paul did not consider the church a school for self-mastery." As God and Christ have accepted the weak and strong alike, so too the weak and the strong must adapt themselves to one another in the same way. The paradigm of the Pauline ethic is ultimately not the "mastery of emotion and desire" but "adaptability to the needs of others."[43]

---

40. Βαστάζειν (15:1) means "to protect and support" (cf. 11:18); see Osiek, "Oral World," 11.

41. See Reasoner, "Potentes," 11.

42. Stowers, *A Rereading*, 66.

43. Ibid., 45, 322, 323, 258.

The Identity of the Weak
and the Strong in Romans 14–15

In a recent article on the weak and the strong, Paul Sampley notes that the direct data about these "groups" is extremely slight.[44] There are only three explicit references to the weak: τὸν ἀσθενοῦντα (14:1), ὁ ἀσθενῶν (14:2), and τῶν ἀδυνάτων (15:1); the use of different terms suggests no formal identification of a group. The "profile of the weak" indicates only that he is "weak in faith" or "weak with respect to faith" (14:1) and a vegetarian (14:2). Paul then opposes anyone interfering "in the relationship of a house servant (οἰκέτης) with his master (κύριος)" and insists "that preferences regarding meat and vegetables are extraneous to one's relationship to one's Lord." A possible third clue in the profile of the weak is that "one prefers one day over another; another regards all days alike" (14:5). Scholars have tended to identify weak and strong respectively here, but Paul does not. So Sampley claims that "even if a modern interpreter insisted on carrying Paul's mention of weak and strong in 14:1–2" into the subsequent verses, "it is not a priori clear who might be better identified as the weak person." Sampley concludes that this minimal information concerning the weak and the strong surely gives us "scant basis to profile them onto either extreme of what was in reality more likely a continuum among the house churches of Rome."[45]

In contrast to the attempts to give precise specific identification concerning the profile of the weak and the strong, Sampley holds that 14:1—15:13 is "laced with exhortations and definitional declarations that are designed to *be equally applicable to all the Roman believers*" (emphasis mine). "These claims rehearse the common ground and calling that all believers share and give a powerful context in which to consider anew individual differences with regard to practice." While we may speculate that "one point of contention among Roman believers was in fact the sabbath," Paul does not actually say this was so. Gentiles also honored special days— so Paul deftly moves the sabbath issue "onto neutral ground." Thus "Paul's rhetorical strategy" involves an "oblique approach" that puts no Roman group in the spotlight. Paul had done the same earlier in this chapter on the issue of keeping *kashrut* by moving the discussion over into the "neutral and mutually accessible grounds of vegetarianism" so that when he "finally brings to the surface . . . what indeed must have been a contentious issue,

---

44. Sampley's paper was read at the 1993 SNTS meeting in Chicago. It has been published as "The Weak and the Strong: Paul's Careful and Crafty Rhetorical Strategy in Romans 14:1—15:13," 40–52.

45. Ibid., 41–42.

viz. what is κοινός ("common, impure, unclean," 14:14), he has assiduously prepared a context within which it can be considered afresh and on different grounds by all the parties among the Roman believers."[46]

While supporting the scholarly consensus that stresses the connection of 12:1–2 with all that follows, Sampley insists that 14:1—15:13 cannot be adequately grasped apart from its links to 12:3. Two elements prepare for what succeeds 12:3: (1) the significant "individuated 'measure of faith'" that "provides the conceptual framework within which one could recognize stronger and weaker faith" and (2) the "caution against over-evaluation"— Paul does not warn against under-evaluation of oneself, so unwarranted "high self-evaluation" must be the problem of all in Rome. Thus, Sampley claims that when "Paul broaches the Roman divisiveness with his figured speech in 14:1—15:13, he urges the strong to welcome the one who is weak in faith—and in so doing assumes that all parties may well identify themselves as strong in faith" ("presuming all will identify themselves as strong in faith"). He also urges them to realize that "each believer has the obligation to welcome and nurture others, just as 'Christ did not please himself' (15:1–3)."[47] We find ourselves in broad agreement with Sampley's approach.

However, we can only accept with reservation the thesis that "the rhetorical notations of 'weak' and 'strong' have no objective referents in the Roman congregations." We can accept the more dynamic notion of a continuum of various "types" of Christians,[48] but this does not necessarily entirely remove the need to posit the existence of certain groups across whose divisiveness Paul proposes to build rhetorical bridges.[49]

It will greatly assist our understanding here if we can be clear about Paul's intention. Is Paul seeking to remove diversity in order to produce a more monochrome Christianity in the Pauline mold? This is certainly not the case. Paul's intention is to promote harmony *within* diversity rather than to remove the diversity—otherwise what could be the significance of saying, "Let everyone be fully convinced in his own mind" or "whatever is not of faith is sin"?

I have previously argued that ethnic distinctions are far from being unimportant for Paul.[50] Although for the apostle, Jew, and gentile are one in

46. Ibid., 42–43.

47. Ibid., 47–48.

48. We need to distinguish "groups" of Christians from "types" of Christians. R. E. Brown refers to "types" in his article "Not Jewish Christianity," but in *Antioch and Rome* he speaks of "groups," reflecting a certain ambiguity.

49. Sampley, "The Weak and the Strong," 48.

50. Paul denies ultimate significance to ethnic distinctions rather than their continuing existence. See Campbell, *Paul's Gospel*, 98–131.

Christ according to Gal 3:28, this statement is too often generalized by correlating it with the twice-repeated thesis in Romans—"there is no distinction"—as if Paul had written the two phrases side by side in the same letter. The Galatian text signifies the equality of access to salvation rather than the removal of distinctions between Jew and gentile (or male and female). I have maintained that it was in fact Paul's own theology that legitimated the right of Jews to live *as Jews* in Christ.[51] The alternative to this is the traditional understanding of Paul's gospel, which inevitably turns out to be a pro-gentile or an anti-Jewish message. Because Paul fought for the right of gentiles to be accepted in faith *as gentiles*, scholars have failed to recognize that Jews have not in fact been allowed a similar privilege—that is, to be accepted in faith *as Jews*. They are expected to become like gentiles and to conform to a gentile Christian lifestyle upon coming to faith in Christ.

Such a gospel is essentially biased and therefore flawed, because it destroys the very equality and correlation it is designed to promote: God becomes the God of gentiles rather than the one God of Israel and the nations. But an even greater consequence of this theology is that theologically Judaism, as such, and Jewishness—even in its manifestation as an element within Christianity—has no longer any actual right to exist.

Paul does identify himself as strong, but he is realistic enough to acknowledge continuing diversity within the house-churches, as Jewett has clearly recognized: "Faith for Paul is not a single dogmatic standard . . . faith in Jesus Christ has pluralistic possibilities."[52]

But the question that now requires answer is: What kind of pluralism? "Let each be fully convinced in his own mind" too readily suggests to modern interpreters the contemporary Western individualistic view of society as comprised solely of separate individuals who freely choose their own particular lifestyles without reference to cultural groupings or corporate loyalties, shared traditions, and so on. It is our contention, however, that Paul is dealing here with conflicting groups rather than with differing types of individual Christians. This perspective will become clearer if we consider the alternative scenario. If Paul is dealing only with a variety of individuals who are situated at various points on a continuum that stretches from "conservative," law-abiding Jewish Christians to radical (possibly Hellenist) Christians, then why should individual believers be vulnerable or threatened? With such diversity of opinion and such freedom for individual conviction, this inherent pluralism of belief should in fact prove to be a source of security for the diverse individuals that produced it. "Weak" and

51. Ibid., 99–100.
52. See Jewett, *Christian Tolerance*, 62.

"strong" would be almost completely relativized. If there were no group-ings or if the groups were so numerous and diverse that everyone could be easily accommodated, then there would be no vulnerable "weak" torn with divided loyalties or troubled conscience.

We need to distinguish here between a continuum of ideas and a con-tinuum of organizations. Doubtless, every shade of Christian opinion was represented among the Christians in Rome. But this does not mean that there was freedom and opportunity in every instance for believers to follow their own individual convictions. The diversity in belief was probably not exactly matched by diversity of organization, and individuals would have to conform to the mores of the group to which they wished to be attached.

The fact that Rom 14 indicates that there are weak Christians who are extremely vulnerable (see vv. 13, 15, 16, 20, 21) may be taken as an indication that there were individuals who were torn between adherence to conviction and adherence to a group. If groups were in contention and in competition with each other, individuals would feel under pressure to con-form to the dominant behavior patterns of such groups, especially if they were well-defined groups.[53]

Paul's clear advice and stance are that the strong ought in some way to support and accommodate the weak (15:1). If his advice had been that the weak should yield to the strong, then the problem would be solved. The Christians with synagogue connections and a Jewish lifestyle would simply relinquish both of these and form one mixed Pauline community. But what then would be the relevance of the measure of faith meted out to each if this inherent charismatic diversity is simply obliterated? The provision for ongoing diversity, which seems to be such a fundamental premise in the discussion, means that yet another possible solution is thereby excluded. If Paul's advice were that the strong should simply accommodate the weak by giving up their own lifestyle and conforming completely to that of the weak, this would mean that the lifestyle of the latter would become the norm for both the house-churches and (Christian) synagogues in Rome, a position that begins to appear very different from the contemporary understanding of Paul.

A radical review of Paul's attitude to Judaism and to the weak has recently been proposed by Mark D. Nanos, who, claims that "the weak in faith" was Paul's phrase to describe the faith of those he still considered part of the people of God but who had not yet recognized that Jesus was the Christ of Israel: i.e., *non-Christian* Jews. Nanos links the stumbling of the weak in chapters 14–15 to 9:30–33, where the stone over which

53. See Tajfel, *Differentiation between Groups,* 61–76.

Jews stumble is the refusal to accept the equal co-participation of gentiles in God's grace because of an ethnocentric definition of entrance requirements.[54] The church in Rome was not yet separate from the synagogue, but this mainly gentile community was becoming arrogant, boasting in freedom from the law as the new people of God in a way that would cause Jewish people "to blaspheme" the grace of God supposedly enjoyed by such gentiles. Paul writes to exhort the strong Christians to help support the weak Jewish brother to prevent him stumbling and thus to encourage him toward faith in Christ. The strong must in fact behave like righteous gentiles for the sake of the weak.

Nanos's arguments are compelling and make excellent sense of many verses and sections of Romans. Reluctantly, I find myself not fully convinced by some aspects of his comprehensive reworking of the letter. I am still inclined to the view that the weak are Christians—the measure of faith of 12:2 in my view implies a christological foundation (rather than just a theological one). Further, Paul argues for the continuance and maintenance of the diversity that springs from the differing measures of faith gifted to believers. This could not be the case if the Jewish believers were not yet committed to faith in Christ.

It seems best therefore to envisage a scenario something like this. Paul is essentially dealing with differing groups of Christians in the context of ongoing links with synagogues. Whether we should envisage the Christians who feel obligated to a Jewish lifestyle as being a *part* of a synagogue or, alternatively, as comprising a separate assembly of Jews who had faith in Jesus, it is impossible to determine. What we can be reasonably sure about is that there were groups of Christians in Rome who by conviction followed the broad lines of a Jewish lifestyle in relation to purity laws, festivals, and so on. Alongside these there were other groups of Christians, probably in the majority, who were mainly of gentile origin, although some at least of these would previously have had contact with the synagogues in some form or another. These despised the scruples of their "Jewish" brethren and were arrogant in their self-confidence as the new people of God. They now worshiped only in their house groups and saw little reason why they should maintain any social contacts with Jews as such.[55]

---

54. Nanos, *The Mystery of Romans,* see esp. chapter 3, "Who were the 'weak' and 'strong' in Rome?" Although Nanos's work was unknown to me when I read the initial version of this paper at the 1993 SBL meeting in Washington, I am delighted that the author has kindly shared his forthcoming work with me.

55. See Jewett, "Tenement Churches." If the majority of Roman Jews were poor—as seems likely from Philo's comment that the Jewish population of Rome was concentrated in the Transtibernine region—then most of them would have lived in mass

Thus, we have a context in which groups of Christians were divided over their attitude toward (and therefore their connections with) the law and the synagogue. The organizational issue that we posited above as a necessary constituent of the situation in Rome could then take the form of the question whether or not gentile Christians and former God-fearers should sever their links with the synagogue. This hypothesis would make even better sense if in fact the troublemakers of 16:17 were suggesting precisely this—that is, advocating a separatist "gentile Christianity." The assumption implicit in this interpretation is that most of the Christian groups in Rome had hitherto been subgroups of the synagogues, even though there is no indication of any pressure to judaize.

We ought also to consider here the role of leaders, especially in relation to synagogue groups. Paul himself was not disinterested in promoting order and discipline in his communities. He urged the Corinthians to submit to such men as Stephanus and to every fellow worker and laborer (1 Cor 16:15–16). Contrary to earlier interpretations of Paul's charismatic theology, the apostle himself saw no inherent contradiction between charisma, structure, and order (to a limited extent at least) within his communities.[56]

Synagogues in Rome were organized independently rather than under a central *ethnarch* or γερουσία (council) as was the case in Alexandria. Each synagogue group may have had its own γερουσία, though there may have been a designated leader (ἄρχων) (cf. Rom 13:3) from within the γερουσία. The house-churches would also have their leaders. If "those who create doubts and cause stumblings (σκάνδαλα) in opposition to the teachings you have been taught" are themselves (gentile) leaders *within* the house groups in Rome (rather than [judaizing] interlopers from outside), then their self-serving associated with the creation of dissensions and the causing of stumbling may consist in their putting severe pressure on weaker individuals to conform to their (new) perceptions of what faith means.[57]

Thus, the role of leaders is a further element in the organizational or supraindividual features of the Roman context that must necessarily be considered alongside any understanding of the continuum of ideas. The attitudes and activities of the leaders may well have accentuated differences

---

housing (*insulae*) rather than in their own *domus* (see Walters, *Ethnic Issues*, 31–32).

56. Cf. Holmberg, *Paul and Power*.

57. The tendency to see all Paul's opponents as Judaizers has not assisted a clear understanding of 16:17, *contra* Kettunen, *Der Abfassungszweck des Römerbriefes*, 192–96. See Campbell, *Paul's Gospel*, 165–70; see also Fitzmyer, *Romans*, 34. Wedderburn (*Reasons*, 54) admits that evidence for the nature of Christian traditions in Rome remains scanty, "that they were originally of a judaizing character must remain a hypothesis, nothing more."

between groups and led to the persecution and stumbling of individuals (cf. 12:14; 14:21). If Nanos's view is correct, then the Roman Christians were to be subordinate to the synagogue leaders, to obey the apostolic decree in keeping the Noachic commandments and to pay the temple tax.[58] Christians subject to the discipline of the synagogue could have suffered prescribed beatings for association with gentiles (2 Cor 11:24). Some of them could have been excluded if others refused to eat or worship with them.

A vital concern for a new religious movement engaged in the process of self-definition is a fresh understanding of its past. This pre-history must be reviewed and reinterpreted in order to affirm the newly acquired identity of the movement. For Christians with a previous association with the synagogue, Judaism itself, its failings and its virtues, must be called in question. The tendency to define oneself over against those Jews still rejecting the gospel would be hard to resist—"branches were broken off so that I might be grafted in" (11:19).

Thus we can envisage a situation in which the significance of the Jewish roots of their faith was being debated by the emergent Christians. Accordingly, the appropriate lifestyle for the members of the new communities would also become a bone of contention. We have envisaged competing communities and leaders along a continuum that stretched from "synagogue Christians" to "gentile" house-churches with an aversion to Judaism and the law.

Our discussion of the identity of "the weak" has revealed a wide diversity of opinion. It is no longer feasible simply to designate them as Jewish Christians. The reference to what is κοινός ("unclean") and to σκάνδαλα ("stumbling[s]") denotes that Jewish purity laws constituted one element in the debate. There is evidence of judging one another's lifestyle and of adherence to practices that may be mainly or partly attributable to Judaism or earlier Jewish socialization of gentiles. But we find no evidence of judaizing. The opponents in 16:17 may as readily be designated "gentilizers" as judaizers, since their identity derives from one's perspective on chapters 1–15.

That Paul sent Romans to "all God's beloved in Rome," but primarily addressed gentiles, must indicate a community(s) of gentile believers living in a context involving some relationship with Judaism. A pronounced gentile ethnic self-consciousness is also evident in 11:17–24. Boasting with an element of ethnic superiority appears both in the latter passage and also in the apostrophe to the Jew in 2:17–29. Our knowledge of the Roman context

---

58. Chapter 6 of Nanos's study, entitled "Romans 13:1–7: Christian Obedience to Synagogue Authority," integrates Rom 13:1–7 into the theme of the letter. For evidence of gentiles with formal links with a Jewish community, see Goodman, "Who Was a Jew," 1–20.

indicates that there were probably also social dimensions to the disunity among "God's beloved" in Rome. Differences in social status (see 12:16) and differences in knowledge related to this may have combined with the unrest resulting from the disturbances under Claudius to create insecurity for a significant proportion of believers. We conclude therefore that the division between "the weak" and "the strong" "did not correspond to the division between Jewish and Gentile Christians, but cut across it."[59]

It is not in fact the differences in lifestyle that concern Paul—the kingdom of God is not meat and drink (14:17). Righteousness and the unity of the church are his concern. Since he clearly states that his policy is "not to build on another man's foundation" (15:20), it must certainly follow from this that he also would have made it his policy not to destroy another man's foundation (even if Rome was somewhat of an anomaly in this respect). Since Paul himself had not founded the churches in Rome, he is faced with diversity as a given factor in the situation, and one he must acknowledge rather than seek to demolish.[60] The fact that Paul's own theological thinking is contextually related and influenced means that the apostle must take into account the Roman context as part of the reality within which he is called to operate.[61] The church for Paul is truly a church of Jews and gentiles, not a third entity that is neither of these. Viewed from this perspective, Rom 12–15 may be adequately described as Paul's argument for the legitimation and maintenance of diversity among the Christians in Rome. We must now consider the theological rationale on which Paul bases his argument for this.

The Rule of Faith: Norms for the Believing Community

Paul provides both a positive and a negative application of faith to everyday issues of conduct. In Romans, faith is not only individuated, as 12:3 asserts; faith is also demonstrated in one's choice of lifestyle and in one's attitude toward the differing lifestyles of other Christians. Both righteousness

---

59. See Ziesler, *Paul's Letter to the Romans,* 325. The approach of the Pauline Theology Group has been to study each letter of Paul separately; on the weak in 1 Corinthians, see Theissen, *The Social Setting of Pauline Christianity,* 137–40.

60. Paul envisages a permanent pluralism in Rome; see Jewett, *Christian Tolerance,* 134.

61. See my essay "The Contribution of Traditions to Paul's Theology," (chapter 2 in this volume). Wayne Meeks ("Breaking Away," 93–115, esp. 108) argues that since Paul's normal practice was to establish house-churches that were, from their origin, fundamentally independent of Jewish communities, then the Roman Christian community would differ radically from the norm in that, unlike the others, this community was shaped by having its origin within a Jewish context.

and faith were practical issues for the Romans. Orthopraxy rather than orthodoxy was a central concern; however, it is not choice but *conviction* that determines how one lives the life in Christ, and one does not lightly change one's convictions.[62] Here Paul is a true charismatic. The Holy Spirit gives gifts to all and through the Christian community will guide each one (whether as individual or group) to live in obedience to Christ.[63]

Thus, to take one's own "measuring rod" of faith—that is, the norm that each person is provided in the appropriation of the grace of God—and to seek to impose it as a norm upon others is to usurp the function of the Spirit and contradict the meaning of "faith in Christ."[64] The nature and origin of one's own charisma should prevent anyone from attempting to force a brother or sister to adopt his or her particular lifestyle. This is Paul's positive rationale, but he reinforces it by a negative argument as well. If people are forced to live other than as they are called, they are being forced to sin, for "whatever is not of faith is sin" (14:23). Paul uses here a particular phrase, ἐκ πίστεως ("from faith"), that he has already employed a number of times in earlier chapters (1:17 [twice]; 3:26, 30; 4:16 [twice]; 5:1; 9:30, 32; and 10:6). This recurring theme is obviously of some significance in the letter.[65]

We first meet ἐκ πίστεως in Paul's citation of Hab 2:4 in Rom 1:17; here the phrase occurs in conjunction with εἰς πίστιν ("into faith") and with the phrase "to the Jew first and also to the Greek." In this citation ἐκ πίστεως embraces both God's faithfulness and the human response in faith. Paul cites this text because he wishes to stress both the source of righteousness and its practice in daily life: note ζήσεται ("shall live," 1:17; cf. also 6:11; 8:13; and 10:5).[66] We find ἐκ πίστεως again in Rom 3:26 and 3:30. The Christ-event is intended to demonstrate that God himself is righteous and that he justifies the one who has faith in Jesus (τὸν ἐκ πίστεως Ἰησοῦ). Paul interprets this to maintain that all boasting is excluded on the principle or rule of faith (note the similarity with 14:23).[67] The alternative to this is to make God "the God of Jews only" (3:29). But

---

62. Fitzmyer, NRSV, and RNEB translate πίστις, as "conviction" in 14:22. The RNEB and Fitzmyer are consistent, repeating this translation in 14:23 and Fitzmyer translates πίστις in 14:1 also as "conviction." For a good discussion of the issues here, see Fitzmyer, *Romans*, 698–700; and Cranfield, *Romans*, 2.698–701.

63. On this, see Käsemann, *Romans*, 334–35.

64. See ibid., 379; Jewett, *Christian Tolerance*, 59–67.

65. See Dunn, *Romans 9–16*, 828–29.

66. We use the terms "Jewish Christianity" and "gentile Christianity" to indicate lifestyle rather than ethnic origin; cf. Gal 2:14.

67. On whether νόμος should be taken figuratively here, see Fitzmyer, *Romans*, 363; but cf. Cranfield, *Romans*, 1.220.

"God is one"; "he will justify the circumcised on the ground of faith (ἐκ πίστεως) and the uncircumcised through faith (διὰ τῆς πίστεως, 3:30)."

If Paul's main purpose in this passage is to argue for the equality of Jew and gentile in salvation, it seems strangely unwarranted for him to use differing prepositions in respect to the two peoples whose distinctiveness he apparently wishes to eliminate. The equality of Jew and gentile in faith must therefore constitute only *one* aspect of Paul's argument; the other is that even as he argues for equality he acknowledges their continuing distinctiveness within the divine purpose.[68]

Paul next uses ἐκ πίστεως in 4:16, where he summarizes a major section of his argument by a cryptic phrase διὰ τοῦτο ἐκ πίστεως ἵνα κατὰ χάριν, "that is why it depends on faith in order that the promise may rest on grace." Only as it is dependent on grace can the promise be guaranteed to all Abraham's seed. "The seed" (σπέρμα) here is not Christ, as in Gal 3:16, but refers to two distinct groups—τῷ ἐκ τοῦ νόμου and τῷ ἐκ πίστεως Ἀβραάμ—those who adhere to the law and those who share the faith of Abraham. Romans 4:16 is essentially inclusive (not only but also), and since it maintains the necessity of faith, the two groups listed here must signify the Jewish Christian and gentile Christian "branches" on "the tree of Abraham." Only thus in Paul's view can God's promise to make Abraham "the father of many nations," the father of us all (4:16–17), be realized.

Paul's emphasis on Abraham as an inclusive figure for all peoples of faith would appear to indicate that the Roman Christians were disputing what walking in the faith and footsteps of Abraham should mean for the pattern of daily life—in particular, how they should relate to the law. What is to be noted here is that although Paul argues for a common paternity for all believers in Abraham, he again acknowledges the difference between Jew and gentile. The implication of this may turn out to be that two differing lifestyles are permissible within the family of Abraham's children. Significantly, Paul in 4:16 uses the phrase τῷ ἐκ τοῦ νόμου ("the adherent of the law") in a neutral rather than a pejorative sense. This description of Jewish Christians demonstrates that in Paul's theology there was no absolute opposition between Christ and the law.

Paul begins a new section of the letter in 5:1, which continues the inclusive emphasis of 4:16. He uses ἐκ πίστεως here in an opening summary in which all believers are included as those who have been justified and who

---

68. See Stowers, "Ἐκ πίστεως and διὰ τῆς πίστεως in Rom 3:30," 665–74. Following Origen and Theodore of Mopsuestia, Stowers holds that Paul's use of different prepositions is significant, concluding that διά appears when the gentiles are in view, and ἐκ when either or both Jews and gentiles are under discussion.

(therefore) should enjoy peace. Their boasting is not of ethnic distinctions but of hope, of afflictions, or of God (5:2, 3, 11).

We find ἐκ πίστεως again in 9:30 and 10:6. Israel's failure in its race toward righteousness is explained as a result of its not being "from faith." In 10:6 this mistaken faith is contrasted with the true righteousness (ἐκ πίστεως). The difference noted here is not that between those who had the law and those who had not, but that between those who *acted* from faith and those who did not.

Significant discussions of faith (and unbelief) occur in 11:13–24 (cf. 11:20) and in 12:3, although the precise phrase ἐκ πίστεως does not recur there. In 14:23 Paul gives a crucial role to faith (ἐκ πίστεως) as the principle or rule by which the lifestyle that is in accordance with the will of God is discerned. If we consider the various occurrences of ἐκ πίστεως noted above, alongside the frequent use of the verb πιστεύειν ("to have faith"), it is apparent that this word group is of central significance in Romans.[69] It is no surprise therefore that Paul's doxological conclusion in 15:13 reads "May the God of hope fill you with all joy and peace ἐν τῷ πιστεύειν ("in believing").

From this cursory survey it would appear that Paul wishes to demonstrate to the Roman Christians that the life of faith is a life of commitment rather than of vacuous freedom, of obligation to Christ and to other humans. Yet the *obedience that faith produces*, though in continuity with Israel's faith, is not the same as obedience to the law.[70] Moreover, although all true faith has one divine source, it may be differentiated in practice in the differing lifestyles of Jewish Christians and gentile Christians.

Paul warns against pressuring people to conform to other people's lifestyles in contradiction to their own faith conviction. Such conformity to the world Paul repudiates in his important introductory exhortations in 12:1–2. The significance that Paul gives to mutual recognition and admonition between Christians with differing lifestyles should not be underestimated. The Christian faith was still very young; the church in Rome was lacking in any unified understanding of what should be normative, and the whole movement would be at risk if it came to the attention of the authorities.

69. As Bartsch has emphasized ("The Concept of Faith in Paul's Letter to the Romans," 41–53). Bartsch notes that the word faith occurs forty times, more often than in any other biblical book, and that the concept appears twice in the beginning of the letter in unique usages (1:5 and 1:17) that Paul obviously assumed his readers would understand (ibid., 45). See also Lindsay, *Josephus and Faith*.

70. We take ὑπακοὴ πίστεως as a genitive of source; see Garlington, *"The Obedience of Faith*, esp. 205–6. See also Fitzmyer, *Romans*, 449. "Obedience of faith" signifies not a polemical thrust against the law but continuity with the faith of Israel; see Nanos, *Mystery of Romans*, chapter 4, *contra* Garlington, *Obedience*, 247–59.

Bearing in mind also the previous disturbances in Rome and the resultant expulsion of the Jews, Paul's call for subjection to the governing authorities in 13:1–7 makes good sense.[71] The Romans are advised to be submissive and obedient citizens meeting all their debts—above all the debt to love one another (13:8). The commandments are summed up in "the Golden Rule" and "love does no wrong to a neighbor—therefore love is the fulfilling of the law" (13:9–10).

In stressing the demands inherent in his gospel, Paul is seeking an "obedience of faith" that seems to bring together somewhat disparate elements. A congruence hinted at earlier in 3:27 and in 8:1–4 (cf. also 10:4) now becomes explicit, and a positive relation between the commandments and Christian love is established. The δικαίωμα of the law is love.[72] This leads us to believe that, in showing the congruence, Paul is seeking to minimize the force of the conflicts about the law and its relevance for the daily life of the Christian community.

Paul has prepared for this emphasis in chapters 5–6 in a major contrast between obedience (Christ) and its effects and disobedience (Adam) and its effects. Righteousness is also linked with obedience and slavery to Christ, while sin and death are linked with disobedience and slavery to sin's rule. Paul's own mission is to win *obedience* from the gentiles (15:18).

This emphasis on the obedience of faith is further strengthened when we note the strong correspondence in vocabulary between chapters 6–8 and 12:1–21, as Victor Furnish and J. D. G. Dunn have emphasized.[73] The imagery of slavery to Christ significantly reappears in 14:18. According to 6:17 the Romans had previously received catechetical instruction. As former slaves who transferred to a new master, they "became obedient to the standard of teaching or *rule of faith* (Moffatt) to which they had been entrusted."[74] Paul writes to bring to their remembrance aspects of this they may have forgotten or neglected (15:15).

---

71. Paul must have been aware of the reaction of people in the empire to the conduct of the *publicani* and the tax situation under Nero. Christian reactions to the cult of the emperor may also be in view here; see J. Friedrich, Pöhlmann, and Stuhlmacher, "Zur historischen Situation und Intention von Röm 13, 1–7," 131–66; also Bammel, "Romans 13," 365–83.

72. See Keck, "What Makes Romans Tick," 3–29; see also Davies, *Faith and Obedience in Romans,* 173–75.

73. Furnish, *Theology and Ethics in Paul,* 103–4; Dunn, *Romans 9–16,* 708–9.

74. See Fitzmyer, *Romans,* 449–50.

The Failure of the Romans to Accept One Another: Boasting in Distinction and Ignoring Common Allegiance to Christ

Our study to this point leads us to the conclusion that diversity in lifestyle was not the most serious problem; it was rather the attitude of Christians to this diversity. Provided their own calling or faith conviction calls them to this lifestyle, Paul has no quarrel with those who continue to observe the law so long as they do not seek to compel others to live like them! *Gentiles must not regard observance of the Jewish law as incompatible with Christian faith, and Jews must not regard it as essential to Christian faith.*[75] *Justification by faith demands freedom of lifestyle in faith.*

But there were some in Rome—evidenced in 11:13–24 as well as in chapters 14–15—who felt that freedom in Christ in no way obligated them to the Jewish law. This attitude combined with other factors already noted to make the gentile Christians feel that they were superior to non-Christian Jews, and probably also to those Christians still committed to a Jewish lifestyle. Paul does not wish to encourage such attitudes. He opposed all boasting in human achievement such as the idealized self-image of the Jew in 2:17–24, but an inflated self-image was not the exclusive prerogative of the Jews in Rome.[76] It is instructive in this regard to consider Paul's use of the verb φρονεῖν and related terms in Romans.[77] The neutral use, meaning "to think, form, or hold an opinion, have an understanding" is found in Paul as in 12:3, but the term can be given a more particular and often negative force by its context; in the New Testament this usage is almost wholly Pauline as in 11:20 and 12:16.[78]

This accusation of "high-mindedness" follows from 11:13–24, where it is specifically gentiles whom Paul targets. In contrast to ὑπερφρονεῖν ("arrogant thinking"), Paul places σωφρονεῖν ("think wisely"); the latter featured widely in popular Hellenistic philosophy, denoting modesty or restraint and would have been familiar to Paul's readers. Paul's wordplay shows he also is aware of this.[79]

---

75. See Watson, *Paul, Judaism and the Gentiles*, 96.

76. See Wedderbum, *Reasons*, 126.

77. Φρονεῖν occurs in 8:15; 11:20; 12:3, 16 (twice); 14:6 (twice); 15:5; φρόνιμος in 11:25; 12:16; and φρόνιμα in 8:6 (twice); 8:7; and 8:27. See Wedderbum, *Reasons*, 76–77. Paul tells his readers "not to be super-minded above what one ought to be minded, but (to) set your mind on being sober-minded" (Jewett, *Christian Tolerance*, 66).

78. See Dunn, *Romans 9–16*, 721.

79. Ibid., 721-22.

Thus, a characteristic of some of the Roman Christians was that they held an inflated self-estimate, and this may have included elements of religious, ethnic, and cultural superiority. They tended to boast in their *distinctions* rather than in their *common faith*. It was arrogant attitudes that were the root of the problem. This arrogance destroyed community harmony and was characterized by a presumptuous pride. Pride and boasting contradict faith, transforming πίστις ("faith") into ἀπιστία ("unfaith"), and Paul in Romans opposes gentile as well as Jewish misconceptions of faith.

Bornkamm noted this drawing of distinctions behind Paul's statements in 1:18—2:29. Paul's strategy was to free the natural understanding of God and the world from its Greek presuppositions through specific Jewish terms and thoughts, and again in the second part of his argument to burst the boundaries of the Jewish understanding of law and judgment through the reference to the law that gentiles know. By dealing separately and in rather stereotyped ways with the traditions and practice of the different groups, whether Jewish or gentile, and by stressing God's judgment upon all, Paul showed that none may boast because the gospel relativizes their exaggerated distinctions.[80]

Judging and despising one another are also for Paul in direct contradiction to the acceptance that the gospel demands (see chap. 2; 14:1; 15:7 [11:15]).[81] The gospel requires of both Jew and gentile that they re-evaluate all their past, including their cultural presuppositions; such "judging" will prevent inflated self-images and self-understanding, and promote a better appreciation of their common humanity as God's creation.[82]

In the face of assumed cultural and ethnic superiority, in opposition to boastful, imperialist faith, Paul uses his weapon of a justifying faith centered on the cross, before which no human may boast of any achievements or attributes. The earliest form of this justification by faith argument may have been formulated in reaction to Judaism or judaizers, but its presentation in Romans has a more universal focus; the target is not just Judaism or judaizers but *all* Christians. So Paul addresses the gentile Christians and reminds them that they do not bear the branches but they themselves are borne on the root of Abraham; they are wild and unproductive olives cultivated by divine grace.[83] And to Israel he says that were it not for divine mercy that

---

80. Bornkamm, "The Revelation of God's Wrath: Romans i–iii," 46–70, esp. 61.

81. The root κριν becomes a leitmotif in Romans and thereby connects the judging in chapter 2 with that of chapters 14–15; see Meeks, "Judgment and the Brother: Romans 14:1—15:13," 290–300, esp. 296.

82. As Marxsen (*Introduction*, 92–109) correctly perceived.

83. See Davies, "A Suggestion concerning Romans 11:13–24," 153–63.

chose not always the firstborn or the mighty, but the weak and younger, then not even a remnant would have been saved.[84]

Before God Jews cannot boast of their Jewishness and gentiles dare not presume. *The lifestyle to which their faith commits them is not something about which to boast* above other believers. Nor is it legitimate to condemn or despise the believer whose convictions bind him or her to a different pattern of life. The harmonious solution to the disputes among the Roman Christians demands a recognition that faith must determine what is the right lifestyle for everyone. Love, rather than domination, will liberate and take care of the weak; diversity is to be acknowledged and allowed to continue.[85] Ultimately it is not birth or public pressure, or even Torah, but only faith that should be determinative of lifestyle.[86]

Conclusion: Paul's Theology of Faith in Romans

Because of the Romans' misconceptions about the meaning of faith, Paul's major concern in writing to them is with the nature of obedient faith. The translation of a Semitic faith into Hellenistic culture may have allowed the Romans to miss some of the content πίστις normally carried for those of Jewish background, familiar with the Septuagint.[87] Paul reinterprets the meaning of faith in such a way as to stress positive continuity with the faith of Abraham and equality for Jew and gentile within this faith.

Instead of positing that Paul opposes judaizing tendencies or "works of law" in Romans, it makes better sense to view the discussion of faith and merit as related to the human problems of boasting and judging, whether by Jew or gentile. A true understanding of faith counteracts arrogance over against one's neighbor and confirms the right of persons to live by their own "rule of faith." To counteract misconceptions of faith, Paul uses both Abraham and Christ as originators and exemplars of faith. Abraham found grace, unmerited favor, but even he had nothing to boast about. He became "strong in faith" because his faith was not determined by earthly realities

---

84. See Thielman, "Unexpected Mercy: Echoes of a Biblical Motif in Romans 9–11," esp. 178–79. Thielman notes that God often communicates his blessing through the very candidate whom cultural norms would exclude.

85. "Paul does not assimilate Jew and Gentile into a generic Christianity" (Stowers, "Έκ πίστεως," 674; see also Beker, "The Faithfulness of God and the Priority of Israel in Paul's Letters to the Romans," 16).

86. On the uniqueness of the "μέτρον πίστεως" for each believer, see Käsemann, *Romans*, 334–35; and Dunn, *Romans 9–16*, 721–22.

87. See Lindsay "The Roots and Development of the 'pist' Word Group as Faith Terminology," 103–18.

such as his old age. Thus the present reality of lack of faith in Christ among the Jews must not lead the Roman Christians into boasting.

To further counteract a presumptuous type of faith, the provisional aspect of salvation is stressed in Rom 8:14–39. Those with faith already enjoy the firstfruits of the Spirit (8:23), but they *await* adoption as sons. They dare not boast over those Jews who reject the gospel, for until God's purpose for Jew and gentile comes to fruition there is no salvation for either. Paul claims that Christ came to *confirm* the promises, but he avoids the language of fulfillment that might encourage presumption. Paul is certain that God's consistency and integrity (ἀλήθεια) are greater than human faithlessness. God's faithfulness is demonstrated in Christ's becoming and continuing to be "servant to the circumcised" (15:8).[88]

Remarkably, Paul does not use the term "Israel" but prefers "circumcision" despite all its ethnic connotations.[89] This surely points to the fact that *ethnicity and cultural divisions were crucial factors in the Roman situation.* Christian leaders in Rome should not selfishly seek their own factional interests thereby causing the weak to stumble but, out of concern for the weak, should follow the example of Christ, the servant of Israel.

Paul's collection for and his relationship to Jerusalem would suffer if anti-Judaism were to develop among the gentile Christians in Rome.[90] Paul seeks to deny legitimacy to a Christianity that defines itself over against Judaism. He secures the new movement to its historical roots in Judaism and that not only at the new point of departure in the revelation of Christ. He binds it to Israel's origins with Abraham and to Israel's ultimate salvation (see 11:25).

88. See Stowers, "Ἐκ πίστεως," 673; and Bartsch, "Concept of Faith," 48–49.

89. See Marcus, "The Circumcision and the Uncircumcision in Rome," 67–81.

90. The importance of the collection within the context of Romans is often overlooked. "It gave concrete expression to Jewish and Gentile Christians' common sharing in the spiritual heritage of Israel" (Wedderburn, *Reasons*, 40).

4

Divergent Images of Paul
and His Mission

Examples from the Reception
of Romans in the Twentieth Century

A CERTAIN DUPLICITY IN PAUL'S Letter to the Romans has been observed by a number of interpreters from C. H. Dodd in his 1932 commentary *The Epistle to the Romans* in the Moffatt series to more recent scholars such as Heiki Räisänen[1] of Helsinki, Francis Watson of London,[2] and Charles Cosgrove[3] in the USA. Although there are several points where lack of clarity or consistency emerge, the most frequently discussed chapters tend to be chapters 9 and 11, which are seen by quite a few scholars as somewhat at odds with each other.

C. H. Dodd sets out the issue with exquisite clarity: "The fact is that the whole argument of 3:1–8 is obscure and feeble. When Paul who is normally a clear as well as a forcible thinker, becomes feeble and obscure, it usually means that he is defending a poor case. His case is inevitably a poor one, since he is trying to show that, *although there is no partiality about God,* yet the Jew's superiority is, somehow, *much in every way.* It is no wonder that he becomes embarrassed, and in the end dismisses the subject awkwardly."[4] Dodd continues in similar vein on Rom 3:9 "Well, now, are we Jews in a better position? Not at all. Though temporarily and relatively the Jews have a certain advantage, yet in an absolute view of the matter, that advantage

---

1. Räisänen, "Paul, God, and Israel: Romans 9–11 in Recent Research," 178–206.

2 Watson, *Paul, Judaism and the Gentiles.*

3 Cosgrove, *Elusive Israel: The Puzzle of Election in Romans.*

4 Dodd, *The Epistle to the Romans,* 46.

vanishes. This is very near to his (Paul's) conclusions in chapters 9–11, and it is at least a possible interpretation of the Greek here."[5]

Dodd's diagnosis of the reasons for Paul's weak arguments was that Paul had argued from the promise to Abraham on two divergent and perhaps inconsistent lines[6] and his logic was vitiated by his emotional interest in his own people. Logically, the Jew can have no advantage whatsoever, but "the trouble is that the 'Jewish objector' is in Paul's own mind. His Pharisaism—or shall we say his patriotism?—was too deeply engrained for him to put right out of his mind the idea that somehow the divine covenant with mankind has a 'most favoured nation clause.'"[7]

A brief glance at Francis Watson's criticisms will illustrate similar problems with Paul's argument: "It is ironic that Paul's arguments for the consistency of God in 9–11 are themselves inconsistent, for Romans 11 is based on the definition of the chosen people rejected in Romans 9."[8] Räisänen's criticisms are similar. E. P. Sanders, on the other hand, maintains that part of the problem with Paul is his method of argument—the apostle does not, as we would normally expect, argue from problem to solution but on the contrary, from solution back to problem. Nevertheless, Sanders too admits in relation to chapters 9–11 that what is noteworthy is not so much the ideas they contain but the feelings of anguish, concern, and triumphant expectation that Paul expresses in relation to his own people.[9] Paul's solution in chapter 11 is a "somewhat desperate expedient" to meet the problem of "competing convictions which can be better asserted than explained": of reconciling native convictions with those received by revelation. Paul's anguish is that he seeks desperately for "a formula which would keep God's promises to Israel intact, while insisting on faith in Jesus Christ."[10] The fact that we are confronted by a variety of readings of Paul's letter is occasioned largely by the difficulty of his topic as much as by his style and method of argument—the use of diatribe style in large sections of the letter and the frequent recourse to the Hebrew Scriptures, especially in chapters 9–11, increase the potential for diverse readings and charges of at least apparent inconsistency. We are particularly interested in the canons of consistency, the standards of measurement, the criteria by which we are to esteem one reading as more acceptable than another. In this regard it is illuminating to

---

5. Ibid., 47–48

6. Ibid., 183.

7. Ibid., 43.

8. Watson, *Paul, Judaism, and the Gentiles*, 168.

9. E. P. Sanders, *Paul, the Law and the Jewish People* 193.

10. Ibid., 197–99.

note the charges or explanations that are stated as reasons for Paul's failure to convince or to maintain consistency.

Consider the following proposed reasons: The apostle has confused relative advantage with absolute advantage, perhaps because of patriotic and emotional attachment to his own people;[11] anguish and concern to solve an insoluble problem;[12] a new revelation received as Paul wrestled with the subject matter in writing Romans;[13] either one has to conclude that Paul was capable of thinking coherently only for very short periods of time, or if one rejects an artificial harmonizing process the only possible solution lies in examining afresh the social context and function of Romans in order to make coherent sense of it.[14] We note in passing the need to be careful lest we seek anachronistically to judge Paul by our standards of logic and consistency and the need also to maintain an awareness of the fact that Paul was operating in a very different culture to ours where somewhat different standards of consistency—perhaps even of rationality—and methods of argument applied. Paul was after all seeking to convince a first-century audience and we must not judge him as if he had targeted us.

But allowing for all the explanations and or reasons that help us to understand the apostle and his letters, it must still be noted that the most powerful voice that can be raised against the apostle is his own. This can have three main forms. The first form of Paul's voice comes from his other letters written prior to Romans. From them, particularly from Galatians, we know the content of Paul's gospel already and we legitimately expect what we find in Romans to harmonize with this, the Early Paul, or at least the Earlier Paul. The second form of Paul's voice emerges not so much from what he said as from what he did—his missionary activity as apostle to the gentiles—we expect him to fight for them and to uphold their rights. The third form of Paul's voice is however the most powerful of all and it is this that raises such difficulties in Romans. In the earlier part of the letter even up to the end of chapter 9, or perhaps for some, the end of chapter 10, many see what they recognize as the familiar (Earlier) Paul. But in chapter 11 another voice of Paul suddenly and surprisingly appears, what we might call the Later Paul. This "Paul" seems to some to be completely at odds with the Earlier Paul, and contrasts sharply with the previously well-known pattern of his life and his publicly proclaimed gospel in his letters to other churches.

11. Dodd, *The Epistle to the Romans*, 43.

12. Sanders, *Paul, the Law and the Jewish People*, 199. Räisänen, "Paul, God, and Israel," 195–96.

13. Noack, "Current and Backwater in the Epistle to the Romans," 165–66.

14. Watson, *Paul, Judaism and the Gentiles*, 170.

Is the different voice the result of the apostle facing a changed situation, or the outcome of a development in his thought?

Which is the genuine voice of Paul? Will the real apostle stand forth! Various strategies may be adopted here. One is to put all the weight on Rom 1–8, 1–9, or even 1–10, and to interpret Rom 11 from the perspective of the rest of the letter, thereby reducing the significance of its specific contribution. This has been a dominant pattern among some Lutheran interpreters,[15] but there are many parallels in Dodd. Dodd was of the opinion that Rom 12:1ff. seems to be the real sequel to 8:39, rather than chapters 9–11, which are a somewhat self-contained unit, a treatise or sermon possibly in existence prior to the writing of Romans.[16] The surprise resulting from the inclusion of 9–11 at this point arises from the fact that Paul has earlier in the letter apparently spoken of the abrogation of the privilege of Israel in a dispensation in which no distinctions are drawn.[17] Effectively this means in practice ignoring or dismissing at least part of chapter 11, and presuming we already know and understand the *authentic* Paul without the wisdom or otherwise of chapter 11. The outcome of this may well produce a view of Israel entirely at odds with Paul's conclusion at the end of Rom 11. Israel is not saved but has lost any special status whatsoever; according to Klein, Paul's theology "radikal entheiligt und paganisiert . . . die Geschichte Israels."[18] Klein's perspective typifies the approach of those who tend to force the contents of Rom 11 to fit the mould of the Paul they already know and understand from elsewhere—the apostle to the gentiles, or more specifically, the Paul of Paulinism.

Klein's essay was written, of course, some thirty-five years ago, and we must allow for the changes and development in interpretation since then. Nevertheless, there are close parallels even in a very recent study. Cosgrove cannot help stressing what a surprise is the content of 11:25f. in an otherwise coherent argument in Romans. Because of this he asks, "If what Paul affirms about Israel in Romans 11 comes as a surprise, that in itself shows how strong the countervailing reading of Romans 9 is."[19] Again he questions, "If Paul's teaching about divine impartiality seems to contradict the notion of a special election of the Jewish people, is it reasonable to affirm

---

15. Dahl, in a review of Bultmann's *Theology of the New Testament*, noted that whilst Bultmann had much to say about Rom 1–8 he had relatively little to say about chapters 9–11, cf. *Theologische Rundschau* xxii (1954), 21–40.

16. Dodd, *The Epistle to the Romans,* 148.

17. Ibid., 151.

18. G. Klein, "Römer iv und die Idee der Heilsgeschichte," 441.

19. Cosgrove, *Elusive Israel,* 29.

that special election when one can also reasonably construe his arguments in a way that does not require this conclusion?"[20]

What emerges from the above overview of opinions is that chapter 11 has become a focal point in the discussion. This marks a refinement of the earlier view that sought to interpret 9–11 from the perspective of 1–8, and thus somewhat neutralize its contribution, but now it is recognized that chapters 9–10 fit reasonably well with the content of 1–8. This in effect isolates chapter 11 and highlights apparent discrepancies between its contents and those of chapter 9.[21] Thus Rom 11, and especially its conclusion, comes as a somewhat surprise intrusion in a letter that can be consistently interpreted in a direction other than what this chapter suggests. This probably indicates that the work done in recent years on the connections between 1–8 and 9–11 has been partially successful in demonstrating real links across these chapters. But the problem of perceived contradictions between the content of chapter 11 and that of chapter 9 or of the whole of the earlier part of the letter, for some scholars at least, remains a serious obstacle.

One possible explanation of this interpretative conundrum that faces us in the history of the exegesis of Romans is not just that there are divergent readings of the letter itself, but rather that there were already in existence, whether implicitly or explicitly, divergent understandings of the significance of Paul's gospel and mission. It may in fact be the existence of these that forms part of the explanation for the parallel, if not conflicting, readings of his letter to the Romans.

Paul, Champion of the Gentiles: The Partisan Paul

If the Romans were aware even indirectly of the contents of Galatians and possibly of some of his other earlier letters, and knew a certain amount of information, reliable and otherwise, about the apostle to the gentiles who had promised to visit them for some time now, then they already would have formed a specific view of Paul and his theological opinions, especially in respect of the gentiles. They would certainly have been familiar with a rough outline of his gospel. We need to differentiate between what Paul knew of the Romans and what they thought they knew about him. Thus although he had not yet been to Rome, Paul was not a complete stranger to the Roman Christians.

20. Ibid., 37.

21. Cf. Watson, *Paul, Judaism and the Gentiles*, 168–72; Räisänen, "Paul, God and Israel", 182, 192f.; and Cosgrove, *Elusive Israel*, 30–37.

It would appear, however, that their perception of the apostle may, in fact, have been slightly suspect, especially as to how they understood the significance of his gentile mission. Paul may have been understood by the Roman gentile Christians as being pro-gentile and conversely as being indifferent to Jews. Paul's inclusion in the letter of phrases such as "to the Jew first" may indicate a correction of their viewpoint in this area. This hypothesis would gain support also from the content of 11:13ff, where it is clear that Paul wishes to correct the gentile Christians' self-understanding in relation to Israel.

If we can project an image of Paul as he can be understood from his personal experience of call, etc., from his writings prior to Romans (or reports of same), and from the impression created by his mission to the gentiles (such as the creation of mainly gentile communities exercising a certain degree of freedom in relation to the Jewish law), then we can envisage how Paul might have been viewed by the gentile Christians at Rome. He was probably seen as the champion of the cause of gentiles throughout the church and at the council of Jerusalem and so forth, a pro-gentile Paul committed to winning the gentile world and indifferent to the concerns of Judaism.

In many ways this pro-gentile Paul is very similar to the Paul of liberal scholarship as reflected in the work of someone like C. H. Dodd. The emphasis upon "no distinction" and upon the universal scope of the gospel are only two aspects of this portrait. But it includes the assumption that Jews who accepted the gospel, even those not situated within the Pauline mission area, would cease to associate with the synagogue community and probably also cease to abide by the Mosaic law. An associated mindset may have been the tendency to view almost all Paul's opponents as Judaizers. At every point of contact, Paul seems to be in conflict with Jewish Christians and the Jerusalem Christian leaders. This reading derived much of its strength from the Lutheran tendency to stress the antithesis between the gospel and the law. It was therefore simply assumed that Paul and his gentile mission were engaged in an ongoing war with Jewish Christians and Judaism, two competing cultures and missions. Existentialist theology such as that of Rudolf Bultmann also did little to challenge the prevailing current of opinion, mainly because of a lack of interest in historical continuity between the old and the new. So the continuity between Paul's gentile communities and the Jewish roots of their faith was seldom stressed whilst radical discontinuity was everywhere assumed.

It is difficult to be precise in broad areas of interpretation such as these, but it would appear that here we have in outline the generally accepted image of Paul and his mission, which continued to dominate until about 1970, and which is still viewed by many as the norm even up to the present time. An alternative opinion was already in process with the work of Johannes Munck in the 1950s.[22] Munck's interest in a fresh appraisal of Paul's thought, especially as represented in Rom 9–11 was, more than a decade later, advanced by Krister Stendahl's timely stress upon Paul's thought and mission as encompassing real Jews and gentiles.[23] The solid mold of Pauline scholarship had been broken and this opened up the way for a fresh appreciation of the apostle particularly from the perspective of Romans, around which an increasing volume of scholarship would rapidly concentrate.

The outcome of this scholarly development has gradually led to a rediscovery of the Jewishness of Paul and therefore to a more balanced reading of his theology and practice. The new perspective on Paul necessarily took account of a fresh understanding of Rom 9–11, particularly as these chapters could no longer be viewed as being simply an appendix of secondary importance in the interpretation of the letter. Assisted as it was by the growing interest in the relevance of the Holocaust for the interpretation of the New Testament, by a blossoming interest in a sociological approach to the study of the Christian origins,[24] and by recent critiques of the Lutheran understanding of faith and works, the scene was set for a revised understanding of Paul's thought and work. This radical reassessment of Paul is well demonstrated by the coining of the now well-known term "The New Perspective on Paul" by James Dunn.[25]

In my opinion, the conflict surrounding the question of contradictions in Paul's thought arises mainly from a debate as to what constitutes the "real Paul." Is he the heroic Paul who is depicted as the champion of the gentiles, or is he the "revised Paul" of Romans, especially of Rom 11? To put it another way: is the real Paul to be identified with the previous pro-gentile image of the apostle, or with the recent more Jewish Paul identified in Romans, particularly in chapters 9–11? Is the apostle really pro-gentile (partial to gentiles and their cause) or is his gospel "to the Jew first and also to the gentile" (inclusive and impartial)?

The answer we give to these questions is crucial if we are not to be left with two very divergent images of the apostle and his mission. Is it really likely that Paul would recognize the rights of Jewish Christians in certain situations to continue to abide by the law? Would he not have advocated

---

22. Munck's study of Rom 9–11, *Christ and Israel*, was completed in Danish in 1952 as a prelude to his better known *Paul and the Salvation of Mankind*.

23. Stendahl, *Paul among Jews and Gentiles and Other Essays*.

24. See for example, Malherbe, *Social Aspects of Early Christianity*.

25. Dunn, "The New Perspective on Paul."

that they forsake the synagogue? Did he recognize continuing distinctions between Jews and gentiles even in Christ, so that ethnic differences remain a consideration in some contexts? Did he stress a certain priority for the Jew in the purpose of God and did he really hold that God had not cast off Israel, but would still save "all Israel" in some miraculous way in the future? It could, of course, be argued that this revised reading of Paul emerges from post-Holocaust guilt[26] and that we are now trying to update our image of him to suit a revised understanding of what constitutes liberal Christianity. We are perhaps, after all, still "discovering" the image of Paul we expect to find. Whatever our response to this issue, it is necessary to look again at some of the texts where our conflicting images of Paul are generated, and to seek afresh to assess to which image they give most support.

Continuity between Romans 3–4 and Romans 9–11

There are obvious links between chapter 3:1ff. and chapters 9–11, which we do not need to discuss in detail here: the advantage of the Jew, the value of circumcision, and the faithfulness of God despite the faithlessness of Israel are clearly common themes noted in chapter 3 to be dealt with in detail later. There are, however, other points in chapter 4 that again point beyond themselves to an anticipated later sequel. Adolf Schlatter correctly perceives the relevance of Abraham in chapter 4 for the rest of the letter. "If this section of the letter were missing, much of the clarity of the second part of the letter would be removed. Why are there two types of sons of Abraham, and why is Israel the olive tree into which the believer is grafted?"[27]

One of the more interesting of these "forward looking" passages is 4:16 where the aim of Paul's discussion of Abraham's faith is clearly indicated. In a tightly constructed argument, Paul asserts that faith and grace were necessary ingredients in guaranteeing that the promise would be realized for all the seed of Abraham, *not only* for those who adhere to the law, *but also* for those of the faith of Abraham. We wish to note the inclusive emphasis and form of argument here, "father of us *all*," designed to specifically include both those who may be of Jewish origin as well as those of gentile origin.[28]

26. See Chae, *Paul as Apostle to the Gentiles*. If there were no intrinsic connection between Christian anti-Judaism and the Holocaust, Chae's thesis would be more convincing.

27. Schlatter, *Romans: The Righteousness of God*, 107.

28. Franz Leenhardt (*The Epistle to the Romans*, 119) rightly criticizes Otto Michel's view (based, probably, on 4:11) that for Paul Abraham is the father of the uncircumcised much more than of the circumcised. Michel (*Der Brief an die Römer*, 167–71), however, correctly emphasizes that the discussion in Rom 4 is not about the faith of individuals but rather about Abraham's "house," "Abrahamskindschaft."

Paul does not argue exclusively (*either* Jews *or* gentiles). He argues inclusively (*not only* Jews *but also* gentiles), and the surprise use of ὁι τοῦ νόμου in a neutral rather than a pejorative sense underlines that he specifically wishes to stress "the national reference,"[29] the inclusion of Jews *as Jews*. We would wish to insist that the emphasis here is not simply on the inclusion of gentiles, but on the inclusion of *both* Jews and gentiles.[30]

This form of argument is fairly typical of Paul's mode of arguing in the entire letter. Another interesting use of the same argument occurs at 9:24, again at the high-point of a discussion. In 9:23 Paul speaks of vessels of mercy as the goal of the divine purpose, and in the following verse he further elaborates on the composition of these vessels as being "not from the Jews only but also from the gentiles." What is obvious here is that Paul uses a Jewish form of argument—not only from the Jews, as if there was no need to discuss this and as if what follows was the surprise element, "but also from the gentiles."[31] Now it could be argued that in both places, 4:16 and 9:24, Paul's concern is to argue for the inclusion of gentiles, as gentiles, in the people of God. This is not in my opinion his primary intention.

It is clear that Paul is deliberately arguing for an inclusive salvation that includes Jews *as Jews* as well as gentiles *as gentiles*. It is pointers such as these—and more could be enumerated—which indicate that there is a real continuity in subject matter as well as intent between Rom 3–4 and 9–11. There seems to be real continuity in substance between these sections. This will become clearer as we turn to consider the relationship between chapter 9 and chapter 11, as well as their place within the letter as a whole.

Romans 9 and the "Surprise" Ending to Romans 11

Räisänen is certainly correct in his comment that "Romans 9–11 has long been a test case in Pauline exegesis. Decisions made concerning the internal consistency or inconsistency of these chapters, or concerning the place

---

29. Dunn, *Romans 1–8*, 216. Dunn also correctly notes that the inverted order, uncircumcised followed by circumcised, is due simply to following the sequence of events in Abraham's case, and does not contradict the "not only but also" pattern we have noted (ibid., 211). Nor does it indicate a complete rejection of Jewish salvation history as Klein asserts ("Römer 4 und die Idee der Heilsgeschichte," 434f.).

30. That this is so should have been evident from the very different understanding of σπέρμα in Gal 3:16f. and Rom 4:13f. In the former it is interpreted in relation to the one seed, Jesus Christ, but in the latter specifically with reference *to two* peoples. Cf. Beker, "The Faithfulness of God and the Priority of Israel in Paul's Letter to the Romans," 327–32 (329).

31. Cf. Dahl, "The Atonement—An Adequate Reward for the Akedah?" 27–28.

of the thoughts expressed in them in Paul's theology at large, will deeply influence—or quickly reveal—one's understanding of many central issues of New Testament interpretation."[32] Some scholars, such as Dodd, have expressed surprise that Paul did not conclude his theological argument with the high point reached at Rom 8:39. This is partly because 12:1ff. seems to be a theological sequel to 8:39 rather than the somewhat self-contained and compact argument of 9–11 that "can be read quite satisfactorily without reference to the rest of the epistle." This section was possibly in existence as "a separate treatise which Paul had by him, and which he used for his present purpose."[33]

Dodd is aware, of course, that the inclusion of Rom 9–11 has been hinted at or envisaged at earlier points in the letter and admits it is likely that Paul already knew that he was going to use his sermon on the rejection of Israel when he briefly discussed the difficulties raised in 3:1–9. The surprise presented by the inclusion of chapters 9–11 is, according to Dodd, that Paul has apparently already spoken of the abrogation of the privilege of Israel, in a dispensation in which no distinctions are drawn.[34] As Dodd understands Paul's argument, the promise is not broken even if the *entire nation* is rejected.[35]

Few scholars would favor Dodd's reading here. Schlatter sees the connection between the two sections of the letter very differently. "The question, for what purpose did God make Israel and what does he make of them now, was precipitated by all of the following: The designation of the message of Jesus for the Jew first (1:16); the rejection of any favouritism for Israel on God's part." Schlatter gives seven more reasons from Rom 1–8 why the new topic rises with compelling urgency from the concluding sentence of chapter 8. He then goes on to note, "How woefully limited the interests of the Reformation's interpretation of Romans remained is demonstrated with unusual force in Calvin. He was completely surprised by the new section and saw no connection between it and the first section."[36]

Those for whom the inclusion of Rom 9–11 are a surprise are obviously missing something that was implicit if not explicit in Paul's reasoning in chapters 1–8. Whether or not the implicit logic of Paul's argument would permit the rejection of "all Israel," Paul himself could not entertain such a

---

32. Räisänen, "Paul, God, and Israel," 178.

33. Dodd, *The Epistle to the Romans*, 2.216.

34. Ibid., 151.

35. Ibid., 155; Räisänen, "Paul, God and Israel," 184; Watson, *Paul, Judaism and the Gentiles*, 162–63.

36. Schlatter, *Romans*, 200.

scandalous notion—"God forbid!" was his response. Schlatter is probably correct in claiming that "only the one who grieves over Israel's fall speaks correctly about it." To Christ Paul attributes the fact that he does not take pleasure in gloating over Israel's misery and that he does not merely stand before them as the angry messenger of judgment.[37]

Implicit in Paul's argument is that the faith of the gentiles in Christ is the outcome of God's promises to Abraham (cf. Rom 4:17ff.), and that Abraham is not merely a fine example of a man who believed as a gentile, but rather the first of the faithful to whom all subsequent believers are deeply indebted. Gentile believers in Christ are deeply indebted also in that they are grafted into the stem of Abraham, as 11:13ff. will make plain. The gentile branches are dependent on the stem of Abraham, and if this ceased to exist, or if they were separated from it, they too would fall.[38] Implicit here is the assumption that God is faithful to his covenant and that he will preserve his people to such an extent that his purposes for them will not fail. The latter is made explicit only in chapters 9–11. The righteous "remnant" concept, to be developed gradually from 9:6ff. through to chapter 11, assumes that God always maintains by his grace a faithful minority, and moreover that he will never cease to do so. The implicit thinking behind this appears to be that it is in and through this remnant that God's long-term goals for Israel will be attained. In Paul's thought, gentiles can share in Israel's inheritance only with and through this righteous remnant. So the salvation of the gentiles assumes the prior realization of the promise for Israel, and therefore excludes the possibility of a salvation for gentiles alongside the *complete failure* of the promise to Israel; that is, even the concept of a gentile "new Israel" is ruled out by this.[39] For Paul, the option of salvation "also for the Greek" presupposed that it is enjoyed by "the Jew first." For Paul, if not for his interpreters, it was meaningless to consider the election of gentiles apart from the election of Israel; it is this that constitutes the priority of Israel.

In fairness to those interpreters whose readings perceive Rom 9–11 as somewhat of a surprise, it has to be acknowledged that it is only in these chapters that Paul spells out what seems to have been until now only implicit. The problem for these, as for the first interpreters to whom the letter

---

37. Ibid.

38. Schlatter (*Romans*, 223; cf. 107) develops this further: "The existence of a people of God is not due to those in the church who believe in Christ; rather, because there is a people of God, they are its members."

39. As Beker ("The Faithfulness of God and the Priority of Israel," 330) notes, "Such a rejection of Israel by God would simply cut the connection of the gospel to its foundation in the Hebrew scriptures and degrade the God of Jesus Christ into the God of Marcion—a 'new God' who has no relation either to creation or to Israel's salvation history."

was addressed, is that we all bring to these chapters preformulated views of the apostle and his thought that may need to be somewhat revised in the light of their content.

Paul appears to be insisting that it is not enough that individual Jews find faith in Christ; he wants the salvation of Israel, but not simply as a small remnant attached to a predominantly gentile church. Thus, although his arguments in Romans may be read in light of the principle "there is no distinction" (Rom 3:22; 10:12), and this might imply that since there can be no favoritism for Israel, then the elect may indeed be a purely gentile phenomenon, this does not appear to be what Paul had in mind. It is here that we must stress again Paul's formula "to the Jew first and also to the Greek," which indicates that what he intends to argue for is an extension of Israel's privileges to gentiles (rather than a transfer of them away from Israel). Paul's formula is thus an affirmation of Israel's status as the covenant people rather than an annulment.[40] But what has not always been realized is that the two elements—affirmation of Israel's covenant and its extension to gentiles—belong together in Paul and are certainly not mutually exclusive, as might have been anticipated. Paul's theme in Romans, therefore, is *not* that the goal of the divine purpose is the salvation of the gentiles; it is rather the salvation of Jews and gentiles both.

This is where unconscious assumptions may color interpretation and lead to very divergent readings of the same text. This is clearest in the interpretation of Rom 9. Watson objects to the content of chapter 11, which seems to suggest that the ultimate purpose of Paul's gentile mission is not the salvation of gentiles, but the salvation of Jews, whereas "elsewhere the salvation of the Gentiles, together with the Jewish remnant, is itself seen as the ultimate goal of God's purposes."[41] The passages that Watson cites in support of his reading are 4:16ff. and 9:24ff. I want to question whether these are in fact supportive, because, as already noted, these are verses that repeat the formula, "not only . . . but also," which I have argued stresses the inclusion of gentiles alongside Israel, as an extension of Israel's covenant. We need to look more closely at 9:24, as this is crucial to our discussion.

---

40. The occurrence of βεβαίος in Rom 4:16 (as also βεβαιῶσαι in 15:8 in a final construction) denotes "legally guaranteed security" (Dunn, *Romans 1–8*, 216). The latter verse with its reference to Christ indicates the intertwined relation of the salvation of Jews and gentiles in Paul's thought; as Fitzmyer (*Romans*, 704) renders it, "Christ became a servant to the circumcised to show God's fidelity, to confirm the promises made to the patriarchs, *and* Gentiles have glorified God for his mercy" (emphasis mine). Note there is no exact parallelism between the patriarchs and gentiles.

41. Watson, *Paul, Judaism, and the Gentiles*, 169.

The dominant theme in Rom 9–11 is the people of Israel, and only indirectly and in relation to this, the inclusion of gentiles. In chapter 9 gentiles are introduced only at two points: 9:24 and 9:30. In 9:30 the reference to gentiles enters merely as a foil to contrast their success with Jewish failure, so we will concentrate on 9:24 to see whether there is any basis here for the view that this chapter sets out a charter for God's election of a new people (as Watson reads).

Watson notes that whereas in Rom 11:1ff. "his people" (τὸν λαὸν αὐτοῦ) refers to the present generation of Jews, in 9:25, in diametrical opposition, "my people" (λαόν) refers to gentile Christians.[42] We need to look more closely at the text. Paul cites from Hos 2:23, "Those who were not my people I will call 'my people,' and her who was not beloved I will call 'my beloved.'" Dodd voices the sentiments of many commentators when he states, "It is rather strange that Paul has not observed that this prophecy referred to Israel, rejected for its sins, but destined to be restored." But it was Dodd's further comment that aroused my curiosity and caused me to look more closely—"strange because it would have fitted so admirably the doctrine of the restoration of Israel which he is to expound in ch. 11."[43] Further evidence for the strangeness of Paul's application of Hosea's words to gentiles is demonstrated in the two further citations that succeed this one. Fitzmyer points out that "whereas Paul quoted Hosea's promise apropos the Gentiles, he will next quote Isaiah's admonition apropos of Israel."[44] Surely, Paul himself must have been aware of the arbitrariness of his application of Scripture in the space of a few chapters. And of course, it seems foolish that he would not avail himself of the benefit of a scriptural text that offered apparent support for the restoration of Israel, a desired outcome toward which his own argument is tending.

An alternative reading of Rom 9 may be required in order to clarify Paul's consistency. According to this reading, the chapter is not a further argument for the inclusion of gentiles—as if 9:24 were the point toward which all of Paul's argument is tending, as if the inclusion of gentiles were in and of itself the goal of God's purpose, the thing in need of justification. But neither the starting point of the chapter, Paul's grief over Israel, nor its contents, such as the emphasis that God can have mercy on whomever he wills, adequately supports this notion. As Räisänen rightly notes, "It is the negative traits in God's dealings that according to Romans 9 cry for an explanation; the salvation of Gentiles is not a sufficient one."[45]

---

42. Watson, *Paul, Judaism, and the Gentiles*, 168.

43. Dodd, *The Epistle to the Romans*, 160.

44. Fitzmyer, *Romans*, 573.

45. Räisänen, "Paul, God and Israel," 184.

That Rom 9:21–22 reaches some sort of a conclusion is clear; it sums up the argument about the divine freedom in relation to Israel: "Has the potter no right over the clay, to make out of the same lump one vessel for beauty and another for menial use?" (9:21). That 9:22 continues this emphasis is not so clear, because here Paul introduces what is apparently a hypothetical statement, "What if God . . . ?" In succession to this in 9:23, he adds a purpose clause but fails to conclude the condition he began in 9:22, thus creating an anacoluthon.[46] So we are left with the unexpected hypothesis "What if God, because he wished to display his wrath and to make known his power, endured with much long-suffering vessels ripe for destruction?" Where Paul could have argued that God had cast off Israel, having first of all established the divine right of freedom, he surprisingly argues for God's right to be patient with Israel. It is only after this proposition that Paul, after a fuller elaboration and explanation of what has already been established in describing the purpose of the divine patience as being "to make known the riches of his glory," proceeds to further elaborate on the identity of its recipients in 9:24.

If we were to proceed into Rom 9:24 without a break, it might give the impression that gentiles are equally if not primarily the object of the divine purpose. With Fitzmyer and others, it is advisable to put 9:24–29 in a new subsection, which Räisänen entitles, "the inclusion of Gentiles."[47] But as he himself notes, the inclusion of gentiles is not the primary emphasis of the chapter. Fitzmyer's heading is therefore more appropriate: "God does not act arbitrarily: Israel's call, infidelity and remnant as foreseen in what God announced in the Old Testament."[48] This heading makes clear what I think is the case, that the topic under discussion is still primarily Israel or, more precisely, God's activity, but particularly in relation to Israel.

I conclude from this that it would be most unlikely for Paul to use the Hosea citation with reference to gentiles when this was not its original purpose and especially since it is immediately followed by two other Scripture citations that clearly apply to Israel. I would maintain that the Hosea citation is taken by Paul to apply *primarily* to Israel and thus the three citations all have the same point of reference, Israel. Rejected Israel, like the northern tribes, will be restored. This is Paul's primary thesis, but in and with the restoration, another "non-people," the gentiles, will also be blessed. Paul does apply the Hosea citation in a secondary sense, typologically, to gentiles also, but only after he has first used it to refer to Israel.[49] Like Hosea, he envisages

46. Cf. Bornkamm, *Das Ende des Gesetzes: Paulusstudien,* 76–92.

47. Räisänen, "Paul, God, and Israel," 183.

48. Fitzmyer, *Romans,* 571.

49. There is some support for this proposal from Karl Barth (*A Shorter Commentary*

the reuniting of the twelve tribes into one people, that is, the hardened and the remnant parts of Israel will one day be reunited.

When we see how minimal are the references to gentiles in Rom 9 and recognize that all the discussion about God's selection in 9:6ff. is not about the choice of gentiles at all but only about selection *within* the people of Israel in their *past* history,[50] then it is plain that another reading is possible; the chapter may now be read as not being about God's choice of a new people, but as being still specifically focused on the people of Israel. Where the gentiles are included at 9:24 and at 9:30, it is either in a secondary reference after Israel, or in 9:30 to contrast the outcome of the gentile mission with the Jewish response to Jesus, as if the two were causally related (as they seem to be in relation to the concept of hardening). The beginning of chapter 10 supports this reading because it refers to bearing witness to "them," where it is clear that the referents can only be the people of Israel.

The most surprising factor in Rom 9 is the somewhat unexpected twist with which Paul makes use of his powerful argument about the divine freedom. Instead of arguing that God is free and therefore can cast off Israel, Paul turns this around and asks, What if, as is the case, God patiently endures his people Israel.[51] When we follow closely the manner and sequence of Paul's argument in chapter 9, and recognize that the primary interest is in God's activity with Israel, then chapter 11 and its ending are not such a surprise after all, because the "surprise" has already been tentatively introduced in 9:22ff.

Recontextualizing Paul's Statements in Romans 9

No other passage in Paul's letters or perhaps even in the entire New Testament suffers so severely from the Augustinian[52] and Reformation readings

---

on Romans, 122–23), who interprets somewhat differently: "To whom did these words originally apply? To the Israel of the kings of Samaria, which had been rejected by God and which had yet been granted such a promise. And because these words have now been fulfilled in the calling of the Gentiles to the church of Jesus Christ, they obviously also speak with renewed force in their original sense; they also speak of the rejected, disobedient Israel. Now that he has fulfilled it superabundantly among the rejected without, how could God's promise not apply also to the rejected within, to whom he had once addressed it?"

50. Cf. Campbell, *Paul's Gospel in an Intercultural Context*, 43–49. There I describe Romans as "a reinterpretation of covenant righteousness in the light of the Christ-event." From a theological perspective, a distorted view of Paul's mission reveals a mistaken view of covenant (ibid., 173).

51. See Barrett, *A Commentary on the Epistle to the Romans*, 189.

52. See Stowers, *A Rereading of Romans*, 293–303. Stowers regards the entire epistle

as does Rom 9. Despite the valiant efforts of Karl Barth (though his own reading has led to further problems), Johannes Munck, Franz Leenhardt, and Krister Stendahl, among others, there is an inherent tendency to regard Paul's words in this chapter as referring to the timeless election of individuals by an arbitrary act of a mysterious and omnipotent deity.

Although there is now general agreement that the purpose of the argument of Rom 9–11 as a whole is to maintain or defend the trustworthiness of God regarding his promises to Israel, there are diverse opinions as to how chapter 9 serves this purpose. Watson sees chapter 9 as offering a different definition of the chosen people from chapter 11: "9:6–29 offers a clear and coherent argument for the view that the salvation of Gentiles and the rejection of Jews was entirely consistent with God's purpose of election as revealed in scripture. Yet in 11:1ff., and indeed throughout this chapter, Paul reverts to the old view of the people of God which he had previously rejected."[53]

Räisänen also, in his reading, finds problems with the content of Romans. Is Paul thinking theologically or historically? "Paul's argument is curious. It implies that empirical Israel—the unbelieving majority—should be identified with Ishmael and Esau. But what seems bewildering in terms of common sense is possible in Pauline theology."[54] Räisänen feels that interpreters eventually have to make a choice between the negative view of Israel in chapter 9 and the positive view in chapter 11. Romans 9:6–13 shows that the majority of Israel never belonged to the elect (and therefore God's promise is not affected by the unbelief of empirical Israel). In fact, "v. 22 implies predestination in damnation."

We can see that Räisänen seems to be dealing here with what he considers to be an abstract doctrine of predestination very similar to that of Augustine or Calvin. But scholarship has progressed radically on this topic since the Reformation. Barth correctly argued that if we start where Calvin started and if we are as consistent as he was, we will inevitably end up at the same point of conclusion.[55] So Barth moved the discussion forward by arguing not for the election of individuals as such but for election *in Christ*.[56]

---

as having been written to gentiles and gives a superb critique of the traditional view of 9–11 in opposition to Räisänen.

53. Watson, *Paul, Judaism and the Gentiles*, 168.

54. Räisänen, "God, Paul and Israel," 182–83.

55. Barth, *Church Dogmatics* 2.2, 35–37.

56. This recognition of Barth's contribution does not overlook its weaknesses. Goppelt (*Jesus, Paul and Judaism*, 163), for example, complains, "He understands election too much as predestination outside of history."

Munck, Leenhardt,[57] and Stendahl, all in differing ways, have stressed the need to see Rom 9–11 as a text of the missionary outreach of the first century, which as such should not be interpreted in the Augustinian and Calvinist manner of dealing with it as abstract and timeless theology.

What is lamentable, however, is that the insights of these interpreters from Barth to Stendahl seem to have been forgotten or overlooked even in some of the most recent studies of Rom 9–11.[58] I am not suggesting that there is no basis for discussing some of these issues (election and predestination) in relation to chapter 9. Paul himself applies these theological categories to his own day: "So too at the present time there is a remnant chosen by grace" (11:5).

Nevertheless, it is legitimate to read Rom 9 as a discussion of God's dealings with Israel in its *past*, as distinct from its present to which Paul specifically refers in 11:5. It is also clear that chapter 9 is not even about the number of the elect in Israel in the past. The categories of "the rest" and "the remnant" are implicit throughout the entire discussion, but these represent categories rather than a specific number of individuals. It is gratuitous to add, as in the RSV translation, "only" before the reference to a remnant in 9:27 ("*only* a remnant of them will be saved"). In point of fact, the emphasis in chapter 9 is not upon individuals *as such* but on chosen leaders and a righteous remnant to secure the future of the people. On this reading, it is an argument to show *how* God has maintained his purpose for this people throughout their history, sometimes through a minority, even by using Pharaoh.

Paul does make general theological statements about the "children of the promise" in distinction from the "children of the flesh." But he is not discussing God's election outside of or beyond Israel; the entire discussion up to Rom 9:24 is about God's elective purpose *within* Israel. It is not until 9:24, and then, as already noted, almost as an aside, that gentiles are mentioned. Thus, it *cannot* be argued that the interest here lies in the ingathering of gentiles. Paul's primary aim is to demonstrate that God is not tied to Israel in any specific way. Despite the covenant, God remains free even in relation to

---

57. Leenhardt (*The Epistle to the Romans*, 249–50) realized that the theme here was not the personal salvation of those who were called, but rather their utilization as instruments in a saving process, and that the interest is not so much in named individuals as much as in peoples who are thus named after their eponymous ancestors according to Old Testament practice.

58. Despite being aware of the problems surrounding these approaches to Rom 9–11, Cosgrove (*Elusive Israel*, 26ff.) frequently reverts to them as if they still had some validity; see also Räisänen "Paul, God and Israel."

Israel—free, that is, within his compassion to do as he wills (9:18).[59] Though it is also part of the divine method of working in the history of his people, Paul's primary interest is not in hardening either. The point Paul makes in both the hardening and having compassion is that God is free in his choice of individuals or groups to use them as he wills for the divine purpose for his people in history. Read from this perspective, Pharaoh's future salvation (9:17–18) is not the issue, but rather the future of Israel as perceived from the perspective of Paul's contemporary mission. The choice of people to serve, whether positively or negatively, God's purpose for Israel in its *past* prior to the coming of the gospel era is by no means the same issue as God's choice of people for eternal life, whatever parallels may legitimately be drawn between them.

If Rom 9 is read as not being primarily concerned with those whom God elects, but rather about his manner of acting in history, then it would be inconsistent to view it as a charter for the election of gentiles as the new people of God. Again, if chapter 9 is primarily about establishing God's freedom in relation to Israel, whether then or in the present and the future, the fact that *only* a remnant was elect *in the past* does not necessarily prevent all Israel, in whatever sense, being within God's purpose of election *in the future*. It appears from this that it is because Paul's use of election terminology is anachronistically interpreted in the light of post-Augustinian categories that a conflict is perceived between the fate of Israel in chapter 9 and a posited future in chapter 11. Theologically speaking, there cannot actually be a contradiction between the content of chapters 9 and 11 as we now have them. The basis for the salvation of Israel in both chapters is the same: God remains free to be compassionate with Israel as he wills. But when this is interpreted as we have already argued in relation to 9:22, God's freedom means that he is not obligated to discard Israel, however unworthy an object of his mercy she may actually be at any particular point in history. The freedom of God in relation to Israel is not a threat to Israel, because God's action toward Israel must then be based solely upon divine steadfastness and compassion rather than on Israel's fluctuating loyalty.[60] Since neither Israel nor the gentiles can constrain God to accept them, because he is free, so too he is not compelled

---

59. Cf. Barth's (*A Shorter Commentary on Romans*, 143) assertion "God remains free as regards the disobedient, just as he remains free as regards the obedient."

60. This is clearly recognized by Leenhardt (*The Epistle to the Romans*, 252–53): "If his reaction had depended on 'man's will or exertion,' . . . then Yahweh could only have punished with the greatest severity. Instead of that he gave to this rebellious people a new revelation of his grace and at the same time displayed its basic principle: my mercy is utterly free."

by their failures to cast them off. A salvation determined by works cannot be denied on the one hand and reaffirmed on the other.

My conclusion on this point is that the perceived contradictions within Rom 9, or in its relation to chapter 11, or in its relation to the letter as a whole, have been at least partly due to interpreting "a missionary's contribution to a discussion"[61] as if it were a timeless theological treatise seeking to solve questions that Paul, at this juncture at least, had no interest in asking. It is, moreover, inconsistent and anachronistic to read most sections of this letter in the light of the contemporary interpretation of Paul's letters as a whole, and yet read this particular section as if we were living in the seventeenth century.

Divergent Understandings of the Significance of Paul's Gentile Mission as a Factor in the Roman Context

In my reading, I have argued with Munck that Rom 9 ought to be interpreted as "a missionary's contribution to a discussion" rather than in abstract theological or philosophical categories. A sociological approach might lead us to regard, with Räisänen and Watson, this chapter as addressed to those who, like Paul, felt the plight of Israel to be a calamity; that is, to Roman Jewish Christians for whom Paul's predestination language would function as consolation for their lack of success among their own people.[62] But 11:17ff. makes it clear that the addressees of Paul's argument are gentile Christians for whom the fate of Israel was of little concern.

A possible scenario is that Paul addresses gentile Christians throughout Rom 9–11, and that Paul, in chapter 9, using himself as exemplar, thus demonstrates what their proper attitude to Israel ought to be. At the same time, this would also provide comfort and reassurance to those who wished to continue to follow a Jewish lifestyle. But why, then, should Paul need to protest so solemnly that he indeed does care for Israel? He appears to be refuting rumors to the contrary.[63]

---

61. Cf. Munck, *Paul and the Salvation of Mankind*; cf. also Dahl, *The Missionary Theology in the Epistle to the Romans*, 70–94.

62. Räisänen ("Paul, God and Israel," 186) rightly focuses on the social function of the doctrine of predestination. However, it seems to point to Jewish Christians as the addressees (ibid., 181). On this view, Paul's real concern seems to be with Jewish Christian queries (ibid., 195). Watson's (*Paul, Judaism and the Gentiles*, 97–98; cf. 151–53, 163–64, 172) sociological approach likewise seems to target Jewish Christians, especially their social reorientation away from the synagogue.

63. "Paul had to dispel suspicions that he is hostile or indifferent to Israel" (Watson, *Paul, Judaism and the Gentiles*, 180). Räisänen ("Paul, God and Israel," 198) notes that

What alternative images of Paul and his mission may have been current at Rome? It had been anticipated that Paul would pay a visit. He protests that despite wanting to come and remembering them continually in his prayers, he has hitherto not been able to do so (cf. 1:9–13; 15:22). It is not until 15:25 that he admits that he is actually not going to visit them even now, but is going instead to Jerusalem with the collection. From Paul's obvious embarrassment here, we can be sure that some of the Roman Christians expected Paul to visit them, and he recognizes that they reside within the sphere of his gentile mission (1:13).

If Paul's reputation depicted him as a champion of the gentiles, it would then probably be gentile Christians who legitimately expected a visit from him, especially if there was conflict between rival groups at Rome. The reason Paul gives for not visiting the Romans is significant: he is a pioneer missionary unwilling to build on another's foundation (15:20–22). But now that this kind of work has been completed in the east, he is heading for Spain to continue in a similar vein. He does not come to evangelize in Rome, but for mutual edification in each other's company (1:11–13), and hopefully to receive support for a new outreach in Spain (15:24).

The crucial issue is this: did Paul delay a visit to Rome because Rome was regarded by Paul as already founded, that is, because in coming there he would in fact not be going to those who had never heard (15:21)? The best explanation is that Rome differed from Paul's normal pioneering areas in that it already possessed Christian communities, most of whom were formerly, and continued to be, in association with the city's synagogue communities. In this context, gentile Christians may have felt, particularly in the earlier days of their communal existence, a need of Paul's support to champion their cause and maintain their rights.

As Paul writes, however, to the Romans, we do not get the impression that they are either weak or dominated by Jews or Judaizers. They are self-confident enough to interpret the world from their own conceited perspective. Paul seeks to prevent this by helping them to understand "the mystery of Israel" (11:25f.). We can be reasonably sure of that. Therefore, they are deficient in their understanding of God's purposes for Israel, and this deficiency is a cause for boasting (11:13ff.). There is an additional factor not sufficiently noted. In 11:13ff. Paul not only warns the gentile Christians against boasting over Jews, but he somewhat surprisingly introduces his

---

besides Rom 9:1, οὐ ψεύδομαι occurs in Paul only in 2 Cor 11:31 and Gal 1:20 (assuming that 1 Timothy is non-Pauline), and that in both cases Paul is refuting rumors, whereas Käsemann (*Romans*, 257) sees this as resulting from Paul's often being accused of hostility to Israel.

own mission as an element in the discussion. Paul, while addressing them as gentiles, wants them to realize that his ministry to gentiles has direct relevance not only to the salvation of his fellow Jews, but also that the salvation of them relates to their own salvation (11:13ff.).

Taking these two factors together, it seems beyond reasonable doubt that a misunderstanding of the significance of Paul's mission on the part of the Roman gentile Christians had contributed to their inflated self-esteem (cf. 12:3ff.) and to their corresponding denigration of Israel,[64] which was manifesting itself in their intolerance of those conscientiously committed to living a Jewish lifestyle.[65]

Paul is implicated in the situation at Rome, in fact, doubly implicated. As apostle to the gentiles, the churches there come within his remit, but beyond this, it is clear that reports of his own gospel and mission have probably been a catalyst in the situation. Based on the knowledge that Paul viewed himself as apostle to gentiles and that he set up congregations that did not force their adherents to observe the Jewish law, it would have been easy for a one-sided, gentile-sided, image of Paul to develop. This, coupled with the frequent hostility of Jewish opponents who regarded him as a disloyal apostate, could soon have assisted the development of an image of the "partisan Paul." By the very location of his work—predominantly gentile territory—it would also be unlikely that Paul would have often needed to discuss the future or even the evangelization of his own people. It would have been very easy for an image of a pro-gentile Paul to gain credibility. His opposition to Judaizers in Galatians in defense of his gentile converts must have had some such outcome. His "face to face" with Cephas in the encounter at Antioch was no doubt perceived in this way and thus served as a pivotal event in the creation of the image of the partisan, pro-gentile Paul.

This was the Paul the Roman gentiles were expecting to visit them. Even allowing for the normal exaggeration of hearsay reporting, it must be recognized that before the letter was sent to them, the Roman Christians could have expected a somewhat pro-gentile apostle—in my view, one very similar to the Paul of Paulinism.[66] But there were new elements in the situa-

64. For further emphasis on the deficiency of the gentile Christians see my *Paul's Gospel in an Intercultural Context*, 170–77. Schlatter (*Romans*, 221) claims, "For those who were Greeks by birth, it was easy to assume that Paul had separated himself completely from the Jews. In this case they also argued . . . that they were under no obligation to the Jews." Theologically speaking, they had misinterpreted the covenant and hence the divine purpose for the world, that is, for Jews and gentiles *both*.

65. See Jewett, *Christian Tolerance*. It is not possible to deal adequately here with the vast literature on the *Sitz im Leben* of the Roman Christians, but see also Nanos, *The Mystery of Romans*, 75ff.

66. Against Watson's thesis (*Paul, Judaism and the Gentiles*, 98) that Paul wants to

tion at Rome as well as possibly in Paul's own mission that were to combine to bring to light a rather different apostle.

However Romans is read, it is beyond dispute that Jewishness in one form or another was an issue among the Roman Christians. If Nanos[67] and others are correct in their reading that there were some Jews there who were at least open to the Christian message, if not already fully committed, then Paul had to take these into account, particularly if, as seems to be the case, they were a minority. Since Paul did not found the churches in Rome, he faces a problem, because he has to accept what already exists there or run the risk of destroying the weak "for whom Christ died" (14:15). Moreover, if he simply supports the arrogant gentiles in their mistaken conceit, such support will have repercussions throughout the church, not least in Jerusalem, where Paul now heads with fear for his own safety. But more serious still, as Stendahl notes, "Paul may have found something unnerving in the missionary zeal of his bragging Gentile converts over against the Jewish people."[68] Perhaps Paul encountered here for the first time a supersessionist form of Christianity that his own mission, at least as it was reported, had helped to produce.

The Inclusive Paul:
The Purpose of God for Jews and also for Gentiles

As Paul writes Romans, he is apparently faced with a dilemma. Not only is he not coming now to Rome, but worse still, he is heading for Jerusalem with a collection from his gentile communities, something in itself open to great misunderstanding. If he alienates the gentile Christians, not only will this help to accentuate their errors but he may also lose their much-needed support for his mission in Spain. This combination of factors resulted not only in the creation of the content of Romans,[69] but also helps to explain the manner of its presentation. Paul is forced to start with the images of himself and his mission that the gentiles actually hold and then to seek discreetly to lead them in the direction he wants them to proceed; hence his employment of the dialogical style of the diatribe.[70] It is this point of departure that helps to explain why the earlier parts of Romans can be read in such a way that Rom

---

convert the Roman Jewish congregation to Paulinism.

67. Nanos, *The Mystery of Romans,* 95–119.

68. Stendahl, *Paul among Jews and Gentiles,* 53.

69. On the combination of Rome, Jerusalem, and Spain, see Käsemann, *Romans,* 405–6.

70. See my *Paul's Gospel in an Intercultural Context,* 136–41.

11, with its *apparently* pro-Jewish conclusion, is not even envisaged, and why many scholars see such similarities between these chapters and Galatians.[71] Paul stealthily prepares throughout the letter for the disclosures concerning his attitude toward and his hope for his own people. If, as Sanders claims, Paul works from solution back to problem,[72] then Romans as we now have it perhaps ought to be read in reverse! In this approach, the content of chapters 9–11 would not be seen so much as a surprise.

For Paul, the entire argument of Romans presupposes the faithfulness of God to his people, and this is made clear at many significant points. See, for instance, Rom 1:16, the gospel is the power of God "to the Jew first and also to the Greek"; 3:26, "it was to prove at the present time that he himself is righteous"; 4:16, "in order that the promise may rest on grace and be guaranteed to all his descendants, not only to the adherents of the law but also to those who share the faith of Abraham." Paul was certain that the faithlessness of Israel could not destroy the faithfulness of God, and he gives only a hint about this in 3:1–8 in order to alert the observant reader that this is a presupposition throughout the letter. For Paul, in contrast to his interpreters, to insist on faith in Jesus Christ while also maintaining God's promises to Israel is not irreconcilable.

It should be acknowledged, however, that despite the many indications already given in Rom 1–8, even a superb exegete such as Ernst Käsemann could still find problems with the Paul of chapter 11. Admittedly, this was in the different intellectual climate of 1961, when the significance of the Holocaust for interpretation was not yet fully recognized. Käsemann holds that Israel has exemplary significance for Paul—"in and with Israel he strikes at the hidden Jew in all of us"—and he finds it fortuitous that "Romans 9–11 repeats the argument of the whole letter." He continues, "Is the apostle contradicting himself when he nevertheless ends chapter 11 with the promise of salvation for the whole people of Israel?" Despite Käsemann's recognition that Paul concedes to Israel "the rights of the first-born," he eventually concludes, "Thus the justification of the ungodly, which is also the resurrection from the dead, is the only hope both of the world in general and also of Israel."[73]

Our conclusion from all this must be that different readings of Romans, especially from chapters 9–11, arise chiefly from those presuppositions we bring with us to this point. Included in these, and of primary importance, is

---

71. See Sanders, *Paul and Palestinian Judaism*, 487–88.

72. Ibid., 443ff. and 499.

73. Käsemann, "Christ and Israel," 183–87. This essay originated from a broadcast talk.

our image of Paul himself and his mission. Also of some significance is our larger understanding of how Christianity, particularly in its origins, relates to Judaism.[74] In Käsemann's reading it is clear that he interprets chapters 9–11 out of chapters 1–8, and Israel becomes an exemplar or symbol for the justification of the ungodly. There may be a parallel here to what happens when Paul commences to write his letter to the Romans. He is faced with the fact that they are already in possession of an image of the apostle to the gentiles and that they therefore think they know how he will respond to their situation. So Paul has to present as discreetly as possible another image of himself, this time one that includes his own understanding of how the gentile mission relates to God's purposes for *both* Jews and gentiles. The image of the "partisan Paul"—the apostle for the gentiles—is thus revised and updated to become the image of the "inclusive Paul" of "not only the Jew but also the Greek," of Paul among Jews and gentiles.

Despite dedicated attempts to get behind the overlay of centuries of readings of Romans, scholars will never be able fully to comprehend its message as it was first delivered to the Romans. But we must give the text its due weight and not interpret it on the basis of Galatians,[75] of an already known gospel, or of a familiar portrait of the apostle at an earlier stage in his career. As far as is humanly possible, we must interpret Paul's mission and Paul himself as they are presented in this specific text before we resort to harmonization or revision from any other sources, however significant. Within the letter, the same principle applies: we must allow, as we are able, each section of the letter to reveal its own peculiar content before we seek to relate it to a coherent view of the whole.

74. As long as Judaism and the Hebrew Scriptures are regarded as simply preparatory to Christianity, then it is inevitable that the gentile mission will be viewed as the climax of God's work, and the Christian church will continue to be confused with the kingdom of God (see Soulen, *The God of Israel and Christian Theology*, 19).

75. Against Cosgrove's (*Elusive Israel*, 88) proposal: "As part of the Christian canon, Galatians 2 now supplies part of the canonical story of the Gentile mission. In a constructive canonical interpretation, it is therefore appropriate to interpret Rom 11:19 within the context of this canonical story."

5

"All God's Beloved in Rome!"
Jewish Roots and Christian Identity

Structure and Content in Romans 8:14—11:36

IN A PREVIOUS ESSAY on the structure and style of Romans, I drew attention to the frequency of questions and responses in the diatribe style in certain sections of Romans, though this feature is absent in others.[1] I had some difficulty in describing chapter 8 in this approach. In some respects it is similar to the proclamatory style some scholars have noted in 3:21–26 and chapter 5.[2] Yet parts of chapter 8, especially verses 31–39, are very similar to chapter 9. This was awkward for someone like myself who wanted to make a major break at the end of chapter 8, thus dividing the letter into chapters 1–4, 5–8, 9–11, and 12–16. Since the first essay was written, I have become increasingly aware of the strong links between chapter 8 and chapters 9–11 and would emphasize them still more.

A major difficulty with linking chapters 8 and 9 is that the latter is very much a discussion of Jewish issues carried out in dialogue with the Old Testament Scriptures, whereas the former usually is read as one of the most explicitly Christian statements in the entire letter.[3] What sort of meaningful links can one discover between chapters of such differing perspectives? Themes in Romans 8—such as the fulfilment of the law in believers, the

1. Campbell, "Romans 3 as a Key to the Structure and Thought of the Letter."

2. Joachim Jeremias, O. Michel, and others investigated the structural and verbal clues in Romans; for details see Campbell, "Romans 3 as a Key." Rhetorical studies such as Jewett's "Following the Argument of Romans" (in *The Romans Debate*, 265–77), and Elliott's *The Rhetoric of Romans* have greatly assisted our understanding in recent years.

3. Robin Scroggs ("Paul as Rhetorician: Two Homilies in Romans 1–11," 271–98) drew attention to differences within Romans, regarding 1–4 and 9–11 as two homilies diverging greatly from 5–8.

witness of the Spirit, the renewal of the creation, and above all the secure destiny of those in Christ—have caused chapter 9 and its concern with the Jewish failure to accept Christ to appear as anti-climax to a story which already has reached its conclusion. Chapter 11, with its conclusion advocating the salvation of "all Israel," appears in fact to contradict the neat conclusion already achieved at the end of Rom 8. Small wonder that C. H. Dodd viewed Rom 9–11 as a sermon on the Jewish issue that Paul previously had constructed elsewhere before inserting it rather arbitrarily at this point.[4]

In fact, the apparent dissonance between Paul's statements in Rom 8 and 9–11 respectively have individually contributed to two divergent understandings of Pauline theology. One is pronouncedly christological, representing an evangelical, existential type of theology and stressing radical newness, while the other is *"heilsgeschichtlich,"* stressing continuity with Israel. The former perspective stresses Rom 1–8 and tends to use 9–11 negatively as witness to the disobedience and rejection of Israel, while the latter sees Paul's argument as progressing cumulatively to a positive climax in chapter 11 or 11–16. Even the figure of Abraham is disputed. In his use of the Abraham tradition is Paul simply providing his converts with a fictive-family connection to an individual significant only as a "punctiliar," exemplary believer?[5] Or is he actually relating them to a particular people of God of whom Abraham was the father? Is Paul, in fact, rooting the gentiles in the ancient stem of Abraham, or is he creating a new people of God?

Recent research on Paul's use of Scripture, and on scriptural echoes in the New Testament generally, has proved illuminating here.[6] Far from using the Scriptures merely as proof texts or as evidence for his view of the gospel, Paul has emerged as a serious student of Scripture who not only uses it frequently and explicitly but whose whole thought is permeated with scriptural nuances and insights. To the careful observer, echoes of the Scriptures are discernible throughout his writings.

In response to Calvin Roetzel in a discussion concerning the origins of Paul's theology, I came to the conclusion that Paul's uniqueness consists not so much in creating absolutely new theological structures as in the creative transformation of his ancestral traditions. Paul both interprets Scripture in relation to contemporary events of his own time, and in turn interprets these events in the light of Scripture. Thus the frequent emphasis on calling (καλέω) in 1 Corinthians reminds us of God's calling of Israel and that

---

4. Dodd, *The Epistle to the Romans*, 148–49.

5. Cf. Martyn, "Events in Galatia," esp. 174.

6. Cf. Hays, *Echoes of Scripture*.

"Paul's theologizing takes place within the specific context of ongoing divine activity in relation to a people who are called."[7]

Paul does not suddenly turn to the people of Israel in chapter 9; already beginning with Rom 7:1, and especially from 8:14–39, the story of Israel provides the background to his argument.[8] Sonship, as it is developed in 8:14–15, builds on the consolidation of themes in 6:12—8:11; this is evident particularly in 8:12–17, where the negative formulations that were applied to the Christian life in 6:1–11 (death to sin, release from slavery to sin) are replaced by the positive theme of divine "sonship." The argumentative unit is therefore 6:1—8:13, which is succeeded by a second unit beginning in 8:14 and continuing through to 11:36.[9]

Commentators have noticed the parallels between terms used in chapter 8 and those that recur again in chapter 9 but, in the latter instance, with their primary reference to Israel.[10] "Calling" in various constructions occurs in 8:30; 9:7, 12, 24–26. The first reference to "sons of God" in Romans occurs in 8:14 (cf. 8:19). In scriptural citations the same or parallel expressions occur in 9:26: "the non-people" become "sons of the living God"; and in 9:27: "though the number of the sons of Israel is as the sand of the sea, a remnant will be saved." Sonship occurs first in 8:15, then in 8:23, and again in 9:4 in the sevenfold list of Israel's privileges. "Children of God" occurs in 8:16, 17, 21, and in 9:8. In 8:28 we have reference to those "called according to his purpose" and in 9:11 "the purpose of God in election." "Those whom he foreknew" is found in 8:29 and recurs in 11:2 in connection with "his people." "Glory" occurs throughout Romans but notably in 8:18, 21; 9:4, 23; and 11:36.[11]

Clearly, Paul does not turn to the attributes and privileges of Israel for the first time in Rom 9–11; rather, many of these already had been introduced earlier in the letter in 7:12 and in 8:14–39.[12] This enables us to

7. Campbell "The Contribution of Traditions to Paul's Theology," 234–54 (chapter 2 in this volume).

8. See Campbell, "Divergent Images of Paul and His Mission," 187–211 (chapter 4 in this volume).

9. Cf. Elliott, *The Rhetoric of Romans*, esp. 271–75 on "The Argumentative Coherence of Romans 5–11."

10. Cf. "brethren" (ἀδελφοί) in 8:29 and 9:3. Mark Nanos (*The Mystery of Romans*, 110) notes that "Paul regards non-Christian Jews as his 'brethren' throughout this letter."

11. Dunn notes many links between Romans 8 and 9 in "Paul's Epistle to the Romans: An Analysis of Structure and Argument," 2842–90, and *Romans 1–8* and *Romans 9–16*.

12. The ἐγώ in Rom 7:9 may refer to Israel rather than to Paul, or to Paul as a representative of Israel, which makes good sense in the context. Thus 7:7–25 refers to Israel's struggle with the law; this view is preferable to a psychological or individualistic

conclude that, firstly, chapters 9–11 are no afterthought and there is no major caesura after 8:39.[13] More significantly, however, another observation is warranted. In 8:1–13 and to a lessening extent as the chapter progresses, the christological emphases of the Pauline gospel are present. But surprisingly an increasing ambiguity in terminology emerges so that the new believing community is described in almost similar terms to Israel. Paul uses terms and attributes in chapter 8, and then in 9:4–5 provides a compact list of these referring precisely to Israel (rather than to gentile Christians), followed by other similar references in chapters 9–11.

This argument from the use of common terms in chapters 8 and 9–11 is greatly strengthened when we take into account not only explicit terms but also scriptural echoes and implicit allusions. The underlying theme of 8:14–39 is the narrative of Exodus, as indicated by such terms as "led by the Spirit," "spirit of slavery," and "freedom from fear." More vivid however is the emphasis on "leading" and "sonship," with Israel as the firstborn son and Israel's sonship as derived from the exodus. Sylvia C. Keesmaat has convincingly argued in a recent study that "Paul echoes the language of the Exodus narrative in a way which is consistent with the prophets, so that the Roman believers have an identity as those who are undertaking a wilderness journey en route to the promised land."[14]

The content of 8:18–39 also has close parallels to Jer 31 with its emphasis on a new exodus event, a new covenant, and the assertion that Israel would exist even if the created order were to disappear.[15] From this we discover that faithfulness to the whole of creation and to Israel is the concluding emphasis of chapter 8 and a fitting link to 9–11.[16] From this perspective it is very fitting to describe 8:14—11:36 as "The Heritage of the Children of

---

interpretation of Paul and prepares for the Exodus allusions in 8:14–39.

13. For an excellent discussion of this and related issues see Engberg-Pedersen, "For the Jew First: The Coherence of Literary Structure and Thought in Romans in Conversation with James D. G. Dunn" (paper presented at the annual meeting of the *Studiorum Novi Testamenti Societas*, University of Pretoria, August 1999).

14. Keesmaat, *Paul and His Story,* 153; see also 136–54.

15. Cf. ibid., 153–54. Keesmaat maintains that Paul transforms the tradition, writing as though the new exodus is now taking place.

16. Cf. ibid., 64: "Paul is concerned with God's faithfulness to all of creation, but in the light of Jeremiah 31, the renewal of creation in Romans 8 is an *affirmation* of God's faithfulness to Israel." Ernst Käsemann and some of his students have been criticized by Karl Kertelge for overemphasizing God's freedom as Creator (in Rom 9), in such a way that faithfulness to Israel is replaced by faithfulness to the creation; cf. Käsemann, "The Righteousness of God in Paul," 177–80; Kertelge, *Rechtfertigung,* 308; and Campbell, "The Freedom and Faithfulness of God in Relation to Israel," 43–59; cf. 4–5.

God."[17] According to Neil Elliott, "connections in vocabulary and themes *across* the artificial boundary at 9:1 constitute the argumentative integration of Rom 8 and 9, and thereby of the larger segments 1–8 and 9–11; . . . the thematic unity of the whole is the hope for the 'glory of the children of God' (8:20–21)."[18]

Although he has transformed the story of Exodus by developing the "new exodus" dimension and applying it to believers in Christ,[19] the intended audience of Paul's address in Rom 8 is no different from that in Rom 9. While the failure of Israel to recognize Jesus as Messiah is stressed and the focus in 9:1–29 (with the exception of 9:24) is Israel, the discussion is nevertheless *about Israel as a third party*. It is not a dialogue with Israel.[20] Thus the eventual import of the argument in chapter 8, and perhaps of the entire letter, despite the allusions to Israel, is in part or in total intended primarily for the gentile believers more precisely addressed in 11:13–14. The goal of the argument is indicated in 11:25. Paul's revelation of a mystery and all that precedes it is to destroy the gentiles' mistaken and ill-founded boasting, based on an imagined superiority over Jews, "lest you be wise in your own conceits" (ἵνα μὴ 'ἦτε' [παρ'] ἑαυτοῖς φρόνιμοι). We may summarize our thesis here: 8:14—11:36 functions along with 14:1—15:13, to provide support for "the weak in faith" and to humble "the strong in faith."

At this point we are forced to ask the question of Paul's intention in a rhetoric involving the use of similar terms across apparently very dissimilar chapters. It would appear that he is deliberately blurring the distinction between the new believing community and the old.[21] Is he saying firstly that God is faithful in preserving and delivering his own people and secondly that only God knows and determines the boundaries of his elect people?

17. When this paper was nearing completion, I was delighted to note that Neil Elliott had thus entitled this section of Romans; see Elliott, *The Rhetoric of Romans*, 253–54.

18. Elliott, *The Rhetoric of Romans*, 257.

19. On this see also Davies, "Paul and the New Exodus," 443–63.

20. *Contra* Beker's (*Paul, the Apostle*, 24–25) comment that "in Romans Paul does not attack Christians for adopting Jewish ways or circumcision but demonstrates instead the way in which Judaism is accounted for in the Gospel. The dialogue with the Jews is at the same time an apology for Israel . . ." Cf. Campbell, *Paul's Gospel in an Intercultural Context*, 137. Elliott's emphasis on dialogue is rhetorically more sophisticated and avoids the problems Beker encounters.

21. Robinson ("The Priesthood of Paul in the Gospel of Hope," 244–45) is one of the few exegetes to note this phenomenon. He sees the theme of Rom 8 as being "the liberty of the Jew who has entered his inheritance in Christ and his hope of glory according to promise and election"; Christian experience and the expectation of final glory are set forth deliberately as "the experience of the justified Jew, indeed of Israel itself in the person of the servant and apostle of the Lord."

Presumably one or both of these emphases would be relevant to the believers in Rome. We will understand the two possibilities better if we set out their significance. If Paul wishes to blur the lines concerning the description of the elect of God, perhaps it is because some Christians in Rome were in danger of being wrongly excluded from this people, and Paul wants to prevent what he sees as a drastic mistake. This would be more serious if in fact all or even some of the Christ-believers in Rome were meeting in the synagogues and functioning wholly within the larger Jewish community (or communities) in Rome. If Mark Nanos is correct in interpreting "weak in faith" as referring to Jews who are yet are not fully convinced about Jesus as Messiah,[22] then Paul wishes in his argument to be inclusive rather than exclusive to enable such people to get support and encouragement to lead them in the right direction according to his gospel.

If Paul wishes to oppose Roman gentile Christians in their mistaken despising of their fellow Jews and Jewish believers in Christ and to prevent their cutting themselves off from the stem of Abraham, then his purpose would be to incorporate them into the story of Abraham and the people of Israel. But this would be done in such a way that they would not be encouraged to "judaize" (though there was little likelihood of that). Rather, they are encouraged to perceive themselves as gentile branches in the family tree of Abraham.[23] In this sense Paul would be encouraging them to see the story of God's elect people as their story also, and to allow their identity to be reshaped in an "Israelitish" reconfiguration while yet remaining gentiles.

Jewish versus Christian Identity?

In his recent interesting article on "Jewish versus Christian Identity in the Church," Bengt Holmberg argues that the conflict in Galatians between Jewish and Christian identity should be restated as a conflict between Christian identity and Jewish-Christian self-definition.[24] Holmberg concludes that "the common, fundamental Christian identity of the church is more important than inherited ethno-religious self-definitions."[25] Holmberg notes (following Ben Meyer's insights) that the early church discovered itself and

22. Nanos, "The Jewish Context of the Gentile Audience Addressed in Paul's Letter to the Romans," 283–304. For a fuller explanation of his argument see Nanos, *The Mystery of Romans*.

23. Is Paul's aim in Romans "to show the Gentiles how their hope rests on Israel's Messiah?" Cf. Robinson, "The Priesthood of Paul in the Gospel of Hope," 232.

24. Holmberg, "Jewish *versus* Christian Identity," 397–425.

25. Ibid., 424.

found its own identity by allowing its dynamic missionary work to feed back into its self-understanding. This meant that previous conceptions about the place and role of gentiles had to be drastically revised in the light of the experience of their participation in the Spirit. Thus it is clear that, "theologically speaking, the Holy Spirit creates the identity of the church and shows it to her, and the church's role in this process is to become aware of and obedient to these experience-based insights."[26] That experience-based insights influenced the theological development of the church need not be doubted. We are not convinced however that Holmberg's insights setting Jewish identity in antithesis to Christian identity are valid, especially when applied to Romans.

If our emphasis that Paul has already introduced the theme of Israel in Rom 8:14–15 is correct, then "it seems clear that one of the things that Paul's evocation of the Exodus tradition accomplishes is firmly to root and characterize the identity and calling of the Roman believers. As sons of God, redeemed and called in the climactic new Exodus in Christ, they have a calling to faithful obedience of the God they serve. As participants in the final Exodus, with its import for all of creation, their calling has cosmic proportions."[27] In chapters 9–11 Paul is seeking to provide the Romans with a revised self-understanding. It would appear that some of them are in the process of, or at least at risk of, developing a new self-understanding that is not only distinct from, but perhaps even in opposition to, their designation as children of Abraham. The conclusion to the main argument in Romans lies in the command to "welcome one another" (14:1; 15:7). This concluding admonition is here explicitly designed to overcome alienation and judging of one another, and thus to encourage mutual acceptance between the various gentile and Jewish Christian groupings in Rome.[28] What is significant, however, is that it is supported by a *catena* of scriptural citations in 15:9–12; and the emphasis in all four quotations is on the gentiles confessing and praising Israel's God, joining with Israel (μετὰ τοῦ λαοῦ αὐτοῦ).[29] This suggests that Paul saw a need for gentiles to recognize and relate positively to their Jewish neighbors.

---

26. Ibid., 421.

27. Keesmaat, *Paul and His Story*, 143.

28. Cf. Meeks, "Judgement and the Brother: Romans 14:1—15:13," 290–300. Meeks (ibid., 291) notes that the root κρίν- "becomes a *leitmotif* in our text."

29. Meeks (ibid., 291) draws attention to this as "one odd thing about this *catena* of texts."

Christian Identity and Negative Self-Definition

Why should there be a reaction against Jewishness when historical evidence demonstrates that Judaism proved very attractive to many gentiles, some of whom became proselytes despite the physical and social barrier represented by circumcision?[30] The most reasonable hypothesis is that, in some instances, this aversion to Judaism arose as a rejection of former proselyte status and everything associated with it upon entering a Christ-believing community. This would represent, therefore, a turning away from an acquired Jewish identity by former gentiles.[31] We have in it an example of the phenomenon of a rejection intensified because of high evaluation of the former affiliation. Now they are self-confident and self-aware in their new identity as gentile Christians, even to the point of despising those Christians, whether of Jewish or gentile birth, who felt obligated to continue practicing a Jewish lifestyle.

Their self-estimate is over-inflated for two reasons. First, because they now know that there is no need for gentile Christ-believers to become Jews; in fact, it is explicitly forbidden by Paul to do so, although it may be that not all the believing proselytes shared this view. Second, they have a new understanding of their own role and status in salvation history in relation to the Jews. "Branches were broken off that I might be grafted in" (11:19) probably indicates traces of group conflict. Whether or not this theological opinion is exactly paralleled by an actual situation in Rome is another highly debated question, but greater consensus now exists concerning the Christ-believing community at Rome, at least with regard to the Roman gentile believers.[32] We can be reasonably confident that at least some of these believers were using their antipathy toward a Jewish lifestyle as a means of negative self-definition.

30. See Rutgers, *The Hidden Heritage of Diaspora Judaism,* 33; cf. Tessa Rajak, "The Jewish Community and Its Boundaries," 9–28.

31. Despite the attractiveness of Judaism to many gentiles, once proselytes became acquainted with the gentile mission, a new option was then available that had not been open to them earlier; and this may have allowed them to return to the inherent resentment prevalent in Hellenistic society, perhaps encouraged by the very strength and self-confidence of Judaism. See Rutgers, *The Hidden Heritage of Diaspora Judaism,* 37; also Barclay, *Jews in the Mediterranean Diaspora,* 444.

32. I have argued for this reading of Romans in different articles, some of which are included in my *Paul's Gospel in an Intercultural Context,* but see also more recently "The Rule of Faith in Romans 12:1—15:13," 259–86 (chapter 3 in this volume). Dunn (*Romans 9–16,* 801–2) also supports the view that the divide between "the weak" and "the strong" basically was along a Jewish-oriented vs. non-Jewish-oriented line—and that Paul is urging the latter to bow to the sensibilities of the former.

What we seem to have evidence of here is a sectarian type of gentile Christianity. We are not suggesting that Paul's communities were sectarian, but Paul did not found the church in Rome. A possible explanation for the emergence of this sectarian attitude is that, because their self-definition in Christ was being negatively valued by Jews who did not share their faith, some Christ-believers sought to justify their inclusion by undermining the place and legitimacy of the practice of Jews. While Christianity in its origins may be accurately described as a messianic sect of Judaism,[33] it was not necessarily sectarian in character, and this group in its negative self-definition is an aberration from the norm of the Pauline communities.[34]

How Paul attempts to oppose this self-designation is extremely interesting. His depiction of the gentiles as branches grafted into the stem of Abraham demonstrates analogically their dependence on the Jewish foundations of the church. They have no entirely independent identity, whether or not they desire such. If they do not show proper reverence, they too will be broken off; they have no absolute independence or security in and of themselves. They remain branches, which in and of themselves do not constitute a tree. Paul in fact relocates the gentiles in the family of Abraham. They have to take on the identity or part of the identity of children or seed (σπέρμα) of Abraham. In Romans, as distinct from Galatians, the σπέρμα is comprised of two peoples (4:16).

What is surprising here is that Paul does fully incorporate the gentiles in the seed of Abraham, but without identifying them as proselytes, despite the connection with circumcision in Gen 17. That this is the case is demonstrated by the fact that Abraham is described as father *both* of the circumcised *and* of those who believe without being circumcised (4:11–12). The latter are not just "righteous gentiles" loosely affiliated with Israel, but neither are they Israelites proper, since Paul reserves this title for those who, like himself, are of Jewish ancestry (9:3–4; 11:1–2).[35] Reports of this aspect of Paul's gospel may in fact have contributed to confusion concerning Christian identity in Rome.

The status of former proselytes who became believers in Christ is a difficult issue on which to speculate. But that there were such need not be doubted

33. Cf. Rowland (*Christian Origins,* 1st ed., 109–10), who describes Christianity as a messianic sect of Judaism,

34. *Contra* Watson's thesis (*Paul, Judaism and the Gentiles,* 19–20) that Paul sought to transform a reform movement into a sect.

35. See Campbell, "Israel"; cf. Dunn, *The Theology of Paul the Apostle,* 525–26, where Dunn suggests that "the identity of Israel as defined by grace and faith included both historic Israel and Gentiles" (ibid., 526); cf. also Donaldson, "Proselytes as Righteous Gentiles," 3–27.

as the reference to Nicolaus, a proselyte of Antioch (Acts 6:5), makes clear. But if among these there were, as we have suggested above, some proselytes who, on joining the Pauline communities, rejected their temporary affiliation to Judaism and its practices, choosing instead to follow a gentile believer's life-style, this would create a very complex situation for both the Christ-believing communities and for the believing proselytes themselves who for a second time had to decide for or against living a Jewish life.

The proselyte believers most vulnerable would be those who were torn between accompanying their fellow proselytes in their rejection of Jewish practices and a conscience loyal to their previously adopted proselyte faith. In a very real sense, as believers in Christ of gentile birth and also as pros-elytes to Judaism, they may not have felt, despite their previous acceptance into the synagogue, entirely at home in either community. They would now literally have been, and also have felt as if they were, in a liminal or even limbo state. Interestingly, Rom 14–15 makes very good sense if it is read as support for those proselytes who were vulnerable because of the upheaval facing them as a result of their abiding Jewish sensibilities. In conjunction with this, scholars have long disputed the too easy, perhaps simplistic, iden-tification of the weak as Jews and the strong as gentiles.[36] Recent research has tended to stress the actual orientation of these groups rather than their ethnic origins. A variation on traditional approaches has emerged in Paul Sampley's suggestion of a continuum of commitments along a wide spec-trum of Jewish-gentile stances.[37] The latter viewpoint would find some sup-port and the insights of previous scholars would be respected by positing the existence of an inner group conflict such as I have described.

Moreover it would answer the question posed to me in a discussion by Lloyd Gaston as to how Paul in a letter conciliatory to Judaism, as Romans is, could still describe Jews with conscience scruples as weak. The "weak in faith" are in this proposal gentile by birth and also Jews by proselytizing. Their weakness is not simply a Jewish conscience but a dilemma caused mainly by others changing and transferring their allegiance. Another strength of this proposal is that Paul's policy of remaining in the state in which one was called (1 Cor 7:17–18) would be welcomed by the "weak in faith."

If a major emphasis in Paul's Letter to the Romans was to promote awareness of the Jewish roots of the new faith and to discourage a separat-ist gentile-oriented breakaway group, we may well ask, what effect did his

36. Rauer investigated this issue many years ago in his *Die "Schwachen" in Korinth und Rom nach den Paulusbriefen.* Elliott's *The Rhetoric of Romans* offers a constructive and fresh approach to the topic.

37. Sampley, "The Weak and the Strong: Paul's Careful and Crafty Rhetorical Strat-egy in Romans 14:1—15:13," 40–52 . Cf. Campbell, "The Rule of Faith," 270–71.

letter actually have on the Roman church, and its subsequent identity? If it was successful, then we would expect a church with harmony between its diverse elements, whether in house churches or in association with a synagogue. We would also anticipate a renewed respect for the Scriptures and for the Jewish roots of the faith.

There is, in fact, evidence of a certain Jewishness in the Roman church both in its origins[38] and in its development, even towards the end of the first century.[39] Perhaps Paul's death in Rome helped to convince some of the believers of the truth of his views and they responded accordingly to make their church(es) inclusive and more harmonious. On the other hand, perhaps differing strands of tradition survived side by side, explaining the origin of the Letter to the Hebrews[40] and, possibly, the arrival and relative success of Marcion in Rome in the mid-second century. But in any case, Paul's letter may have helped the church to decide against Marcion's views at a crucial moment in its history, even if the issues raised are still a matter of debate—emerging at the moment around the issue of the basic identity of Christianity. We have, in fact, still not solved the problem faced by Paul so many centuries ago.[41]

That this is still very much a matter of debate is demonstrated by the contrast between Holmberg's view that the issue is one of "Jewish versus Christian Identity" and Dunn's claim that the identity of Israel included both historic Israel and the gentiles. According to Holmberg, "we see both Jews and Gentiles in the Christian movement slowly sliding out of their earlier identities, and becoming something no one had ever been before. This *reciprocal identity displacement*, which is at the same time a *unification process*, started early in the history of the church—actually on Easter morning—even if we do not see it completed in the history of the writings of the New Testament."[42] In my view, this is not an adequate understand-

---

38. Ambrosiaster tells us about Roman Christians: "It is evident then that there were Jews living in Rome . . . in the time of the apostles. Some of these Jews, who had come to believe [in Christ], passed on to the Romans [the tradition] that they should acknowledge Christ and keep the law. . . . One ought not to be angry with the Romans, but praise their faith, because without seeing any signs of miracles and without any of the apostles they came to embrace faith in Christ, though according to a Jewish rite." On this and related issues see Fitzmyer, *Romans*, 25–39. Cf. also Brändle & Stegemann, "The Formation of the First 'Christian Congregations,'" 117–27.

39. On this see Lane, "Social Perspectives on Roman Christianity," 196–244.

40. Cf. ibid.

41. Cf. Soulen, *The God of Israel and Christian Theology*, 25–26, 57–58.

42. Holmberg, "Jewish *versus* Christian Identity in the Early Church," 422. On the issue of Christianity as a "third race," see Campbell, "Religious Identity and Ethnic Origin in the Earliest Christian Communities," 98–12. My opinion on this issue was greatly

ing of the complexity and diversity of the process by which Christian identity has been formed.

The issue concerning the true nature of Christian identity is as yet not very clear.[43] One may express it in this way. If we were to follow Holmberg's reading of Galatians, how then should we read Romans? A certain kind of Christian imperialism has always shown frustration and impatience with Jewish sensibilities. But that same imperialistic spirit is also impatient with the diversity which continues to exist, and which according to Robert Jewett ought to be allowed to continue to exist within Christianity.[44] Käsemann warned us against making our faith the norm for others,[45] an excellent summary of Paul's position in this matter. Ben Meyer attempted to clarify the issue of Christian identity by distinguishing between "identity" and "self-definition."[46] He also acknowledges "that Christian identity was culturally incarnated . . ." and therefore "incarnated diversely."[47] Despite these useful insights, Meyer still tends to operate with a rather static understanding of identity.

Diversity in Christian Identity

It is of considerable relevance to the issue of divergent identities between first-century Jewish and gentile Christians that modern research demonstrates that identities are neither monolithic nor fixed.[48] This correlates well with recent studies of Diaspora Judaism.[49] While it is true to recognize that, through the gospel, Paul to some extent relativizes cultural specificities, yet he does not present the gospel "as if it carries a whole new cultural package,

---

influenced by Rader's *The Church and Racial Hostility*.

43. In a recent article on Jewish-Christian identity Dunn ("Who Did Paul Think He Was?" 193) concluded that "ambiguity and confusion remain at the heart of Christian identity today." Cupitt ("Identity versus Globalization," 285–91) deplores the fact that today we are absorbed in trying to conserve our separate identities; Cupitt (ibid., 289, 291) claims, "In Western society at large, 'the Christian tradition' has become just one more strand in everybody's cultural heritage."

44. Jewett, *Christian Tolerance*, 35–42.

45. Käsemann, *Commentary on Romans*, 379.

46. Cf. Holmberg, "Jewish *versus* Christian Identity," 422–23.

47. Meyer, "The World Mission and the Emergent Realisation of Christian Identity," 188–89.

48. See, e.g., Boyarin, *A Radical Jew*, 235, 244, and 257. It is possible to have a dual identity—as, e.g., Mendes-Flohr (*German Jews*) has argued for German Jews in the nineteenth and twentieth centuries.

49. See Barclay, *Jews in the Mediterranean Diaspora*, 443; also his "Neither Jew nor Greek," 197–214.

designed to eradicate and replace all others. It is rather a cluster of values, focused in love which enables the creation of a new community in which variant cultural traditions can be practiced."[50] It would seem that for Paul commitment to Christ did not mean installing Christ as the founder of a new culture in opposition to Judaism. Rather this commitment can simultaneously encompass various cultural particularities.

The legacy of F. C. Baur[51] is still visible and influential even in current understandings of Paul's universalism. Paul inevitably appears to be in opposition to particularism, especially that of his own people. Even Boyarin's description of the apostle's subtle "particularist claim to universalism" distorts the variegated vision of Paul in Rom 11.[52] It is only relatively recently that New Testament interpreters have recognized that Paul argues strongly in defense of Jewish-related scruples in Rom 14–15, requiring that each be fully convinced in one's own mind (14:5). Rather than insisting that there is no difference between Jew and gentile in Christ, Paul is in fact affirming abiding differences between the two, actually recognizing their particular identities, regardless of the way the gospel relativizes them.

The fallacy in the traditional understanding of Pauline universalism is that the transformative influence of the gospel is seen as relativizing particular identities to the point that they form one common new identity. But this relativization requires neither the complete obliteration of prior identities nor their complete coalescence into one new identity. One might even ask whether such a conception of a common identity without inherent diversity would allow for the adequate formation of any kind of identity. Jenkins defines social identity as "the ways in which individuals and collectivities are distinguished in their social relations with other individuals and collectivities. It is the systematic establishment and signification, between individuals, and collectivities, of relationships of similarities and difference. Taken—as they can only be—together, similarity and difference are the dynamic principles of identity . . ."[53] This would suggest the necessity of an "other" in identity-formation.

It would appear that the paradigmatic character of Paul's "conversion" seems to demand that all Christians ever since should experience a similar religious and cultural transformation to a new identity. Since commitment

50. Cf. ibid., 211.

51. See Baur, *Paul the Apostle of Jesus Christ*, Vol. 1., 3–5. The image of Judaism as tribalistic and opposed to all forms of universalism has proved difficult to displace; this conception is the product of a modern cosmopolitan outlook. Cf. Munck, *Paul and the Salvation of Mankind*, 7.

52. Boyarin, *A Radical Jew*, 205–8.

53. Jenkins, *Social Identity*, 4.

is necessary for every Christian it is assumed that a similar cultural transformation is also obligatory for all. But as Jenkins notes, there are "primary identities" (such as selfhood, gender, and, in Paul's world, kinship and ethnicity) that are established early in a child's experience, which are particularly resistant to change, whereas transformation of secondary identities can be more easily accomplished.[54]

It is therefore of some significance whether we consider Paul to have received a call to apostleship or to have experienced a conversion to a new religion. Did Paul in fact experience "a resocialisation process in which 'one universe of discourse' or set of shared social meanings was replaced by another"?[55] Should we not rather consider Paul and other Jews as undergoing a process analogous to secondary socialization since their Christian identity was super-imposed on a pre-existing Jewish identity? Thus Richard Travisano distinguishes between this, which he terms alternation, and conversion as a radical change of universe of discourse. For him alternation is a less radical form of identity transformation and conversion.[56]

The degree of continuity that we perceive between Paul and his Jewish roots is thus greatly determined by the model of his Damascus road experience that we utilize. Only if we greatly exaggerate the degree of change that was effected in his life are we obligated to consider him as necessarily exchanging a Jewish identity for a Christian one.

If our assessment of Paul's aim in Rom 8:14—11:36 as a continuous argument is correct,[57] it would appear that already in chapter 8 he is beginning the attempt to incorporate gentile believers in Christ into the story and identity of Abraham's descendants.[58] But this does not mean a common

54. Ibid., 20–21. Jenkins' insights are particularly relevant to our hypothesis concerning gentiles who became proselytes and who later reacted on becoming Christbelievers against their acquired identity.

55. See Taylor and Wanamaker, "Paul and the Construction of Christian Identity" (paper presented at the annual meeting of the *Studiorum Novi Testamenti Societas* at the University of Pretoria, August 1999), 3. Cf. Taylor, "The Social Nature of Conversion in the Early Christian World," 128–36.

56. Travisano, "Alternation and Conversion as Qualitatively Different Transformations," 595–606.

57. Jewett ("Following the Argument of Romans," esp. 276–77) has argued that we should follow the argument of Romans as a whole to its goal, made explicit in the peroration in chapters 15–16.

58. This means that we should not separate Romans too rigidly into separate subsections that are apparently only slightly related to each other. Meeks ("Judgement and the Brother," 291–97) has shown, with reference to the use of the κρίν- root, that themes may be continuous throughout the letter, whatever its construction. Meeks notes ὁ κρίνων in 2:1 and 14:4, κρίνω in 2:1, 3, 12, 16, 27; 3:4, 6, 7; 14:3, 4, 5, 10, 13, 22; κρίμα in 2:2, 3; 3:8; 5:16; 11:33; 13:2; cf. also διακρινόμενος, and κατακέκριται

undifferentiated identity for all. In Paul's understanding, Abraham is the father of us all (i.e., of differing peoples such as Jews and gentiles). If all were to become Jews or all were to give up their Jewishness, Abraham could not be the father of two different peoples. But whereas the apostle's strategy in Rom 14–15 for those with Jewish-related scruples is to allow them to follow their convictions, in his use of the analogy of the olive tree he seems to be affirming that there is no option for gentile believers to separate completely from some form of Israelite if not Jewish identity.

However, the gentile believers still are not called Israelites, as this would mean one common, undifferentiated Jewish identity for all. On the other hand, the universalizing of gentile Christian identity, as has tended to be the norm in the later history of Christianity, simply constitutes another kind of common, undifferentiated identity for all. The complexity of Paul's perspective on diversity, unfortunately lost so quickly in the history of the church,[59] is that although he attaches gentiles to the stem of Abraham this does not mean their proselytization to Judaism nor the universalizing of their gentile Christian identity. Thus, originally there was no one inclusive term to describe all believers in Christ. There were simply groups of Jewish and gentile believers distinguished by their differing lifestyles.

I trust that this essay is in keeping with the perspectives Robert Jewett has continued to emphasize in his writings on Romans—such as the individuation of faith, "Not to be super-minded above what one ought to be minded, but to set your mind on being sober-minded, each according to the measuring rod of faith that God has dealt out"—and also that "there are political, ideological, racial, and temperamental components that are legitimately connected with faith . . ."[60]

---

in 14:23.

59. On this see Kahl ("Gender Trouble in Galatia? Paul and the Rethinking of Difference," 70–71): "Within the framework of Jewish identity Paul thus develops a concept of descent, nation, religion and culture which fundamentally subverts any closed and separatist group identity. By clothing Paul with a Christian identity in the later sense and after driving the circumcised out of the church we have silenced and buried this highly challenging discourse on identity and difference, which today could be one of the most precious contributions of Paul to the dialogue of religions and cultures, especially to the Jewish-Muslim-Christian encounter."

60. Jewett, *Christian Tolerance*, 62, 66.

6

"As Having and as Not Having"[1]

Paul, Circumcision, and Indifferent Things in 1 Corinthians 7:17–32a

Introduction

IN HIS LETTERS TO the Corinthians, Paul faced the challenge of certain kinds of over-realized eschatology. To keep this issue in mind is most important in the interpretation of individual chapters or sections of the letters. In particular, I would suggest that this context strongly influences the model Paul utilizes to describe the transfer to the new life in Christ. In my view Paul operates, not with a concept of new creation in the sense of a complete reconception of the self but, on the contrary, with a model of *transformation* of the person or self through Christ.

In adopting a model of transformation in Christ rather than of "new creation," it may be possible to avoid triumphalist tendencies that exaggerate or misconceive the reality of what it means to be in Christ in Corinth in the first century, or even in our contemporary era.[2] For Paul, "the fundamental story of God's gracious dealings with humanity reach their zenith in the

1. Following Bultmann, *Theology of the New Testament*, 1.240.

2. A strong tendency continues in contemporary Christianity to present an over-realized eschatology that exaggerates the inauguration of the end-time as if this were already fully present, and the new creation already here. Fulfillment terminology can contribute to this form of exaggeration when not used with precision; in particular, a certain framing of apocalyptic can also be used as a means of destroying the relevance of the past so as to permit interpreters via an exaggeration of the concept of the church as "new creation" to diminish or even ignore indebtedness to Jewish traditions and heritage, as for example, Martyn, "Apocalyptic Antinomies in the Letter to the Galatians," 410–24.

Christ-event, itself the generative centre of this story, which then provides the paradigmatic story with which Paul shapes his telling of any other stories, including those about himself."[3] This reading suggests a reconfiguration of the history and identity of those in Christ rather than simply the obliteration of their past. In the case of Paul this would involve a re-evaluation of himself in the context of his Jewish heritage—that is, a transformation of his person and of his self-understanding, rather than the creation of a totally new person with a new identity. Thus it is significant that Paul, as transformed in Christ, can still call himself an Israelite. But this means that for non-Israelites (i.e., gentiles in Christ) Paul's experience cannot be universalized to become the template for one undifferentiated identity in Christ.[4] Jews like Paul must "learn Christ" (cf. Eph 4:20) as gentiles must also do, though these must learn what it means to be gentiles in Christ,[5] rather than simply copying Paul. He does call upon Christ-following gentiles to imitate him, but this means something other than mere replication of the apostle. Paul cannot replicate the sufferings of the Christ whom he imitates and neither can his gentile converts copy the life of an apostle. He sends Timothy with the commission "to remind you of my ways in Christ" (1 Cor 4:17), and these ways were meant to be *guidelines, not prescriptions.*[6]

Transformation in Christ

If the Christ-event is truly ultimate, then for Christ-followers every aspect of their existence must be related to and affected by it.[7] Paul's concern in his mission is primarily with gentiles, and he attempts by every possible means to influence their understanding of the new possibilities now opened up for them in the divine activity in the Christ-event. Here it is important to differentiate the various different forms of learning that may be involved in discipleship to Christ in the Pauline tradition. The primary emphasis in this process is on relational learning and, as Eph 4:20 indicates, what is to be learnt is Christ himself rather than knowledge about him.

A similar emphasis is found in Phil 4:9. Paul says "What you have learned and received and heard and seen in me, do." The terminology used

---

3. Horrell, "Paul's Narratives or Narrative Sub-Structure?" 168.

4. As I have maintained in my book, *Paul and the Creation of Christian Identity,* 86–96.

5. See Fowl, "Learning to Be a Gentile," 22–40.

6. Cf Ehrensperger, *Paul and the Dynamics of Power,* 152.

7. We use the term Christ-event as shorthand for the life, death, and resurrection of Christ coherently understood within the divine purpose, following the emphasis of Beker, *Paul the Apostle,* 204–11.

here reflects four different aspects of Paul's understanding of the learning-teaching process. Firstly, the learning terminology (ἐμαθήτε) implies that learning and discipleship (μαθητής) are intrinsically related. Then we find reference to παραλαμβάνω, the technical term for learning through the transmission of tradition. This is clear evidence that the learning process involves participating in a previously existing and living tradition, a narrative concerning Israel and the nations, into which these gentiles must be socialized. The reference to ἀκούω—to hear—brings to mind Paul's proclamation of the gospel and the Philippians positive response to it. Lastly we have a reference to Paul as a visible exemplar of living the way of Christ ("what you have seen in me"). Thus the entire learning-teaching experience though mediated by Paul does not focus on Paul but on practicing the way of life in Christ.[8] This in my view justifies using the term "Christ-followers" rather than "believers" as the more appropriate term.[9] The combined occurrence of these four dimensions alerts us to the fact that we are not simply discussing normal didactic learning, but rather a learning process that encompasses the entire person, one that involves doing the faith rather than simply assenting to it in a propositional form, hence my choice of the term Christ-followers rather than believers.

A similar emphasis is found in 1 Cor 4:6 where Paul says, "In writing this much, brethren, with special reference to Apollos and myself, I have done so for your sakes in order to teach you by our example what those words mean, 'which say nothing beyond what is written'—so that you may cease to take sides in boastful rivalry, for one teacher against another" (Weymouth). Jealousy and strife abounded in Corinth in the various house church factions, so Paul applies to himself and Apollos the new standards and status they now have as servants of Christ. By means of several different analogies he demonstrates in a very clear argument what being Christ's servants means for the status of Paul and Apollos, as well as for their relationship to one another and also to the Corinthians. In this Paul is demonstrating how the advent of the kingdom of God in Christ implies a radical re-evaluation of the whole of life. In Christ the significance of everything must be revalued, that is, compared with the values of the kingdom. It is not just, for example, circumcision and

---

8. As noted by Ehrensperger (*Paul and the Dynamics of Power*, 153), "To accommodate to him/her in his/her difference as Paul does (1 Cor 9:19–23) is proper imitation of Christ. This does not mean the giving up of oneself. . . . Accommodation to the other and seeking the advantage of the other should not be confused with giving up oneself. . . . In as much as imitation is not identical with copying, accommodation is not the same as becoming identical with the other."

9. Notwithstanding the fact that, as Sanders (*Paul and Palestinian Judaism*, 463) notes, in Paul "[t]he most used and most general term is to 'believe.'"

uncircumcision that this applies to but also to the role of leaders. This too must be revalued in terms of the kingdom.[10]

Rudolf Bultmann, in relation to 1 Cor 7:29–31, speaks of what he terms the "eschatological reservation." Believers, though they are in the world, must live "as if" (ὡς μή) they were not.[11] They are to live like ordinary people who have and enjoy the gifts of God in normal human existence but with this essential difference—though having they are to live "as if" not having. They are and yet they are not part of this world. This does not mean that the world is completely denied or negated. Nevertheless the re-orientation is complete and universal—all has to be reassessed in the light of the Christ-event. This helpful insight from Bultmann demonstrates that whilst there is a general perception amongst scholars that being in Christ involves a radical change of perspective, there is much less agreement on how this change ought to be described.

I now find re-evaluation a more fruitful term than relativization, despite my earlier use of the latter.[12] I am troubled by the negative effect a term like relativization may imply for the understanding of Judaism and how Paul's former life is to be valued. Every aspect of life in Christ must be subject to the lordship of Christ. This is fundamental. But Christ is the Promised One of Israel, so for faithful Israelites, his claims should not be inconsistent with prophetic hopes as enshrined in the Scriptures. A term like relativization suggests that somehow the past has lost its value and is in some sense redundant. But the Scriptures, however we view them, are those texts that testify in some form or other to the confirmation of messianic hopes for Christ-followers. As such they may receive a fresh perspective when read in the light of the Christ-event, yet this in no way diminishes but rather *enhances* their value.

The ultimacy of the Christ-event is difficult to express with any degree of precision. Sanders perceptively noted that, in relating the old dispensation to the new, Paul's "thought is dominated by the surpassing value of life in Christ."[13] As noted above, I have previously discussed some of the very diverse terms by which Christian theologians have attempted to express both the

10. As Ehrensperger (*Paul and the Dynamics of Power,* 179) has noted, "The transformative dimension of power . . . has emerged as a decisive aspect for understanding how Paul and other leaders of the early Christ-movement related to the communities, whether as 'weak' apostles, 'nursing fathers' and 'teaching mothers,' models to imitate, and messengers who transmit God's call to response-ability."

11. Bultmann, *Theology of the New Testament,* 240. In 1 Cor 7:29–31, ὡς μή appears no less than five times.

12. Campbell, *Paul and the Creation of Christian Identity,* 89–93.

13. Sanders, *Paul, the Law and the Jewish People,* 140.

relation of Christianity to Judaism and the differences between these.[14] Tran-scended, abrogated, annulled, rendered obsolete, relativized are frequently used terms. Somewhat differently, E. P. Sanders speaks of "a revised view of God's plan of salvation."[15] My view is that none of these are very satisfactory, in that there is a general tendency to devalue Judaism either incidentally or for the express purpose of assuring the ascendancy and superiority of Christian-ity. The difficulty lies in expressing the newness of the Christ-event in such a way as not necessarily to denigrate Judaism. Sanders offers a classic example of the problem in his brave attempt to insist that what Paul found wrong with Judaism was only that it was not Christianity.[16] But at least he succeeded in demonstrating that in any comparison between religions, one's starting point and commitments are crucial. As a New Testament scholar, I cannot nor would I want to, deny my Christian commitment, but that does not mean that I have to denigrate Judaism. I must be aware of what Paul is saying in the text before me rather than assuming that he will agree with my presuppositions. What is clear in the history of Christianity, especially since the Reformation, is that most scholars tend to maintain a line of interpretation that is in ac-cord with the historic Christian tradition in which they have been nurtured. So some scholars stress newness more than continuity, but that gives us no reason for an uncritical reading of Paul or blindness to our point of origin and particular stance.

Continuity and consistency in divine revelation lie at the core of the question concerning continuity and discontinuity between Christianity and Judaism as well as in the assessing of the continuity between Saul the Pharisee and Paul the apostle. If we are content to claim that whereas God in earlier times permitted a salvation by works, but then in spite of this, of-fered in Christ a contrary salvation though faith and grace, then the major problem lies in the reliability, consistency, and faithfulness of God, a central theme in Paul's letter to the Romans.[17] It would appear that for Paul even the inauguration of the new creation in Christ is not more important than the

14. Campbell, *Paul and the Creation of Christian Identity*, 89–93.

15. Sanders, *Paul, the Law, and the Jewish People*, 47.

16. Thus Dunn ("The New Perspective on Paul," 101) critiqued Sanders's revised perspective on Paul "The Lutheran Paul has been replaced by an idiosyncratic Paul who turns his face against the glory and greatness of Israel's covenant theology and abandons Judaism simply because it is not Christianity." Sanders, in *Paul, the Law and the Jewish People*, did go on to elaborate on Paul's critique of Judaism, pointing out that his real attack on Judaism is against the idea of the covenant, but adding "and that what he finds wrong with Judaism is that it lacks Christ" (ibid., 46–47).

17. Since the Christ-event demonstrates that God himself is righteous (Rom 3:26) and hence the gifts and the call of God are irrevocable (Rom 11:29), we must take care in assessing and re-evaluating the past in respect of the divine purpose in the call of Israel.

faithfulness of God, both must be affirmed simultaneously.[18] The revelation of God in Christ must thus be related to the prior revelation to Israel, and not be expressed in such a form as to indicate opposition or competition with it.[19] To hear the gospel concerning the beginning of the messianic era, and particularly for Jews, this must be expressed in such a way that its origins in Jewish hopes must be recognizable.

Paul's solution, not often stressed by his interpreters, is to view Christ as the one who affirms the promises and who is also the servant to the circumcised (Rom 15:7–8). Thus for him the Christ-event is a further revelation of God that simultaneously affirms the past and opens up a way to the future already envisioned to some extent in the promises. This event is obviously of some significance for gentiles, but likewise has significance also for Israel. Thus for Paul there is positive continuity even within the new activity of God as represented by Christ. But how is this continuity to be expressed in life and action by those following Christ? This is where scholars differ. Thus some regard ethnicity or nationalism as particularly repugnant to the way of life in Christ, especially as these are represented in Judaism.[20]

Such views are often based on assertions by Paul that, for example, circumcision or uncircumcision are "nothing"(1 Cor 7:19; Gal 6:15). According to Anthony C. Thiselton, "in the terminology of Pauline studies new creation terminology affirms an eschatological status for believers on the basis of which issues of circumcision and 'Jewishness' have become

18. Similarly, the New Testament cannot be fully understood without the Old, and likewise the latter for Christians is incomplete without the sequel of the New.

19. Heinrich Bullinger, the Swiss Reformer, in his 1533 commentary on Romans stresses the continuity between the Testaments in such a way as to avoid the strong dichotomy between law and gospel characteristic of Luther and Melanchthon. Bullinger gives real value to the Old Testament in and of itself, stressing the need for a knowledge of Hebrew, not only in relation to reading it, but also for the exegesis of the New Testament, since the New is nothing less than an exegesis of the Old. In his disputes with the Anabaptists, who negated the validity of the Old Testament, Bullinger stressed that the New Testament must be read within the faith tradition of the Hebrew Bible as a corrective to the subjectivity of biblical interpretation. On this see my essay, "Built on Tradition but not Bound by Tradition," 148–70.

20. For example, Dunn ("The New Perspective on Paul," 114–15)—in his attempt to give content to Paul's critique of Judaism (in light of Sanders' failure to do so)—proposed that "the covenant is no longer to be identified or characterized by such distinctively Jewish observances as circumcision, food laws and sabbath. *Covenant* works had become too closely identified as Jewish observances, *covenant* righteousness as *national* righteousness. . . . To insist on such works of the law was to ignore the central fact for Christians, that with Christ's coming God's covenant purpose had reached its intended final stage in which the more fundamental identity marker (Abraham's faith) reasserts its primacy over against the too narrowly nationalistic identity markers of circumcision, food laws and Sabbath."

obsolete . . ." However, although these things have now been rendered *obsolete* "they are not *abrogated* wholesale" (emphasis mine).[21] Others claim that Paul no longer regards himself as living within "Judaism"[22] and that "a total demolition and reconstitution of the self" is required.[23]

It is thus worth noting that Paul in 1 Cor 7:17–24 does not use explicit "new creation" terminology as he does in Gal 6:15 (but cf. also 2 Cor 5:17). Although in both instances we have the same formulaic assertion that neither circumcision counts for anything, nor uncircumcision, surprisingly in 1 Corinthians, instead of simply repeating a "new creation" response as in Gal 6:15, Paul stresses "keeping the commandments of God" (1 Cor 7:19). If all laws and constraints are not annulled in the Christ-event,[24] should circumcision (for Jews) not be considered as included in those still valid? In Paul's assertions, it is not just circumcision that is at issue, but the whole of life as is indicated by his inclusion of both circumcision and uncircumcision, and by his express statement in Phil 3:7–8 that he counts "everything" (πάντα) as loss compared with Christ. The fact that there is no uniform emphasis on "radical newness" in two passages both offering an apparently similar perspective on circumcision suggests that we must be careful in assuming some generalized concept of newness as always and everywhere operative in Paul's letters. It is entirely unwarranted to import the content of Paul's statements from Gal 6 into 1 Cor 7, as James Dunn does,[25] since Paul himself does otherwise. We cannot infer that all that is included in Gal 6:15 is to be presumed as present in 1 Cor 7:19 since Paul expressly changes his formulation to fit new circumstances. In short, Paul's ethical guidance is normally particular and contextual rather than general. If we fail to follow the precision with which Paul relates the demands of the gospel to each

21. Thiselton, *The First Epistle to the Corinthians*, 550–52.

22. Cf Horrell's critique of Barclay in this respect in "Paul's Narratives or Narrative Sub-Structure?" 157–59.

23. "This is because he now sees with utterly different eyes, from a perspective that radically relativises, if it does not wholly obliterate, all social and historical categories" (Barclay, "Paul's Story," 139–40).

24. As Thiselton (*The First Epistle to the Corinthians*, 551–52) recognizes.

25. Although Dunn ("Paul and the Torah," 450–51) recognizes the fact that circumcision for a Jew would be part of keeping the commandments of God, and notes that this means that Paul both devalued some aspects of the law whilst regarding others as obligatory for his converts, he interprets what is categorically stated in 1 Cor 7 by way of a partially similar statement in Galatians. "We can deduce therefore that the negative side of the contrast echoes the emphasis Paul made in Galatians: in each case he was warning against the claim that identification with Israel by circumcision was essential." He thus effectively generalizes statements from very divergent contexts that Paul himself clearly distinguishes.

specific context, we make Paul's theology into a "Paulinism" that is at risk of being a harmonization based on some of Paul's statements but ignoring the force of others.[26]

This is further born out by the guidance Paul gives in 1 Cor 7:17–24. Instead of ignoring situation and circumstance, what may be termed one's social locatedness, Paul surprisingly asserts that each person should remain in the status/situation in which she or he was when God called them, and this after a previous statement, "Was anyone already circumcised when called?" Similarly "Was anyone uncircumcised when called?" "Whatever be the condition in life in which a man was, when he was called, in that let him continue" (1 Cor 7:18, 20; Weymouth's translation). And lest there should be any doubt, Paul repeats his exhortation in almost identical wording in verse 24, "Where each one stood when he was called, there, brethren, let him still stand . . ."[27]

Thus, despite the apparent re-evaluation of everything in Christ, the status (the point of receipt of call—κλῆσις) in which one received the call to faith has a specific significance in Paul's ethics.[28] This remains a vital factor in determining future conduct even in issues as significant as whether or not to accept or reject circumcision. One's situation may not be the decisive factor, but it is still significant. This is a clear demonstration that circumcision or lack of it continues to play a role in the ethical decisions of those in Christ.

Some disagree with this perspective stressing that for Paul circumcision really means "nothing"(οὐδέν) to him.[29] It seems somewhat strange, however, that a busy travelling apostle should have spent so much of his time discussing circumcision, and opposing its application to gentile Christ-followers if it really was of no significance for him. How then should we interpret in its first-century context this apparent indifference expressed in Paul's rhetoric that both circumcision and uncircumcision are nothing?

---

26. As Stendahl (*Paul Among Jews and Gentiles*, 72–73) has critically commented, "For the richness of revelation could not be maintained if the apologetic needs for harmonization were allowed to swallow up the uniqueness of the distinct messages." Cf. Sanders' claim in relation to the law (*Paul, the Law and the Jewish People*, 86) that "All Paul's statements cannot be harmonized into a logical whole."

27. 1 Cor 7:25ff. (concerning the unmarried) is also relevant here, as Rudolf Bultmann (*Theology of the New Testament*, 240) notes, conduct "according to the flesh" need not be immoral conduct, "rather it may consist of normal human affairs whenever a man devotes himself to them without the reservation of 'as if . . . not' (1 Cor 7.29ff.)."

28. On this see my "The Contribution of Traditions to Paul's Theology," 245 (chapter 2 in this volume).

29. Cf. Horrell, "No Longer Jew or Greek," 320–44, 338. Whilst Horrell agrees that Jews need not remove the signs of circumcision and that gentiles should not be circumcised, the reason for this is simply that circumcision and uncircumcision are nothing.

What does Paul mean by "nothing" or "of no account"? Is it absolutely or only *comparatively* nothing?

Some have noted in Paul's approach here certain similarities with Stoic reasoning and ethics. Thus Will Deming compares Phil 1:20–26, 1 Cor 7:25–38 and 1 Cor 7:20–23 with a view to identifying Stoic parallels *generally*, not just with reference to Stoic ideas about indifferents.[30] Paul rarely uses the principal terms of the Stoic discussions, and rarely, if ever, in a manner that would mark their usage as distinctly Stoic; moreover, comparison of Paul's list of indifferent things with those used by the Stoics is difficult because both of these are often incomplete and use common material not exclusively Stoic. However, Deming does find some traces upon Paul's thought of Stoic influence generally and concludes, on the basis of this, that Paul's treatment of indifferents in the selected passages is likely to owe a debt to Stoicism as well.[31]

In relation to circumcision, Deming seeks to show that there exist conceptual similarities between the basic assumptions of Stoic thinking on indifference and the way in which circumcision functions as an indifferent for Paul. He finds it helpful to interpret Paul's approach as a "functional" or "dynamic" equivalent of the Stoic approach. There is nothing inherently implausible in Paul's making use of Stoic and other popular philosophical conceptions. Within the tradition of Israel, he was a flexible, dynamic thinker, and also eclectic in that he would use whatever material he could find to better communicate his gospel to the gentiles, as is likely indicated by 1 Cor 9:19–23. His letters illustrate that he seeks by every means possible to relate to the context of his addressees, and his use of popular Greek or Roman concepts would be very much in keeping with this. Without denying some general influence from Stoicism, we note, however, that in one respect, Paul's ethics do not accord with, nor can they be explained by, Stoic thinking. This is with reference to a limitation Paul specifically sets out with respect to the point of receipt of the call to Christ, which suggests that for Pauline ethics, circumstances form part of the criteria for ethical decision in Christ.[32] Whether we see Paul's ethic as leaning towards the rule to "remain as you were" or conversely towards "eschatological freedom," the

---

30. Deming, "Paul and Indifferent Things," 387.

31. "Even if the evidence with regard specifically to 'indifferents' is too weak to make the case on its own" (Deeming, "Indifferent Things," 387).

32. As in Gal 3:28, Paul works not only with the issues of gender, sex, marriage, and celibacy but also with the parallel "pairs" of Jew and gentile, slave and free. Following the emphasis of Cartlidge ("1 Cor. 7 as a Foundation for a Christian Sex Ethic," 220–34), Thiselton (*The First Epistle to the Corinthians*, 544) claims, "Paul does not want the addressees who may have a lack of realism and unhelpful priorities in the first area to fail to notice how the same stance would impinge on the other two related categories."

particularity of one's situation is crucial.[33] Whatever eschatological freedom Christ-followers may enjoy, this freedom is limited by one's situational starting point when called to faith. This represents a contextual factor that is precise and particular to each one called, whether gentile or Jewish, and thus sets them in a particularly defined and restricted status in which they are to follow out the call of God.[34] So if wives remain wives and slaves remain, temporarily at least (since Paul makes an exception in their case), slaves even in Christ, one's status at the call to faith has real and abiding significance; it is certainly not *obsolete*, and cannot adequately be described as such without encouraging some of the very problems, emanating from an over-realized eschatology, that Paul was seeking to overcome in Corinth.

The fact that Paul uses call (κλῆσις) for the point of receipt of the call to faith indicates that he is actually giving a christological significance to the human status and condition at this crucial juncture. Thus although circumcision and uncircumcision are rhetorically "nothing," this means only that one's standing at the receipt of Christ's call is re-evaluated rather than having no further significance. That circumcision and uncircumcision remain decisive elements in Pauline hermeneutics is demonstrated by a strange omission in Paul's vocabulary. Nowhere in his letters do we find the term προσήλυτος. Since circumcision or lack of it plays such a prominent role in Paul's argumentation, one would anticipate that the status of former gentiles who have become proselytes would require some precise explanation. But the absence of such implies in my opinion that Paul's view of circumcision/uncircumcision remains a key element in his "in Christ" hermeneutic. There is no discussion of proselytes because they are regarded by Paul as now part of Judaism. Their acceptance of circumcision denoted a major transition for them that remains a feature of their future existence. They do not require a recognition as a "third entity" that is somehow both gentile and Jewish, but are subsumed under Paul's general designation of circumcision and its antithesis, uncircumcision, respectively indicating the Jewish and non-Jewish peoples. The force of Paul's theologizing must not be overlooked, since in his perspective the act of circumcision actually changes the status of proselytes. In similar fashion, calling takes place at a particular time and place and that status remains a given, an essential component of one's ongoing identity in Christ, subject only to the Lordship of Christ. This could even suggest that the calling to which converts are called is in fact

33. The main exponents of each of these stances are fully documented by Thiselton, *The First Epistle to the Corinthians*, 544–66.

34. Barth, *Kirchliche Dogmatik* 3.4, 669–70.

itself specific. Even though they are all called into relation to Christ, individuals are called specifically *as circumcised or uncircumcised* rather than in an unspecified designation.[35]

If this factor is considered in association with the stress on the particularity of each Pauline letter, then *particularity rather than universality* becomes the mark of Paul's ethical guidance. Thus his churches are not governed by universal generalized principles despite the fact that there are patterns that apply in all the churches of the gentiles (1 Cor 7:17).[36] So whilst, eschatologically, there is no longer Jew or Greek, this does not mean that these are not abiding realities in ethical matters in the everyday life of the churches. Thus Dale Martin, dealing with the issue of slavery in 1 Corinthians concludes,

> Paul does not here destroy the divisions between persons of different statuses. He first redefines the arena for status by taking it out of normal discourse and placing it within the symbolic world of the household of Christ, then reversing the status giving higher status within the household to those who held lower status outside the household.[37]

The Process: The Interaction between Continuity and Transformation

The new creation presupposes the old and transforms it. In Paul's theologizing it is the renewal of creation that we encounter rather than its obliteration. Thus whether we speak of "call" or "conversion" in relation to Paul's Damascus road encounter, we are still dealing here with issues of continuity as well as of discontinuity. As Alan Segal notes, "The one expression that Paul uses most comprehensively in his own writing to describe this experience is *transformation*."[38]

Thus, despite the required "biographical reconstruction" and the "change in universe of discourse"[39] there is real continuity between past and

35. On this see chapter 3 above, "The Rule of Faith in Romans 12:1—15:13," following Stowers, "Ἐκ Πίστεως and δία Πίστεως in Rom 3:30," 665–74.

36. For example, the demand that each remains in the calling in which they were called is an imperative that could apply universally without restriction due to particular exigencies.

37. Martin, *Slavery as Salvation*, 66.

38. Segal, *Paul the Convert*, 73.

39. Segal (ibid., 75) claims, "No convert forgets everything previously known. Rather, the convert changes a few key concepts, revaluing everything else accordingly. Old

present in the life of believers. The issue that continues to be disputed is the actual extent of the continuity with the past. Beverly Gaventa offers several ways of describing the degree of personal change that occurs in the life of the newly committed. The change can be described as an "alternation," a relatively limited form of change such as moving within Christianity from one denomination to another. This change can also be typically described as a conversion experience—a radical change in which past affiliations are rejected in favour of a new commitment and identity. The third option is described as a transformation, also a radical change, but one in which an altered perception reinterprets both present and past.[40] Of course the problem is that these ways of describing our contemporary understanding of the "conversion phenomenon" is that, as Krister Stendahl especially has argued, Paul's experience is possibly best described in terms of a call from God in line with that of the ancient prophets.[41] What I am arguing for is simply that there is continuity with the past however great the degree of change required.

Because there is real continuity, those who are in Christ cannot be presumed to become all the same. This means that all differentiation does not disappear in Christ. Being in Christ can be likened to being one body or one universal family. As Paul maintains, "there are many parts yet one body" (1 Cor 12:20). Again, a family, however close, is not a group of identical members, but by definition presupposes diversity of various kinds as, for example, among siblings or between parent and child. Being one in Christ rather demands difference since, if all were identical there would be no need to seek for oneness or unity.[42]

This means that unity in Christ also allows for differentiation between Jews and the nations, and likewise also differentiation between diverse ethnic identities. Thus there is no real basis in Paul for denying the ongoing relevance

doctrines often remain intact but are completely changed in significance through the imposition of a new structure." We note here the role played by "revaluing everything," a process that I find key to understanding Paul's hermeneutical stance, though I prefer the term re-evaluating.

40. Gaventa, *From Darkness to Light*, 1–9. Gaventa explores the Lofland-Stark and the Berger/Luckman models and other definitions such as those of W. James, A. D. Nock, and R. Travisano. She is careful to point out that the distinctions she notes are not hard and fast (ibid., 12).

41. Stendahl, *Paul among the Jews and the Gentiles*, 7–12. Stendahl (ibid., 7) asserts, "The emphasis in the accounts is always on the assignment, not on the conversion. Rather than being 'converted', Paul was called to the specific task—made clear to him by his experience of the risen Lord—of apostleship to the gentiles."

42. That diversity is implied in the quest for unity is not always recognized. A great debt is owed to Hannah Arendt for the clarity with which she perceived this. In her perspective, "Human plurality, the basic condition of both action and speech, has the twofold character of equality and distinction" (*The Human Condition*, 175–76).

of ethnic differentiation. This is due to the fact that though everything is re-evaluated at the point of entering the body of Christ, since there cannot be complete obliteration, transformation is still possible. The creation in Paul is not so corrupt in a dualistic sense that only its complete obliteration and destruction will be adequate—thus care must be taken with phrases such as dying and rising with Christ as, for example, in Rom 6:1–14. Paul does not hold that Christ-followers are already resurrected to new life, but that this is a *future* reality, "we believe that we *shall* also live with him" (Rom 6:8). Nor, as we have argued above, does he hold that in turning to Christ, all the past is left behind as totally corrupt. Instead one's previous life, its culture, and its social context are viewed by Paul as *the raw material of a transformed existence.*

Thus the previous life with its commitments, whilst undergoing a radical testing by the encounter with Christ, nevertheless abides as a formative and defining element in the new existence. Culture and life are transformed by the Christ-encounter but not obliterated or displaced by some new culture descending from heaven, or otherwise mystically achieved. It is one of the most tempting yet intellectually-weak theological or social conceptions that the past can somehow be obliterated. When an individual takes on a new self-understanding whether in terms of social and/or religious identity they are sometimes now represented as becoming an entirely new, sometimes hybrid, person, a fusion or amalgam of two cultures. But the one fact that is not taken into account in this representation is that the past that preceded the transition to the new identity cannot be thus easily annihilated, or presumed to have no ongoing influence throughout the whole of life. What we have been puts limits to the potential of what we can be, and in terms of moving forward or upward, we can only start from where we are, not from where we might like to be or where we envisage we might be.

Another significant factor that needs to be taken into account is that the modern world and its diversity, however similar, is still very different from that of Paul's time, and it is anachronistic to read Paul from a post -70 CE perspective. Thus it is most appropriate to see the life in Christ as confirming much in the previous life of those now in Christ, but at the same time transforming it, this outcome being dependent on the nature of the previous way of life. The past is not completely obliterated but "baptized" into Christ at a given point which can neither be ignored nor eliminated, because one enters the community of Christ once and for all. The outcome is that Jews remain Jews in Christ, as likewise gentiles. Each retains their identity in Christ and both are transformed, but not into some super Christian identity, a new creation that is neither Jewish nor gentile. All are identical only in that they were called, yet their prior existence is not erased but provides a differing point of departure for the ensuing life in Christ. Those in Christ do not become the same nor need their cultures be identical. In fact, within the sphere of Christianity, there can be no identical universal Christian culture, but only differing cultures more or less transformed by the presence of people in the process of being transformed by the presence of Christ living in them.

Resocialization and Reversal of Values

Wayne Meeks has drawn attention to the corporate dimension of the transfer to the new life in the Christ-following communities:

> the image of the initiate being adopted as God's child and thus receiving a new family of human brothers and sisters is a vivid way of portraying what a modern sociologist might call the re-socialisation of conversion. The natural kinship structure into which a person has been born and which previously defined his place and connection with society is here supplanted by a new set of relationships.[43]

This draws our attention to the fact that the resocialization of Jews is not identical with that of gentiles. Radical change is demanded of both, but in differing degrees and in differing ways as part of the process of transformation. The Corinthian gentile context offers us a good example of this process especially where "new creation" terminology is operative. A striking example of paradoxical reversal appears in the Corinthian letters when Paul asserts, "I am content with weaknesses, insults, hardships, persecutions, and calamities for the sake of Christ; for when I am weak, then I am strong" (2 Cor 12:10). Earlier, in 1 Cor 4:10, Paul had contrasted the Corinthians' self-perception with his own, "We are weak but you are strong! You are held in honor, but we in disrepute!" Paul's linking of being regarded as "strong" and worthy of "honor" would make good sense in this context where young men were taught from infancy to strive for honor and high social status, where lessons in competing and dominating began at home, and were intensified in adolescence.[44]

Paul's problems possibly resulted from his first visit to the city, "I was with you in weakness and in much fear and trembling," (1 Cor 2:3). He had not appeared to offer a good model of leadership because he appealed to them "by the meekness and gentleness of Christ" (2 Cor 10:1). But the effect

---

43. Meeks, *The First Urban Christians*, 88.

44. I am indebted here to Bartchy's excellent essay, "'When I'm Weak I'm Strong': A Pauline Paradox in Cultural Context," 49–60.

of this counter-cultural leader image[45] was exaggerated beyond measure because Paul when criticized, instead of fighting for more honor and repute, embraced his "dishonorable" situation with a perverse satisfaction (2 Cor 6:10; 12:10). He not only happily accepts such shameful circumstances for himself but also apparently wishes all Christ-followers to imitate his example in embracing enthusiastically this "shameful" way of life (4:8–21 and 11:1).[46] We note here that what Paul does has precedent in biblical passages such as Ezek 34, which shows the Lord taking the side of the weak sheep and judging the strong shepherds in a theology of reversal.[47]

The outcome was that when so-called "super-apostles" arrived in Corinth, Paul had to embark on a fierce struggle against these "false apostles" in defense of his brand of leadership and its basis in following the example of Christ. Scott Bartchy concludes that:

> The sharply counter-cultural perception of power that Jesus taught and demonstrated, with his execution on a Roman cross as the central symbol, had created a profound upheaval in Paul's own sense of honorable behavior. As one who had been liberated by the Spirit of Jesus from the need to dominate and control others, Paul became motivated to use his power, training, and gifts to empower, to build up, to reconcile, to befriend the socially inferior and to encourage the weak . . .[48]

From this discussion of Paul's reversal of certain Corinthian values, it is clear that in these gentile societies, resocialization represents a major transition to the values of the new creation, and the reconfiguration that life in Christ entails. But this does not permit us to make a generalized statement about the *reversal of all values*. In my view Paul is not consistently counter-cultural.[49]

45. As Scott Bartchy ("When I'm Weak I'm Strong," 56) reminds us, it was Edwin Judge who in his article, "St Paul and Classical Culture" first called attention to Paul's "pursuit of radical self-humiliation," which Judge finds running through all Paul's work "in theology and ethics alike, and on into his practical relations with both followers and rivals," an attitude that was "in violent reaction to much that was central to the classical way of life."

46. As Bartchy ("When I'm Weak I'm Strong," 56) notes, "In each case he was challenging behavior that he regarded as spiritually arrogant and divisive, behavior characterized by competitive honor seeking and lack of concern for the loss others might suffer thereby."

47. As Gäckle has demonstrated in his recent study *Die Starken und die Schwachen in Korinth und in Rom*, 64.

48. Bartchy, "When I'm Weak I'm Strong," 56–57.

49. Paul Sampley in his discussion of "Two Models of Paul's Ambiguous Relation to Traditions and Conventions," comments in relation to the convention of honor and

"As Having and as Not Having"

Thus the re-evaluation of all things in Christ and the resulting trans-formation of those in Christ, need not imply an abandonment of Paul's Israel-centered convictions, which though radically revised in Christ were by no means completely abandoned.[50] Keck asserts, "As Paul sees it, Gentiles abandon their religion when they accept the gospel (1 Thess 1:9-10), but observant Jews who accept it do not change religions but *reconfigure the religion they already have.*"[51] Whether we should then speak of conversion within a single religion, as Segal does in relation to Paul,[52] or use another term for gentiles converting to an entirely new faith is disputed. But since we have recognized a major difference in Jews' and gentiles' respective ini-tiation into Christ, we must follow out the significance of this for our view of Israelite identity and culture. Is the culture and identity of Israel relativized, rejected, or re-evaluated and in some sense retained? And what happens then to "prior mutual obligations" concerning ethnicity, status, and gender that differing Christ-followers inevitably share?[53]

We can state the issue in this way: if Israel is obliterated with the com-ing of Christ and the gospel, then there can be no continuity within the people of God.[54] On the other hand, if Israel remains the same, then the

---

shame, "Paul's relation to this dominant social dyad is exquisitely complex," and he concludes that "at every point, . . . it is Paul's convictions that govern and trump the cultural conventions and social values of his world" (ibid., 11 and 15).

50. On Paul's convictions and their revision in Christ see also the useful investiga-tion by Donaldson, *Paul and the Gentiles*, especially 17–27. An important aspect of using the terminology of convictions and taking these into account is that this draws atten-tion to deeply held beliefs *and attitudes* from which people cannot easily be dissuaded, thus hindering a simplistic perspective on conversion or transfer to a new belief system. We take into account here Pierre Bourdieu's insightful emphasis that people are initially influenced by the world they inhabit, and that their actions cannot escape this particular history, since we all learn through the body in a permanent interaction with our social context that "inhabits us" (*Pascalian Meditations*, 141). However, we do not intend to suggest that convictions are relatively static. Paul does have deep convictions but these are held within a flexible dynamic under the guidance of the Spirit (Cf. J. R. Wagner, *Heralds of the Good News*, 3 n.11). On the outworking of convictions in practice see my "The Con-tribution of Traditions to Paul's Theology" (chapter 2 above), especially the conclusion.

51. Keck, *Romans*, 286. Cf. also Dunn's comment ("The New Perspective on Paul," 105–6), "Justification by faith is not a distinctively Christian teaching. Paul's appeal here is not to *Christians* who happen also to be Jews, but to *Jews* whose Christian faith is but an extension of their Jewish faith in a graciously electing and sustaining God."

52. Segal, *Paul the Convert*, 63–71.

53. As noted by Thiselton, *1 Corinthians*, 547.

54. Thus we have argued in chapter 2 above that Paul inherited in Judaism a frame-work of meaning that enabled him to make sense of the new divine activity manifested in the Christ-event. The interpretation of God's activity in the history of Israel, whether perceived as judgment or mercy, held the clue to understanding the Christ-event.

Christ-event as a new act of God in the world is apparently denied any significance, at least for Israel if not for the gentiles.

It has been asserted that Paul actually "subverts the basis on which Jewish law-observance is founded and thus precipitates a crisis of cultural integrity among the very believers whose law-observance he is careful to protect."[55] By demanding of the weak "Christians," commitment to a church in which the Jewish mode of life is tolerated but not required, Paul threatens what he appears to support, thus undermining the theological and intellectual foundation of their tradition. There is, however, no evidence in Romans that Paul intended or deliberately planned to subvert Jewish traditions and thus to seek to eliminate the difference between the ethnic groups. At best it may be claimed that this in the long term may have been the effect of Paul's strategy, but certainly it cannot be seen as his intention.[56] Esler notes the pro-Israelite dimension of Paul's thought evident in Rom 11 and 14:1—15:13, and claims it is "inaccurate to attribute to him the positive aim of destroying the differences between Judeans and non-Judeans."[57]

Thus Paul, whilst seeking *to transform* Israelite convictions in relation to the interpretation of recent divine activity which he perceived in the Christ-event, does not seek their *abandonment* nor does he actually *subvert* them. Transformation by implication implies retention in a renewed form. Also since the Scriptures of Israel are so determinative of Jewish identity prior to any encounter with Christ, the transformation effected is an inner-Jewish reconfiguration, a re-focusing within the narrative of God's dealings with Israel rather than a negation of that scriptural narrative.

The case of gentiles in Christ is even more complicated, because as Keck notes there must be a major change in their basic life patterns. Yet it should also be noted that aside from the practice of idolatry, which was almost all pervasive, Paul does not recommend or demand the abandonment of *everything* in gentile society. We remind ourselves also that religion/cultic activity was not easy to separate from the rest of life as it is now possible

55. Barclay, "Do We Undermine the Law? A Study of Romans 14:1—15:6," 308.

56. On this see Esler's clear distinction, in *Conflict and Identity in Romans*, 354–56. Esler affirms that the new Pauline groups require a distinct identity, one that will be lodged as social identity in the minds and hearts of the members—meaning that sense of who they are that derives from belonging to this group, but concludes "yet such identity will need to co-exist with whatever remains of the member's original Judean and Greek identities" (ibid., 140).

57. "Paul does not tell the Judean members of the Christ-movement to stop being Judeans. He does not ask them to sever any ties they may have with the Roman synagogues, and he is tolerant of their continued practice of the Mosaic law, at least in regard to provisions relating to food, wine, and holy days" (Esler, *Conflict and Identity*, 364–65).

in contemporary society. Nevertheless, Paul can state without qualification that following his example and using the discernment that Christ-followers must exercise, they can pursue "whatever is true, whatever is honorable, whatever is just, whatever is pure, whatever is lovely, whatever is gracious . . ." (Phil 4:8). These goals are not further defined and thus demonstrate that within Greco-Roman society, there were elements that were not in opposition to the gospel, as Paul understood it, and which could continue to offer moral guidance for gentiles under the discipleship of Christ through the transforming power of the Spirit.[58]

Circumcision, Transformation, and Christ-Identity

What can then be demonstrated to be Paul's stance on circumcision? Although he insists that neither circumcision nor uncircumcision counts for anything in comparison with keeping the commandments of God (1 Cor 7:19), we have already noted a significant difference in almost identical statements on circumcision in Gal 6:15 (Cf. also Gal 5:6). Paul stresses in Galatians that what is important is "a new creation," but to the Corinthians with an over-realized eschatology, he stresses "keeping the commandments of God." Notably, Paul does not make a separate statement saying simply "circumcision or uncircumcision are of no account" as might be assumed if we split the two parts of Paul's single sentence in 1 Cor 7:19. Rather, there is a strong element of comparison involved that functions to bring out the relative significance of the differing items noted. We note here that there are three items involved in Paul's statements. A) circumcision is nothing, B) uncircumcision is nothing, C) *but* keep the commandments of God. These three items are misread if taken separately. Paul does not say "circumcision is nothing" and he does not say "uncircumcision is nothing" but rather that neither of these count for anything *in comparison with* keeping commandments of God.

What tends to happen is that these two apparently paradoxical or even contradictory statements are taken as somehow cancelling out each other, with the effect of undermining the significance of circumcision in Paul.

---

58. But see Esler's essay, "Paul and Stoicism: Romans 12 as a Test Case," in which the differences are expressly emphasized rather than the parallels, since he claims "Paul's paramount concern with the nature of face-to-face contacts between Christ-followers . . . is so radically different from anything in Stoic thought that it brings into sharp focus his distinctive vision of moral life in Christ" (ibid., 124). Esler is critical at a number of points concerning Engberg-Pedersen's book, *Paul and the Stoics*. Cf also Engberg-Pedersen's response to some of these issues, "The Relationship with Others: Similarities and Differences Between Paul and Stoicism," 35–60.

Similarly, only one half of Paul's statement here concerning circumcision is often heard, i.e., "circumcision is nothing," thereby effectively radically perverting Paul's intended statement. Such a process has the effect of creating through these verses an image of Paul as decidedly anti-Jewish, a reading not at all justified in the context of 1 Cor 7. Paul's statements, interpreted in the specific rhetorically balanced relation to each other, and of both together in a joint comparison to keeping the commandments of God, have the total effect of levelling distinctions between Jew and gentile in face of the judgement of God. Thus, though Jews and gentiles come from very differing ways of life, and though in Christ aspects of the lives of both are affirmed, in differing but parallel ways their everyday lives are changed by the call of Christ particularly in their relation to and understanding of one another's role in the purpose of God.

The crucial point of this verse is *not a comparison between circumcision and uncircumcision but a comparison of both with the call of God*. This is illustrated by the strong ἄλλα after the first two elements. Thus since both circumcision and uncircumcision are revalued, in fact the whole of life is viewed differently. What one is and what one has is taken away with the call of Christ but it is then given back to be regarded differently, as Bultmann stresses, as "having and yet as not having."[59] Thus Paul is not concerned about certain things and indifferent to certain others. Re-evaluation of all things in Christ does not mean their obliteration or being rendered obsolete because *all* is transformed at the call of Christ and will continue to be transformed until the completion of the new creation. Indifference is not an attitude that Paul advocates. In 1 Cor 7:25–35 he claims that he wants the Corinthians to be "free from anxieties" (v. 32) and, as already stated in verse 28b, he wants them to "avoid worldly troubles." But in verse 29 he stresses that "ὁ καιρὸς συνεσταλμένος." It is due to the seriousness demanded by this interim time that Paul exhorts them to live ὡς μή.[60] For Paul, the ultimate value is Christ

59. On this see n.11 above. As Bultmann stressed in his formulaic "As Having and as Not Having," this attitude to life seems to be a strong element in Paul's thought. What is significant is that in relation to this formula, "ὡς μή," Bultmann does not just discuss a new attitude to Judaism, but rather to the whole of life, as Paul does. This particular aspect of Bultmann's thought contrasts vividly with much Christian discussion concerning transcending, abrogating, or annulling the former existence, which tends to concentrate on Jewish life patterns only. The latter would be valid had Paul stated only that circumcision is nothing, and had not included uncircumcision as well.

60. Giorgio Agamben (*The Time That Remains,* 43) understands this messianic time ἐν τῷ νῦν καιρῷ as "the revocation of every worldly condition, released from itself to allow for its use." For Agamben "the tension toward what lies ahead is produced on and out of what lies behind; forgetting the past, only on and out of this straining toward the future." He translates Phil 3:12 as "It is not that I have already seized hold of it or have already reached fulfilment, but I strive to seize hold because the Messiah once seized

and his kingdom and *all else has to be set within this framework of values and reassessed accordingly.*[61] Since for Paul circumcision is synonymous with Jewish identity (Christ became a servant to the circumcision, Rom 15:8) then Jewish identity is transformed in Christ and not obliterated or rendered obsolete, just as in the case of the identity of those from the nations.[62] A transformed Greek is still a Greek and a transformed Jew is still a Jew!

For Paul, although all things have been re-evaluated in Christ, this does not prevent these things being given ethical status and significance even for those who are in the process of being transformed in Christ. Quite the opposite. To "learn Christ" is not simply learning about certain things that may have to be reduced in their significance but rather about how a new perspective challenges every aspect of thought and behavior,[63] refusing to value anything in a way not in keeping with the standards of the kingdom, the values of Christ who gave up his own life for the sake of others.[64] But although this discipleship of Christ involves "learning in relation" as the primary focus, rather than didactic learning, the scriptural messianic hope and especially the narrative of the people of Israel in interaction with the God of Israel also had to be learned by gentile Christ-followers as part of their identity formation. "As Ephesians makes clear, however, although becoming a Christian does not require the erasure of one's ethnic or cultural past, it requires the remembering of that past as a gentile past. It demands an understanding of one's past and present in relation to Israel and the God of Israel."[65] They had to learn why, despite following the Messiah of Israel, and learning that Israel's Scriptures were written for their instruction, they must not accept circumcision, the sign of the covenant. They needed to know

---

hold of me" (ibid., 78).

61. Cf. E. P. Sanders's claim (*Paul, the Law and the Jewish People,* 140) that "Paul's thought is dominated by the surpassing worth of life in Christ."

62. Although we use the term "Jew" here, we are very much aware of the spatial or geographical element in group/social identity. Human beings are affiliated in some sense to a particular social location even if, as in the case of Diaspora Jews, they do not actually live in their ancestral land. For a good discussion on the use of the term "Judean," see Esler, *Conflict and Identity in Romans,* 67–74.

63. We are reminded of Matthew's scribe who was compared to a householder who brought out of his treasure things both new and old (Matt 13:52).

64. As Ehrensperger has emphasized, having Christ as the pattern involves the deconstruction of hierarchies of values, particularly the thought and value system of the dominant Greco-Roman society. Indeed, "the guidance and teaching provided by these examples has been seen to cohere with the content of imitation in a way which actually demands the creativity and self-responsibility of Paul's converts in the formation of their lives in Christ" (*Paul and the Dynamics of Power,* 154).

65. Cf. Fowl, "Learning to Be a Gentile," 39.

the meaning of circumcision in order to know it did not apply to them as gentiles. As such, even for gentiles, it was not an indifferent thing.[66]

Thus despite what affinities may be acknowledged between Paul and Stoic thought, which time does not permit me to discuss in this contribution,[67] it must be recognized that at some points, and particularly in relation to circumcision/uncircumcision, Paul's thought takes a very different path. Paul does not view his mission as the minimizing or the overcoming (by declaring irrelevant) of diversity in human societies. The divergence between peoples, especially as perceived from the perspective of traditional Jewish theology concerning Israel and the nations, is not something that can be eliminated or perhaps even minimized by being declared irrelevant despite the serious conflicts that sometimes ensue from failure to appreciate one another by either or both parties. This historic animosity arises not from the fact of difference, but by virtue of the unwillingness to recognize and accept difference. In the announcement of reconciliation in Christ, Paul believes that he has a message that enables both the achievement of mutual acceptance and continuing diversity. The apostle views the goal of his mission not as the erasure or rendering irrelevant of ethnic distinction as such, but the enabling of all those who are called, whether from the nations or from Israel, to glorify God together in their transformed particular identities and in mutual recognition of their abiding differences (Rom 15:7–13).

Harmony within the diversity marked by circumcision/uncircumcision, rather than indifference to it or even the erasure of such diversity, is Paul's eschatological goal.

66. The fact that the term "disciple" is not common in Paul's letters is interesting— one possible explanation is that since the first disciples were all Jewish and maintaining a Jewish identity, these were not suitable models for gentile Christ-followers.

67. As this essay was first delivered as a Short Paper at an SNTS annual meeting, and slightly revised for a similar lecture in 2007, the length of the paper was limited to a maximum time of half an hour. As already noted, some scholars hold that Stoic ethics have a heuristic value for interpreting Paul, and Paul possibly does share certain conceptual assumptions with the Stoics, but this could not be adequately dealt with here. For a useful summary of some of the main issues, cf. Engberg-Pedersen, "The Relationship with Others: Similarities and Differences between Paul and Stoicism," 35–60. As Engberg-Pedersen (ibid., 37) notes, "differences only stand out *interestingly* on the background of similarities. It is the similarities that give the differences their distinctive character . . ."

7

Unity and Diversity in the Church

Transformed Identities
and the Peace of Christ in Ephesians

Introduction

OVER THE LAST TWO decades and in my recent book on *Paul and the Creation of Christian Identity*[1] I have argued that Paul's gospel declares that everything is relativized in the coming of the Christ—circumcision is nothing and so too is uncircumcision.[2] The practical significance of this is that those who are married, because of their dedication to Christ, are to live as though they are not. Yet despite this, wives and husbands still remain married, slaves by and large likewise, and one's ethnic identity at the receipt of the call of Christ is not to be denied or forsaken—everyone should remain in the calling, ἐν τῇ κλήσει, in which they were called (whether as circumcised or uncircumcised) (1 Cor 7:20).

Pauline transformation in Christ does not mean the creation of a new group without ethnic identity but rather the transformation of those who are Greeks into transformed Greeks, and of Judeans[3] into transformed Ju-

---

1. 2006. This essay is also based on papers delivered at SNTS Annual Meeting, Aberdeen Aug 2006, and at SBL Annual Meeting Washington, Nov 2006, subsequently revised again in 2007.

2. See esp. my *Paul and the Creation of Christian Identity*, 89–93.

3. In the ancient world the Enlightenment concept of religion as a separate realm of human experience was not recognized, and one's geographical location was crucial in the depiction of identity. See Esler's excellent discussion (*Conflict and Identity in Romans*, 64–71) of this issue, giving preference to terming "Jews" of New Testament times as Judeans. For further discussion of this issue, see my *Paul and the Creation of*

deans in Christ. Paul thus cannot be said to be indifferent to ethnic identity in the way this might be postulated of Stoic thinkers,[4] since his stipulation to remain as you were means that *for Paul ethnicity is not an indifferent thing*. He does state that both circumcision and uncircumcision are nothing, but the crucial point of this passage (1 Cor 7:17-24) is not a comparison between circumcision and uncircumcision, but a comparison of both with the call of God.[5] In light of this call, the whole of life is relativized, and it is neither better nor worse to be circumcised or uncircumcised. With the call of God, what one is and what one has is taken over by Christ, but then given back to be regarded differently so that all of life can be transformed by God, whether as Jews or gentiles in Christ.

The issue I wish to explore in this article is whether Paul's stance on retaining one's ethnic identity (remaining in the calling in which one was called), which eventually was lost when the church became predominantly gentile, was already lost by the time the letter to the Ephesians was written around 90 C.E. at the latest.[6]

Unity is Both a Cause for Celebration and a Process to Be Worked At

Ephesians advocates a distinctively Christian identity—Christ is central and the hero of deliverance. As Karl Barth brilliantly recognized, Ephesians more than any other letter stresses that election, in fact the whole of redemption, takes place *in Christ*. It is in him that believers are elect and have everything that is gifted to them by God. But how is this deliverance in Christ presented? We will return to this later, but the reading adopted here is derived from the

---

Christian Identity, 3–10.

4. See Deming, "Paul and Indifferent Things," 387.

5. On the concentration on the root καλ- in this passage and in 1 Corinthians generally see Roetzel, *The Letters of Paul,* 211–33, and my response, "The Contribution of Traditions" (chapter 2 in this volume).

6. The differences between Ephesians and the generally accepted Pauline letters are numerous. The concept of the church as the church universal (as distinct from local churches) is one of the most obvious, but the distinct vocabulary of Ephesians with some ninety words not found elsewhere in Paul's undisputed letters and some forty words not found elsewhere in the New Testament is also significant. On authorship, etc., see Best, *Ephesians,* 2, and Lincoln, *Ephesians,* lxxxi–lxxxii. John Muddiman (*Ephesians,* 298) notes that "Ephesians uses slightly different words in the same sense as Paul and the same words in slightly different senses from Paul." This acknowledgement does not prevent Muddiman claiming that "there are fragments in Ephesians of what Paul originally wrote to the Laodiceans alongside statements and omissions that he would not have made."

macro image of Ephesians, that of the new temple. Christ has broken down the dividing wall on the cross. That is, he has removed the balustrade that prevented gentiles from having access to the temple courts the same as Jews. But now gentiles in Christ are built into a new temple, without division, in which God's glory dwells. They have a new identity in him being built on the foundation of apostles and prophets, Christ being the corner stone or, as I prefer, coping stone that holds the entire building together.[7] His reconciling work has thus removed the partition of hostility between Israelites and gentiles.

As Dahl notes, "In comparison with nearly contemporary writings, Ephesians contains no expression of anti-Jewish sentiments."[8] The law is not mentioned at all in Eph 1, there is only one reference to the law in the letter at 2:15, and even that is not simply to the law *per se* or as a whole—it is the law, τῶν ἐντολῶν ἐν δόγμασιν, literally *the law of instructions through rules*.[9] It looks more like a specific *aspect* of the law that is abolished rather than the law in total.[10] But for the author it is not a central issue and he gives it little attention. This is because he prefers to stress, as Barth alerted us, the overall purpose of God, in which believers are chosen in Christ before the foundation of the world, and are now being created into a new temple in him.[11]

But the gentiles are not alone in this building, they are fellow-citizens with Israelites; there is strong emphasis that they are no longer foreigners or resident aliens; this is part of a deliberate and prolonged critique of pagan culture, with four separate descriptions of gentiles, designed it seems to distance the gentile Christ-followers from pagan culture.[12] Negative self-definition in Ephesians is not against Jews as such but only against the rest of humanity outside of Christ (3:2). The author does describe his addressees in 2:11 as

7. Kreitzer notes that an association is made in the *Testament of Solomon* between King Solomon as Temple-builder and the ἀκρογωνιαῖος as the focal point of the Temple's construction in a way similar to how Ephesians refers to Jesus Christ as the key component, the cornerstone, of the new temple, thus suggesting that the writer of Ephesians is deliberately associating him with the person responsible for the construction of the first Temple.("The Messianic Man of Peace," 505).

8. Cf Dahl, "Gentiles, Christians, Israelites," 37.

9. See Olson, *Deuteronomy and the Death of Moses*, 151–53.

10. Cf. Yee, *Jews, Gentiles, and Ethnic Reconciliation*, 157. Yee argues that the stark depiction from a Jewish perspective of the depravity of gentile society is evidence of the effects of Jewish exclusivity upon Jew/gentile relations, thereby attributing the onus for enmity to Jews rather than to both groups, as I would prefer. He reads Ephesians as written from a Jewish world view where the "far of" language of 2:13a echoes the view of the periphery as a place of negative extremes and the Jews as central, (118).

11. Barth, *The Doctrine of God*, 60, 110.

12. Ephesians "seeks to impose a worldview which involves transformation of identity, resocialization, and increasing social distance from a non-Israelite heritage and culture," Shkul, "Religious Identity", 10.

"gentiles in the flesh," or by birth in a purely descriptive way. They are labelled as "the foreskin" or the "uncircumcision" by those called "the circumcision" (that made in the flesh by hands). But this represents merely inter-group distinctions in a context that stresses what benefits now come to gentiles in Christ.

There is no equivalent distancing from Israelite culture and identity. The word "Jew" does not appear at all, so there is no criticism of Jewish identity as such except in the passing reference that Christ abolished the law of instruction through rules.[13] Can the fact that there seems to be no explicit reference to Jewish communities not be seen as proof that Jewish identity is being negated? The answer to this lies in our presuppositions. Thus some will assume automatically that to be in Christ means to be in opposition to any kind of Jewish identity. But although Ephesians stresses a Christ-centred identity, we must not presume that any Jewish Christ-followers would no longer be able to follow a life according to the law because Ephesians also stresses Israelite identity as central.[14] Thus it does not follow that the abolishing of the law of instructions through rules means the abandonment of law observance in general.

Here we need to look at the probable context of Ephesians somewhere before 90 C.E., whether this is Ephesus itself or somewhere nearby in the province of Asia. In the area of Ephesus, as Paul Trebilco[15] and others have demonstrated, there were certainly some Jewish Christ-followers from the earliest days until the time of Ignatius. There were Jews in large numbers in Ephesus itself and the seven churches of Revelation give clear evidence of these in the areas surrounding. Without arguing in detail, it may be confidently claimed that Jewish Christianity existed, and continued to exist in or alongside the diverse groups that can be identified from the Pastoral Epistles, the Johannine Epistles, the book of Revelation, and later from the letters of Ignatius. There are references to those who claim to be Jews and are not, but despite not being Jews, are stereotyped as "a synagogue of Satan" (Rev 2:9). There is even evidence that Ignatius had to point out the inconsistency involved in confessing Christ and practicing Judaism simultaneously.[16] Thus, what some regard as impossible was not impossible in actual life

---

13. "Ephesians . . . insists on the relation of 'saved by faith' to the issue of 'good works.' (Paul's) doctrine of justification has been separated from the issue of the Jewish law and ethicized," (Muddimam *Ephesians*, 18).

14. Cf MacDonald, "The Politics of Identity," 421.

15. Trebilco, *Early Christians in Ephesus*, 712–17.

16 Cf. Ign. *Magn.* 10:3; Ign. *Phld.* 6:1. On this see Campbell, *Paul and the Creation of Christian Identity*, 151, and Zetterholm, *The Formation of Christianity*, 203–8.

at the period of Ephesians. Jewish Christ-followers could and did continue to keep the law and at the same time follow Christ.

There is, however, a unique feature concerning the work of Christ, first introduced in 2:15, which has certainly some bearing on law observance. Here the previous statements in relation to the law are seen as part of Christ's intention to make the two—the "far off" and the "near," at this point obviously identity references to Jews and gentiles respectively—into one new ἄνθρωπος thus making peace. This reconciling peace-making proclaimed by Christ echoes in 2:13 and 2:17 the words of Isa 57:19 and Isa 52:7 where divine blessing was proclaimed to Jews in the land (those who are near) and also to Jews who were dispersed in the exile (those who are far away).[17]

We note here the etymological and other associations between shalom, or peace, and the traditions concerning the figure of King Solomon. Solomon was celebrated as the one who brought peace, having united the northern and southern tribes in the worship of God in a newly built temple. In light of these traditions, Isa 57:19 is thus read as proclaiming a vision of a united Israel, of "all Israel," much in the same vein as Solomon had created a united monarchy, but in Ephesians the two thus united are now Jews *and non-Jews*.[18] Kreitzer draws attention to the fact that in Eph 2:17–19 there are some remarkable similarities to one of the petitions made by Solomon to YHWH in connection with his Temple dedication speech in 2 Chr 6.[19] The use of the rare word for God's dwelling place, κατοικητήριον, in 2:22 is significant. Thus Kreitzer concludes that "the writer of the letter to the Ephesians turns to the traditional descriptions of Solomon as a Temple-building king who ruled over a unified people in order to stress his point about the need for unity within the congregation he addresses."[20]

What then is the significance of the work of Christ in relation to ethnicity and the creation of one, new *anthropos*? As noted already, unity through Christ across ethnic difference is a dominant theme in this letter. Being addressed to gentiles, the significance of the work of Christ is highlighted by calling to remembrance their former way of life in the pagan

17. Kreitzer, "The Messianic Man of Peace," 501.

18. Ibid., 500.

19. Kreitzer (ibid., 501) notes that in Solomon's petition there are references to foreigners who come to worship at the Temple in Jerusalem (found in 1 Kgs 8:41–43/2 Chr 6:32–33). These resonate via the Hebrew root *nokri* with Ephesians' references to ξένος and πάροικος (though a different word, ἀλλότριος is used in the LXX). In addition, 2 Chr 6:32 speaks of these foreigners as coming from a land "far away." The description in 2 Chr 6:33 of the Temple as "your dwelling place" also uses the rare word κατοικητήριον (θεοῦ), which is found in Eph 2:22 for the dwelling place of God (and elsewhere only in Rev 18:2 in the NT).

20. Ibid., 502.

world—"then" in contrast to "now" in Christ (2:13).[21] What function does the denigration of gentile society serve in this context? Can it be argued that the condemnation of their gentile past is an indication of a *new non-gentile identity*—a new status to which they should adhere, stressing instead a *"Christian" identity in Christ*? The evidence for such a view depends on how the one new *anthropos* of 2:15 is to be understood.

The New *Anthropos* is not a "Third Entity"

Is the author claiming in 2:11–22 that ethnicity has no longer any actual significance in the church? Is it now entirely irrelevant whether one is a Jew or a gentile? Have Israel's privileges, responsibility, and identity been transferred to the gentiles?[22] Is ethnicity really a thing of the past in Christ? There is indeed strong emphasis here in putting one's gentile life truly in the past, making it passé. Can it also be inferred from this that the author of Ephesians is in this way seeking to distance his audience not just from sinful patterns of life but from their ethnic ancestry as well? And thus might there be some truth in the suggestion that what is proposed is essentially a "third entity"—a newly constituted group of people who are neither Jewish nor gentile but Christian, to all intents and purposes, a third "race," as a few scholars still hold?[23]

This concept has a mixed ancestry and has tended in practice towards anti-Judaism, not least because *it fails to stress continuity with Israel*. In the nineteenth century the term "higher unity" was often used with reference to the situation in which the difference between Jew and gentile was overcome; according to F. C. Baur, Ephesians presents Christianity as "a unity standing above the antitheses of Jew and Gentile."[24]

---

21. Cf "at one time" (2:11), "at that time" (2:12), "but now" (2:13), "no longer" (2:19) "no longer as the gentiles" (4:17).

22. As argued by Garlington, *The Obedience of Faith*, 253.

23. Cf Best, *Ephesians*, 42. Cf also Lincoln, *Paradise Now and Not Yet*, xciii. E. P. Sanders (*Paul, the Law, and the Jewish People*, 178) asserts that "Paul's view of the church, supported by his practice, against his own conscious intention, was substantially that it was a third entity." The concept of a "third race" is problematic. For the history of the concept see the thorough work by Rader, *The Church and Racial Hostility*. It seems it is difficult to hold a theory of the church as a third entity beyond Jewish and gentile identity without some vestiges of anti-Judaism. The attempt to rid the church of Jewish influence drove such aspirations in the Third Reich. As Jacob Meuzelaar maintains, "an 'abolition of all differences' in the body of Christ has in the past . . . again and again led to the 'Christian' view that the Jew as Jew no longer has a right to existence" (cited in Rader, *The Church and Racial Hostility*, 223. Cf. also Campbell, *Paul's Gospel*, 110–16).

24. Cf. Rader, *The Church and Racial Hostility*, 171–72.

The point needing to be noted here, however, is that all the emphasis is upon negating one's *gentile* past, rather than that of both Jews and gentiles. There are no specific opponents and certainly no reference to Judaizers; Israelite identity seems to be accepted without explicit criticism. The saints, ἅγιοι, is used both for Jewish and all believers, but the "we" reference at 1:12 has primary reference to Israelites. Apart from the strong emphasis upon the breaking down of the dividing partition, it could be claimed that an Israelite-related identity is being presumed, even promoted. Whereas Paul in Romans enumerates the advantages of the Jews, the analogous list in Eph 2:12 presents this indirectly as the privileges that the gentiles did not have.[25] And yet the gentile Christians though closely related to Israel are not quite completely identified with Israel.[26]

It is proclaimed in Eph 2:11–22 that Christ's work is such that the two groups of Jews and gentiles are made one in him, yet a question remains concerning what form this "becoming one" is going to take. The language of two into one implies the existence of two entities, but do these two entities continue to exist after the uniting, or are they entirely fused into one new entity? Do they in fact become not only one but *one and the same?*

Alternatively, do they continue as discrete and distinct entities but now without hostility and in a harmonious relation?[27] It is explicitly stated in 2:16 that it is hostility, τὴν ἔχθραν (rather than ethnic status) brought to an end by the reconciliation of both to God in one body in Christ. As Yee asserts, "The author's endeavour ought not to be read as a levelling and abolishing of all ethnic differences . . . but as a repudiation of the ethnocentric perspective which perceives the differences as grounds for estrangement and discrimination."[28]

---

25. Cf Dahl, "Gentiles, Christians, Israelites," 35.

26. "They and the Jews now share the same socio-political space" (Yee, *Jews, Gentiles, and Ethnic Reconciliation,* 197–98). This might be significant if, as some interpreters argue, the aim of the letter is to emphasize to gentile Christians, tending to drift away from their roots, the Jewish context of their faith.

27. As Gerhardsson (*Memory and Manuscript,* 279) states in relation to decisions at the summit meeting at Jerusalem, "This decision did not mean that two churches had been set up side by side. . . . The Church, the apostolate and the gospel were regarded as being one. In support, we need only recall the vital importance of Paul's conviction that Christ is not 'divided,' and that the church is undivided in essence, and must therefore stand as a unity, though inclusive of diversity . . ." According to John 10:30, Jesus claims "I and the Father are one" (ἕν as in Eph 2:14). But there could be no question in John, a text nearly contemporary with Ephesians, of the Father and the Son being confused in essence, or becoming the same, a point that seems not to be considered in relation to the two becoming one in Ephesians.

28. Yee, *Jews, Gentiles, and Ethnic Reconciliation,* 166.

If, as seems plausible, the dividing wall image reflects the notion of the balustrade in the temple that limited the access of gentiles,[29] then this is, in fact, a metaphorical statement. Similarly the new *anthropos*[30] image is a metaphorical representation of the reconciliation effected by Christ between Jew and gentile. There could be no new man, a fusion of Jew and gentile in natural or actual terms. Nor could there have been one new *anthropos* who was neither Jewish nor gentile, a culture-free clone (despite the RSV's gratuitous addition of "in place of the two"). We must not essentialize what is basically metaphorical. Though the celebratory style and sustained rhetoric suggests that the one new *anthropos* is already realized[31] rather than merely announced, it must also be recognized that this verse refers to the purpose of God in Christ (ἵνα), "so that he might create one new *anthropos*, so making peace."

The "not yet" is clear when read in light of 4:22–24 where readers are exhorted to put off the old *anthropos* and to put on the new *anthropos*. The baptismal imagery of putting off and putting on clothing is dangerous when applied carelessly to identity. Clothes can be easily or quickly discarded, but identity is something else, "a task rather than a possession."[32] When the strong emphasis on putting on the new *anthropos* in 4:22–24 is set alongside the parallel emphasis on growing in 2:21 and 4:15–16, an ongoing process is plainly denoted.

Ephesians is suggestive of a building site on which a previously existing dividing wall has been demolished and in which a new building is now taking shape. However, whilst the design of the building is already evident, the building itself is still very much in process of construction. So too is the identity of the members of the ἐκκλησία. The alienation of the outsiders and the enmity between insiders and outsiders has been overcome by

---

29. *Contra* Yee (*Jews, Gentiles, and Ethnic Reconciliation*, 151), who holds that whilst the wall may refer to the *soreg* in the Temple, or the law *per se,* more likely it "refers to the social barrier which is closely associated with some of the boundary markers used by the Jews to separate themselves from the gentiles."

30. We will not use the terms, new personality, new humanity, new man but instead retain the Greek word "ἄνθρωπος" transliterated, so that, as far as is possible, we do not read modern presuppositions into the text. Cf M. Barth, *Ephesians*, 292 and 301–2. Marcus Barth does use "new person," arguing that Gal 3:28 should mean "you are all one *person*, not one *thing* (meaning rather the bride of Christ)." Thus Barth claims, "The members of the church are not so equalized, leveled down, or straightjacketed in a uniform, as to become a '*genus tertium*' that would be different from both Jews and Gentiles."

31. Association with baptismal celebration might explain these emphases, cf. Dahl, "Jews, Gentiles, Israelites," 31–39.

32. As Tanner (*Theories of Culture,* 124–25) maintains regarding Christian identity.

Christ, and the church, the household of God,[33] is truly destined to become a "home for the homeless."[34]

Belonging to the household of God as to any group involves ongoing identity construction, rather than a brand new identity. Philip Esler has recognized that in the case of the Pauline groups the development of a distinct identity is required, one that will be lodged as social identity in the minds and hearts of the members—meaning that sense of who they are that derives from belonging to this group, but he nevertheless concludes *"yet such identity will need to co-exist with whatever remains of the member's original Judean and Greek identities."*[35]

Ephesians Constructs an Alternative Society in Implicit Contrast with Roman Imperialistic Claims

The consistent emphasis on the church (rather than on local churches) in Ephesians arises not from a preference to look inwards in deference to political involvement. Ephesians on both the implicit and explicit level is one of the most political of New Testament texts.[36] Principalities and powers (3:10) are to be understood as relating primarily to social and political forces in pagan society.[37] Though defeated by Christ, these are forces that Christ-followers must oppose in their daily lives, and which must relate in the first instance to Roman domination. The symbols of domination—victory temples and imperial and other cults—were all-pervasive in cities such as Ephesus. As in Israel, Iraq, and even Northern Ireland today, it would

33. It is significant how words with the "οἰκ" stem proliferate in Ephesians. In 2:19–22 alone there are no less than six occurrences to accentuate the new status of gentiles no longer as πάροικοι (foreigners) but οἰκεῖοι (household members). Cf. Gombis, "Ephesians 2," 417. Cf also Horrell, "From ἀδέλφοι to οἶκος θεοῦ," 305.

34. In the Greco-Roman world, where one's culture was associated with citizenship in the *polis*, the use of the terms ξένοι, aliens, and πάροικοι, resident aliens, contrasts sharply those at the centre and those on the margins, thus serving unequivocally as "signals and emblems of difference." See Yee, *Jews, Gentiles, and Ethnic Reconciliation,* 191–92 and Elliott *A Home for the Homeless.*

35. Esler, *Conflict and Identiy,* 140.

36. But see Finney's comment ("Christ Crucified," 20–33; 31; see also 29–30) concerning 1 Corinthians: "For Paul, the sheer paradox of the crucified Messiah becomes the paradigm for an identical paradoxical relation between life in the *ekklesia* and the established structures of the Greco-Roman world—central to which was the seeking of honour, power and status." For a comprehensive overview of this theme, see Carter *The Roman Empire.*

37. For a discussion of the possible meanings of "powers" in Ephesians, see Yee, *Jews, Gentiles, and Ethnic Reconciliation,* 24–28.

have been impossible to escape political and social pressure in "a society saturated with symbols of imperial power."[38] Yet whilst separation from certain gentile patterns of life is strongly advocated, there is no pressure for a complete withdrawal from society. In fact, in contrast to the Qumran community, "there is every good reason to suspect that Ephesians was addressed to a community that remained integrated with the urban fabric of society." Yet, despite this, a hidden transcript in Ephesians sets God, not the emperor, as the Father of all and the language of principalities and powers designates Christ, not Augustus, as the true peace creator,[39] the victor over every political entity by the construction of a new universal *anthropos*. Christ not Caesar is the Savior of the world.[40]

The political consciousness of Ephesians emerges also in the emphasis on the household, the smallest legal unit in Greco-Roman society but which is simultaneously both the focal point of Christ-followers, and the template for the household of God.[41] Whatever the extent of the takeover of the model, the fact remains that for this author the church is the household of God, and to that extent not subject to another Lord. As is increasingly being recognized, the situation of the Jews and Christ-followers (Jew and gentile) vis-a-vis their pagan neighbors cannot be treated in isolation from each other.[42] So at some periods in the Ephesus region, it may have been beneficial for Christ-following households to be perceived as

38. Cf. MacDonald, "The Politics of Identity," 423 and 426 respectively.

39. This is a clearly intended contrast between the "gospel" of the "salvation" and "peace and security" established by Augustus and his successors with the peace achieved by Christ in line with the vision of *shalom* for Israel according to LXX Isaiah 57:19. On the Roman imperial ideology generally and its links with Pauline theology, see Finney, "Christ Crucified," 27–31; Georgi, "God Turned Upside Down," 92.

40. See Reed, "Rethinking John's Social Setting," 93–106.

41. For a history of the household code and its use in New Testament interpretation, see Bauman-Martin, "Women on the Edge," 253–79. This article is critical of the thesis of Balch (*"Let Wives Be Submissive"*) that the *Haustafel* form in general, and the Petrine code in particular, was derived from an Aristotelian *topos* of "household management" (*oikonomia*), which urged that the patriarchal household order must be maintained for purposes of state order (cf. Bauman-Martin, "Women on the Edge," esp. 262–63). Bauman-Martin (ibid., 262, 263 n.37) argues that whilst the codes of Hellenistic Judaism present the closest correlate to the *Haustafeln*, the codes should not be grouped together, but each read in context (following Elliott, *Home for the Homeless*, 210).

42. The association of the term ἄθεος, a *hapax legomena* in the New Testament, with civic loyalty is found in Josephus's *Against Apion*. Macdonald ("The Politics of Identity," 430–32) suggests that it is quite feasible that the term may have been applied to church members as early as the first century by outsiders who perceived that the movement was closely associated if not coterminous with Judaism. She considers that the unusual use of the term to refer to the past life of believers may reflect a response to non-believers who had previously applied the label to church members.

groups of Jewish communities despite the diversity in terms of the actual membership. The destiny of the smaller groups of Christ-followers with varying links to, and attitudes towards, Judaism could not always be easily dissociated from the effects resulting from imperial application of particular policies towards Jews. The political context under Domitian was such that flexibility in association and perhaps even in identity construction was a necessary attribute for survival as well as for growth.[43]

What needs to be noted in relation to the complicated triangle of Jews, Romans, and Christ-followers is that the political forces of the period under Domitian's rule were such that the creation of a distinct identity for the church was not a simple task.[44] A hasty separation from Jewish communities and a public opposition to Jewish-related identity may have been in some instances beneficial, but in others exceedingly counter productive. The freedom to manoeuvre was very restricted when both Christian and Jewish communities were under severe constraints because of the *Fiscus Judaicus* and its collection for Rome, but even more so because of the long-term suspicion that Jewish groups were guilty of disloyalty to the state, particularly in relation to the increasingly significant imperial cult.[45]

In some instances it might be wiser to strengthen links with Jews rather than weakening them, and thus not be publicly perceived as an isolated new religious movement without the traditional right to exist customarily enjoyed by Jewish communities.[46] Thus the celebration of the one, new *anthropos* and the peace that Christ had achieved, whilst a cause for rejoicing within the household of God, may have been a cause for persecution from the wider society. But the author of Ephesians is no blinkered ideologist without any contextual or even pragmatic concerns; rather, the opposite is true. It might even be suggested that the lack of explicit reference to actual problems between Jews and gentiles in the church may be perceived as a deliberate silence so as not to give increased attention to this type of conflict; *that enmity needs to be removed is a basic assumption of the text*. The author

43. "The picture that emerges is one of flexible and dynamic shifts in social posture in relation to a variety of forces, including the changing fate of Jewish communities in the empire" (MacDonald, "The Politics of Identity," 422).

44. On this see my chapter on "The Tripartite Context: Paul's Mission between State and Synagogue" in *Paul and the Creation of Christian Identity*, 68–85.

45. For a careful study of the origins and development of the Roman imperial cult and the differences in its form and expression between the East and the West, see Finney, "Christ Crucified," 21–26.

46. Carter maintains that there was no such concept as a *religio licita*, "John's Gospel and the Imperial Cult."

may be deliberately depicting an enhanced scenario of actual relations between groups for the sake of the desired hope of a positive outcome.

Whatever the actual circumstances in front of the text in Ephesians—whether there was real hostility between differing groups, and a fear of persecution if the wrong links are made or maintained, the wrong image projected, the author offers the reconciling work of Christ as the key to peacemaking, and the end to ethnic hostility. This alternative community based on "the gospel of peace" (6:15) proclaimed by Christ (2:17) stands in sharp contrast to the imperial value system promoted by Rome.

The Reconciliation Advocated Involves Diverse Communities of Christ-Followers

Ephesians addresses a community in process of construction and hence one in which identity is also somewhat fluid. This is reinforced when we note the frequent use of συν-compounds and a corresponding emphasis upon oneness and unity. There is *one* Lord, *one* hope, *one* faith, *one* baptism (4:4–5), *one* body (2:16, 4:4), *one* Spirit, (2:18; 4:4), *one* new ἄνθρωπος (2:15b), *one* God and Father of us all (4:6), *one* (universal) church (3:10; 5:24–32).

The corporate dimension is central here—it is group acceptance rather than individual peace and reconciliation that is emphasized by the frequent use of συν-compounds. The primary dimension is union with Christ and then union with others as demonstrated in 2:5–6—it is *together with Christ* that believers are made alive, raised up and made to sit in the heavenly places. The συν-compounds proliferate at certain points in the letter; the gentiles are fellow-citizens (συμπολίται) with the saints (2:19), joint-heirs, joint-members of the same body, and joint-partakers of the promise (3:6). Believers are joined together and built together with Christ, the coping stone, and with the Jewish Christ-followers into a holy temple, a dwelling place of God in the Spirit (2:20–21). Developing in parallel with the temple imagery, is the image of the body.[47] Christ followers are to grow up together into Christ, the head of the body, from whom the whole body is joined and knit together (4:15–16). The συν- constructions are even used negatively to advocate dissociation from the evils of pagan society.[48]

47. Another difference between the image of the body in Paul's generally accepted letters and in Colossians/Ephesians is that in these, the head and the body are distinguished (i.e., as two distinct entities).

48. The negative use of συν-compounds in 5:7 and 5:11 indicates an intensification in the emphasis on separation from the pagan world, reflecting some similarities with Qumran. Cf. Perkins, *Ephesians*, 147. And yet Ephesians is not advising withdrawal like Qumran. Singing and worshipping continue without advice to hide (despite some

It must be strongly emphasized that the force of all the συν-compounds, when taken together with the parallel stress upon one and becoming one, is lost if they are to have no more significance than a recognition of, and possibly encouraging a return to, the Jewish roots of the faith without any contemporary relevance for growing together or reconciliation with groups of Jewish Christ-followers.

The concern in Ephesians is not simply about acceptance and reconciliation between *individual* Jewish and gentile Christ followers,[49] but extends beyond that. The force of the concentration on συν-compounds is diminished and even misunderstood if they are taken to reflect relations between individuals rather than groups. In the region around Ephesus—the third city of the Empire with a population around 200,000[50] (and a strong Jewish minority who possibly had rights of citizenship[51])—there would be substantial diversity among the population, probably also reflected in the Christ communities, not least in attitudes to the practice of magic and worship in the Artemis cult. There would also be strong pressure to conform to the established forms of civic loyalty and practice deemed necessary to the well-being of the state.[52]

Without resorting to "mirror reading," it is possible nevertheless to draw *correlations between Ephesians and its social context.*[53] Thus we do think that there were real social problems among the gentile Christ-followers whom the author addresses. There are texts that suggest that these gentiles were weak, infants still, being rendered unstable by differing forms of teaching, and not growing up together in Christ with their fellow Jewish Christ-followers, whether in one household or, more likely, in several households (cf. 2:14–16; 4:17—5:21).

---

insecurity), advocating wisdom in the world rather than separation from it. Cf. MacDonald, "The Politics of Identity," 428.

49. Cf. Perkins, *Ephesians,* 71.

50. Muddiman, *Ephesians,* 35 (following Koester, *Introduction*)

51. Ibid., 120.

52. In order to guarantee their survival, Christ-followers would be involved in the same cultural negotiations as Jews, with the added complication that they may have operated either as a sub-group within the Jewish community or as a *collegia* subject to the rules governing such groups. On this see Ascough's view (*Paul's Macedonian Associations,* 190) that, "although there is no one association inscription that has all the features of either Philippians or 1 Thessalonians (and thus no one association that is exactly the same), the comparative process reveals that on the social map of antiquity the associations provide a ready analogue for understanding the community structure of Paul's Macedonian Christian communities."

53. E.g., MacDonald, "The Politics of Identity," 436–37.

The rhetorical function that the unflattering image of gentile life serves here is that of exaggerating its radical difference from walking with Christ. It serves to distance, not only in time but also in spirit, these gentile Christ-followers from the life and patterns of living they formerly practiced. Yes, what the author says may resonate with Jewish critiques of gentiles, but that is a secondary factor here in a pastoral concern that views distancing from former gentile life patterns as crucial to being joined in fellowship to Jewish Christ-followers,[54] whether in one household or in other parallel households. It is for this reason that, in sharp contrast to previous concerns for unity, the συν-compounds are used negatively in 5:7 ("do not associate with" the sons of disobedience) and 5:11 ("do not share" these works of darkness).

In the limitation of *ekklesia* to refer only to the universal church we have clear indication that thinking on this theme has developed substantially since Paul's day. The church is an established fact, and it is only its composition and identity that still require construction and/or elaboration. The frequent imagery of buildings' construction is not accidental but pointedly focuses attention on process rather than product. And yet, despite the unified concept of the church, there is much vagueness and possibly deliberate imprecision as to the actual house churches or assemblies addressed. It is most likely that there were a number of varied groups in loose association with each other. The author's use of varying metaphors denoting unity in diversity—as for example, the one body, the one household of God, and the one universal *ekklesia*—are symptomatic of a need for diverse groups to acknowledge what they have in common, rather than the distinctions and enmity that divide them.

Thus we are led to the hypothesis that Ephesians, like Romans,[55] though addressed to gentiles in Christ, nevertheless envisages contacts with synagogues or household assemblies of Jewish Christ-followers. Even if there

---

54. There arises an issue here as to the identity of "the saints" or "the holy ones" with whom the gentiles become fellow-citizens, cf. 2:19 and 3:6. Paul describes the collection as "aid for the saints," διακονῶν τοῖς ἁγίοις (cf. the general references in Acts 9). This reference indicates Jewish Christ-followers in Jerusalem. Does Ephesians also sometimes use the term ambiguously in order to be as inclusive as possible? In 2:19, it seems most reasonable to take as a reference to Jewish Christ-followers, especially in light of the distinction between "we who first hoped" and "in whom you also . . ." of Eph 1:12–13. On this see Perkins, *Ephesians*, 70–71. Shkul ("Religious Identity," 2) claims that "Ephesians articulates identity and social guidance in the absence of opponents while conflicts or internal power struggles within early Christianity are silenced." Cf. Trebilco, *Early Christians in Ephesus*, 554–69.

55. On this see chapter 8 in this volume. Cf. also Best, *Ephesians*, 13. Although he does not support this reading of Eph 1:1, Best notes that the positioning of "in Christ Jesus" in the sentence "appears to imply the association of 'saints' with Ephesus and 'in Christ Jesus' with 'faithful,' so as to suggest two groups of recipients, 'the saints' and 'the faithful.'"

were a few Jews among the Christ-followers this would not be adequate to account for the emphasis upon oneness, stressed so powerfully throughout Ephesians. If, on the other hand, there were no Jewish assemblies of any kind in the region around, then the emphasis upon Jew and gentile being one would have little real social significance.[56]

But if we posit for Ephesians, rather a context with varieties of Christ-groups, then the references to unity and the συν language indicating joint association are given more validity. The "we" in Eph 1:2 would then refer to Jewish Christians in association with the author (usually regarded as being himself Jewish), whilst the "you" would indicate the gentile addressees. The Jewish roots of the church are thus taken as given, and not only in the sense of events in the past with present significance. At times and places it would have been political to emphasize Christian distinction from Jews, but at others it was wise to keep silent and allow the civic and/or the Roman authorities[57] to determine how they were to be labelled.[58]

This seems to be the situation reflected in Ephesians. There seems at places to be an almost complete appropriation of Jewish identity by Christians despite a gentile majority church membership. This could serve the function of encouraging Jewish Christ-followers to feel at home in the gentile majority Ephesian households.[59] It could also help justify the existence of Christian sub-groups under the umbrella of Jewish identity, whether temporarily or for a longer period. The text of Ephesians taken along with the envisaged context of Ephesus around 90 C.E. indicate a strong Jewish milieu for the gentile believers who are the main addressees. Far from being indifferent to Jews, whether inside or outside the church, Israel is presented as *central* to the identity of the believers.[60]

The church in Ephesus, though mainly gentile, appears to have both past and present associations with Jews and Jewish institutions, and may

56. Cf. Fischer, *Tendenz und Absicht des Epheserbriefes*. Fischer (ibid., 79–81) seeks to avoid any suggestion of a "third entity" that is neither Jewish nor gentile, but posits a specific post-Pauline context where gentiles are losing the vision of Paul and were in danger of repudiating Jewish tradition which needed to be reasserted.

57. See Wilson, *Related Strangers*, 9–16; Macdonald, "The Politics of Identity," 429–30.

58. Labelling can be both a labelling by outsiders, and also a projection of a group's preferred identity, involving some self-labelling in keeping with the perception of identity creation as self-conscious. Shkul ("Religious Identity," 8) concludes that "naming involves ingroup identification of saints as well as defining outsiders, 'non-Israelite sinners' and 'the circumcised' who are allocated stereotypical roles in promoting Christianness and in group identity."

59. Cf. Roetzel, *The Letters of Paul*, 142–43.

60. Cf. Macdonald, "The Politics of Identity," 434.

even also sometimes be associated with Jews by outsiders. It is entirely plausible to presume that the gentile Christ-followers continue to share some aspects of community life with their fellow-Jewish believers. *It may also be plausible that whereas in an earlier period, the acceptance of gentiles qua gentiles was the issue, it may be that now the issue may concern the acceptance of Jewish Christians qua Jews.*[61]

The reference to "winds of doctrine promoted by cunning" (4:14) and the exhortation in 5:11 not to be co-participants in "unfruitful works of darkness" would suggest that there is much diversity in Ephesus and that the addressees of the letter are not immune to influences, whether from within or outside of the Christ communities. The fact that the συν-compounds previously used positively recur in 5:11 in negative form might again suggest a relation to differing groups rather than merely to individuals.[62] Thus boundaries may still be permeable and group designations ambiguous as the process of identity construction in face of the Empire and in relation to Israel continues.[63] Acceptance and recognition at the social level of widely differing groups of Christian or Jewish assemblies in the Christ movement may be causing problems,[64] not the least of these being animosity from some gentiles who were tending to find their social acceptance with their own ethnic groups outside the church.

We need to be cautious in interpreting the "two become one" simply as evidence of the strife *of an earlier era*.[65] As already noted above, the announcement of reconciliation achieved is more likely also meant as an impetus towards contemporary reconciliation, and an indication that enmity has not been entirely overcome. The affirmation that Jews and gentiles are one in Christ does not mean this is an accomplished fact but might well

---

61. Cf. Roetzel, *The Letters of Paul*, 142.

62. The negative use of συγκοινωνεῖτε in 5:11 echoes the positive use in Rom 11:17 (referring to the gentile and Jewish branches sharing in the one tree).

63. As MacDonald ("The Politics of Identity," 442) notes, "under Domitian's reign the fate of members of the *ekklesia* may have changed depending on whether they were being viewed as Jews, apostate Jews, or as distinctly 'Christian,' and at times there may have been advantages to being viewed as one, but not the other."

64. Schmithals ("The *Corpus Paulinum*," 122) proposed that the letter's purpose may be "to seal the acceptance by the gentile Christians from the Pauline communities of their Christian brothers who came from the synagogue and also at the same time to acquaint the latter with the Pauline tradition." Alternatively, as Muddiman (*Ephesians*, 37–41) suggests, the motivation for our present Ephesians, may be the reconciliation of Pauline and Johannine Christian groups.

65. See Kittredge, *Community and Authority*, 146–49, *contra* Dahl, *Studies in Ephesians*, 446. Trebilco (*Early Christians in Ephesus*, 716) claims that the drawing of internal boundaries within the Christian movement was a feature among groups at Ephesus.

imply the opposite.[66] We have argued that this is borne out by the fact that the one new *anthropos* announced in 2:15 refers to the purpose of God in Christ, rather than to an already completed project. We have found here a community under construction and a corresponding constructing of identity in Christ. The work of Christ has achieved reconciliation in principle between Jew and gentile, and a new humanity of Jews and gentiles reconciled in Christ is being created, but rather than having being achieved, it is still very much in process. For this reason alone, Jewish and gentile identities are not factors only of the past.

Being in Christ and Israelite Identity are Interdependent in Ephesians

Christian identity is not a substitute for previous Jewish and gentile identities. As Esler claims, "belief in Christ was made additional to, not in substitution for, Israelite law and identity."[67] The church is not equated with Israel. There is no sign in Ephesians that the author sets out to undermine Jewish identity. He does not perceive this negative foil to be necessary for the creation of a specifically Christian identity. He is self-conscious in the use of ethnic-related terms, so he is by no means ethnically naive. He favors Israelite and Israelite-related identity and there is no doubt concerning the central role of Christ and being in Christ. But there is no sign that a negation of Judaism is essential to the affirmation of a distinctive Christian identity. The Israelite symbolic universe is foundational to his thinking and Christ is not depicted in opposition to it. If we demand a negation of Jewishness, we must import this somehow into the text because the text presents Israelite identity as central and it is contradictory then to try to negate "Israeliteness." Likewise if gentiles are presented as joint-heirs with Israelites, this cannot refer merely to their being built on apostles and prophets as something in past history. Israelite identity cannot at one and the same time be presented as foundational and simultaneously undermined, since it is in this direction gentiles are to proceed.

On this scenario, circumcision or uncircumcision are not indifferents for this author. Like Paul, he recognizes their reality and ongoing presence. But also like Paul, he does not envisage the church as a third group neither Jewish nor gentile, but has rather developed the work of Christ in an ethnically significant direction[68] so that the two are not con-

66. Muddiman, *Ephesians*, 19.

67. Cf. Esler, *Conflict and Identity*, 276.

68. Cf. Yee (*Jews, Gentiles and Ethnic Reconciliation*, 170): "The author's skill consisted

fused, their past nor present identities, however qualified, are not entirely negated,[69] but the new association, the church, in which they glimpse a new humanity in Christ is now paramount.

The silence concerning relations with Jews whether inside or outside the church cannot be interpreted as indifference to circumcision or uncircumcision. It would be difficult on the basis of Ephesians alone to envisage the "one new *anthropos*" in isolation from Israel. In fact, Israel's place in the symbolic universe of the text is simply presupposed. It is presumed that gentiles, whilst remaining gentiles, instead of creating a new humanity in opposition to, or displacement of, Israel must develop a deeper understanding of their links with Israel and thus a more Israelite-related identity, though they are never identified as co-Israelites. The new *anthropos* is thus new in the specific sense that difference is no longer a cause of hostility but a cause for celebration.

Most significant is the role played by Paul in Ephesians. He is celebrated as the recipient of a profound mystery hitherto unrevealed; the content of this mystery is that the gentiles are fellow heirs through the gospel. As the author looks back to Paul, who identified himself as an Israelite, he writes that what Paul's mission was to accomplish was not to make the gentiles Israelites like himself, but co-heirs *as gentiles* with Israel. If Paul's mission had been described as making the gentiles into Israelites, then it would follow that this Jewish and gentile combination could be a displacement of historic Israel. But one cannot be a joint heir with Israel if Israel is an entity only of the past. This is not the case since 2:22 claims, "you *are being built up* (συνοικοδομεῖσθε) into a dwelling of God by the Spirit." As Gombis asserts, "just as triumphant deities in the ANE had temples or palaces built in their honour, so here in Eph 2 the triumphs of the exalted cosmic Lord Christ are memorialized with the building of his temple, the people of God made up of both Jewish and Gentile believers."[70]

Conclusion

The movement we have noted in and through this text is not one away from Israelite inheritance and identity, but one in which this is positively recognized in groups with a developed ethnic consciousness due to their impingement upon one another, both in the past and in the present. The

---

of his ability to draw into use the technical language of ancient political rhetoric in such a way that he could speak of Christ as a fervent campaigner whose ultimate aim is to create a mankind which is in concord by bringing to an end human enmity and estrangement."

69. Cf. Dahl, "Gentiles, Christians, Israelites," 34.

70. Gombis, "Ephesians 2," 403–18.

preferred identity the author seeks to construct is one based on resolution of ethnic enmity by depicting Christ as the peace-maker between those who are alienated from one another due to ethnically significant issues. His solution is not to downplay ethnic awareness or to ignore the hostility usually associated with it, but to seek resolution in that reconciliation and peace with difference, which he presents as the outcome of the Christ-event.

For those of us who were born or reside in Northern Ireland, the vision of Christ as peace-maker between divided communities—as the one who truly can remove the enmity and hostility associated with abiding differences, whether in religious, political, or cultural affiliation—the letter to the Ephesians has something significant to say. Christ does not merely bring peace of mind, psychological well-being, but *shalom,* the total health and well-being of being right with God and finding peace even with enemies. To depict the peace that Christ enables merely as a sentimental, internalized emotion experienced only in worship, is to deny the gospel of Christ and its power to transform even the most depraved societies or individuals. "He is our peace" can be a real political challenge, as dedicated groups and individuals of differing persuasions have already demonstrated in the last three decades without concern for their own welfare. It is a real political and social peace that Christ enables and which, moreover, he demands of those who truly belong to his kingdom. This cannot be a one-sided peace, favoring one group over another, but must take account of the ethnic/cultural differences that cause hostility and end in death and destruction. As Eph 1–2 indicates, through the power of Christ hostility arising from difference can be turned into a cause of celebration of the blessings of God in Christ.[71]

71. This essay is written in appreciation of Professor J. C. McCullough's work in Union Theological College, N. Ireland and in gratitude for his help in translating into English (for private use) J. Munck's *Christus und Israel* when we were just commencing postgraduate research.

8

The Addressees
of Paul's Letter to the Romans

Assemblies of God in House Churches and Synagogues?

Introductory Issues

THE PUBLICATION OF THE edited volume on *The Romans Debate* in 1977 offers a window into the ongoing interpretation of the identity of Paul's addressees and the variety of opinion that has developed since then.[1] In one of the essays in this volume, R. J. Karris, in response to K. P. Donfried's article on "False Presuppositions in the Study of Romans," questioned that even "if Rom 14:1—15:13 is actual paraenesis, to what concrete situation in the Roman church(es) is it addressed?"[2] Karris demanded a clear explanation of what *theological situation*—as distinct from a sociological situation relating to synagogues and house churches—Paul addresses in Romans.[3] Karris's own stance was that "Rom 14:1—15:13 (should) be read as general paraenesis, not in Dibelius's sense that it has nothing to do with Paul's own theology"; rather, it is "intimately connected with the theological principles of Paul, but at the same time it is general."[4]

---

1. Donfried, *The Romans Debate.*

2. Karris, "The Occasion of Romans: A Response to Prof. Donfried," 127. See also Karris' contribution to the debate "Romans 14:1—15:13 and the Occasion of Romans."

3. Karris, "The Occasion of Romans," 125–26.

4. Ibid., 83.

It is hard to comprehend fully the changes that have taken place in the interpretation of Romans since 1977. The issue of chapter 16 as part of the letter is now recognized as satisfactorily resolved. The place of chapters 9–11 as an integral part of the letter has been firmly established. The new perspectives resulting from Jewish/Christian interaction—in particular E. P. Sanders' research on the nature of Palestinian Judaism[5]—and from feminist, post-colonial, and liberation approaches, all now have an accepted place among our options. Rhetorical perspectives have been developed to a stage where a rhetorical overview of Romans can find a measure of agreement and provide a framework for more detailed exegesis.[6] In other respects also, the older consensus emphasizing a more theological approach has had to be refined and become more differentiated as scholars take into account social scientific insights on issues such as ethnicity and identity alongside historical and theological concerns.[7] Ongoing research into the nature of Paul's letters has helped to overcome the tendency to universalize Paul's statements and to regard the universal as displacing the particular.[8] Nils Dahl has in fact demonstrated that attention to the epistolary features "shows that in Romans 9–11 Paul not only unfolds the theological theme of the letter as a whole but also addresses the epistolary situation more directly than in most parts of Romans 1–8."[9] We are now, therefore, in a very different situation from that of viewing the *paraenesis* in Rom 14–15 as general rather than as specifically addressed to Rome. It may not be an exaggeration to claim there is now a consensus that although Paul may use similar wording and even terminology in differing letters, his language is always specifically adapted and applied to the distinctive context.[10] The parallels between the weak in Corinthians and Romans may still be disputed, but it is generally

---

5 E. P. Sanders, *Paul and Palestinian Judaism*. Sanders' research on this topic has been disputed but one feature of his contribution will abide, that is, as Dunn ("The New Perspective on Paul", 185) has described it, alerting us to the fact that the Judaism Paul was traditionally depicted as opposing had been "read through the grid of the early sixteenth-century Catholic system of merit."

6. Most recently well exemplified in Jewett's *Romans*.

7. See especially Stendahl's *Paul among Jews and Gentiles*; Stowers, *A Rereading of Romans*; Esler, *Conflict and Identity in Romans*; Campbell, *Paul and the Creation of Christian Identity*; Elliott, *The Arrogance of Nations*.

8. See, e.g., Ehrensperger, *That We May Be Mutually Encouraged*.

9. Dahl, "The Future of Israel," 141.

10. Much progress in this area was made in the decade-long SBL consultation on Pauline theology published in four volumes from 1991–97 to which Chris Beker (among others) was a significant contributor on this topic: *Pauline Theology* Vols. I–IV, edited by D. Hay, J. Bassler, D. Hay, and E. E. Johnson, and E. E. Johnson and D. Hay respectively.

agreed that the occurrence of similar terminology in the two letters does not indicate that Paul faced the same situation as he did in Corinth. In order to set the scene for our investigation, we will briefly consider several general issues that impinge on any consideration concerning the context to which Paul addresses Romans.

Historical Issues and Possible Inferences Arising from These

There can be little dispute that the early history of the Christ-followers in Rome indicates that these were in some way closely related to Jewish patterns of life. This would support the contention by some (e.g., Mark Nanos) that there was continuing interaction between Christ-following gentiles and synagogues in which there were also Christ-following Jews.[11] At least this is a probability that is strong enough that it ought not to be ruled out. As J. C. Walters states, "Peter Lampe's study of the early Roman Christians has reinforced the conclusion that many scholars had already reached: that earliest Christianity in Rome was an intra-Jewish phenomenon."[12]

There is also a real historical probability that there may have been a temporary disruption in relations between Jewish and gentile Christ-followers because of political factors during the reign of Claudius (cf. Acts 18:2).[13] There were earlier political events involving Roman relations with Jews that meant the latter had to be careful lest they be seen to cause offense to those in power. Since there is evidence that Paul believes (at the time of writing Romans) that there were ongoing issues that were disturbing social relations within the groups of Christ-followers, these may possibly in some way be linked to the influence of political realities.[14] Thus there most likely existed ongoing tensions in which political factors and ethnic affiliation may have played a role.

The fact that Paul had not yet visited Rome when he penned his epistle is another historical factor that must be taken into account in determining

11. Nanos, *The Mystery of Romans*.

12. Walters, "Romans, Jews and Christians", 176.

13. Despite its attractiveness to many, we are cautious about following the reconstruction offered by Wiefel in his "The Jewish Community of Ancient Rome and the Origins of Roman Christianity," in which he proposes a combination of the evidence from Suetonius, Acts, and Rom 16. Giving an outline of Wiefel's reconstruction, Keck (*Romans*, 30) is very hesitant about adopting it, as he states, "The interpretation of Romans in this commentary takes this widely accepted reconstruction not as established fact but as a plausible, though unverifiable hypothesis."

14. See my chapter, "The Tripartite Context: Paul's Mission between State and Synagogue," in Campbell, *Paul and the Creation of Christian Identity*, 68–84.

the situation he is thought to have addressed, even though we may not come to the same conclusion as Karris. But this failure to have visited does not of itself prescribe or determine how the letter should be interpreted.

Interpretative Factors

Romans has tended to be regarded as an outline of Paul's theology, as a measuring line for what can be claimed in all the apostle's other letters.[15] This way of representing Romans as the essence of Paul's theology is now most frequently achieved by regarding references to Paul's gospel as implying that he is setting out his theological principles. This reading is most easily adopted when Romans is regarded as a letter of self-introduction and when justification is viewed as central in Paul. References to his gospel are, however, better viewed as relating to Paul's mission in its widest sense rather than to some deposit of apostolic doctrines. The long history of viewing Romans as opposing "Jewish works righteousness" also operates as a backcloth that inevitably predisposes some scholars to reject otherwise convincing readings.[16] It may also encourage accusations of subjectivity in that when critical attitudes to Jews and Judaism are not emphasized in the interpreting of Romans,[17] this is viewed by some as taking the Holocaust too much into account out of a sense of guilt. But so long as scholars live in the real world of sin and death, politics and suffering, there can be no escape from these realities. How frightening it is to consider the possibility of a scholarship immune to the pangs of humanity!

The Approach Adopted in this Study

In view of the complicated and unclear historical and interpretive factors surrounding Paul's letter to the Romans, specific decisions must be taken and adhered to in any attempt to offer a probable description of the

15. A significant exemplar of this tendency is John Calvin, who used Romans as the hermeneutical and theological framework for his *Institutes*. Cf. Hansen, "Door and Passageway," 77–94.

16. Cf. Elliott, *The Arrogance of Nations*, 19.

17. Thus, the Swiss Reformer Heinrich Bullinger was dubbed a Judaizer because he interpreted Rom 9–11 as a warning against boasting, addressed to both Jews and gentiles. Although Bullinger sees a threat from false prophets who do not hold fast to *solus Christus* but add to their confession of Christ the demand to do the works of law, he is not explicitly anti-Jewish, whilst refusing to adopt the faith-works dichotomy as the key to understanding Paul. Cf. Opitz, "Bullinger on Romans" and Campbell, "Built on Tradition but Not Bound by Tradition," 148–65 and 166–70.

addressees and of their relations with one another and with the Roman authorities. This means taking into account all those factors that have some definite historical foundation, whether in historical accounts or from the text of the letter itself. But since these factors, by themselves, are unlikely to offer a convincing scenario of the Roman Christ-followers whom Paul addressed, they must be related to differing exegetical options from the text of the letter so that the resulting combinations might together provide the most precise and coherent explanation possible in relation to available data.

But before embarking on this quest, however, one other item must be dealt with, namely, the presuppositions that lie behind our interpretation of the text. What is amazing to discover is how Paul's (presumed) lack of direct knowledge of the Roman Christ-followers and their local situation is used to "smuggle in" interpretive options. Thus the fact that Paul has not visited Rome is given as a reason why he would offer them an outline of his gospel (i.e., his theology); and yet the frequency of εὐαγγέλιον or its verbal form is no greater in Romans than in Paul's other main letters.[18] That Paul might explain his mission policy is conceivable, perhaps likely, but not that he would resort to give them an outline of his theology (if in fact Paul himself would actually carry around in his head or otherwise such a theoretical construction). It is fairly clear from Paul's other letters that his words are always "words on target"; that is, applied theology, rather than general treatments of theological topics.[19] This tells us that where we have no really definite knowledge, we must recognize that what we derive from this absence of knowledge is hugely speculative and should be treated as such. Thus, other more substantial reasons than the historical fact that Paul has not yet visited Rome (though this is an important consideration) must be offered for perceiving Romans as an outline of his theology.

Instead of assuming that an arbitrary interpretation of the letter as Paul's theology is somehow warranted, if or when we are unable to offer any solid contextual link between this letter and the situation of the addressees, we must then recognize that we do not have authority to relate the text *to any situation*. Scholars have frequently dismissed the reconstructions of those who have sought to offer some scenario that would explain why Paul said what he did in this letter.[20] Such critiques give the impression that only those who offer a possible "situation" for the Roman "Christians" are guilty of circular reasoning. This is precisely not the case. If it is not feasible to

18. Cf. Stegemann, "Euangelion bei Paulus," 1–24.

19. See esp. Beker, "Recasting Pauline Theology," 15–24.

20. Such a dismissal is not new, since Bullinger had to fight against it at the time of the Reformation and insisted on viewing Romans as a fully contextual document. Cf. Opitz, "Bullinger on Romans," 152ff.

offer a credible context for the letter, then the honest response would be to acknowledge that we do not know how to interpret Paul's statements in such an interpretive vacuum. Yet this is not what actually happens, for after criticizing possible contextual interpretations they disagree with, some scholars then resort to interpreting the letter theologically *within their own imagined context* as, for example, that Paul would wish the Romans to be acquainted with an outline of his gospel or theology. What in fact must be recognized is that *all* interpreters have an envisaged "context," even it if is described as not being a context! In that sense we are all equal, and what remains to be done is to test the validity and appropriateness of our envisaged contexts.

Evidence Concerning the Historical Context Prior to Paul's Writing to the Romans

The problem with any attempt to reconstruct a *Sitz im Leben* for the Roman Christ-movement is not a complete lack of evidence but rather, as with Romans itself, the interpretation of the evidence we have. The most important single factor that has caused considerable divergence and debate concerning the situation of the Roman Christ-followers is the Edict of Claudius, dated probably around the year 49 C.E. What this edict actually implied is, however, already a matter of differing interpretations in antiquity. Luke in Acts 18:2 states that Claudius expelled all the Jews (πάντας τοὺς Ἰουδαίους) from Rome; Suetonius' report (second century), however, allows for two interpretations, leaving it unclear whether all Jews or only the troublemakers were expelled.[21] In addition, the third-century writer Dio Cassius reports that at the beginning of his reign in 41 C.E. Claudius did not drive out the Jews but ordered them not to hold meetings. Precise conclusions from these varied reports cannot be drawn but they do indicate that measures were taken against the Jews because of conflict amongst them which caused repercussions from the Roman authorities.

Whether the source of this conflict was of a messianic nature is also unclear. Suetonius is interpreted as ascribing the cause to an individual referred to as "Chrestus"; it is perhaps possible that this is a reference to Christ, thus offering evidence for the existence of the Christ-movement in Rome at an early date, at least as early as 41 C.E.[22] Different reconstructions

---

21. See Fisk, "Synagogue Influence and Scriptural Knowledge," 165.

22. The reported association of Peter with Rome after a period of twelve years residence in Jerusalem (and other traditions noted by Riesner) point to the persecution under Agrippa I in 41 or 42 C.E. as a factor in the spread of the Christ-movement away from Jerusalem, see Riesner, *Paul's Early Period*, 117–23.

of these historical events may be developed, depending on how much credence and what interpretation one gives to the differing sources. Perhaps the most probable scenario is that there were disturbances amongst the Jews in 41 C.E. that led to an edict by Claudius in 49 C.E. when his patience was exhausted. These disturbances may or may not have been messianic, and may or may not have anything to do with the Christ-movement.[23] H. D. Slingerland convincingly opposes a Christianizing interpretation of Claudius's edict, which he regards as arising from the instigation of someone called Chrestus, who urges Claudius to expel the Jews; that is, Chrestus' action was a reason for the Jews being expelled rather than the cause of their disturbances. As L. Rutgers and more recently N. Elliott have convincingly argued, "Rome's measures against the Jews had straightforward political causes."[24]

Which of these scenarios one adopts significantly shapes how one envisages the impact of these events on the history of the Roman Christ-followers prior to Paul's writing his letter. At a minimum, we know that there were disturbances among Jews to which the Romans reacted. This probably led to some of the Jewish leaders being expelled from the city, which in turn may have affected the stability of the congregations if still in contact with the synagogues,[25] and possibly also the relations between Jews and gentiles locally in the Christ-movement. But it should be noted here that expulsion of Jewish Christ-followers from Rome constitutes a political decision by Roman authorities rather than a doctrinal split between Jews and the Christ-movement. Whatever the effects and outcome of this temporary (geographical) separation it must not be confused with intra-Jewish debates, which might have continued had it not been for Roman intervention. In view of this, a return of Jewish leaders need not necessarily have provoked a final separation between synagogues and house churches.[26] On

23. Slingerland, *Claudian Policymaking*, 167.

24. Rutgers, "Rome's Policy towards the Jews," 93–116; Elliott, *The Arrogance of Nations*, 96–99.

25. As argued for instance by Walters ("Romans, Jews and Christians") who constructs his understanding of the Roman situation around the posited effects of the Claudius edict. For a critique of this stance, see Nanos, *Mystery of Romans*, 372–87.

26. The Jewish term for their place of worship was προσευχή. According to Philo the Alexandrian Jews met in such προσευχαί and he assumes that such also existed at Rome (*Legat.* 23 §§ 156–57). There is as yet no consensus concerning whether there may have been purpose-built synagogues in Rome. If there were not, it is difficult to distinguish groups of Jews from groups of Christ-followers merely in terms of physical location since both would then meet in private houses or tenements. For a good discussion of the significance of the synagogue building at Ostia, the original structure of which possibly dates as early as the reign of Claudius, see Esler, *Conflict and Identity*

the other hand, the evidence from history is that even the existence of separate meeting places did not in the first few centuries prevent real association from continuing to take place between Jews and Christians.[27]

We cannot say with any degree of confidence when and how the Christ-movement first arrived in Rome. Ambrosiaster writing in his commentary on Romans around 375 C.E. claims that there were in the times of the apostles Jews in Rome who believed in Christ but kept the law. They had, he claims, without seeing any signs and miracles and without seeing any of the apostles, believed in Christ "although according to a Jewish rite."[28] That Ambrosiaster is content to write such a description of the beginnings of the church of Rome at a time when the church was becoming increasingly gentile and enjoying recently acquired official status is strong evidence for a tradition of Jewish foundation at an early date.[29]

The Evidence from the Letter Concerning Those Whom Paul Addresses

The early foundation and importance of the Christ-movement at Rome is confirmed by Paul's own statements stressing these things in Rom 1:8–13. According to Paul their faith is proclaimed in all the world (καταγγέλλεται ἐν ὅλῳ τῷ κόσμῳ, 1:8), and he has often intended to come to visit them

in Romans, 88–97. On house churches versus synagogues, see Das, *Solving the Romans Debate*, 190–93. Kee ("Defining the First Century CE Synagogue," 11–23) opposes the view that synagogue referred to public buildings prior to 70 C.E. Claussen ("Meeting, Community, Synagogue," 144–67) perceives most Diaspora synagogues as being meeting places in private houses in the context of large families. Further, see Runesson, *The Origins of the Synagogue*.

27. Whilst it is difficult to disprove Nanos's contention that gentile Christ-followers might have constituted sub-groups within synagogue communities it must be acknowledged that ongoing contact with Jews does not require such a scenario for this to be possible. Cf. Das's comment (*Solving the Romans Debate*, 143), "Nanos's cogent reasoning would remain equally applicable for communities that may not have worshipped together but were otherwise proximate."

28. Cited in Knox, *The Epistle to the Romans*, 362.

29. Thus Fitzmyer emphasizes that the Jews of Rome preserved strong links with those of Jerusalem. He notes that there would be descendants of those Jerusalem Jews taken to Rome by Pompey as prisoners of war in 63 B.C.E. and that in rabbinic writings of later date there is mention of rabbis who visited Rome. If some of the Roman pilgrims mentioned in Acts 2:10–11, 41 as present at the events of Pentecost were part of the origins of the Christ-community in Rome then, Fitzmyer (*Romans*, 29) suggests, "the Roman Christian community would have had its matrix in the Jewish community, possibly as early as the 30s, and thus made up at first of Jewish Christians and God-fearing gentiles or even of *proselytoi*."

but has hitherto been hindered. "Now at last" he plans to come (1:10). This temporal emphasis regarding Paul's long-term intentions to visit Rome indicates that the Christ-movement there must have already been in existence a reasonable length of time, probably at least a decade or more. Such an interval is required both to make sense of Paul's frequent planning to visit and likewise to allow sufficient time for these Christ-followers to be so widely acclaimed. Since Paul acknowledges that he himself has not been previously involved in the Christ-movement at Rome and offers no suggestion as to a founder there, this means that other Christ-followers must have brought the message of the gospel to Rome. Whether these emanated from Jerusalem or from Antioch is not clear, but these seem to be the most likely sources of the gospel for Rome because of the early origin of the Christ-movement there and because of its "Jewish rite."

Paul makes it clear in 15:14ff. that he has no foundational claim on the communities at Rome. He has written to them very boldly only by way of reminder (τολμηπότερον δὲ ἔγραψα ὑμῖν . . . ὡς ἐπαναμιμνῇσκων ὑμᾶς) and because of his designation as apostle to the gentiles, which they are and in which sphere they live. He boasts only of what Christ has wrought through him to win obedience from the gentiles (15:18). His ambition has been to preach the gospel only where Christ has not already been named. It seems Paul feels obliged to give an apology for his visit to Rome, probably because he needs them as a base for a continuing mission to those living where Christ has not been named in Spain. His consciousness of conceivably being regarded as wrongly interfering in a mission field where he has no right to work is very obvious.[30] This would suggest that possibly the Christ-movement at Rome had roots in the mission to the Jews led by Peter and thus that it maintained links with Jerusalem. This is not Paul's sphere of work. But what he is clear about is that there are gentile Christ-followers in Rome and they are legitimately within his sphere of interest; that is, the apostleship to the gentiles as the emphases in 1:5 and 1:7 and throughout the letter indicate (cf. 11:13ff; 15:13ff.).[31] In fact, they need his guidance critically at this time. Thus Paul may be writing mainly to the gentile Christ-followers because the Jewish members of the movement, whether connected with the synagogues or not, do not fall within his sphere of authority.

Although, not surprisingly, there are over twenty references to τὰ ἔθνη in Romans, the interpretation of the evidence from these is not in

---

30. Cf. 2 Cor 10:13–16 in the light of Jewett's thesis that Epaphras missionized the Lycus Valley and was also the author of the letter to the Laodiceans, *Letter to Pilgrims*, 5–8.

31. Cf. Moo, *The Epistle to the Romans*, 54 n.79.

every instance as clear-cut as might be expected.[32] The first reference in 1:5 is to gentiles as the sphere of Paul's mission thus designating the Romans themselves as gentiles. This is developed somewhat in the next reference in 1:13, where Paul claims he wishes to have some fruit "among you as among the rest of the gentiles." This reference clearly designates the Romans as consisting at least of a majority of gentiles. The most explicit reference to gentiles is in 11:13—"Now I am speaking to you gentiles." This is most significant for understanding the content of Rom 9–11. I take this to mean that Paul here is stressing the fact that he is directly addressing gentiles, rather than that previously in this letter he may have been addressing Jews.[33] It is also significant that in these chapters, Paul's specific apostleship to the gentiles is developed in relation to its bearing upon and implications for the future of Israel. The link between Paul's apostleship and the Romans as gentiles seems to be a central focus of concern throughout the letter.

In addition to these two clear references indicating that Paul addresses gentiles, the implication of 15:16 is that Paul writes to the Romans "very boldly so that the offering of the gentiles may be acceptable," which implies that these Christ-followers are themselves part of that offering and hence gentiles. These texts are probably sufficient for us to maintain that the Roman Christ-followers are at least in the majority of gentile origin. However, the groups and individuals named in chapter 16 indicate that there also were Jewish Christ-followers in some numbers at Rome.

Yet it is quite clear from both chapters 11 and 14–15 that the stress in Paul's letter falls upon his gentile apostleship as his legitimate link with the Romans, and hence upon his guidance to gentiles. He anticipates that it is they who have the capability to adjust or repair the major deficiencies that Paul envisages in the community.[34] Thus it may be put forward as an hypothesis at this point that Paul holds that the gentiles are not just more numerous but also more powerful socially than are the Jewish Christ-followers.

---

32. This is due to the debate about whether Paul's focus is on gentile peoples or on gentile regions; for the geographical emphasis, see Cranfield, *The Epistle to the Romans I*, 68.

33. There has been a tendency to try to find evidence for Judaizers in Romans. I think this arises from the interpretive stance that Paul promotes a law-free gospel in Romans and a resultant inference from this can be that there were those in Rome who needed this guidance (see, e.g., Kettunen, *Der Abfassungszweck des Römerbriefes*, 182–86). Although not supporting the hypothesis of a Judaizing opposition to Paul, Wedderburn (*The Reasons for Romans*, 61) argued that Paul must at least be opposing "mild Judaizers." Sometimes also the fact that Paul talks about Jews in the third person is misappropriated as evidence for the claim that Paul is directly in dialogue with Jews, as Beker (*Paul the Apostle*, 89) claimed.

34. Cf. Nanos, *The Mystery of Romans*, 96–97.

This would suggest that Paul has some specific information concerning the Roman Christ-followers that he must have gained from some sources that he regards as reliably well-informed, possibly, for example, Aquila and Priscilla. Paul is able to list nearly thirty people by name, most of whom are leaders in the congregations at Rome. Of these at least half are known personally by Paul, close personal friends, fellow prisoners, and coworkers in the Pauline and other mission fields who now reside in Rome and probably continue to work in the Christ-movement in Rome, but who must necessarily, through their acquaintance with Paul, be also fully conversant with his gospel. Jewett holds that of those greeted by Paul, nineteen have Greek names and eight Latin, seven are almost certainly of Jewish identity, with only one name, Miriam, being clearly Jewish.[35] In only one case, that of Aquila and Priscilla, is it clearly stated that they have a church (ἐκκλησία) in their house (οἶκος), thus making them its patrons. Others in the group of those mentioned, because of their slave or associated low social status, more likely belonged to tenement churches that, Jewett believes, practiced a kind of agapaic communalism in which the members shared their space and provisions with one another.[36] From this long list of people known to Paul, it would seem that even though he had not yet visited Rome, this by no means meant that he was not in touch with friends and fellow workers there who kept him informed concerning the congregations.[37] What is striking from the list of those named and briefly described is their great diversity, whether in place of origin, gender, social class, ethnicity, or even possibly in their connection with missions led by others than Paul. Some, like Priscilla, were obviously of high social status; some were free-born, while many must certainly have been slaves or emancipated slaves. Women feature prominently in Paul's appreciation, especially Junia who is said to be "outstanding among the apostles" and who was "in Christ" even prior to Paul (16:7). Thus, she and her husband are almost certainly Jewish.[38] Diversity in places of meeting is also possible.[39] As noted there is only one named house-church with tenement churches posited alongside this. Is it possible that some of these

35. Cf. Jewett, *Romans*, 952–53.

36. Ibid., 971.

37. Cf. Judge and Thomas, "The Origin of the Church at Rome," 81–94.

38. *Contra* Das, *Solving the Romans Debate*, 99. To hold that Paul primarily addresses gentile Christ-followers does not require that there are no Jews at all in the groups since obviously almost all leaders of this period would be Jewish, as was Paul himself despite working with gentiles.

39. On the household setting of Roman Christianity that continued even beyond the first century, see Lane, "Social Perspectives on Roman Christianity," 208–14, 223–24.

groups were also sub-groups of some of the various synagogues in Rome?[40] If so is it likely that Paul might have given any hint of this in his greetings? The group referred to as "all 'the saints' who are with Olympas" might well be a group of this kind. Thus the diversity among the Roman Christ-following groups may have been constituted by more than Jew-gentile factors since even in Trastevere there was some diversity in housing.[41] Thus the diversity among the Roman Christ-following groups may not be confined to differences arising from ethnic issues but also those arising from social issues, as evidenced in different types of house groups in richer and poorer settings.

This overview of the composition of those in the Christ-movement at Rome is not an attempt to re-import Jewish "Christians" into the discussion, nor to produce a conjectural reconstruction that actually pays only scant attention to the way that the letter itself depicts its readers, as Stowers criticizes commentators for doing.[42] I seek simply to be descriptive in showing that Paul addresses the gentiles almost if not completely exclusively.

Evidence Concerning
the Addressees within Romans 9–11

It is clear from Paul's statements concerning Israel in 9:3–5 that though Paul is deeply concerned about his brethren, his kindred in the flesh, he is not addressing them but discussing them in the third person. "*They* are Israelites, and to *them* belong the sonship," etc. But even though he speaks *about* them, he does not distance himself *from* them and everything in this catalogue of designations is positive, including the συγγενῶν μου κατὰ σάρκα—his kindred (v. 3).[43] Nor are these attributes valid only in a previous era; rather, they retain their ongoing significance.

40. Note the strange term ἐπισυναγωγή in Heb 10:25 as a possible designation for church meetings as subgroup additional meetings related to a synagogue, cf. Wedderburn, *The Reasons for Romans*, 52–53. There is little clear evidence concerning precise patterns of worship, both Jewish and in the Christ-movement at the time of Paul. See Wick, *Die urchristlichen Gottesdienste*.

41. Despite the recent consensus that the Jews in Rome were concentrated mainly in Trastevere there is some evidence that they may have been more widely dispersed and thus would have offered more points of contact for interested gentiles, whether in organized synagogues or private meeting places. Even in Trastevere there was better quality housing on the higher land (cf. Cogliolo, "Jews and the Origins of the Church in Rome in the First Two Centuries").

42. See Stowers' useful discussion on "The Audience in Traditional Ways of Reading Romans," in *A Rereading of Romans*, 22–33.

43. The phrase κατὰ σάρκα is purely descriptive of common origin and carries no negative overtones.

Later in chapter 9, Paul does speak descriptively in the third person of both Jews and gentiles as constituting the Christ-communities, without directly addressing either (9:24–31). Throughout chapter 10 he continues to emphasize his concern for Israel in his "prayer to God for them" that "*they may be saved*." The same stance is apparent in 11:1 where he asks "has God rejected his people?" The immediate repudiation of this suggestion begins with the fact that Paul, himself an Israelite, has not been rejected. In 11:7 he continues, "What then? Did Israel fail to obtain what it sought?" Similarly in 11:11 he continues "so I ask, have they stumbled so as to fall? By no means! But through their trespass salvation has come to the gentiles . . ."

At this point the discussion in the third person suddenly changes to a direct address: "Yes I am speaking to you gentiles . . ." (11:13). But even here he continues to address the gentiles *about the Jews*: "However in as much as I am an apostle to the gentiles, I glorify my ministry hoping somehow that I might make my kinsmen jealous, and I might save some of *them*" (11:13–14).[44] This pattern continues throughout chapter 11, including the olive tree image: "And you, a wild olive shoot were grafted in amongst them" (σὺ δὲ ἀγριέλαιος ὢς ἐνεκετρίσθης ἐν αὐτοῖς, 11:17).[45] Similarly from verses 21–24 Paul claims "if God did not spare *the natural branches*, neither will he spare *you*," meaning the wild olive tree grafted "contrary to nature" and contrasting this with "How much more will these natural branches be grafted back?"

We may summarize our discussion up to this point by noting that whilst Paul clearly distinguishes Israel and the gentiles, at no point does he address Israel directly; his guidance concerns only gentiles to whom he addresses a severe warning about their attitude toward Jews. He warns them specifically against boasting over against the other branches (11:17–24). Again he says, "Do not become proud but stand in awe." This strong condemnation of gentile arrogance in face of the apparent failure of the Jews is given as the reason for Paul's explanation of the mystery of God's dealings with Israel and is central to the entire letter. His conclusion is that the "unsearchable and inscrutable ways of God" mean that Jews and gentiles are inextricably intertwined in the

44. Following Stowers' translation of this verse, which leaves no gap between the first and second parts of the verse. Stowers (*Rereding Romans,* 288) summarizes his translation of 11:13–15 thus, "Yes, I am addressing you gentiles in this letter but *you* should understand that my very ministry to the gentiles has direct relevance to my fellow Jews and their salvation to your own." Stowers concludes, "11:13 makes it transparently clear that the letter addresses itself only to gentile believers."

45. The presence of the image of the olive tree branches and of diatribe style does not alter the overall address within the chapter. On diatribe see Stowers, *The Diatribe and Paul's Letter to the Romans,* and Elliott's modification and development of Stowers' proposals, *The Arrogance of Nations,* 101–7. Proper recognition of diatribe style allows us to dismiss the suggestion that Paul directly addresses real Jews in Rom 2:17ff.

purposes of God so that one may not boast over the other and so that one without the other cannot find the salvation of God. This emphasis is continued in chapter 12–15, but especially in 14:1—15:13.

The recurrence of παρακαλῶ and ἀδελφοί in 12:1 suggests that Paul is perhaps addressing all the Christ-followers under the general theme of transformation in Christ in contrast to conformity with surrounding society. But in 12:3, with the reference to Paul's apostleship ("the grace given to me"),[46] he returns to his condemnation of arrogance, which in 11:13–24 was specifically directed against gentiles. The fact that this is followed by a reference to diversity within the one body might suggest that though he is addressing gentiles he does so in the context of Jewish Christ-followers. The stress on humility over against unbridled arrogance recurs again in concentrated form in 12:16, where they are commanded to live in harmony with one another and not to be arrogant or conceited. Somewhat surprisingly, there seems to be a change of address in 12:19 where Paul addresses "the beloved" in striking similarity to 1:7, "to all God's beloved in Rome." It could be argued on the basis of 11:28, where the Jews are designated "beloved for the sake of the fathers" (ἀγαπητοὶ διὰ τοὺς πατέρας) that both in 1:7 and 12:19 the use of the term "beloved" is an indication of a Jewish presence. In any case, it seems that the address to gentile Christ-followers takes place in a context where Jewish Christ-followers are presumed to be present.

The Weak and the Strong in 14:1—15:13

Our intention in this section is to draw attention to the continuity of address to gentiles from 11:13 on. The several references to φρόνειν and related terms from 11:20—15:5 indicate that the issue of weak and strong is not to be separated from this focus but is an essential part of it. Similarly, the emphasis upon divine faithfulness to Israel stressed in chapter 11 (particularly in verses 25–32) is developed and reinforced in chapter 15 (especially in verses 8–13)[47] to demonstrate the need for gentiles to associate with Israel.[48] Thus if we are not to be inconsistent, it must be maintained that these groups of weak and strong can all be addressed within the overarching theme of gentile arrogance already strongly opposed by Paul in 11:13–24.

Paul's sympathies clearly lie in the protection of those who are weak and vulnerable, and it would appear that any reduction in opportunity to continue to maintain diversity would, in his opinion, adversely affect the

---

46. Cf. Ehrensperger, *Paul and the Dynamics of Power*, 91–97.

47. As is clearly demonstrated by Wagner, *Heralds of the Good News*, 307–29.

48. Cf. Schaller, "Christus der 'Diener der Beschneidung,'" 261–85.

weak, who appear to have little social power or room in which to manoeuvre. To some extent these weak groups are self–limited in that, like
the strong, they have their own "measuring line" of faith assigned to them
by God through the Spirit (12:4). Diversity is further demonstrated in the
variety of functions within the body of Christ: "having gifts that differ according to the grace given to us" (12:4–7). The emphasis falls on what has
been assigned or given by God, rather than on the options to choose for
oneself. This likewise supports an argument for maintaining the convictions
and recognizing the rights of those at risk in the tensions between the differing groups. If there is any stress on freedom, it is on freedom to exercise the
gifts God has given and to live out the convictions to which one feels bound.
Thus there can be no suggestion that Paul forces or puts pressure upon the
weak to make them conform. Nor does he advocate a mere tolerance that
allows them temporarily to continue as they now live, yet only for a very
limited time when such a way of life must be adjusted or given up.

But having established that Paul argues to support the weak, what does
this tell us about their identity. Formerly, it was customary to view the weak
as of Jewish origin but facing opposition from more liberal gentiles. I have
argued earlier that the division between "the weak" and "the strong" did not
correspond to the division between Jewish and gentile Christ-followers but
cut across it.[49] Thus Rom 12–15 represents Paul's argument for the legitimation and continuance of diversity within the Christ-movement at Rome. It
might be argued that there are Jewish Christ-followers present in the Roman
congregations, as indicated by the term "the weak," but that Paul, whilst trying to protect these, addresses his exhortations only to the strong because
both the fault and the (social) power rests with these. The alternative reading
is that whilst there obviously are Jewish Christ-followers present in Rome,
these are not addressed directly nor are they those identified as "the weak,"
despite having things in common with them. Thus, although the people to
whom Paul sends greetings in 16:3–15 (whether leaders of house groups or
individuals) certainly include some Jewish Christ-followers, these need not
be among those directly addressed within the letter.[50] If the returning Jews
are socially weak and despised and they resume attendance at synagogues,
is it possible that those within the Roman congregation who continue to
associate with them share in the designation "weak" with which the for-

49. Campbell, "The Rule of Faith in Romans 12:1—15:13," 277–78 (chapter 3 in
this volume).

50. See Stowers, *Rereading of Romans,* 33. Similarly Thorsteinsson (*Paul's Interlocutor in Romans 2,* 98–99), who claims that "instead of being descriptive of the letter's
audience, these greetings suggest that the persons meant to be greeted should *not* be
counted amongst those to whom Paul wrote the letter . . ."

mer have been labelled?[51] It seems that an element of discrimination with regard to food must be involved in the debate concerning the weak and the strong. In this case, the weak include those from among the gentile Christ-followers who, in association with Jews in the synagogues, also are careful to eat only food that is clearly not contaminated in any way by idolatry. Though not themselves Jews, they associate with Jews and adhere to Jewish food patterns. Such a scenario would be consistent with the history of the Christ-movement in Rome as originally associated with "Jewish rites" and it would fit with the likelihood that there were many God fearers, possibly also proselytes, linked to the synagogues at Rome.[52]

This reconstruction leaves us with Paul directly addressing Christ-followers all of whom are of gentile origin, but who are severely divided in their attitudes to Jews and Judaism and who label each other with reference to perceived preferences for and against association with Jewish groups (which may have been still an option for gentile Christ-followers in this period).[53] This scenario is quite plausible in view of the fact that there it would have been quite normal for gentiles to congregate around a synagogue community without any pressure being put on them to proselytize.[54] With the growth in numbers of these and changes in the social and political scene in Rome, diversity developed, but so too did opposing factions. It is fairly easy to find traces amongst these factions of differing attitudes toward Jews in the synagogue, particularly toward those not embracing the gospel concerning Jesus Christ, as already noted in 11:19.

But why then should Paul associate himself with the strong, especially since we can find no trace of a policy advocating separation from the synagogue? The issue causing confusion among the gentile Christ-followers in

51. For a full discussion of Jews and the perception of them in contemporary Roman culture, see Reasoner, *The Strong and the Weak,* 57–61.

52. See Lampe, *From Paul to Valentinus,* 69–71.

53. This would imply that no "decisive split" had as yet occurred between the Jews and the Christ-followers in Rome. *Contra* Das, *Solving the Romans Debate,* 148. The fact that a temporary separation between Christ-followers and the synagogues may have already taken place earlier does not correspond to a final or decisive split with Judaism nor should it be interpreted as such. Paul's form of argument in Rom 14–15, coming after his open attitude towards the future of the Jews in 9–11, certainly would not lead to such a conclusion even if the next two centuries of church history suggested otherwise (which they do not).

54. Fredriksen draws attention to the remarkable degree of social and cultural integration that was possible in the ancient city thanks to the Romans' deep respect for the *mos maiorum.* Also the fact that most activities in a Mediterranean city would not have taken place indoors but in the areas around buildings, thus being somewhat open to the public, assisted cultural exchange. See Fredriksen, "What 'Parting of the Ways'?" 54–56 and 60–63.

Rome is that whilst they themselves know that according to Paul's gospel they do not need to, and in fact ought not to, become Jews on becoming Christ-followers, some of them have become fully convinced that they must not adhere to any Jewish practices even when associating with Christ-following Jews. But this viewpoint has caused dissension and the source of this dissension may have been traced back to Paul—and not without some basis. Not all Christ-following gentiles in Rome had a close association with Judaism prior to faith in Christ. Others, who had been associated with Christ-following Jews, felt obligated to maintain prior patterns of life but were criticized for doing so by the "strong," who regarded such behavior as inconsistent with the Pauline gospel of being in Christ. So Paul acknowledges that he is on the side of the "weak" (15:1). He even may have felt obligated to write at this time because his gospel is implicated in the dissension.[55] He feels obliged to make it clear that accommodation to those living a Jewish way of life, far from being in conflict with his gospel, is demanded by it, if the conviction of fellow Christ-followers so requires. Thus the freedom for all groups of Christ-followers in Rome is safeguarded not by a theology concerning "indifferent things"[56] but rather by the obligation to the weaker brother for whom Christ also died (14:15).

Thus Paul is not merely supporting people in their prejudices. He does identify with the strong, yet his primary concern is with the plight of the weak. The whole section, 12:1—15:13, is prefaced in 12:1–2 by a call for the renewal of one's mind—a transformation in relation to Christ and a call not to conform simply to human social patterns. The emphasis is on not judging one another, or destroying one another, but instead on recognizing the convictions of others and supporting them in their differing way of life. The recurrence of παρακαλῶ in 12:1 indicates Paul's goals in writing.[57] It would

55. See my essay, "Divergent Images of Paul and his Mission" (chapter 4 in this volume).

56. Convictions of Christ-followers regarding Jewish life patterns are by no means matters of indifference for Paul since these may result in the division of communities and thus hinder the gospel and the development of converts. On the positive side, Paul respects the origin of Christ-followers as Jews or gentiles and takes account of this in his guidance to them, as in 1 Cor 7:17–24 (see my *Paul and the Creation of Christian Identity*, 89–96).

57. Bjerkelund (Παρακαλῶ, 158–61) noted in Rom 1:8ff and 15:3ff. that a typical feature of Paul's letters, in parallel with ancient epistolary practice, is that an introductory thanksgiving is followed by an appeal introduced by παρακαλῶ; usually the subject matter of the thanksgiving is directly connected to that of the request in that the former somehow paves the way for the latter. Despite the fact that in Romans the normal thanksgiving in 1:8ff. is widely separated from the concluding παρακαλῶ in 15:3ff., Bjerkelund has claimed that the mention of a visit to Rome in 15:22–24 serves the function of restoring the connection between the subject matter of the thanksgiving

appear that Paul is seeking peace and harmony in a situation of great diversity, but in such a way that the vulnerable are secure and protected, so that all those in the community will be able to support one another to the glory of God (15:5–6). Paul's solution is that the strong must make concessions and accommodations to the practices of the weak since it is in their power to promote harmony by this gesture of communal concern. If they do have such power, this would indicate that they are not meeting in this instance in a synagogue group, since otherwise they would not be in a position to compromise the weak at the communal meals.

Whilst it may be somewhat speculative, the occurrence of οἰκέτης (house servant) in 14:4 may indicate the fact that some Christ-followers do live as servants in a master's house, and that, consequently, their freedom or lack of it with regard to disputed practices is not under their own control. The various house groups Paul lists in chapter 16 add credence to this suggestion concerning a possible source of strife.[58] Doubtless the leaders of groups could have put pressure on Christ-followers to conform to particular household patterns, and if they did not wish to do so, they would have been in an unenviable position.[59]

The climax of Paul's exhortation emerges in the imperative to welcome one another (προσλαμβάνεσθε ἀλλήλους, 15:7)[60] based on the work and example of Christ, "who became a servant to show God's truthfulness and

---

and Paul's request in 15:3ff. Thus, the fact that these verses echo the introductory thanksgiving demonstrates the importance and purpose Paul has in mind for his visit to Rome. Wedderburn (*Reasons for Romans*, 67–91) built on Bjerkelund's research but argued that Paul's purposes in addressing the Romans may be more than simply one. He traces the occurrences of παρακαλῶ not just in 1:8ff and 15:30ff but also in 12:1–2. Bjerkelund (Παρακαλῶ, 161) had noted that both of the latter passages contain prepositional phrases whereas after the first occurrence of παρακαλῶ in a letter this is not usual. Wedderburn holds that this points to Paul's *purposes* in writing Romans and thus situates the collection visit closely within these purposes.

58. Whether house church groups should be considered as *collegia* is unclear; Jews did not refer to their meetings as *collegia* (cf. Gruen, *Diaspora*, 26). Levine (*The Ancient Synagogue*, 129) notes that there was no single model for Diaspora synagogues during this period.

59 Cf. Lampe, *From Paul to Valentinus*, 164–65. I have argued (Campbell, "The Rule of Faith," 276 ff., now 51–57 in this volume) that if we perceive the situation only in terms of individuals, this might not seem as complicated as it would have been if ordinary members of the movement were under pressure from differing leaders who were pressing them to conform to their imposed constraints.

60. Cf. Fitzmyer, *Romans*, 688–89. The basic meaning is unconditional acceptance into one's household (at the fellowship meal), full and free acceptance after the pattern of Christ with no suggestion of temporal limitation, i.e., until such time as others grow or learn to conform to the householder's pattern and practice (*contra* those who continue to suggest that the weak must eventually learn to live like the strong).

to confirm the promises given to the patriarchs." This resonates with the conclusion of Paul's argument in chapters 9–11, where he has previously affirmed God's ongoing purposes for Israel.

The Collection and the Jerusalem Aspect of Romans

A notable feature of Paul's letter to the Romans is that it is situated within Paul's missionary activity beginning from Jerusalem and that it concludes with the forthcoming visit to Jerusalem with the collection.[61] It is quite feasible in fact that the earliest church in Rome had its roots in Jerusalem.[62] There are members of the Christ-movement in Rome at the time Paul writes his letter who were in Christ prior to him (16:7). The reference to a body or form of teaching (τύπον διδαχῆς) to which the Romans had been committed (6:17) is possibly to some kind of early catechism or rule of faith that had helped to build up the earliest group of Christ-followers in Rome. But it seems that the Romans required a reminder (15:15) about their earlier commitments, which Paul's letter suggests may well have been forgotten, thus perhaps indicating some loss of connection between the present Christ-followers and their earlier roots.[63] It would be somewhat presumptuous to maintain that this teaching coincided exactly with that of Paul, but it must at least have been consistent with it, since Paul seems in fact to endorse it, and to acknowledge a policy of non-interference in the mission field of another (15:20).

With changing situations in Rome, whether due to external or possibly internal circumstances (including a significant influx of gentiles), some of the Christ-following groups may have felt that they no longer needed a relationship to a synagogue, or had even come to believe that links with Jews and Judaism were, in the current social and political climate, less than beneficial.[64] Perhaps there had already been a move to break free from the influence of earlier leaders, and to be more conformed to the Roman context in which they had to live.[65] These leaders may have had close historical

61. Dunn (*The Theology of Paul*, 706–11) also emphases the significance of Jerusalem for Paul, and he highlights how the collection offers a visible link between Paul's theology, missionary work, and pastoral concern.

62. On the close historical links between the Jews in Rome and those in Jerusalem, Cf. Cappelleti, *The Jewish Community of Rome*, 22 and 38–44. On Jerusalem as the point of departure for the gentile mission (cf. Rom 15:19), see Riesner, *Paul's Early Period*, 263, and 253–56.

63. Which some might attribute to the effect of the edict of Claudius, though this is almost impossible to demonstrate.

64. Cf. Elliott, *The Arrogance of Nations*, 97.

65. Paul's strong assertion that he is not ashamed of the gospel draws our attention

links[66] to, and a deferential attitude towards, the Jerusalem "Urgemeinde" that were now no longer shared by all of the Christ-followers. Thus Paul, in excusing his long delay in visiting Rome, may also be demonstrating simultaneously in word and action the significance Jerusalem still holds for him,[67] whether or not this attitude is shared by the Romans. A major difference between Paul and the leaders of the gentile Christ-followers at the time of writing seems to be that they differ from Paul in being unwilling to accommodate those who wish to adhere to Jewish food laws.

Thus, by linking his purpose in writing to them so closely with his collection visit to Jerusalem[68] Paul may, at the same time, be testing their attitudes, i.e., to find out whether the Romans will become inflated with their own new self-understanding or return to a transformed existence by the renewing of their minds as debtors to both Jew and Greek,[69] and above all to the spiritual riches emanating from Jerusalem. This should by no means be perceived as an attempt to establish a client-patron relationship in either direction since the gifts are described in terms of mutuality.[70] Even if they do not participate in the collection, they are still exhorted to pray for Paul and his safety and for the acceptance of the collection. These outcomes will

---

to the important role of honor and shame in the Hellenistic world. From 1 Cor 1–2, we can see how Paul portrayed the gospel in opposition to the Roman civic cult. Perhaps the Roman Christ-followers viewed some aspects of Paul's gospel concerning a crucified Jewish Messiah as unacceptable in their context, but Paul because of the revelation of divine righteousness rejects the shame that Roman culture attributed him on this account, see Jewett, *Romans*, 33–39.

66. Antioch is really the only other candidate as a source of origin for the Christ-communities at Rome, cf. Riesner, *Paul's Early Period*, 108ff.

67. On the collection and its significance for Paul, see Georgi, *Remembering the Poor*. Georgi was influenced by Karl Holl's famous essay, "Der Kirchenbegriff des Paulus," 44–67. Keck ("The Poor among the Saints," 103ff.) is not convinced that "the poor" is a technical term for the Jerusalem church.

68. Käsemann (Käsemann, *Commentary on Romans*, 405) notes the combination of Rome, Jerusalem, and Spain and offers a good discussion of this tripartite connection. He notes the "desire for solidarity" in relation to Jerusalem but feels it should be made more precise, and holds that if "Paul through his epistle could win over the Roman church and especially its Jewish-Christian minority, or at least dispel in part their existing suspicions, he would get rear-guard protection in relation to Jerusalem too." He stresses too much, in my view, the weakness of the posited Jewish-Christian minority and leans too heavily on the reconstruction based on Wiefel and the Claudius edict, but he does demonstrate his awareness of the mediating function of Rome. Käsemann could have added more precision to the desire for solidarity in relation to Jerusalem by adopting the proposals of Bjerkelund as outlined above.

69. On indebtedness and its significance in Romans see my *Paul's Gospel in an Intercultural Context*. 207 n.20.

70. See Ehrensperger, *Paul and the Dynamics of Power*, 79.

facilitate the other outcome relevant to the Romans, that Paul may be able to come to them with joy and be refreshed in their company (15:30–32).[71] Will their participation in these prayers, with its explicit recognition of their indebtedness to Israel, be rejected, or will they join in the prayer and goals of Paul who is the apostle to the gentiles, and hence their legitimate leader? Or will they see this as "dependence upon or subordination to a church or a centre with which they felt they had few ties and towards which they felt little loyalty or reason for gratitude?"[72] Is it better to distance one's group from all things Jewish in conformity with some prevalent attitudes in Rome? Their response will determine how Paul will be able to rely upon their help for his proposed mission to the barbarians in Spain.

Moreover, in the light of chapter 15, the image of the olive tree now emerges as not simply a very appropriate image from the tradition of the Scriptures, but as a concrete depiction of the indebtedness of gentile Christ-followers in Rome to the earliest representatives of the faith in Jerusalem. They represent the branches but Jerusalem represents the stem, and it is necessary to maintain a living relationship between them.

Conclusion

One of the characteristic features of Romans is its double character, addressed to gentiles but at many points dealing with Israel and how gentiles in Christ are related to God's purposes for Israel and the world. The ongoing conversation with the scriptural traditions of Israel is a particular feature of Romans, but the specific discussion of the relation of the Jews to the gospel in chapters 9–11 and 15:8–10 is unique amongst Paul's letters. A striking feature of the letter is not just the absence of ἐκκλησία, coupled with the address to "all God's beloved," but also the duplication of similar terms that are applied to Jews and gentiles in Christ respectively, e.g., ἀδελφοί (8:29; 9:3), υἱοί 8:14; 9:26–27, τέκνα θεοῦ (8:16–17; 9:26–27), κληρονόμοι (8:17), καλέω (8:30; 9:24–26) and ἀγαπητοί (11:28; 12:19). The fact that Paul deliberately and self-consciously uses the same term to apply to the Jewish people and to those in Christ means that he is emphasizing links between them.[73]

However, this does not mean—although the boundaries in places seem to be blurred—that Paul is confusing their identities. It seems rather that

---

71. Cf. Wedderburn, *The Reasons for Romans*, 141–42.

72. Ibid., 74.

73. Cf. Kettunuen (*Abfassungszweck*, 36–37) who notes how Paul, in the proem of Romans, addresses them "with highly expressive predicates appropriate to the promised people of God" and echoing Hos 2:23 and 1:10 (LXX 2:25 and 2:1) cited in Rom 9:25–26.

he is suggesting that Jews and Christ-followers cannot avoid being related within the purposes of God through the work of Christ, and because of this ought to be living in peace with one another in submission to the overall purposes of God. Two readings are possible from this duality of terminology. One that is clearly ruled out is that Paul sees Israel as now containing gentile Christ-followers, with the result that the identity of these gentiles has been incorporated into that of Israel. This is manifestly in opposition to what Paul says about Israel and the relation of gentiles. The other reading is that those in Christ are, through him, related to a divine purpose in which the destiny of Christ-followers and Jews are intertwined. The conclusion to be drawn from the same terminology with reference both to Jews and to Christ-followers is that the meaning of these terms is not exhausted when applied only to those in Christ, since this would amount to an exclusion of others to whom Paul also applies the terms. For Paul, Christ's mission can be described as a ministry to the circumcision (15:8), and thus Christ's mission cannot be accomplished merely through the salvation of gentiles. In Pauline eschatology, salvation can only be complete when God's purposes for both Jew and gentile have come to fruition. And this, according to Rom 11, has *not yet been accomplished*.[74] To stress the "already" of the Christ-event and to omit the Pauline "not yet" is to misrepresent Paul.

This may account for the ambiguity in the address of the letter to "all God's beloved in Rome" (1:7). As argued earlier, the address throughout is to gentiles but it seems also that they are in the context or presence of Jews. Does Paul's rhetoric intend to signal this to us by his use of sonship language, etc.? Or does his careful address only to gentiles originate from the fact that he is addressing congregations he did not found, which owe their origin in some way to Jerusalem? What is ruled out by Paul's use of parallel language referring to Christ-followers and to Jews generally is an anti-Jewish interpretation of Rom 9–11. For such an interpretation to be plausible, either Paul should have used the terms to apply univocally to Christ-followers only, or he should have not used them at all.[75] But since he

74. Cf. Wagner, *Heralds of the Good News*, 279 n.194.

75. The fact that in Romans Paul uses, and that deliberately, terms for Jews and gentiles in Christ that parallel similar designations of Jews generally has a significance not annulled by the fact that he adds "κάτα σάρκα" to his reference to "my brothers" in Rom 9:3; see my "All God's Beloved at Rome" (chapter 5 in this volume). If Paul had regarded gentile Christ-followers as an integral part of Israel, then his use of parallel terms for Jews and Christ-followers would be understandable, but since he did not designate gentiles as *Israel*, such use of language may indicate a deliberate blurring of boundaries for his rhetorical purposes in Romans. This is not to deny Paul's normal use of ἀδελφοί, as noted by Gagnon ("Why the Weak at Rome Cannot Be Non-Christian Jews," 67–68), but rather to interpret the evidence differently and to look at other terms as well.

did use the terms in this dual manner, it seems that he meant to be as inclusive as possible within the terms of the gospel and that he meant to leave the future open to God rather than limiting the options by more precise application of terminology.

On a number of issues, we have considered the options but have not found sufficient evidence to come to definite conclusions. The political situation indicates that, rather than being singled out by the Romans as a distinct group, the Christ-followers' earlier history was intertwined with that of the Jews. Whilst there is evidence of Jewish προσευχαί in existence at this period, and whilst it is perfectly feasible that some gentile Christ-followers continued to worship with Jews, whether they actually did so remains an open question. If instead of synagogues as buildings we focus on groups of Jews meeting in various modes for various purposes and gentiles associating informally with them, this offers a more open scenario of association.[76] Gentile Christ-followers as subgroups attached to synagogue communities is one possible reading of the evidence,[77] but we must be careful not to give the impression of greater institutionalization than is probable at this period. What is demonstrable is that there was ongoing contact with and influence from Jewish groups and that some Christ-followers resented this, possibly because they associated such a negative attitude with Paul. The history of the Christ-movement at Rome does provide evidence of an ongoing conversation with Jews and Judaism to such an extent that strong evidence to the contrary is demanded of those who would view them in complete dissociation. What can be asserted with some confidence is that Paul writes to gentile Christ-followers about Jews in God's purpose in such a way that the Jews (whether Christ-followers or not) seem to be listening in to the conversation.

76. This conclusion is in harmony with the findings of Lane ("Social Perspectives on Roman Christianity," 214–18), who concludes that because the Greco-Roman household played a central role in Roman Christianity, the latter remained fragmented long after the reign of Nero. Even in Hebrews the primary image of the church is "the household of God." Like Romans, Hebrews is also addressed to "all the saints throughout the city," and "there continues to be a Jewish presence in the church at Rome" (ibid., 223).

77. But if it is a possible reading, then it cannot be asserted with confidence that the Christians were meeting separately in their own houses, *contra* Das, *Solving the Romans Debate*, 148. Romans 14–15 depicts a very fluid situation with varying degrees of association with synagogues, both from those valuing Jewish identity, and those distancing themselves from this. See my *Paul and the Creation of Christian Identity*, 113–20.

9

"Let Us Maintain Peace" (Rom 5:2)

Reconciliation and Social Responsibility

Introduction: Why Focus on Reconciliation in Paul?

In my book on Christian identity[1] and in a subsequent article on Ephesians 2,[2] I argue that the retention of Jewish identity in Christ is not only tolerated by Paul but explicitly commanded, as in 1 Cor 7:17ff.[3] Despite the use of terms such as hybrid identity,[4] and despite my acknowledgement that this hybridity may well represent a useful categorization in recent or contemporary society, I wish to emphasize that as I understand Paul, in Christ Jews remain Jews and likewise gentiles (though no longer pagans, in that they are obliged to give up idolatry) remain gentiles, related to the family of Abraham as gentiles, but not as hybrid Jews or Jewish other than in sharing a Jewish symbolic universe.[5] The recognition that gentiles in Christ are related to Abraham via Christ does not mean that they become Israelites or lose their status as gentiles. It is only as gentiles (i.e., as non-Jews in Christ) that these have access to God's grace. It is in and through their identity as believing gentiles that they are simultaneously related to, but also differentiated from, the people of Israel. Paul and other first century Jews saw the

1. Campbell, *Paul and the Creation of Christian Identity*.

2. Campbell, "Unity and Diversity in the Church" (chapter 7 in this volume).

3. Augustine was one of the first to recognize the right of Jews to retain their Jewishness, cf. Fredriksen, "Judaizing the Nations," 232–52.

4. Cf., for example, Johnson Hodge, *If Sons, Then Heirs*, 134–35 and 149–51.

5. To share the Jewish symbolic universe is to view the world from the perspective of God's promises to Abraham, rather than to become identical with Israel, and should mean that gentiles are brought near to God and also to Israel, cf. Fowl, "Learning to Be a Gentile," 28–32.

maintenance of clear boundaries between Jew and gentile as essential for the identity of Judaism.[6] As Pamela Eisenbaum asserts, "All will be kin; none will be strangers, but the gentile will not become Jew, and the Jew will not become gentile."[7]

My view is that Romans addresses the gentile Christ-following groups in Rome with greetings to other groups added in chapter 16.[8] However, an objection could be raised against my proposal concerning the retention of particular identity in that this could be read as support for some kind of ethnic apartheid or ethnic cleansing.[9] I take this very seriously, just as seriously as I do the prejudice against any retention of Jewishness in Paul's theology. I was particularly attracted by the notion in Ephesians of Christ depicted as removing hostility,[10] where the three essential elements of the discussion—identity difference, the work of Christ, and reconciliation in face of hostility—are interlinked. Here I found the connection I needed to make between retaining one's identity in Christ and the necessary corollary to ensure a cessation of hostility against those who are and who remain different. In the world of the first century, where Paul lived and worked, this meant above all the hostility between Jew and gentile.[11] If one believes that one's identity in Christ is subsumed into a new identity that is neither Jewish nor gentile, it would seem that the problem of hostility resulting from abiding difference is solved only by the escape from particular identities. I am not convinced that it is a real existential option to leave behind one's actual social identity in order to take on this new "in Christ" identity, but in any case, the posited new identity, supposedly surpassing all earthly identities,

6. But Paul's perspective was lost to a great extent when the Christ-movement changed rapidly towards the end of the first century due to the fall of the Temple, growth in the number of gentile adherents, and other social and political factors. Paul's letters must not be anachronistically interpreted from the perspective of the texts of this later period as is frequently done, particularly when identity issues are discussed in relation to texts only, without due contextual correlation. Cf. Holmberg on "Identity as a Textual Phenomenon" in his essay, "Understanding the First Hundred Years of Christian Identity," 7–10.

7. Eisenbaum, *Paul Was Not a Christian,* 254–55, cf. also 98.

8. For a detailed argument see my "The Addressees of Paul's Letter to the Romans" (chapter 8 in this volume).

9. On this issue see esp. Volf, "Exclusion and Embrace: Theological Reflections," 230–48; see also his extended study, *Exclusion and Embrace.*

10. As Fowl asserts in relation to Eph 2:14–15, the best theological option will require us to take the term "hostility" as the direct object of the verb "nullify"("Learning to Be a Gentile," 29). It is not the erasure of particular identities that is demanded but of the hostility resulting from these.

11. Cf. my article, "Unity and Diversity in the Church" (chapter 7 in this volume). Cf. also Heckel, "Das Bild der Heiden," 282.

no more resolves the problem of abiding differences than does the retention of one's identity in Christ, because these real differences *do* still abide despite the rhetoric, and are all the more serious because it is claimed that their effects are somehow overcome. Idealism offers no solution here.

Thus I realized that alongside the claim to retain one's identity in Christ, there must be a necessary link with the demand for an ongoing life of reconciliation. In the case of Ernst Käsemann, in stressing justification by faith he argued that the gifts of God through justification cannot be enjoyed in Christ apart from his lordship; the gift cannot be separated from the giver.[12] The advantage, however, of using the image of reconciliation is that the work of Christ is described in such a way that there cannot remain any ground whatsoever for the inconsistency of claiming to be in Christ and simultaneously being at enmity with one's brother or sister (and that means all humans, not merely those in one's own denomination). *Reconciliation presupposes enmity arising from difference but simultaneously demands its demise.* Indeed the demand for Christ-followers to be conciliatory towards those who differ from them is basic to the gospel—"blessed are the peacemakers."[13] Yet sadly our contemporary society offers abundant evidence to the contrary, evidence, that is, of "conflictual" Christians rather that conciliatory. This I think is associated with a sectarian attitude to life and to the world. "I alone am left, and they seek my life" (Rom 11:3). But God never leaves himself without thousands who have not bowed the knee to Baal and, in any case, such a negative "conflictual" attitude is detrimental in the extreme for Christian witness. Of course the gospel may lead to conflict, but conflict by itself is no proof of grace but often only of its absence. In the UK as in North America the fragmentation of Christian faith into innumerable splinter groups with ongoing hostility and in-fighting, coupled with the Western World's confrontation with Islam, has rightly led some thoughtful people to question the connection between current "Christianity" and the crucified Christ.

Militant, and aggressive in many of its forms, contemporary Christianity needs to look afresh at the gospel of reconciliation, and consider carefully what has produced such paradoxical expressions of its gospel of good news for the world. Irrespective of whether or not reconciliation can be claimed as significant as justification by faith, I nevertheless embrace the emphasis on reconciliation as a most appropriate metaphor for proclaiming and promoting the gospel without compromise both by conciliatory attitude and

12. Käsemann, "The Righteousness of God in Paul," 174.

13. Davina Lopez (*Apostle to the Conquered*, 168) maintains that theological reflection on justification by faith should be re-imagined as "reconciliatory justice-making through solidarity."

example. In how many parts of the world today does it not sound ironic when Christian groups claim to have peace with God even when they are hostile to one another, to people of other faiths (or none), and to those who dare to disagree with them? Surely the claim to have peace with God ought to mean something in terms of human relations, a peace that is with God alone has, I suggest, no earthly or social significance. The peace we are speaking of in Paul's letters has real social and political significance, its roots are in the Hebrew term *shalom*, in which there is a posited harmony throughout the world, with neighbor as well as God.[14]

If we view the differing images of atonement and redemption as simply differing ways to express what God in Christ has done for the world, then these ought not to be seen as in opposition, but as parallel images which, unlike differing concepts, can coexist side by side without contradiction. Thus I do not see the metaphor of reconciliation as subsidiary to justification, even though the latter precedes it in Romans; there is no necessary exegetical reason to subordinate reconciliation to justification. The chapters of Romans are not written in ascending order, and some excellent interpreters have suggested a reverse reading order starting with the concluding chapters and then reading the rest of the letter in the light of these.[15] Paul went to great lengths to relate his gospel to the particular needs of his communities, and today in the contemporary world there is a need for a conciliatory brand of Christianity so great that reconciliation should become the dominant image. As Ralph Martin has noted, whereas Paul employs traditional atonement language without explanation in Rom 3:24–25 and 5:6–8, it is only with the introduction of the word καταλάσσω in 5:10 that he moves

14. The politicization of religion in Northern Ireland has resulted in ongoing community conflict so tragic in communities where religion historically has held such a significant status. Cf. Megahey, *The Irish Protestant Churches*. It is to be hoped that the reconciliation process so seriously undertaken in South Africa will provide a model for the ongoing resolution of conflict in Northern Ireland, and that current visits by Northern Irish politicians to South Africa will prove fruitful. Cf. Battle, *Reconciliation: The Ubunbtu Theology of Desmond Tutu*.

15. Stendahl's innovation in his *Paul among Jews and Gentiles* was to argue for chapters 9–11 as "the real centre of gravity" (ibid., 28), if not the climax to Paul's argument in Romans, a stance similar to that which I had proposed in my unpublished PhD thesis "The Purpose of Paul in the Letter to the Romans" (submitted to the University of Edinburgh, 1972). The older more traditional view had meant in practice that chapters 1–8 were considered the core of the letter and that 9–11 were by one means or another effectively marginalized. This perception, coupled with a view of chapters 12–16 as general paraenesis, produced an interpretation of the letter amenable to theological reflection but divorced from and immune to many of the real issues with which Paul had to wrestle in his mission. Stendahl challenged the tendency of contemporary scholarship by questioning whether chapters 1–8 were in essence a preface to the central revelation of chapters 9–11 (ibid., 29).

into an explanatory mode, thus providing a larger context for righteousness, one that easily extends to the reconciliation with fellow human beings.[16]

The Source of Paul's Imagery of Reconciliation

The roots of the reconciliation motif lie in the vision of Isaiah who saw a time of universal *shalom* when the lion would lie down with the lamb, when the nations would be reconciled to God and to one another. The restoration of Israel from exile will usher in a new era, described symbolically in Isa 43:18–19 and Isa 65:17 in terms of a new creation. In my view, it is not a serious problem that scholars have found it difficult to link Paul's thought concerning reconciliation with precise texts of Scripture, since there is here a clear connection with the Isaiah context in Paul's thought, suggesting this is the source of Paul's imagery. As Gregory Beale has demonstrated, what is especially striking in 2 Cor 5:17 is the unique contrast in the New Testament between τὰ ἀρχαῖα and καινά, connected by ἰδού plus creation vocabulary.[17] It appears that prior to writing Romans, Paul had found an understanding of Christ's death as reconciliatory, which he uses in a revised form to address problems in Rome. This is in keeping with Beale's conclusion that both in 2 Corinthians, Ephesians and most likely also in Romans, "the emphasis of reconciliation is upon both the restoration of alienated human relationships and the reconciliation of alienated people to God."[18]

It is quite probable that Paul's use of reconciliation language has a specific link with his own experience of Christ on the Damascus road. He was at that time zealously persecuting the followers of the fledgling Christ-movement. He was their enemy prior to joining the movement himself. It makes good sense for Paul, reflecting later on his earlier behavior, to describe himself from his new perspective as having formerly behaved as an enemy of God. Kim argues that Paul's conversion provides the likely location for the development of the concept of reconciliation and therefore of his experience of Christ.[19] Through his vision of the risen Christ, Paul discovered that God had taken the initiative and overcome this enmity by reconciling Paul to himself through Christ. And even those who still are

16. Martin, *Reconciliation,* 148 and 152.

17. Beale, "Reconciliation in 2 Corinthians 5–7," 553–55.

18. Ibid., 579; similarly see Lambrecht, "Reconcile Yourselves," 263–68.

19. Cf. Kim, *The Origin of Paul's Gospel,* 13–20. Wolff ("True Apostolic Knowledge of Christ," 93) claims that, "this experience of reconciliation shaped Paul's apostolic existence."

enemies of the gospel (not "of God," despite the RSV and NRSV readings of Rom 11:28) can be reconciled by divine initiative.

We are seeking at this point to give some coherence to Paul's theologizing by avoiding a dichotomy between belief and experience.[20] Thus Paul's own personal experience on the Damascus road and even during his mission work[21] may have combined with his reading of the Isaiah passage *to provide a vivid understanding of divine activity,* first with Israel at the time of exile and then also in the mission to the gentiles, which in turn would lead to the restoration of Israel. It is of great significance that all of these items occur together in Romans 11, especially since Paul's own mission activity is included at a point where it might not have been anticipated (vv. 13–14).

This step in the argument is strengthened by Cilliers Breytenbach's thesis that Paul drew the reconciliation language from the political sphere of creating peace between warring parties showing that diplomacy in particular employed such terminology.[22]

Moreover, John T. Fitzgerald argues that Paul, in a radical paradigm shift, in contrast to the normal view that the offending party must take the first step toward peace, makes God the offended party, the one who takes the initiative in reconciliation.[23] Both of these insights fit with our understanding of Paul who sees himself, particularly in the context of chapters 9–11, like the prophets of old, exercising his ministry among the leaders of nations rather than just in reconciling individual Jews or gentiles to God.[24]

Locating Reconciliation Language within the Structure of Romans

The fact that reconciliation terminology tends to be regarded as located primarily in chapter 5 of Romans can be very misleading. The stance taken in this paper is that the motif of reconciliation is much more prevalent in

---

20. I have argued earlier on the problems in interpreting Romans arising from reading chapters such as Rom 9 as consisting primarily of abstract theological language without a concrete contextual setting, "Divergent Images of Paul and His Mission" (chapter 4 in this volume). Cf. also Kraftchick, "Death's Parsing," 144–66.

21. Although we do not agree with C. H. Dodd's view of the nature of Paul's radical spiritual crisis as a result of his illness combined with the problems at Corinth, it is important to note that the apostle, like other humans, had to learn by experiences, both good and bad, and that it makes good sense to view Paul as becoming increasingly conciliatory in his human relations. Cf. Kraftchick, "Death's Parsing," 152–54.

22. Breytenbach, *Versöhnung*, 40–104.

23. Fitzgerald, "Paul and Paradigm Shifts," 241–62.

24. On collective identity see Reckwitz, "Der Identitätsdiskurs," 21–38.

Romans than the frequency of occurrence of specific terminology might suggest. Thus the explicit use of reconciliation language in 5:10–11 is taken up again in 11:15, but recurs in differing form in 15:7 with the call to accept one another as Christ accepted you. If reconciliation terminology is meant to convey to gentiles the meaning of atonement—this would help to explain why this terminology is not used previously in Romans, but only introduced in Romans 5.[25] It is possible that the atonement language of chapter 3 represents a more Jewish understanding of the work of Christ expressed in justification terminology, whereas the reconciliation terms in chapters 5 and 11 represent Paul's way of expressing the gospel to gentiles. This is explicit at least in chapter 11 where the ἀποβολή of the Jews results in the reconciliation of the *kosmos*, here clearly referring primarily to the gentile world. It is also now no longer necessary to separate the doctrinal and paraenetic sections of the letter as earlier scholarship insisted. As recent scholarship has demonstrated (see, for example, the work of Dunn[26] and Haacker[27]) the pastoral and doctrinal sections are closely interlinked and interrelated. This allows a much more flexible understanding of the letter and enables a more coherent interlinking of all its parts. It is also now more recognized that the actual explicit occurrence of specific terminology cannot be the sole carrier of meaning in a letter since the same meaning can be transmitted implicitly as well as explicitly and without being limited to the same choice of words. Thus the terminology of righteousness, peace, and joy in Romans 14, as well as of life and peace via the Spirit in Rom 8 are to be taken into account alongside the explicit references to the reconciliation word group in Romans chapters 5 and 11. I will argue therefore that the theme of reconciliation re-emerges in chapters 12–15 and thereby connects back to chapters 5–11, and that it is by no means unwarranted to describe Romans as a letter about reconciliation of differing groups as well as reconciliation to God.

Inter-Group Conflict among the Roman Christ-Followers

I have dealt at length with this interpretation elsewhere.[28] My view is that the text of the letter, especially chapters 12–15, read in light of what can be known of the history of the Roman congregations in this period, requires

25. Cf. Achtemeier's suggestion (*Romans*, 91–92) that it is another dimension of God's righteousness.

26. Dunn, *Romans 1–8*, lv–lviii.

27. Haacker, *Der Römerbrief als Friedensmemorandum*, 25–41.

28. Cf. Campbell, "The Rule of Faith in Romans" (chapter 3 in this volume).

for its explanation, the posited existence of some measure of inter-group hostility and conflict. It seems there was much diversity among the Christ-followers at Rome, and that Paul is seeking to persuade them to accept one another despite their abiding difference (15:8). We stress the *continuing* difference here, rather than as sometimes has been the case, a temporary tolerance of the other who is different until such times as they give up their differing patterns or gradually grow out of these. But true reconciliation cannot occur where either or any of those requiring reconciliation is unable to retain their own identity and integrity.[29]

Reconciliation occurs not by the removal of the offending differences but by their acceptance and a willingness, where possible, to accommodate to the other in their abiding difference.[30] If we take Paul's exhortation for mutual acceptance individualistically, then there would seem to have been an easy solution if individuals in their diversity would simply acknowledge the right of others who differ to, as it were, do their own thing, provided each was fully persuaded in their own mind that this was right for them (14:5b). But Paul was speaking to groups of Christ-followers, and address-ing a problem that some individuals amongst them were being seriously damaged by inter-group division (14:15). This was possibly accentuated by leaders who were putting pressure on individuals to conform to group norms of behavior, including differing eating patterns (14:15–23). A typical feature of human activity when people act as members of groups, is that they tend to take sides stressing the differences that constitute each group rather than what is held in common.[31] One central issue in these disputes concerned what it means to live Jewishly in Christ (14:1–6). What is to be retained of Jewish life patterns in relation to hospitality with outsiders, etc., and should gentile Christ-followers take on or even recognize anything re-vered by their Jewish brothers and sisters in Christ?

Paul's solution here, as it was already in 1 Cor 7, is that everyone re-main in the state in which they were called, whether as Jewish or gentile. Thus the Roman Christ-followers should keep their patterns of life except

29. Cf. Lee, "Paul and Reconciliation in Romans: From A Korean Postcolonial Perspective," a paper read at the Romans through History and Cultures seminar SBL annual meeting, New Orleans, Nov 2009.

30. Cf. Georgi's claim ("The Early Church," 68), "Biblical identity means solidarity with all other creatures, the respect for their otherness included. Their otherness is an essential part of their integrity, their independent and equal worth, and only in respect-ing that do we retain and maintain our own integrity and identity."

31. Tajfel, "Social Categorizations, Social Identity and Social Comparison." This tendency is typical of group dynamics today and reminds Christians and others not to be needlessly divisive but to acknowledge and to promote our common historical heritage.

in those cases where these might injure a weaker person: in this case the stronger and more powerful should relinquish their freedom out of love for those at risk. Thus we are not positing only two groups (e.g., Jewish and gentile) in the congregations at Rome.

As noted, whilst the issue of living or not living Jewishly, and the compatibility of this with being in Christ was central, there was greater diversity than this. Since, initially, Rome had been a Jewish foundation, although the letter as a whole is primarily addressed to gentiles, it is addressed to gentiles who had been, and almost certainly still are, in close contact with other Christ-followers of Jewish background. An earlier Jewish form of the faith is now probably in the process of evolving into a more diverse phenomenon in which differing patterns of lifestyle may be partially in conflict. Part of the complication may have also resulted from powerful leaders, possibly a minority of these being of higher social status, or from meeting separately in differing venues, whether in basement workshops or members' homes, or in differing areas of the city with only occasional (if any) joint meetings. It is apparent that the most powerful and possibly the more numerous were those of gentile life-patterns who needed persuasion that rather than continuing to please themselves, they should please their weaker colleagues, just as Christ did not please himself. The use and application of Christ's example demonstrates the seriousness with which Paul regards the divisions affecting the Christ-following groups at Rome (15:1–3). Paul's prayer for the disparate Roman congregations is that they will live in harmony with one another in accord with Christ Jesus so that with one voice—the one voice of harmonious existence between those who are and remain different—they may glorify God (15:5–6).

Such a scenario fits well with recent research that suggests that instead of looking at particular models such as synagogues, house-churches, trade guilds, or philosophical schools to help us understand the issues Paul addresses in his letters, and since there is also a certain amount of overlap between these comparative models, we ought perhaps rather to focus on the generic features of first-century groups.[32] Each involves the coming together of people on a regular basis; each is a distinct unit with a sense of social identity; in each members have or develop relatively close ties with each other; each has its own norms and ethos; each meeting takes place in a regular physical setting, relevant to the group's activities; each imitates to some extent patterns in the wider civic area. Adams concludes that "If the most telling similarities between the Pauline churches and the different comparative models are at the generic level, the quest for the most

---

32. Cf. Adams, "First-Century Models for Paul's Churches," 77–78.

appropriate first-century analogy may be somewhat misguided."[33] Our conclusion on this issue is that groups following the Pauline patterns of the Christ-movement have encountered at Rome differing patterns of life with resultant conflict such as might be anticipated in the dynamics generic to group activity in Rome at this period in history.

It is not just individuals who are called upon to accept one another but groups who differ substantially in their group norms and possibly behavior patterns.[34] This is my envisaged context to which Paul addresses his Roman letter, and to which his call for reconciliation is directed.

Reconciliation in Practice

Thus the outcome of Paul's argument ending in 5:11 is that if God shows his love in that Christ died for us while we were yet sinners, then Christ-followers are secure because through Christ they have received reconciliation. But this leads into a call for obedience following the example of Christ with whose death his followers are now united. "So you also must consider yourselves dead to sin and alive to God in Christ Jesus." Both exhortation and command call for a cessation of yielding one's limbs as instruments of sin. So Romans ought not to be artificially subdivided into doctrine in the first part (chapters 1–8) and ethics in the final (chapters 12–16), with chapters 9–11 in brackets (concerning the Jewish issue). To allow later doctrinal formulations to determine the reading of Romans by interpreting it thematically rather than exegetically is clearly anachronistic. But this newer approach means that the ethical demands of being in Christ begin at the latest with the reconciliation language in chapter 5:1ff. Read in this way, Romans has as its essential agenda the reconciliation of Jew and gentile to God and to his kingdom through Christ, both theologically and socially, through the obedience that faith demands.

But that raises the issue as to why Paul does not specifically apply καταλάσσω/καταλαγή language in Romans as he does in the more personal and direct manner of 2 Corinthians. It cannot be because Romans may be viewed as a doctrinal treatise with only general paraenesis, which has no specific connection with the situation at Rome. This outdated and unlikely view has, I believe, been partly responsible for reconciliation not being accorded the significance in Paul's thought that it rightly deserves. I believe

33. Ibid., 78.

34. Thus Jewett's view ("Romans as an Ambassadorial Letter") of Paul as an ambassador and Breytenbach's emphasis on Paul's use of the language of diplomacy point to the communal and political significance Paul accords to his conception of reconciliation.

there are two main reasons for Paul's presentation of reconciliation in Romans.

The first is that Paul's primary focus in Romans is on the relation of Jew and gentile both in theology and in life. Thus reconciliation is explicit in chapter 11 where it is structured again, as it was already in chapter 5, in a *qal wachomer*, lesser/greater type of argument. Grammar and content together indicate specific continuity between these two chapters. At this point the reconciliation of God in Christ of chapter 5 is combined with the reconciliation of Jew and gentile in God's purpose—i.e., how the coming of Christ has reconfigured the operation of God in relation to these peoples, and thus their relation to one another. The basis for good relations in chapters 12–15 and especially in chapters 14–15 is argued already in explicit reconciliation terms in chapter 11. Instead of pessimism over the emerging fact that only some of the Jewish people have as yet responded positively to the Christ-movement, Paul in a brilliant refusal to accept the apparent failure of God's covenant promises and the resultant mistaken boasting of gentile over Jew, turns the situation on its head by arguing that since from Israel's failure, a positive outcome has emerged in the gospel going to the gentile world, how much more blessing is guaranteed when the final acceptance of the rest of Israel takes place. (11:15). Thus gentiles in Christ must not boast over the apparently faithless Jews but humbly stand in awe of God's plan for them to share in the richness of the olive tree (11:17–20). Then in the later chapters, the symbolic field of reconciliation is more discreetly or implicitly fed into the conversation.

Secondly, the reasons why Paul is not so explicit in using reconciliation terminology as in 2 Corinthians is that he does not know the Romans so well, that he has been slow in coming to visit them, that he is presently going instead in the opposite direction, to Jerusalem, and thus they might feel that it is they who need to be reconciled with him. Also he does not want to be too explicit because there are differing views of himself and possibly also concerning the nature and scope of his mission in circulation at Rome to which he does not want to add and thus contribute to further tension.[35]

Paul in 2 Corinthians is estranged from this community, and he uses the Hebrew Bible background to enforce his argument that the readership needs to be restored or reconciled to him as God's authoritative representative, which amounts to a reconciliation to God himself.[36] But, in this case with the Romans, unlike in 2 Corinthians, Paul cannot include himself here along with the Romans as ambassadors for peace. The problem arises

---

35. Cf. my "Divergent Images of Paul and his Mission" (chapter 4 in this volume).

36. Cf. Beale, "The Old Testament Background of Reconciliation," 579.

amongst the Romans themselves, and from their context in the center of the Empire rather than being mainly the result of Paul's reception by the Romans. So he approaches the conflicts indirectly rather than head-on as he did in 2 Corinthians. The emphasis in Romans is not so much on the process of reconciliation itself as on its desired outcome in unity and peace in place of conflict. This becomes apparent in the manner in which peace becomes a recurring theme in the letter, reaching its explicit climax in chapters 14–15, as Haacker has strongly asserted.[37] Whether we maintain that Romans is a letter that stresses reconciliation or, alternatively, peace there can be no doubt that in it the kingdom of God is presented as closely linked to both righteousness and peace as well as to the outcome of these in everyday life, joy in the Holy Spirit (Rom 14:17).

After the normal introductory "grace and peace" in 1:7, εἰρήνη first occurs in a general reference in 2:10, "glory and honour and peace to all those doing good," etc., then in a negative reference in a Scripture citation in 3:17, "the way of peace they did not know."

But it comes center stage at 5:1, "we have peace"—or more appropriately, as we shall argue, "let us have peace," or better still "let us maintain peace." Then in chapter 8 the contrast is made between the mind (φρόνημα) of the σάρξ, which is death, and the mind of the Spirit, which is life and peace.

Most significantly in 12:18 the exhortation emerges, "If possible inasmuch as you are able, live peaceably with all." The present participle form of the verb εἰρηνεύω appears here and the second person present imperative of the same verb occurs in the other reconciliation letter, 2 Corinthians, at 13:11 (τὸ αὐτὸ φρονεῖτε, εἰρηνεύετε) and similarly also in 1 Thess 5:13. Interestingly, in the latter passage the command to "be at peace amongst yourselves" occurs immediately after a call to respect those who are over you and who labor among you, suggesting that the possibility for peace was related to acknowledgement of the leaders.

What could well be regarded as the most important reference to εἰρήνη occurs in the powerful summarizing statement in 14:17, "for the kingdom of God is righteousness and peace and joy in the Spirit," followed in 14:19 by the programmatic exhortation, "Let us then pursue what makes for peace and for mutual upbuilding." The recommended pursuit of peace has as its fruit and desired outcome, the edification of the other and the up-building of the community. After this point we find three significant occurrences of similar peace terminology in 15:13, firstly at the end of a sub-section, "May the God of hope fill you with all joy and peace

---

37. Haacker, *Der Römerbrief als Friedensmemorandum.*

in believing" and then two important final references in 15:33 to "the God of peace" (which we interpret as "the God who promotes peace"): "May the God of peace be with you all," and in 16:20, "Then the God of peace will soon crush Satan under your feet."

Indirect evidence concerning reconciliation and peace is to be noted in the references to enmity/hostility at 8:7,[38] i.e., the opposite of peace occurs here in relation to the mind of the *sarx*. Jewett finds it rather puzzling that a reference to peace occurs in 8:6 where one would anticipate life to occur in contrast with death. Jewett goes on to acknowledge, however, that peace is extremely relevant for the congregations. Thus, he asserts, Paul draws stark distinctions so that it can become clear in 11:17–25 and 14:1—15:13 that the habits of the old age of the flesh, still visible in the arrogant and discriminatory behavior of competitive congregations, entails serious consequences.[39] Thus the explicit reconciliation language of 11:13–15, is followed by the warning against competitive boasting of gentile over Jew, and the effects of this arrogance on relations between differing groups at Rome.

Even in this contrast with its opposites, the theme of living in peace and the semantic connection with this is still implicit. As Joseph Fitzmyer reminds us, in thinking of reconciliation we must bear in mind that "The notions of enmity, hostility, estrangement and alienation, as well as their counterparts, reconciliation, atonement, friendship and intimacy are derived from social intercourse of human persons or from the relations of ethnic and national groups, such as Jews and Greeks . . ."[40] Thus we cannot make a firm separation between the vertical and horizontal dimensions of Paul's thought. The horizontal presupposes the vertical and the two are inseparable images of divine activity and its impact on human behavior.[41] From this we conclude that peace language in Romans is nothing other than reconciliation language.

---

38. As Jewett (*Romans*, 487–88) notes, the nominal form φρονέω (be minded) is used here for the first time in Paul's letters and indeed in the NT— φρόνημα has the same meaning as the infinitive—to be minded—namely the mindset or orientation itself. Note the use of ἔχθρα in 8:7, the φρόνημα of the flesh is hostile to God whereas the mind of the Spirit is life and peace (8:6) .

39. Ibid.

40. Fitzmyer, *Pauline Theology*, 162, Cf. similarly also Beker. Beker (*Paul, the Apostle*, 259–60) argues that despite differing metaphors, "the levels of symbolic interaction do not justify a view that there is a dichotomy between juridical and mystical language, or an emphasis on one as opposed to the other." On the contrary, he maintains that "Paul interprets the coherent apocalyptic core of the gospel in a variety of metaphors that interact and interweave to form an organic whole, so that a developmental or atomistic analysis of the various metaphors bypasses his hermeneutical intent."

41. Martin, *Reconciliation*, 229.

Since the majority of manuscripts support the subjunctive here and in καυχώμεθα in 5:3, I follow the proposal of Erich Dinkler to translate 5:1 as "let us maintain peace," putting the emphasis upon the anticipated outcome of reconciliation with God as reconciliation with those who differ.[42] Jewett makes an excellent case for the subjunctive reading. "Rather than a triumphalist argument about the current possession of peace and hope by Christian believers that the indicative interpretation has traditionally assumed, the subjunctive produces an admonition about the correct embodiment of faith in the life of the congregation. The formulation in the first person plural includes all the members of Paul's audience as well as Paul and his colleagues in a common obligation."[43] What is more, their common corporate experience of living as a community of reconciliation is how they learn together its meaning, not only for themselves, but also for those who disagree with them, whether about forms of corporate activity in house-congregations or synagogue groups. It is here that the meaning of reconciliation becomes intelligible and understandable in *the experience of striving to live peaceably*, not just with everyone individually, but particularly with differing groups divided by strong opinions and equally strong practices. In the obligation to live peaceably, the link between the doctrine of reconciliation with God and Christian social ethics is bridged, and the body of Christ becomes recognizable and effective in a world where enemies coexist side by side with Christ-followers.[44]

Reconciliation and Paul's Purpose in Romans

Paul asserts he is not ashamed of the gospel for it is the power of God to everyone who believes, but then surprisingly adds to the Jew first, and only then "and also to the Greek." This suggests that there are some gentiles in Rome—since they are the addressees—who are criticizing Paul, claiming that he is ashamed of the gospel for gentiles "apart from the law" and that he still wants to retain his troubled association with Judaism. But this image

42. For Dinkler's proposals see Jewett, *Romans*, 345–50. Jewett also interprets 5:1 as subjunctive, "let us have peace." Porter ("The Argument of Romans 5," 655–77) also has made a good defence of this reading, .

43. Jewett, *Romans*, 348, cf. also Schütz's emphasis (*Paul and the Anatomy of Apostolic Authority*) that for Paul the "singularity of the gospel" and the "unity of the church" are the top priorities.

44. Thus faith and politics cannot be separated, and despite its failings the attempt at political reconciliation of differing peoples in South Africa must be recognized as a valid experiment in communal reconciliation. Cf. Tutu, *No Future without Forgiveness*; also Battle, *The Ubuntu Theology of Desmond Tutu*. Also Volf, "Forgiveness, Reconciliation and Justice," 861–77.

of the apostle is unwarranted in that although Paul will not permit gentiles to become Jews, this does not mean that they are to separate from all things Jewish or from all relations with Jews and Judaism.[45] So Paul gives the standard Jewish view of gentile society in Rom 1:18–32, stressing that God gave up the gentiles to their idolatry. After a discussion of judging one another, Paul turns in 2:17 to the question of who is a true Jew—simply to call oneself a Jew will not do. So here is reflected the dilemma of those gentiles who had acquired a Jewish pattern of life. Some gentile Christ-followers in Rome ask a question, implying they will receive a negative answer: What then is the advantage, if any, of being a Jew? "Much in every way" is Paul's answer. There is no need to be ashamed of being a Jew or of being related to Jews as children of Abraham. Abraham is not someone to be despised for the sake of Aeneas or other Roman forefathers. Abraham is ultimately unique in Paul's genealogy. He is the bearer of the promise—he left his pagan origins and after believing the promise God gave him, accepted circumcision, thereby making him truly the father of many nations.

Thus Abraham is a uniting figure for believing Jews and gentiles, because he has become the model for all those believing without circumcision and likewise also of those circumcised who also believe. There is now no need for hostility and enmity between circumcised and uncircumcised in Christ because of this shared ancestry. The atonement through the life and death of Christ, explicit in 3:21–26, is implicit here. The promise to Abraham and to his descendants did not come through the law but through Christ and the words "it was reckoned to him as righteousness" were written also for those who trust in Christ in whom the promises were confirmed (4:22–25). We can paraphrase Paul's emphasis as follows "having obtained access to this grace in which you as gentiles stand, let us then seek to maintain peace and to live peaceably with all those who are different" (whether they are Christ-followers or not).

This grace in which we stand is moreover the obedience that faith enables—Christ is contrasted with the disobedience of Adam, and then gentile believers are exhorted and commanded in chapter 6:1—7:6 to live a life of obedience, following the leading of the Spirit into peace and righteousness in chapter 8.

---

45. See Fredriksen, "Judaizing the Nations," 232–52. Fredriksen argues against the concept of Paul's gospel being described as a "law-free" gospel, since he imposes Jewish ritual demands of no worship to native gods, thus "Judaizing the nations." Only common usage prohibited Paul from using the term "Judaizing" positively. But Fredriksen still insists, as I do, that Paul strongly maintained the division of humanity into Jew and gentile and that this perception was not done away even in Christ.

Then in chapters 9–11 the relation of gentile Christ-followers to the *whole of Israel* is explicitly considered. This suggests that some gentile Christ-followers in Rome were hostile to Jews and Judaism generally, not just to those gentile Christ-followers who choose to continue to live a Jewish life pattern. Thus it seems that the question of eating and drinking, of the weak and the strong—an issue in my view among gentile Christ-followers in particular—becomes center stage. However, it is not just a matter of food and drink but rather of *food and drink as perceived symbols of Judaism* that some Christ-followers in Rome were keen to leave behind them. They were mistakenly beginning to despise the heritage of Abraham, but Paul over- turns their gentile view of the world by depicting them as wild olives receiv- ing their enrichment not from the Greek world but from Abraham.[46] There is possibly real hostility from some gentile radicals as is glimpsed briefly in 16:17, "I appeal to you, brethren, to take note of those who create dissen- sions and difficulties, in opposition to the doctrine (διδαχη) which you have been taught; avoid them."

Note the echo here of 6:17, "the standard of teaching" (τύπον διδαχῆς). If the Petrine mission from Jerusalem led to the foundation of the church at Rome, then that Jewish foundation would have taught its first converts a Jewish Christian pattern of life; that is why Paul is so careful how he builds on another's foundation—he has learned from Antioch, and he desires peace, not the hasty martyrdom brought on by conflict between Jew and gentile, or by the refusal to pay one's taxes.[47]

Conclusion: The Pursuit of Peace

The quest for peace must not be confused with a sentimental aspiration. In Paul it is a powerful exhortation "τὰ τῆς εἰρήνης διώκωμεν" (14:19), or as in 1 Cor 14:1, "pursue love" (cf. Rom 12:13 "pursue hospitality," and Paul's own testimony concerning what he himself "pursues," Phil 3:12–16). This denotes not just a passive pious acceptance of what might be termed the peace principle, but active and self-conscious living by the "mindset" of the Spirit—"To set the mind on the flesh is death (τὸ φρόνημα τῆς σαρκός) but to set the mind on the Spirit (τὸ φρόνημα τοῦ πνεύματος) is life and peace" (8:6). Paul's goal is that the minds of the Romans should be transformed so that groups do not think of themselves more highly than they ought to think, but to think with sober judgment, each according to the measure of faith that God has assigned (12:2–3). The emphasis on the mindset

46. Cf. Davies, "A Suggestion concerning Romans 11:13–24," 153–63.

47. Cf. my *Paul and the Creation of Christian Identity,* 77–79.

already introduced in chapter 8 is now related back to the pride of gentile Christ-followers noted in 11:17–24, indicating that it is the super- or hyper-mindedness of some gentiles that is causing conflict between the groups. Such an attitude corresponds to the mindset of the flesh denounced in 8:6 as contrary to the mindset of the Spirit that brings life and peace.[48] "Live in harmony with one another; do not be high-minded, but associate with the lowly; never be conceited" (12:16—note here the recurrence of φρόνιμοι). The renewal of the mind in Christ is Paul's response to community conflict. So the response to persecution, to those who do evil, is never to avenge or retaliate but in "so far as it depends upon you, to live peaceably with all" and thus "overcome evil with good" (12:14–21). Thus Paul links life and peace indicating that the latter is a prerequisite for the former and essential to the well-being and growth of the communities.[49]

So whilst Paul acknowledges that he teaches freedom in Christ as some of his gentile followers in Rome were confident he would, yet at the same time, he actually takes the side of the weak—"associate with the lowly" and "stop being conceited." He commands those in power not to destroy the weak persons caught between conflicting life patterns and between differing factions at Rome. His advice is reconciliation and full acceptance of each other's differing stance. "Accept one another as Christ has accepted you," freely, with no qualifications, no reservations, no limitations as to Jewish affiliation or lack of it. His warning is that "you who have power in your gentile Christ-following groups, do not endanger the brother" (who is not able or willing to renounce his previous pattern of living in Christ after a Jewish fashion). Thus, the cause of the perpetuation of hostility is not difference but rather the refusal to accept the other in his/her difference and to be reconciled to them as they are.

This is because contrary to what some gentile Christ-followers think, Judaism is not annulled, nor are the branches lost that were apparently broken. God has plans still for all Israel, and *gentile obedience can assist or hinder those plans*. That is why, says Paul, I plan to visit Jerusalem prior to coming to see you because I need to witness still to the order of the gospel, to the Jew first and also to the Greek. You gentiles have obtained the riches of the God of Israel and the gospel of his Son, the Messiah of Israel, so it is necessary for you as gentiles to share your material blessings with those through whom the promises of Abraham were transmitted to the world. So Paul invokes the Roman gentiles to follow his example of a reconciliation offering to the Jews in Jerusalem as evidence that the offering of Christ had

---

48. Cf. Jewett, *Romans*, 487–88.
49. Cf. Schütz, *Paul and the Anatomy of Apostolic Authority.*

brought reconciliation to the gentile world and still holds out hope for the salvation of all Israel. Paul himself was no stranger to conflict and for the sake of Christ would not shirk to oppose anyone, but despite this, his advice to all is to pursue peace "pleasing his neighbor for his good" in a reconciling pattern of life even as Christ did not live to please himself (Rom 15:2–3). It is most fitting therefore that in Ephesians Paul is depicted not only as the champion of the gentiles, but significantly also as an apostle of peace, "eager to maintain the unity of the Spirit in the bond of peace" (4:13).[50]

50. I offer this study of reconciliation and peace in a world of diverse identities and much conflict in appreciation particularly of the biblical contribution of John T. Williams but also for his deep and abiding respect for the reformed and cultural traditions of his native Wales.

Universality and Particularity in Paul's Understanding and Strategy of Mission

Introduction

THE THEME WE ARE investigating in this essay is the extent to which Paul's molding of his missionary communities in Christ should be viewed as a culture-transforming or a culture-transcending activity. The fact that Paul's gospel is both universal in outreach (he sees himself as apostle to the gentiles) and yet always directed to a particular context is one of the potentially most confusing aspects of Paul's missionary policy/practice. Thus it has been of great advantage in the more recent study of Paul's letters that there has been a growing recognition of the fact that his words are "words on target," not merely generalities with universal application.

Yet there are, on the other hand, elements that indicate that Paul himself did have certain general patterns of communication and teaching that applied in all the churches of the gentiles, as is found in, for example, 1 Cor 4:17, where he speaks of "my ways in Christ, which I teach in every church" (cf. also Phil 4:9). This might suggest that the foundational element in Paul is the claim to be "in Christ," which is then to be regarded as a fixed or recurring entity that does not vary wherever a Pauline congregation is founded. Yet there are strong arguments against holding that being in Christ represents a conformist element in his followers.[1] While it is clear that human beings ought to be molded by the constraints of the gospel, rather than

---

1. Cf. Kim's criticism (*Christ's Body in Corinth*, 37) that "a traditional theological approach to Paul's 'in Christ' language fossilizes Christian identity, fixes it as exclusive, and removes any possibility of a genuine, open-ended engagement with others or of seeing community in multiple context and through the lens of diversity."

adjusting the gospel to fit within their culture, it is also true that following Christ has been as much a cause of diversity as of uniformity. Historically, it has not been particularly evident that being in Christ necessarily leads to a distinct form of cultural expression. But perhaps it is simplistic to argue from what is, as distinct from what ought to be, the case. Should diversity be recognized and celebrated or simply condoned or tolerated? Was there originally a uniformity in Christianity that later broke down due to human weakness? Ought not the one Christ to be regarded as the common element in the faith and thus necessarily the predominant source of uniformity? This is an important issue as we reflect on Paul as a planter of communities of faith around the Mediterranean. Did he, despite the contextual focus of his letters, intend these communities to have a common pattern *irrespective of their cultural context*, or did he promote freedom to develop diversely but in Christ? We need first of all to look at the evidence that would indicate Paul's own pattern of activity.

Commonality in Paul's Teaching

The immediate context of Paul's statement in 1 Cor 7:17, regarding ordaining something similar in all the churches,[2] relates to the state in which the call of God was experienced. The claim seems to be that God has assigned (ἐμέρισεν)[3] a form of life to each individually within the Christ-movement. A parallel use of this verb can be found in 2 Cor 10:13 where the emphasis appears to lie on geographical limits that God has measured out for differing apostles/evangelists. The term ἐμέρισεν also occurs in Rom 12.3 where what God has assigned is denoted as the "measuring rod of faith" (μέτρον πίστεως).[4] Christ-followers are not to be "super-minded" but "to set your mind on being sober minded" even as God has distributed grace within the body of Christ. (12:4–8). According to Jewett's exegesis, the primary meaning of μέτρον is that by which anything is measured, and thus it indicates

---

2. We note, but cannot discuss in detail, that although the verb here is διατάσσομαι, in 4:17 it is διδάσκω (as also in some manuscripts of 7:17). We take both to be a reference to authoritative teaching by Paul.

3. The verb μερίζω means to divide into parts prior to the distribution of these, cf. n.5 below. Here as elsewhere the sovereignty of God as the giver of all gifts via the Spirit is being stressed.

4. On this see Cranfield, *Romans*, 613–18. Cf. Jewett's claim (*Romans*, 742) that "There are political, ideological, racial and temperamental components that are legitimately connected with faith, comprising the peculiar 'measuring rod' that each person in the church has been given."

"the norm that each person is provided in the appropriation of the grace God apportions."[5]

Despite 1 Cor 7:17–24 appearing somewhat of a digression within its wider context,[6] this compact passage is basic to the understanding of Paul, in that it indicates that a recognition of the status[7] at the point of call is a determining factor in the living out of the divine calling.

The immediate theme in this passage concerns being called as circumcised, as uncircumcised, or as a slave, and the clear indication is that each is expected to remain as they were when called, only with the caveat that slaves should avail themselves of freedom if the opportunity arises. What is common in the three passages, 1 Cor 7:17–24, 2 Cor 10:13, and Rom 12:3–8, connected by the recurrence of ἐμέρισεν, is that in all three there is a given element that is to be taken as determined by God. Thus it appears that everything in these new communities is not as undetermined and open as is sometimes assumed. It is not acceptable to give up being a Jew or a gentile for personal preference and certainly not as a means to social mobility. But slaves who have an opportunity of manumission, should take advantage of it,[8] probably as a sign of God's will for them. In the first instance, in 1 Cor 7, the given element appears to be more to do with social status, in the second with a designated sphere of work, and in the third it is with spiritual gifts, which of course would include leadership qualities.

---

5. Ibid. Jewett's emphasis is upon individuation in the distribution of grace, which need not necessarily demand an individualistic interpretation of Paul if construed in the context of Paul's understanding of charismata as God's gifts experienced and exercised within the body of Christ.

6. But it only appears to be a digression since it concerns calling, a central theme of the letter (see the article by Roetzel, "The Grammar of Election" and my response "The Contribution of Traditions," chapter 2 in this volume). It is also taken up again in 9:19–23, which Tomson (*Paul and the Jewish Law*, 270 and 281) regards as being the example in the Apostle's person of the same "rule for all the churches."

7. State or status is not a misleading translation of κλῆσις here. The proposal that this means only to remain in one's call as a Christ-follower is not sufficient since the advice Paul gives is about being Jewish or gentile—debates about vocation are secondary to this primary call.

8. The transition from slavery to freedom, or vice-versa, was normal practice in ancient society. It is just possible that Paul left the issue of seeking release from slavery entirely open, it is certainly not forbidden; see Thiselton's translation (*1 Corinthians*, 110), "If, when God called you, you were a slave, do not let it worry you. Even if there is a possibility that you might come to be free, rather, start to make positive use of the present." Thiselton (ibid., 112) stresses that freedom is not necessary for acceptable Christian service. But see also Bartchy, *Mallon Chresai: First-Century Slavery.* See also Byron, *Recent Research on Slavery*, and my article review of this, "'Remain as you were when called' and Paul's Stance on Slavery," 205–7.

What is apparent from this brief glance at this aspect of given-ness in important areas of Pauline thought, is that within the Pauline mission, the calling, gifts, and spheres of mission were regarded as being ultimately under the direct determination and control of God. A new way of life was opened up for gentiles who followed Christ in the movement, but they were subject to the free distribution of divine gifts to them via the Spirit; they were to remain in the state of calling in which they were when called, and they were to work in the sphere of mission to which God would apportion them. To put it briefly, they were free in Christ, but this freedom was for specific service as determined by God and his gifts through the Spirit. It can be better represented as freedom to do the will of God in Christ rather than just freedom in Christ. Seen in this light, Paul himself as apostle to the gentiles is not free to say "yes" and "no" as he feels appropriate but "yes" can be his only response to the call of God and the commitments that entails (cf. 2 Cor 1:17–19).

Common Content across Paul's Letters

We can argue from such references as 1 Cor 7:17 that Paul did consciously teach similar things throughout his churches and actually used this fact, as he does in Corinthians, as a reason for conformity with his practices. But should such perceived commonality signify that in view of it the letters of one writer (i.e., Paul) can be interpreted as a group rather than only individually, on the presumption that the commonality is greater than the difference? Whilst we would not wish to deny that we can discover from each letter elements that can reinforce or give more probability to a particular understanding of another letter, we need to be very careful in how we relate the contents of individual Pauline letters to each other.

A good example is discernible in the attempts to identify Paul's opponents in 2 Corinthians. The evidence that these people boast in their Hebrew background and their Jewish heritage generally can be combined with information from Galatians and Philippians to create a picture of a mobile opposition group who, with or without official backing from Jerusalem, dogged Paul's footsteps in a concerted attempt to force gentile Christ-followers to judaize and thus to thwart the Pauline mission. This pattern of grouping the evidence of several letters to presuppose an organized and active anti-Pauline movement contemporary with Paul's mission—starting from F. C. Baur and followed by modern scholars such as W. Schmithals in relation to his conception of Gnostic opponents[9] and G. Lüdemann[10]—has

9. Schmithals, *Paul and the Gnostics.*

10. Lüdemann, *Opposition to Paul in Jewish Christianity.*

been, whether implicitly or explicitly, highly influential in the formation of what can broadly be termed Paulinism. In this construction, Paul becomes the self-styled champion of the gentile mission over against a tribalistic Petrine mission to the circumcision. The division into two opposing or competing missions[11] with powerful leaders and differing ideologies can now only be regarded as over-simplistic and somewhat institutionalized, entirely unrepresentative of the great diversity normally accompanying a vital and transitional religious movement. Such criticism does not rule out the possibility of similar developments emerging in differing regions and churches, but it does negate the view that opponents of Paul could equal his tenacity and commitment to travel very long distances in dangerous and difficult circumstances and at great expense. We will return to consider the identity of these opponents at a later point, but now we wish simply to affirm that the individual letters, prior to their being correlated with the contents of others *and thus the importing of what might be considered an overload of meaning from elsewhere*, must first be allowed to reveal their own information, particularly in relation to a specific context. To fail to do this is to create a decontextualized body of disparate items of information, which can then be reused (and thus probably misused) in the service of the construction of a desired uniformity.[12]

Imitation in Paul

In a passage very similar to 1 Cor 7:17–24 Paul states that he sent Timothy to remind the Corinthians "of my ways in Christ Jesus as I teach them everywhere in every church" (1 Cor 4:17). This obviously refers to a pattern of teaching promulgated by Paul. Here it is based on Paul's status as church planter, as "your father in Christ" (4:15) (though not as the Roman "paterfamilias").[13] Because of this he urges them to "be imitators of me" (4:16). Paul as the one who laid the foundation of the Corinthian church ought to be imitated by the Christ-followers there. This is an element in Pauline teaching that is very obvious once we become conscious of it. He encourages imitation of himself to provide a living model for his converts. Thus there is an expectation within the Pauline communities that all the members, together with Paul and other

---

11. Cf. Goulder, *Paul and the Competing Mission*, 211–21.

12. "Paul's reflections . . . become building stones for an abstract system that constitutes the essence of his thought,' in service of 'a topical-dogmatic method that . . . moves away from the contextual meaning of Paul's themes and language" (Beker, *Paul the Apostle*, 34–35 and 351).

13. Cf. Ehrensperger, *Paul and the Dynamics of Power*, 117–19.

co-workers, will adopt a common *pattern* for their lives. It can be concluded from this that a common *practice* of the faith would soon develop across the Christ-movement, or at least the Pauline section of it. It is a way of life that is to be imitated, not simply an adherence to a form of teaching. Paul does commend the Corinthians for maintaining the traditions even as they had been delivered by him to them (1 Cor 11:2b). But this is immediately preceded by the comment, "I commend you because you remember me . . ."! So it is Paul and his practice of the faith that is primary, rather than the content of the traditions, however significant. Yet this is also not quite correct, since Paul qualifies the call to imitate him by the words, "inasmuch as I imitate Christ" (1 Cor 11:1). Thus it has been cogently argued that imitating Christ or Paul must not be viewed as simply copying but rather *embodying the gospel anew in each particular context*.[14]

Hence, despite commonality in the pattern of living, the possibility of diversity within the Christ-movement is not therefore ruled out by the practice of imitation, whether of Christ or of Paul. The application of this common basis in daily life actually necessarily involves diversity.[15] Both Jesus and Paul are of Jewish birth, not gentile, and if we are correct in following Paul's own advice to the Corinthians to stay as they were at the point of call, then it can only be imitation, not copying, that is intended, since gentiles would then be copying Jews and thus judaizing. Also the freedom of charismatic leadership within communities such as Corinth disposes us to the view that Paul could not force just anything on these communities— they too, or at least their leaders, had also to be convinced that what they were urged to do was the will of God for them. Hence Paul's forceful and persuasive forms of argument—the rhetoric of persuasion was really necessary in his attempt to win the churches to his point of view.[16]

Common Destiny—Conformity with the Image of Christ

It can rightly be asserted that, more than any other argument, being in Christ constitutes commonality among Christ-followers in that it contributes to a common identity for Christ-followers. Yet recent research into

14. Cf. ibid., 137–46. Even though the content of Phil 4:9 includes a reference to being taught (ἐμάθετε), to receiving tradition (παρελάβετε) as well as to seeing and hearing, the focus is what has been learned from Paul (ἐν ἐμοί) and the stress is not merely on knowledge but on practicing (πράσσετε) these things. Thus this verse is very similar to what we are arguing from 1 Cor. 4:17 in that both are experientially and personally focused on Paul and, via him, on Christ.

15. Cf. 9:19–23 and n.5 above.

16. Cf. Ehrensperger, *Paul and the Dynamics of Power*, 174–78.

the understanding of identity has raised interesting questions in relation to how being in Christ determines or affects identity. Some scholars stress the creative aspect of identity formation and see individuals and groups as potentially having several sub-group or nested identities. Taken alongside this view, being in Christ can potentially be regarded as an overarching identity that holds together a diversity of human identities. Thus Philip Esler sees the Roman Christ-followers as a mixed group of Jewish and gentile origin with ongoing differing identity, but joined together by an overarching "in Christ" identity.[17] This scenario might be taken to suggest that being in Christ will eventually diminish the significance of sub-group identities and the growing significance of commonality with corresponding decrease in diversity. But it can also be argued that being "in Christ" is more like a transnational identity such as European that need not necessarily diminish local or national identity, but is intertwined with them. It is open to question, however, whether "being in Christ" can thus be regarded as somehow creating a status or station "above" the particularity of context. Most probably the concept of a new entity,[18] a new "people of God" that is neither Jewish nor gentile, has its origin in some such supra-contextual vision.

In a somewhat different vein, E. W. Stegemann, influenced by A. Schweitzer,[19] sees identity in this world as being hybrid through Christ, but leading to a new transcendent identity that overcomes difference finally in the world to come.[20] This implies a transformation of humans into the form of the heavenly Son of God. It should be noted however that this transformation, though it may begin in this world, is not complete until the *eschaton*. But how is identity to be defined in the interim? If this transformation has only begun, then we would be left with Christ-followers already in process of being partially transformed, but still retaining an identity as Jews or gentiles in Christ. Does it make sense then to think in terms of Christ-followers as having a hybrid Christ/Jewish or gentile identity? I am not sure that being in Christ functions in the same way in terms of identity as other geographical and or cultural identities. It would seem to diminish the significance of

---

17. Esler, *Conflict and Identity in Romans*, 49–50, 152–53, and 190.

18. Although emerging only in the post-Pauline period, the patristic idea of Christianity as a "third race" re-appeared in Harnack, *Die Mission und Ausbreitung des Christentums*, 259–81. Sanders (*Paul the Law and the Jewish People*, 29 and 178–79), however, views the church as a "third entity" already in Paul.

19. Schweitzer, *Die Mystik des Apostels Paulus*, 178–99.

20. Stegemann, "Reconciliation and Pauline Eschatology in Romans," paper read at the 'Romans through History and Cultures Group', SBL Annual Meeting, New Orleans, 2009.

Christ identity somewhat if it is regarded as functioning only in the same way as human identity-creating factors.

Should "in Christ" identity be regarded as the invasion of the coming age into this one, and as such something above and beyond contextuality, or ought it to be considered, like Paul's gospel, to be fully contextualized and thus as contributing identity-creating forces in a similar way to other human contexts? If we think, for example, of Christ as being the image to which gentile followers are destined to be conformed (Rom 8:29) then it could be contended that this means all Christ-followers will be transformed into one Jewish identity in keeping with that of the (earthly) Christ?[21] But though we are emphasizing that Paul introduced his converts into a Jewish symbolic universe, this need not mean that these acquire a corresponding Jewish identity also. Paul certainly did not share this perception.[22] The terms in which Paul speaks of being conformed to Christ do not offer much information on the effect of such transformation in this present life. We learn only that "the creation waits with eager expectation for the revealing of the sons of God" (Rom 8:19). It is a hope that is not yet seen but in which we wait with patience. Even the full adoption as sons is not a present reality— the redemption of our bodies is still awaited (Rom 8:23–25). If it is claimed that believers do share already this future identity in Christ, it is still not yet visible, and present only in hope. It seems that too much weight is given if we maintain as an already realized state what, at best, is a hidden identity that thus differs radically from other visible and tangible identities.

We conclude therefore on this issue that whilst the concept of hybrid identity may offer some insights, there are still unresolved problems with it in addition to the incompleteness of the hybrid/Christ identity in this life. The basic problem is that the categories Paul uses are not normally Jew and Roman/Greek, etc., but Jew and gentile. Gentile thus represents the sum of humanity outside of Israel. To be categorized as a hybrid gentile becomes somewhat meaningless in identity terms. The only solution to this would be to insist that for most purposes, gentile operates for Paul as equivalent to Greek and thus it could be argued that to be in Christ as a gentile is to have a hybrid Greek/Christ identity. I remain convinced, however, that it makes best sense to speak not so much in terms of hybrid identity between human

21. *Contra* Johnson Hodge (*If Sons, Then Heirs*, 150), who sees being in Christ as not "involving shifting or mixing for Jews (since) it is already a Jewish identity," but "being in Christ requires a more radical blending for gentiles." I find this very unclear. If Jews remain Jews, then it seems only gentiles have to have hybrid identity through being in Christ. I consider it more apt to regard both Jews and gentiles as remaining Jew or gentile, as they were when called, but both sharing a Jewish symbolic universe.

22. See my "Gentile Identity and Transformation according to Paul."

identity and "in Christ"-identity, but to regard Jewish and gentile identities as continuing to be maintained in this life, but within a vision of a common destiny to be conformed to Christ's image in the world to come.

Being Linked with Christ for Paul Means Being Inducted into a Jewish Symbolic Universe

While, as I have argued, Paul advocated the retention of identity in Christ, whether Jewish or gentile, he nevertheless consciously sought to integrate gentile Christ-followers into a Jewish symbolic universe. Thus it is the God of Abraham, Isaac, Jacob, and of the prophets who is the father of us all, both Jews and gentiles in Christ (Rom 4:16). The Scriptures of Israel become the Scriptures of the Pauline communities for their instruction also. It can, in addition, legitimately be argued that some Noachide laws applied in Paul's communities to enable good social relations between Jew and gentile in Christ.[23] Also a major challenge posed to gentile Christ-followers was that for them, as for Jews, idol worship in any form must be anathema. In view of these factors then it is small wonder that some of Paul's converts were surprised that he did not advocate that they become also proselytes to Judaism.[24] Indeed, the framework of Paul's own mission is centered around a particular understanding of the destiny of Israel and the interplay within this of the mission to gentiles led by the apostle. It would seem then that his universal mission is to be finally located within the purposes of the God of Israel in which the people play a specific and inalienable role. Gentiles have their particular place in this pattern, but it is in an intertwined relationship with Israel, rather than as an integral part of it.[25] This reflects aspects of Paul's Jewish particularity that we anticipate were shared with many other contemporary Jews.

23. Cf. Nanos, *The Mystery of Romans*, 198.

24. On Paul's role in the creation of gentile identity see my *Paul and the Creation of Christian Identity*, 54–67. Cf. also Donaldson (*Paul and the Gentiles*, 236–48) who proposes that Paul's gentile converts should be regarded as proselytes in a reconfigured Israel.

25. My view (Campbell, "Covenantal Theology and Participation in Christ," 41–60) is that gentiles do not become part of the covenant but receive God's blessings through their status "in Christ" in whom God's covenantal purposes are actualized—they have thus no independent existence apart from the covenant of God with Israel.

Universality and Particularity in First-Century Judaism

Philo

Scholars tend to diverge on the extent and nature of Paul's Jewish identity.[26] In my view, identity is a better vehicle to discuss his relation to Judaism and Hellenism, rather than try to estimate the extent of the precise cultural influence in either direction.[27] In this respect a comparison with Philo has often been used to portray Paul as deeply immersed in Hellenistic values. Alongside this there emerges a tendency to view both Paul's and Philo's universalism as "a spirituality which transcends national specifics at the cost of particular traditions."[28] However, recent research on Philo has not demonstrated conclusively that this previous claim can be substantiated. In fact, Philo himself would probably reject such an interpretation.[29] John Barclay concluded that Philo represents an example of "medium assimilation," someone who was thoroughly integrated into the surrounding culture without sacrificing his link with the Jewish community, a good example of cultural convergence.[30] Whilst it cannot be demonstrated that Philo practiced negative self-definition in relation to the other who is different, it can be claimed, at least in respect of Jewish worship, that although he did not draw boundary lines and separate from the dominant culture of Greco-Roman Hellenism, he did use positive self-definition in terms of excelling the surrounding culture. Thus, in his attempt to explain Judaism against the background of Greek philosophy, Philo viewed Jewish traditions as relevant for the entire world and Jewish ethics as of particular excellence.[31] Indeed, Israel is presented by Philo as the destiny of the whole of mankind in the service of the one God, offering a priestly service in the place of the nations

26. For a similar discussion in Historical Jesus research see Ehrensperger, "Current Trends in Historical Jesus Research."

27. Cf. Leonhardt-Balzer, "Jewish Worship and Universal Identity," 31.

28 On Philo see Leonhardt-Balzer, "Jewish Worship and Universal Identity," 34. This same tendency, also apparent in many interpretations of Paul, Hock rightly traces back to F. C. Baur (*The Social Context of Paul's Ministry,* 12) who held that "the reason for Paul's importance is that he was responsible for the doctrine of universalism, the offering of salvation to Jew and Gentile alike that allowed Christianity to break loose from the particularism of Judaism and to become a new and independent religion."

29. Cf. *Migr.* 89f. Leonhardt-Balzer, "Jewish Worship and Universal Identity," 40, and Barclay, *Jews in the Mediterranean Diaspora,* 89–93.

30. Barclay, *Jews in the Mediterranean Diaspora,* 113–17, 173, and 176–80.

31. Cf. Tomson's claim (*Paul and the Jewish Law,* 43) that "Halakha organizes and structures life into Jewish life. Structuring Philo's life, it stamped his Hellenistic philosophy as being Jewish." Cf. also ibid., 45. Similarly Dawson, *Allegorical Readers,* 74.

who do not know this God. By virtue of Moses' unique prophetic insight into the working of the divine Logos, the Jewish Torah corresponds to the universal cosmic order, it is the legislation for the whole world.[32] "For Philo, the question of identity is not so much a matter of distinguishing between 'them' and 'us', but one of integrating the whole intellectual and cultural universe within the Jewish traditions and conversely of giving Judaism its proper place—at the top—in the Hellenistic culture of his time."[33]

Philo and Paul: Commonality and Difference

From the above, several conclusions can be drawn: for Paul as for Philo, universality and particularity need not imply absolute opposition since these are for both not mutually exclusive. It is also to be noted that although Paul is very similar to Philo in some of the respects noted above, the extent to which he sees God as God both of Jews and gentiles and himself as apostle to the gentiles raises the question as to whether Paul's understanding of God is truly representative of Judaism after his call by Christ. Does his subsequent conviction, now substantially refashioned, not represent an entirely fresh understanding of the God of Israel? This may not necessarily be the case. We must distinguish what was already implicit or known by Jews prior to the Christ-event, and what only became clear in and through the action of God in Christ. From Paul's perspective as a Christ-follower, he can argue that the activity of the gentile mission is part of the purposes of God already discernible in the Scriptures. Like Luke, he can see the hand of God in the birth and expansion of the church (cf. Acts 3:17–26).

But in my view what distinguishes Philo from Paul is that in Philo's conception of Israel there is still a destiny to be realized, whereas in Paul something of God's purpose has already been actualized or set in motion in the work of God in Christ. This had specific relevance for the status and hope of gentiles, so that instead of finding a destiny as Jewish proselytes or as gentiles receiving a supplementary status derivative from Israel, they now can become co-heirs with Jewish Christ-followers without the requirement of the law. Through the commission of Paul and other apostles they have a mission and a destiny of their own. But it is questionable whether even this fully represents Paul's perspective. He fought continuously for the rights of gentiles, for their unique status as sons and heirs, but this is always in conjunction with their association with Christ-following Jews. Thus even after the Christ event and the changes it brought into play, gentiles do not in

32. Cf. Leonhardt-Balzer," Jewish Worship and Universal Identity," 33–35 and 39.
33. Cf. ibid., 53.

Paul's view enjoy an independent salvation in which a mission to Jews may or may not have relevance. Freedom for gentiles from Israel's law does not for Paul mean freedom from association with Israel and the divine purpose, because the latter involves both Jews and gentiles, but not one without the other.[34] Thus Paul is at loggerheads with those Christ-believing Jews who do not acknowledge that gentiles in Christ are sons of God without becoming Jews. But he likewise also opposes, and this has not been sufficiently realized, those gentile Christ-followers who no longer see any reason to relate in any fashion to Jews, as Rom 11:13–25 demonstrates.

Thus Paul, in the end, though differing from Philo in respect of gentiles, nevertheless shares the perspective that Israel is the hope for the whole of humankind,[35] and this entity as a whole benefits from the destiny of Israel, and (in my view) *only* in association with Israel.

Similarly, a parallel with Paul can be found in the recognition that Philo's concept of universal spirituality does not mean a transcending of national specifics such as, for example, the significance of the Temple and Jewish worship in accordance with the Torah. The apostle is able to contemplate a "spiritual circumcision" but this need not imply that he opposes circumcision for the sons of Jews. Nor does the recognition of believers as shrines of the Spirit necessarily imply that for Paul they represent a replacement of the Jerusalem Temple just as a law written on the heart does not require a termination of the Torah and its requirements.

Having considered Paul's perspective on the universal and the particular alongside that of Philo, it is clear that despite their distinctiveness, they do have some significant elements in common. Most of all, the particularity that results from Israel's special role in the divine economy is not seen as causing contradiction or anomaly in their vision for the gentiles. Nor does commonality in teaching across the churches, inspired by Paul's universal vision, actually result in a decontextualizing of his thought. He can be *both* universal in perspective *and* contextualized in detail in relation to any one of his gentile communities. This in itself should help to convince us that the perceived dichotomy between the universal and the particular is, as J. Munck stressed, a modern invention. "The opposition between particularism and universalism is the product of a modern cosmopolitan outlook, and has nothing to do with the biblical conception of the mission"[36] (to the gentiles). Munck is clear that both the primitive church and Paul were

---

34. Cf. Fowl, "Learning to Be a Gentile," 41–57, *contra* Magda, *Paul's Territoriality and Mission Strategy*, 187–92.

35. Cf. Wagner, *Herald of the Good News*, 381.

36. Munck, *Paul and the Salvation of Mankind*, 71. Munck is citing B. Sundkler.

universalistic, as was Jesus, but the later Catholic Church lost that universalism because it no longer divided the human race into Israel and the gentiles, but turned instead to the gentiles.

The Contextuality of Paul's Universal Mission— Recognizing the Limits

It is clear from 2 Cor 10 that Paul is aware of and fully acknowledges that there are limits to one's missionary activity. Plummer translates verse 15b, "we are not straining to exceed the limits of our province" (κανόνα).[37] Paul has claimed earlier that we will not exceed our legitimate limits, "but will keep within the limits of that sphere which God has assigned to us as a limit, and which certainly meant that we should extend our labours so as to include you" (v. 13). The sphere or length (κανών) that God apportioned Paul extends to and includes the area of Corinth.[38] Paul is clear that he has been commissioned to come as far west as Corinth; indeed he was the first to proclaim the gospel in Corinth (v. 14). He is not invading nor would he ever trespass on the (geographical) territory of another,[39] taking glory for what others have done, since it is his policy not to build on another's foundation (vv. 13–15, cf. Rom 15).

In the instance of Rom 15, where Paul acknowledges that he did not found the Christ-movement there, it may be surmised that the early date of Christianity's arrival in Rome may indicate a Jewish and most likely a Jerusalem connection. This would explain Paul's hesitancy and concern about being seen as interfering in the foundation of others (15:13–16), especially if Rome were known to be associated with the Petrine mission.[40] Paul's rationale or explanation is that the Romans are within the sphere of his gentile mission and also that he needs them for a planned mission to

37. Cf. Plummer, *2 Corinthians*, 287. Plummer refers to Lightfoot on Gal 6:16, the only other place in the NT where this word occurs. Interestingly there also the meaning has reference to committing oneself (and thus limiting oneself) to a particular pattern or rule of life. Cf. διατάσσομαι as used by Paul to describe how he rules about certain things in every church (1 Cor 7:17). Cf. also Gal 6:15 in relation to this—is this text another way of saying in differing words that Paul has specific universal rules that apply for all the churches? Interestingly, Furnish (*2 Corinthians*, 471–72) uses the English term "jurisdiction" to translate κανών since it carries both the idea of legitimate authority as well as the area over which authority is exercised.

38. Cf. Plummer, *2 Corinthians*, 285–87.

39. I was unable to deal with the issue of ethnic as opposed to geographical limits, cf. my *Paul's Gospel in an Intercultural Context*, 104–6.

40. See my article, "The Addressees of Paul's Letter to the Romans" (chapter 8 in this volume).

Spain, in order to complete a circle to the West and return again to Jerusalem (cf. κύκλῳ, Rom 15:19). But in the case of Corinth, it is not Paul who is interfering, but his opponents. There is, however, a parallel with Rome in that Paul wishes to use Corinth also as a base for expansion westwards to Rome.[41] Here we pause to ask whether Paul is claiming that his opponents at Corinth are interfering since they were not the first to preach here, or because they have no right at all to preach in the gentile mission where he is the commissioned leader. Is it a dispute concerning the allocation of territory within the sphere of the gentile mission, or is it rather a dispute concerning interference from outsiders from the Petrine mission? The answer depends on whether τὸ μέτρον τοῦ κανόνος οὗ ἐμέρισεν ἡμῖν ὁ θεὸς μέτρου is taken to refer only to Paul's territorial area within the gentile mission, or to the larger domain of the mission to the gentiles as a whole (as distinct from that to the circumcision).[42] Sumney rightly stresses that though these people claim to be and are of Jewish descent, there is no indication that they are Judaizers, advocating law-keeping for gentile Christ-followers, or that the letters they carry are evidence of a connection with Jerusalem.[43] On this basis, it appears that they have arrived in Corinth, and caused trouble for Paul by their emphasis on pneumatic status, particularly strong personality, powerful speech, and other characteristics likely to appeal to gentiles influenced by certain Greco-Roman images of important teachers. Paul's refusal to accept pay is viewed as unacceptable for a real apostle and likewise his weak appearance. Paul does debate the qualifications of a legitimate apostle,[44] but his basic stance is that as founder of the church at Corinth he occupies an indisputable status and jurisdiction and that these newcomers, despite their grand airs, are interfering in his God-given apostolate and mission field.

It is interesting to compare Paul's response to these opponents with his previous reaction to Apollos, which by comparison was quite gentle. Does the difference originate in the fact that Apollos did not attack Paul personally or seek deliberately to undermine his apostolic status? Apollos is referred to as our brother Apollos (1 Cor 16:12) and thus in an inclusive reference, which implies that despite whatever factions may have developed around him, he was still perceived as a fellow worker alongside of Paul. Apollos also is of Jewish origin like the interlopers of 2 Cor 10–13, but there must be a

41. See Martin, *2 Corinthians*, 322.

42. See Sumney, *Identifying Paul's Opponents*, 151; Barrett, *2 Corinthians*, 262; Furnish, *2 Corinthians*, 481.

43. Cf. Sumney, *Identifying Paul's Opponents*, 177 and 184. Cf. also his *"Servants of Satan,"* 78–133.

44. Cf. Ehrensperger, *Paul and the Dynamics of Power*, 102–4 and 114–16.

substantial difference between him and these, which can only be accounted for by the behavior of Paul's opponents and their deliberate intention to attack Paul in every way possible, rather than by their Jewish origin, which is shared. What we need to clarify is whether they are also attacked by Paul for interference in his mission field without acknowledging his priority as apostle to the gentiles and as founder of the church there. Or is the issue that as Jewish "apostles" they have no right to interfere in Paul's churches of the gentiles? It is virtually impossible to determine this with any degree of certainty. Thus all we are left with here is the fact that Paul claims that Corinth is part of his gentile mission area, and that he has priority there since he is the founder. It is possible that Paul implies that even as apostle to the gentiles he has agreed certain areas in which he will work leaving the rest to others (see Acts 15:36–41). Is this covered by his claim to go only where the gospel has until now not been preached, or was the territory of the gentile mission sub-divided into certain portions where differing apostles would continue to operate and exercise jurisdiction?

My conclusion on this issue is determined mainly by Paul's reference to God's apportioning to him and his associates a certain sphere of mission. As we have noted above, those things that are apportioned by God—whether *status* at the point of call to thus determine where one would remain as a Christ-follower or the *charismata* one is apportioned or, as here, the *sphere of mission*, whether to circumcision or uncircumcision—are all items of great import, life-determining in a grand sense. Such appear to carry more significance than a sub-division of work within the gentile mission would merit. Thus, although this dispute does not warrant a claim of competition between Peter and Paul, it does give evidence of the possible conflict arising from unwarranted interference from zealous workers.[45] The sovereignty of the divine call and commissioning in the end overrules human preference and plans.

Conclusion

The commonality and the universal scope to which we have drawn attention above are not lost in the particularity of daily life in the Pauline communities. In fact, the universal scope of Paul's gospel and mission imply both particularity and diversity in application, though not sameness. No dimension of life remains untouched by Paul's gospel but this does not mean that all are touched in the same way. Since Jews can remain Jews and gentiles continue as gentiles, the gospel affects both of these but not necessarily in identical fashion. This is because Paul re-evaluates both the states of circumcision and uncircumcision

45. Cf. Ehrensperger, *Paul and the Dynamics of Power*.

equally in that he regards *neither* as ultimately significant in comparison with being in Christ.[46] What is common is that both states of existence, whether as Jew or as gentile are re-evaluated. Yet continuing diversity is not thereby ruled out because Paul in this re-evaluation does not give preference to either state. This common treatment does not result in uniformity of lifestyle as would be the case if Paul had valued the state of uncircumcision above that of circumcision (still a tendency in much NT scholarship). In Christ both Jews and gentiles are transformed, yet their particularity and hence difference remains even after the process of transformation is in process. Thus "in Christ" does not represent an abstract universal designator but is a deeply contextualized description of one's present earthly identity. It functions as an identity trigger mechanism that interpenetrates existing identities and transforms aspects of those identities, though in differing ways for Jews as compared to gentiles.[47] This transformation takes place when apostles like Paul are imitated to the extent that they imitate Christ in their pattern of life. What Jews and gentiles share is being in Christ, even though they continue to be different in their practice of discipleship. Thus Paul, whilst he did have a concern that his gentile communities would learn Christ (cf. Eph 4:15), did not present to them such a blueprint for their development that he was actually trying to force them to copy him in everything. To some extent, even after he had done everything he could to ensure that they were imitating Christ after his example, he had to wait in hope to see how Christ would be formed in them and how this would be expressed in their daily life together. The context in which Paul had been called to work, the gifts that God through the Spirit apportioned to Christ-followers individually, and their starting point when they were first called, whether as Jews or as gentiles, would together combine to produce a work of God peculiar to Corinth or wherever else the gospel was proclaimed,[48] and in keeping with how God himself had determined.

Our discussion has sought to clarify that the universal scope of Paul's mission and his particular contextualization of the gospel throughout his mission field do not represent two contradictory tendencies in view of the fact that these were successfully coordinated in Paul's own vision and activity.

---

46. See my essay, "I Rate All Things as Loss" (chapter 11 in this volume), an address given at the University of Villanova as the Opening Lecture of the Celebration of the Jubilee Year of the Apostle Paul, September 2008.

47. See Tucker, *"You Belong to Christ,"* and also my "Gentile Identity and Transformation in Christ according to Paul."

48. As Meeks (*Christ is the Question,* 4–5) notes, "Whenever and wherever followers of Christ have spoken of incarnation, that has necessarily entailed an incarnation in culture—the culture of a particular time and place and set of social forms. How could it be otherwise?"

11

"I Rate All Things as Loss":
Paul's Puzzling Accounting System

Judaism as Loss or the Re-evaluation
of All Things in Christ?

Introduction

IN THIS ESSAY, I am seeking to answer three questions:[1] (1) how did Paul evaluate Judaism in relation to Christ? (2) how could he have one rule for all his churches? and (3) how are his statements related to our contemporary understanding of his theology? I will consider these issues in relation to three texts: 1 Cor 7:17–24, Gal 6:11–16, and Phil 3:3–8. A common feature of these texts is that in each of them Paul makes comparisons related to life in Christ. Because of his practice of comparing various items with one another, Paul has been very much misunderstood. By looking at these texts individually and then assessing our findings, I hope to be able to show that Paul's comparisons are a key to central themes of his theologizing. It is within this process that I will attempt to show how Paul's statements in his letters are related to our contemporary understanding of his theology.

The starting point for recent study of Paul's letters is to view the statements made by Paul as targeted to a specific audience at a particular time. The nuance here, and the contrast, are between the *general* and the

---

1. Since this contribution was first delivered as a public lecture, I have retained the original format but supplemented the argument in greater detail in the notes in relation to the ongoing scholarly discussion.

particular.[2] What we are arguing is this: although there is evidence, at a later time than that of Paul, of general letters being circulated to more than one church, Paul's policy was to address a specific church or group of churches with a document *specifically directed to them and to their particular local problems.*[3] Thus, the letters to the Corinthians address problems within that community of Christ-followers, though what Paul says there may indirectly have a wider reference to other places facing similar problems. So too with Galatians and Romans, even though the latter addresses a church Paul had not yet visited.[4]

Despite this, Paul shows he is quite well informed about what is going on in Rome, even though not all parts of this letter, as is the case also in Galatians, have equal application to issues in Rome. Some parts of Paul's letters only *indirectly* address local issues but serve a subsidiary function in that they are designed to support arguments that do directly address *local* issues. Though each individual section may not have "words on target," the contents of the letters as a whole do have local and particular implication and significance.

In this sense, therefore, Paul's letters are real letters that require a particular response on the part of those addressed. They are not simply theological treatises, though everyone agrees they contain marvellous theological concepts. They contain theology but they are not to be read simply as abstract theological statements, detached from the context they actually address. If they are read as general statements made to address all and every context, they are easily misunderstood and can, in this way, be grossly misinterpreted and even made to appear contradictory, as is the case, for example, when Paul forbids gentile Christ-followers in Gal 5:2 to accept circumcision but states elsewhere, in answer to a question, "Then what

2. A pioneering study in this regard is Jewett's *Paul's Anthropological Terms* in which he refuses to assume a standard meaning for each anthropological term throughout Paul's letters, but insists on the particularity of their use in differing contexts. For a classic instance of a discussion of this issue, see the debate between Karris and Donfried (Donfried [ed.], *The Romans Debate*, 65–84, 102–27) in their essays, "Romans 14:1—15:13 and the Occasion of Romans" and "False Presuppositions in the Study of Romans" respectively.

3. Since some scholars hold that Colossians is written by Paul, then the reference to having this letter read also to the Laodiceans may be an exception; but see Mustakallio, "The Very First Audiences of Paul's Letters," 236.

4. Hence my opposition to viewing the content of Romans as arising from Paul's own situation at the time of writing, or as a letter to Jerusalem or even as a circular letter. Despite having been written some years ago, an earlier essay of mine ("Why Did Paul Write Romans?" 14–24) offers strong arguments against such views. For a more recent discussion of this issue, see my essay "The Addressees of Paul's Letter to the Romans," 171–96 (chapter 8 in this volume).

advantage has the Jew? Or what is the value of circumcision?" "Much in every way" (for those who keep the law) (Rom 3:1–2).

But are we, by this claim, not greatly devaluing Paul's letters, which have been regarded as *addressing the whole church and as containing univer-sal truth* rather than advice for local congregations? Certainly not. We are recognizing more and more that, for Paul, the best way to do theology, to theologize, was to address local issues in the light of the gospel message of Jesus Christ, and thereby create theological statements, contextually rooted, but with the potential to be reinterpreted in other contexts and even applied to other issues in ever-changing circumstances. The letters of Paul are not to be considered as theology in and by themselves but as the raw material for creating theology for new situations and new issues in other contexts.[5]

But this still does not allow us to escape the problem that those let-ters we do have from Paul, however valuable and however treasured in the church, are still all addressed to *particular* churches in *local contexts*.[6] How then can Paul specifically speak, as he does in 1 Cor 7:17–24, that "this is my rule in all the churches?" How can an apostle who addresses specific churches concerning their particular local problems claim still to have a rule he applies to *all* the churches? This is the first problem we must seek to unravel by looking in more detail at the text of 1 Cor 7:17–24.

"Remain as you were when called": Reading 1 Corinthians 7:20 in Context

In a previous study of 1 Cor 7:19 ("circumcision is nothing, and uncircum-cision is nothing; but obeying the commandments of God is everything"), I argued that there is a strong element of comparison in this text, which func-tions to bring out the relative significance of the different items involved.[7] The crucial point of the verse is not a comparison of the relative merits of circumcision and uncircumcision, but a comparison of both with the call of God.[8] The text does not end with the statement, "circumcision is nothing

5. On this see my *Paul and the Creation of Christian Identity*, 159–73, and Roetzel's comment ("The Grammar of Election," 233) that "Paul did not begin with a developed theology that merely shifted its emphasis from place to place." The other volumes in this series also deal in differing ways with this same issue, see especially Beker, "Recasting Pauline Theology," 15–24.

6. As Fitzmyer (*Paul and His Theology*, 96) has noted, the beginnings of the use of the term "the church of God" in the wider sense, referring to the whole church, can possibly be glimpsed in 1 Cor 10:32 and 11:22.

7. *Campbell, Paul and the Creation of Christian Identity*, 91–93, 103.

8. As Fruchtenbaum ("A Danger of Throwing Out the Baby with the Bathwater,"

and uncircumcision is nothing." Thus, it is not a comparison between A and B, between circumcision and uncircumcision, but a comparison of A and B with C. Paul asserts, "for circumcision is nothing (οὐδέν) and uncircumcision is nothing but keeping the commandments of God." Gal 6:15 is similar in some respects, οὔτε γὰρ περιτομή τί ἐστιν οὔτε ἀκροβυστία ἀλλὰ καινὴ κτίσις ("for neither circumcision counts for anything, nor uncircumcision, but a new creation"). In Galatians, the focus of Paul also is not merely circumcision or its opposite, but rather a new creation perspective in which all of life is re-evaluated in the light of Christ. This rhetoric of comparison is also present in Phil 3:3–8 in a slightly different form, as we will argue later.

The reference to circumcision in 1 Cor 7:17–24 occurs in a chapter in which Paul continues to respond directly to issues that were causing tensions in the community in Corinth. Paul chooses to stress the life in Christ in terms of *calling*—the stem καλ- appears and reappears frequently in this section and throughout the letter.[9] In responding to the issue of whether a woman should divorce a husband who is not a follower of Christ, he stresses that believers are "called to peace" (7:15). Immediately after this emphasis, Paul lays down a policy to let everyone lead the life that the Lord has assigned (ἐμέρισεν) to each,[10] and in which God has called each (κέκληκεν), adding that ἐν ταῖς ἐκκλησίαις πάσαις διατάσσομαι ("this I rule in all the churches," 7:17). The repetition of the rule in verse 24 shows that Paul intended to stress this policy of remaining as one was when called; it also leaves no doubt that he intended people to remain as they were, even in Christ, at least in terms of their ethnicity.[11]

---

67) has asserted in relation to Paul's comparisons, "There is a danger of throwing out the baby with the bathwater. . . . Paul compares what he has in the Messiah to what he had in Judaism—what he declares rubbish. . . . But what he declares rubbish is only in comparison to what is so much greater—not that the thing itself is by nature."

9. See Roetzel, "Grammar of Election," 232–33. As will be noted later, I do not entirely agree that identity lies only in the call of God, as if this by itself could adequately describe the Christ-follower in historical and social context (see n.14 below).

10. See also the similar use of ἐμέρισεν in 2 Cor 10:13 and Rom 12:3 in relation to God's apportioning of *charismata* and determining geographical limits to mission respectively. See my "Universality and Particularity in Paul's Understanding and Strategy of Mission" (chapter 10 in this volume).

11. The issue of whether to remain a slave is complicated by the fact that Paul adds a qualification on this matter in 1 Cor 7:21. The RSV translates this verse, "Were you a slave when called? Never mind. But if you can gain your freedom, avail yourself of the opportunity." Problematic is whether the words μᾶλλον χρῆσαι (which we might translate, following Harrill, "do not worry") mean "do not worry about it" (that is, the reference is back to the state of being a slave when called) or "do not be concerned about" taking advantage of an opportunity for freedom, should it occur. The latter reading puts Paul on the side of favoring freedom should this become an option, whilst still

"I Rate All Things as Loss": Paul's Puzzling Accounting System

That remaining in the state of circumcision or uncircumcision means remaining as Jews or gentiles in Christ is clear once we acknowledge that Paul can claim Christ became a servant to the circumcision (Rom 15:8), meaning, of course, the Jews.[12] We must recognize therefore that the references to circumcision/uncircumcision are here not simply *to the act of circumcision,* but rather *to the state of being a circumcised or an uncircumcised person.*[13] Also, we should note that despite listing various topics such as splitting into factions around differing leaders, which were causing conflict among the Corinthians, and despite addressing these directly, Paul does not respond by simple *ad hoc* advice, but rather with context-related theological guidance. He situates all his advice—whether on marriage and celibacy, slavery and ethnic affiliation—within the framework of the divine calling,[14] obligation, and status, yet still emphasizes the abiding difference at the point of call. Surprisingly, Paul even has a theology about remaining in the state of circumcision or uncircumcision in which one was called, which gives coherence to his understanding of what might have been viewed in Corinth as unrelated issues. Nonetheless, these differing issues must not simply be submerged in some theological overview with the result that Paul's actual statements on each of these entities are submerged to such an extent that the

---

counseling those who remain slaves not to be anxious because slaves in Christ are God's freedmen (1 Cor 7:22). On this, see Harrill, *The Manumission of Slaves,* 118–27. Yet, this leveling in Christ of the status of slave and free does not contradict Paul's general thesis, "remain as you were when called." Also, the qualification only applies to slavery, not to the states of circumcision/uncircumcision, etc. See the excellent treatment of 1 Cor 7:21 in Byron, *Recent Research on Slavery,* 92–115.

12. See Schaller, "Christus, 'der Diener der Beschneidung,'" 261–85.

13. As Martin ("Apostasy to Paganism," 85) has noted, the verb περιτέμνω and the noun περιτομή "refer either to an act, a state, or a practice." As an act circumcision relates to the physical operation itself. Following this surgery, a person then lives in a state of circumcision. But . . . circumcised persons . . . must still decide if they will practice the distinctions associated with the covenant of circumcision."

14. Bartchy (ΜΑΛΛΟΝ ΧΡΗΣΑΙ: *First Century Slavery,* 152 and 132–36) noted that Paul uses some variant of the word "call" (καλέω) no less than nine times in eight verses in 1 Cor 7:17–24, thus setting the entire discussion within that framework. Harrill (*Manumission,* 101) criticized Bartchy for maintaining that slaves had no opportunity to accept or refuse manumission and for making "calling" generally Paul's basic theme here. But Bartchy rightly perceived that Paul was no advocate of slavery, arguing that he did not want any enslaved Christ-followers to think that their legal-social status could negatively influence their status in Christ—"it is a question of their primary identity. Being 'in Christ' trumps all other identifiers." (This citation is from a paper read by Bartchy at the SBL Annual Meeting in Boston, Nov 21–25, 2008, entitled, "Paul Did Not Teach 'Stay in Slavery': The Mistranslation of κλῆσις in 1 Corinthians 7:20–21.")

issues become mere exemplars—losing all individual significance as specific exhortation on how to live.[15]

In an earlier paper, I have argued that the reference to circumcision here does not quite fit with the Stoic concept of "indifferent things."[16] Obviously, if Paul's arguments are to have real force in the Greco-Roman world of first-century Corinth, where the influence of Stoic philosophical values was widespread, he must take these into account when he is teaching in that context. Thus, it may be important to consider the parallels between Paul and Stoic philosophers, especially in relation to such items as life and death, marriage, or slavery. Commonly, such a comparison leads to the conclusion that Paul, who has found a new value system in Christ, like the Stoics, considered some things he formerly valued now unimportant; they are not priorities but "indifferents," that is, matters of indifference.[17] It is quite likely that Paul was somewhat influenced by common Stoic ideas current in his time; but in one respect at least, this particular valuing of aspects of human life as indifferents does not facilitate a coherent understanding of the apostle. As we have seen from 1 Cor 7, there are certain aspects of life that for Paul surely cannot be termed "indifferents": he gives his converts a ruling that they must hold on to the state in which they were called.

What we are in the process of demonstrating here is that the concept of indifference to life, of a certain detachment from life, is not really typical of Pauline ethics and theology. Paul is, on the contrary, deeply involved in human issues—whether he stands for something or against it, it is not really good Pauline theology to view him as *indifferent* to life choices.[18]

As just mentioned, one of the choices where Paul is clearly not indifferent is in his opinion that those who became followers of Christ had to remain as they were when called. Of course, they had found a new faith in Christ that provided them with a new self-understanding, on the way to a transformed

---

15. I see this danger in Thiselton's treatment of 1 Cor 7, in which there seems to be a certain lack of clarity in relation to remaining in a circumcised/uncircumcised state. After a good discussion of 1 Cor 7:17–24, he surprisingly asserts (*1 Corinthians,* 551), "The new creation . . . in the terminology of Pauline studies affirms an eschatological status on the basis of which issues of circumcision and 'Jewishness' have become obsolete." If one inserts marriage or celibacy in place of these, the minimizing of the situational aspect of Paul, and its replacement by theological generalization, become clear. See also my *Paul and the Creation of Christian Identity,* 88–93.

16. "'As Having and as Not Having': Paul, Circumcision and Indifferent Things in 1 Corinthians 7:17–32," a short paper read at the Annual Meeting of the SNTS, University of Aberdeen, 2006, revised for another lecture in 2007 (chapter 6 in this volume).

17. See Deming, "Paul and Indifferent Things," 384–403.

18. See Käsemann, *Commentary on Romans,* 375–76 (on Rom 14:13).

identity.[19] But their way of life was not changed completely, however much they were being transformed. This observation applies to all those in Christ, as Paul states: καὶ οὕτως ἐν ταῖς ἐκκλησίαις πάσαις διατάσσομαι (1 Cor 7:17). Most surprisingly, circumcision is also included in the list of things in which converts are called to remain as they were. It might have been beneficial for a Corinthian church member to hide the marks of his circumcision so as to appear more in keeping with the rest of gentile society and, thus, to become more upwardly mobile. But for Paul, even circumcision is by no means an indifferent thing, hence his ruling about remaining in it. Nor is this rule concerning circumcision/uncircumcision, in the Pauline communities, an option that may or may not be followed on the basis of social or political context, as Paul's argument in Galatians makes clear.[20]

Circumcision and Glorying in the Flesh (Gal 6:11–16)

Unlike 1 Corinthians, where circumcision was mentioned only briefly, in Galatians it is actually a central focus of the letter and, thus, must have been a significant issue among the Galatian churches. In whatever form we attempt the reconstruction of the *Sitz im Leben* of this letter, the issue of circumcision for gentiles remains central. Paul's response is a definite rebuttal of any attempt to impose circumcision, with or without the concomitant observation of the law, upon gentile Christ-followers, "if you receive circumcision," Χριστὸς ὑμᾶς οὐδὲν ὠφελήσει ("Christ will be of no advantage to you") (Gal 5:2; see Rom 3:2).[21]

Paul's own handwritten conclusion in Gal 6:11–18, however, gives a reason for this complete rejection of circumcision for gentile Christ-followers. Here he states the motive that causes some to advocate compulsory circumcision of Christ-followers: "so that they may glory in your flesh" (6:13). Paul responds by emphasizing that his only ground of boasting is "in the cross of our Lord Jesus Christ by which the world has been crucified to me, and I to the world" (6:14). Then he defines what I consider to be his summary hermeneutic in relation to circumcision: "For neither circumcision counts for anything nor uncircumcision, but a new creation" (6:15). The first part of this

---

19. Yet this identity is in some continuity with their former lives; see my *Paul and the Creation of Christian Identity*, especially chapter 6 (86–103), and also my "Gentile Identity and Transformation according to Paul," 23–56.

20. See Runesson, "Inventing Christian Identity," 81. On this see also Fredriksen, "Judaism, the Circumcision of Gentiles, and Apocalyptic Hope," 235–60.

21. As I note below, Paul's discussion here as in Phil 3 is framed in terms of profit and loss.

verse is similar to what Paul has already said in his comparative statement in 1 Cor 7:19, but with a different application to the context.[22]

We note here some important features of Paul's response to the Galatians. In rejecting circumcision for gentiles, he asserts that what is of *primary* importance is not circumcision or uncircumcision but a new creation; this is in contrast to 1 Cor 7, where he asserts the same principle but with a different conclusion: not "a new creation," but instead "keeping the commandments of God" (v. 19). The different emphasis here may be geared particularly to the needs of Christ-followers in Corinth, some of whom may have held the belief that the resurrection had coincided with their conversion so that, for example, they no longer needed to marry or give in marriage because they were already supposedly living in the world to come, that is, in the new creation. So Paul adds a different conclusion to his statement about circumcision/uncircumcision in 1 Corinthians—what matters for them is not, as in Galatians, new creation but instead "keeping the commandments of God" as the way to life.

It would appear that Paul, in both Corinthians and Galatians, is seeking to put things into proper perspective, circumcision included. Thus, he also rejects "glorying in the flesh" in Gal 6:13. His stated reason for this is, as noted, "the cross of Christ" (6:12), from which he develops his understanding of both circumcision and uncircumcision. He is then able to introduce a general hermeneutical principle: "neither circumcision counts for anything nor uncircumcision" but "keeping the commandments of God" (as in Corinthians) or "a new creation" (as in Galatians). Here again we have in Gal 6, as in 1 Cor 7, an element of comparison or evaluation, which leads to the view that in a hierarchy of values, fleshly attributes—be the flesh Jewish or gentile—are not cause for boasting *when compared with* the glory of Christ on the cross. It seems also that Paul, whilst taking human flesh as his starting point, with "flesh" is actually talking metaphorically about spiritual entities, because he speaks of the "kosmos" being crucified as well as himself.[23] Paul's argument thus develops as follows. Circumcision is rejected for gentiles because boasting in one's flesh is the motive behind the call for circumcision, rather than boasting in the cross of Christ. The cross means

22 I am broadly in agreement with Nanos's argument ("What Was at Stake in Peter's 'Eating with Gentiles' at Antioch?" 300–303) that what was at stake in the Galatian controversy was essentially the equality of gentiles as equal members of Christ apart from proselyte conversion.

23. My view is that Paul's understanding of flesh as a power possibly developed from opposition to a demand for the circumcision of gentile Christ-followers, which contradicted and, thus, perverted its original covenantal significance; see further Dunn, *The Theology of Paul*, 62–73; also Jewett, *Paul's Anthropological Terms*.

the crucifixion and, therefore, death of all confidence in flesh of whatever origin. Thus, circumcision and uncircumcision are both ultimately repositioned in comparison with the value system demanded by the cross by which the whole world is re-evaluated. It is not surprising, if we follow Paul's argument carefully, that uncircumcision, the very state for which he argues so fiercely throughout Galatians, is nevertheless also re-evaluated alongside circumcision so that the focus does not abide either on Jewish or gentile existence, but on living a transformed life in Christ.

In light of these findings, we now proceed to look afresh at Phil 3:3–8 to compare Paul's teaching in differing contexts. This passage is all the more significant since, as E. P. Sanders points out, in this text (Phil 3:3–11), as in 2 Cor 3:4–18, "Paul directly compares, in an evaluative way, the old dispensation and the new."[24] The context of Phil 3 evokes commercial metaphors, hence my rendering of 3:8 as "I rate all things as loss because of the surpassing worth of knowing Christ Jesus my Lord."[25]

So, here we have three texts—1 Cor 7:19, Gal 6:16, and Phil 3:2–4—in three letters written to diverse communities, all of which feature circumcision/Jewishness to varying degrees in comparative (rather than oppositional or contrastive) contexts. I hope that a careful thematic look at what the texts say or leave unsaid will uncover, if possible, a more nuanced way of understanding Paul's views—not just of circumcision/Jewishness but, even more importantly, of the whole of life from the perspective of being in Christ.[26] In other words, what was the standard or hermeneutic by which he valued all things, whether in Judaism or in the gentile world?

24. E. P. Sanders, *Paul, the Law and the Jewish People*, 137. Sanders views this as possibly resulting from conflicting convictions in Paul, which he, at this juncture, does not try to reconcile. He (ibid., 138) also notes that Paul goes on to draw a contrast not only between the dispensations of life and death but also between "degrees of whiteness: what was glorious and what is more glorious." *Contra* Sanders, this is not a contrast between the old dispensation and the new in the sense of Judaism and Christianity, but a total contrast, which of course includes the gentile world as well. Thus, what Paul says is not to be taken simply as a critique of Judaism from the perspective of being in Christ, but as a critique of *the whole world and its life* outside of, and in comparison with, Christ.

25. See the New Jerusalem Bible's translation of verses 7–8a, "but what were once my assets I now through Christ Jesus count as losses. Yes, I will go further: because of the supreme advantage of knowing Christ Jesus my Lord, I count everything else as loss."

26. See my criticism of Thiselton in n.15 above. See also Fredriksen, "Paul, Purity, and the *Ekklesia* of the Gentiles," 215 n.24. Fredriksen notes the irony of Barclay's article in Dunn's edited volume (*Paul and the Mosaic Law*, 287–308), which, though citing as its title Rom 3:31, "Do We Undermine the Law?" comes to an affirmative conclusion, in contrast to Paul.

"I rate all things as loss": Philippians 3:8

What about Phil 3? I am not entirely convinced as to the integrity of Philippians as we now have it. Nevertheless, I am convinced by recent research that maintains Phil 3 emanates from Paul himself.[27] In my view, the content of chapter 3 certainly confirms this.

It is not surprising to students of Paul that the whole of the apostle's previous life must be judged and reassessed in light of the coming of Christ. This is especially true if Phil 3 was written towards the end of Paul's life and possibly in prison as he anticipated imminent death.[28] Whatever Paul's circumstances may have been at that time, I am quite clear that his "rating or reckoning of all things as loss" (3:8) is not simply an expression of resignation of a man at the point of death for whom the whole of life more or less has passed. Even if he was in prison, he would not yet have "suffered the loss of all things"; hence, we are dealing here with a principle that relates to all of Paul's life, not just to the end of it, or to his imprisonment.

The verb used here (ἡγέομαι) functions, as Jerry Sumney notes, "to show that Paul had adopted this new perspective with which he re-evaluates all the previously listed privileges in the past."[29] As Sumney further points out, this re-evaluation of all things in Christ is not a past event but an ongoing principle of the life in Christ, and "this continues to be the way he views them" (i.e., all things). What is at issue here is not simply Paul's reiteration of the outcome of his Damascus road experience, however much of a revision of perspective or of pattern of life that must have been. If that were the case, it would explain why Paul goes on to list his superior status in terms of Jewish ancestry and upbringing (3:3–6). We could then think of Paul's "rating all things as loss" as a clear indication that points to a former life as a Jew, albeit in terms of a revision, in his estimate, of that life rather than an abandonment.[30] This assessment might indeed have proven valuable for the community at Philippi who would thus have been reminded of Paul's Jewish past and his subsequent call to be apostle to the gentiles. But if most of the Philippians were of gentile

27. See Standhartinger, "'Join in imitating me' (Philippians 3:17): Towards an Interpretation of Philippians 3," 417–35. Standhartinger has outlined the issues clearly in this article, which I found convincing. She is quite clear, despite positing a varied history of sections of the letter, that chapter 3 is Pauline.

28. See Standhartinger ("Join in imitating me," 427), "the belligerent or desperate tone of 3:2–4 and 3:18–19 would at least indicate great distress."

29. See Sumney, *Philippians,* 77.

30. As Donaldson (*Paul and the Gentiles,* 27) asserts, this new estimation about Jesus resulting from God "revealing His Son to (in) me," means undoubtedly "a revision, but by no means necessarily an abandonment, of Paul's earlier Israel-centered frame of reference."

origin, of what actual relevance would it have been to these gentile Christ-followers to be told that Paul continues to view his Jewish upbringing and values as worthless compared to being in Christ?

However, Phil 3:8 indicates that Paul has re-evaluated not just Jewish privilege but *all* things and found them to be ζημίαν, loss (again probably a commercial metaphor).[31] The present tense of the verb ("ἡγοῦμαι") points to the fact that this is a continuing process of evaluation, not limited to his previous life in Judaism (see Gal 1:13). Thus, as Paul makes clear, it is not just Jewish privileges that are re-evaluated but everything else in life, even in his life after his Damascus road experience. Here the issue certainly includes the rating or evaluation of Jewish life and lineage. Paul asserts, "Whatever gain I had, I counted as loss for the sake of Christ" (3:7), and continues, "Indeed I count everything as loss because of the surpassing worth of knowing Christ Jesus my Lord" (3:8). Yet again, what is re-evaluated is not limited to Jewish factors, but as in 1 Cor 7 widened to include everything, both what is Jewish and also all that is gentile. Still, the question arises as to why Paul, in Philippians, refers specifically to these Jewish values if he does not intend to demonstrate animosity toward his ancestral faith. He does claim, in Rom 3, the advantage of the Jew and the value of circumcision (3:1–2).[32] Yet the passage in Philippians is basically developed around the thesis that even those things that are most highly beneficial lose their value or worth *in comparison with* the new value system that operates in Christ.

The topic under debate is, thus, the things that are of prime importance in Christ. The things Paul lists (Phil 3:3–6) are those regarded as honorable, valuable, or at least profitable—the cherished things that might compete with loyalty to Christ; they are not in outright opposition to "in Christ" values (which, as such, ought to be given up in any case). The comparison is, as Sanders noted, "between degrees of whiteness."[33] These are the most significant things that Paul valued highly, perhaps even treasured. However, if the time of valuing these things is now past, and if they represent only a catalogue of things Paul *formerly* valued, then the comparison is very much weakened. If becoming a Christ-follower requires the obliteration of previ-

31. See Bockmuehl's comment (*The Epistle to the Philippians*, 205), "It is also instructive to note that in rabbinic Judaism the terminology of profit (*sakhar*) and loss (*hephsed*) could be applied to the observant Jewish life: one should balance the loss incurred by observing a commandment against the superior profit it entails . . ." There appears to be a parallel already in Paul in that he uses similar categories in evaluating Jewish practice, which suggests that he still viewed himself as an "insider" rather than as an "outsider" now judging Judaism.

32. As clearly demonstrated by Fitzmyer, *Romans*, 326–31.

33. See n.24.

ous "worlds"[34] and the relinquishment of previous identities, then the things formerly treasured can have no *comparative* value—they have already lost their value entirely. However, the verb used in verse 8 ("rate/count") is in the *present tense*.[35] Paul is not just reiterating things in the past that were beneficial and that he used to value in the days prior to being in Christ. Rather, they are still being valued/re-evaluated by him, but from a new perspective and, thus, cannot possibly have been obliterated; this factor actually strengthens the comparison. If there possibly was pressure on the Philippians, from whatever source, to take on Jewish patterns of life, Paul's prayer and goal for them is that they take as their ultimate value the "superlative worth of knowing Christ" (3:8).

Thus, one possible explanation of Paul's list of profitable and treasured items can be ruled out: that he now discarded them because, in the new accounting, these are no longer regarded as assets. Paul's utter devotion to Christ, as expressed here, could be, and certainly was, interpreted as promoting asceticism.[36] However, although Paul repositions these treasured values in the light of Christ, in his perspective, they certainly retained some value, as is very clear when one takes into account his emphasis, in all the churches, on "remaining as you were when called." If one does not accept this conclusion, one would have to ask what kind of existence a person leads who remains in a state with absolutely no value? In this sense, Paul is by no means counter-cultural, nor dismissive of his Jewish heritage. His theology is indicative of this approach: it is one of transformation rather than obliteration, and of new creation in the sense of transforming the old.

Consequently, we must note that the list is not so much concerned with things to give up or retain, that is, with the value of circumcision as compared with uncircumcision and vice versa, but rather with the ultimate priority of the listed items, and the question as to where in the list living Jewishly or as a gentile should be positioned. If it was already widely known that Paul had turned his back on Jewish life and practice, for whatever

34. In contrast, Gaventa (*Our Mother St Paul*, 68) maintains in relation to Gal 3:28: "The only location for those grasped by the gospel is 'in Christ'; as the gospel's arrival *obliterates* the law, it also *obliterates* those other 'places' with which people identify themselves, even the most fundamental places of ethnicity, economic-social standing and gender."

35. The verb here, ἡγοῦμαι, is first person singular present indicative. In association with the infinitive εἶναι, it does not merely indicate Paul re-evaluated his Jewish heritage on first adopting the new perspective of being in Christ (indicated in verse 7 by the use of the perfect tense ἥγημαι); rather, it shows that he now continues to re-evaluate everything from that perspective; see Sumney, *Philippians*, 76–78.

36. For a good discussion, see the chapter, "The Model Ascetic," in Roetzel, *Paul: The Man and the Myth*, 135–51.

reasons, then, by using his former life in Judaism as a negative foil for the new life in Christ, Paul could rightly have been seen as pro-gentile (and, at least implicitly, as anti-Jewish). Also, there would then seem to be no good reason for his addressing such matters in gentile assemblies, other than a prejudiced attitude, and for his continuing to include Jewish elements in his comparisons in such a context. It is hard to see specifically how this practice might have benefited gentile Christ-followers, but just as easy to imagine the negative effects it might have had on his attempts to give his converts a positive understanding of the Jewish roots of the faith.

Re-evaluating All Things in Christ:
The Rhetoric of Pauline Comparisons

In my opinion, the above observations suggest a different explanation of Pauline comparisons. Specifically, Paul was still continuing to practice his Jewish way of life, even as a missionary to the gentiles (with whatever legitimate adjustments this might require). If there was pressure, as it appears in at least some of Paul's letters, for his gentile converts to begin to live like Jews and to possibly proceed to full proselyte status, something entirely unacceptable to Paul, then his own practice of Judaism could have become a lever in the arguments of his opponents: Paul, the founder, and others of these communities did not live like gentiles but as Jews.

That this was the case is, in my view, beyond doubt. How could Paul as a teacher requiring real credibility teach his converts to remain as they were when called, if he himself, though called as a Jew, then renounced Judaism and lived, to all intents and purposes, as a gentile? The fact that Paul, as apostle to gentiles, still lived as a Jew could then be used as a powerful lever in any attempt to force gentiles in Christ to become Jews.[37]

Such a scenario would give a good explanation as to why Paul, in Philippians, chose to compare life in Christ with his previous life as a Jew. It can be argued that Paul's listing of his own treasured values as a Jew is not just incidental, but deliberately chosen for contextual relevance and effect and to defeat the aims of opponents.[38] The point of Paul's rhetoric here is not to

37. Although we do not have space to deal with this interesting and important issue here, it is relevant to note that if, at the time of his call, Paul was unmarried or widowed, according to his own logic, he should have remained thus. See Murphy-O'Connor, *Paul His Story*, 15, and (in more detail) by the same author, *Paul: A Critical Life*, 62–65; see also Roetzel, *Man and Myth*, 149–51.

38. But if the status, nature, and even the existence of such opponents are not really clear, then it does not make good sense for Paul to devalue his Jewish heritage to gentile Christ-followers who perhaps were not at all tempted to become Jews; see Sumney,

offer a simplistic comparison of Judaism and Christianity via the medium of his own life and experience. However, it must be recognized and explained why the issues used in the comparison in all our three texts (1 Cor 7:17–24; Gal 6:11–16; Phil 3:3–8) include elements relating to Paul's life as a Jew, as, for example, circumcision (1 Cor 7:18–19; Gal 6:12–15; Phil 3:3–5), "glory-ing in the flesh" (Gal 6:13), and "confidence in the flesh" (Phil 3:3–8). The latter text also includes a list of credits (beginning with circumcision) that would make most Jews proud.[39]

Yet, it is significant that in 1 Cor 7 (and in the rest of this letter),[40] there is no strong emphasis on Jewish attributes. The references to circumcision occur as part of a broader theme, which is, "leading the life in which one was called by God," a rule that Paul applies in all his churches (1 Cor 7:17).[41] Galatians differs somewhat in that there is, to a certain extent, a focus on the act or practice of circumcision,[42] which is set under the motif of liv-ing by the Spirit or by the flesh (3:1–2). But at the end of the letter (as we

---

Servants of Satan, 316–22. It is quite possible that the reference to evil workers in asso-ciation with prophetic rivalry between Elijah and the false prophets (1 Kgs 18:22–40) is echoed in Paul's choice of language against certain opponents who may have been Cyn-ics (κύων; ὁ κυνικός) as suggested by Philo and later also by Clement of Alexandria. In any case, it would be most atypical of Paul to draw a parallel between circumcision, ἡ περιτομή, as a revered covenantal requirement and part of his treasured heritage, and the mutilation, ἡ κατατομή, as is done in Phil 3:2–3. Instead, Paul plays on the shared lexical element of being cut (τομή) to emphasize the *contrasting identities* of false prophets and genuine prophets such as Elijah and himself. "These two ways of being in the world are as different as day and night, (males) being cut around (περι-τομή) to be set apart to the God of Israel, as commanded in Scripture, versus being cut into (κατα-τομή) in order to invoke the gods, as supposed to be effective by the rest of the nations. The contrast is with the uncircumcised, the 'pagan' world of the addressees, about which Paul is expressing a specifically Jewish—i.e., *circumcision*-oriented—point of view" (Nanos, "Paul's Reversal of Jews Calling Gentiles 'Dogs,'") 479.

39. This is one of the reasons why Paul's opponents have tended to be generalized as Jews or Jewish Christ-believers. See Johnson Hodge, *If Sons, Then Heirs,* 60–62.

40. Similarly, on 2 Corinthians, see Duff, "Glory in the Ministry of Death," 313–37. Duff asks, why would Paul mount an argument against Judaism here (in 2 Cor 3)? He argues convincingly that Paul was not intent on proving the superiority of Christianity over Judaism, nor the inferiority of the Torah to the gospel, or the inadequacy of the Jewish reading of Scripture compared to the reading of the church. Duff (ibid., 314–20) asserts that 2 Cor 3:6–18 has virtually nothing to do with Judaism's attachment to the Torah—it focuses on the Corinthian gentiles.

41. Because the reference to "remaining as you were" occurs as part of a broader theme, the significance of Paul's assertions on circumcision and uncircumcision here has been overlooked, especially since these do not appear to be specially relevant to the context of 1 Corinthians. Even the references to Cephas in 1:12 and 9:5 do not provide sufficient grounds.

42. On this see Troy W. Martin's distinctions as in n.13 above.

shall see later), Paul resorts to "new creation" terminology and re-evaluates both the state of circumcision and that of uncircumcision (6:15). Paul did not merely contrast life as a Jew with being in Christ, but proceeded, as he does in Phil 3, to include "everything" in his comparisons. This passage thus parallels the use of the terms "circumcision" and "uncircumcision" in 1 Corinthians and Galatians, indicating Jewish and gentile ways of life in their totality. If Paul had simply contrasted life as a Jew with life in Christ, we would be left, at minimum, with an implicitly anti-Jewish Paul. Such an apostle would have little to offer in terms of cultural critique to those modern Christ-followers in the Third World who have had no experience of Judaism in their own history. But Paul's wisdom as a pastor and theologian emerges in the breadth of his comparison: not only Jewish values and virtues are to be revised in Christ, but also all other things, whether living as slave or as freedman, including the values and virtues of the Roman world in which his converts were immersed.

In fact, Paul's theological and ethical strategy gains considerably if, in re-prioritizing all human virtues and fleshly achievements, he used his own case as the primary example. Thus, when facing the challenge of Greco-Roman honor and shame ethics at Corinth or Philippi, he was able to speak with more power and effectiveness because he re-evaluated not just his previous, pre-conversion existence, but also the life that he now continued to lead. Thus, he was able to provide a telling example by using himself as a teacher and exemplar,[43] as he has already done in 1 Cor 4:16–17, where he speaks of "my ways in Christ" as "I teach in all the churches." This observation is not aimed at *devaluing* either Hellenism or Judaism as such, but at their *revaluing* to teach the Corinthians and others that the whole of everyone's life, be they Jew or gentile, must be reassessed in the light of Christ.[44] As Georg Eichholz and E. P. Sanders affirm, Paul views his own experience as paradigmatic.[45]

---

43. On differentiating between "imitating" Paul rather than "copying" Paul, see Kathy Ehrensperger, *Paul and the Dynamics of Power*, 151–52. For Paul, Christ is the primary example, but disciples cannot possibly copy the unique sufferings of Christ. Neither can they copy the apostle to the gentiles in his specific (and possibly unique role); see Stegemann, "'Set Apart for the Gospel' (Rom 1:1): Paul's Self-Introduction in the Letter to the Romans."

44. In this sense, Paul is not a model ascetic, because the revaluation of life in the light of Christ is affirmative rather than negative in keeping with scriptural views of life as God's creation.

45. Eichholz, *Die Theologie des Paulus*, 224–26; Sanders, *Law and Jewish People*, 139. Sanders, in affirming the view of Eichholz, continues, adding "The comparative statement is this: 'Whatever gain I had, I counted as loss for the sake of Christ' (Phil 3:7). This reflects precisely the same view as that of 2 Cor 3:9–11, where the law lost its glory only because of the surpassing glory of the new dispensation."

Thus, the abiding principle Paul teaches is for both Jew and gentile to "put no confidence in the flesh" (Phil 3:2; see "glorying in the flesh," Gal 6:13). It is under the rubric of confidence in the flesh that Paul, in Phil 3:4, begins to apparently devalue his Jewish heritage. But in his wisdom, Paul widens this reference to Jewish flesh to serve as an example for all his communities, so that the form of one's past and present existence, whether Jewish or gentile, and despite its continuance in Christ, is not allowed to become something in which one can boast, and thus threaten the unity of the community. Since this principle applies to everyone's past, whether Jew or gentile, it can then operate, as we have already noted in relation to "remaining as you were when called" in 1 Cor 7, as "a rule in all the churches"—this is probably as near as Paul gets to a universal application of his gospel.

The Re-evaluation of All Things in Christ: A New Paradigm for Pauline Studies?

Essentially, this rule involves both a recognition of difference and, simultaneously, rules out any boasting in the difference. Removing the signs of circumcision for the sake of upward social mobility would lead to boasting in the superiority of gentile identity. In Galatians, there is a parallel: demanding circumcision for gentiles would lead to a boasting in the difference that circumcision makes, that is, in the superiority of Jewish identity. Unlike contemporary Greeks and Romans boasting in their advanced culture over against so-called barbarians—that is over everyone except Greeks and Romans—Paul recognizes and validates each one's particular fleshly existence in Christ, whether as Jew or gentile, but in no way seeks to make everyone the same. The difference is acknowledged and remains, even though in Christ it is re-evaluated differently for Jews and gentiles.

Paul's examples may seem to be anti-Jewish because Jewish practice is part of the actual comparison he creates. But this is only incidentally so, since he, as a Jew, necessarily refers to what is most cherished by him in his Jewish tradition. It is also a part of Paul's strategy to drive a wedge between Hellenistic honor and shame values, and so distance his converts from pagan practices by using himself and his Jewish virtues as an example. But with this example he is not encouraging his mainly gentile converts to develop an anti-Jewish attitude—particularly not in an area such as Corinth where perhaps there were few Jews (and even fewer Jewish or Jewish Christian counter-missionaries).[46] Rather, he is setting up boundaries that are generally applicable in all the churches: whatever one's past, in Christ it has been re-evaluated, and one must

46. See Nanos on this as in n.38 above.

recognize this fact in the new creation values by which all in Christ, whether of Jewish or gentile extraction, must now live. And this way of thinking has even more significance if circumcision and uncircumcision function, in Paul, as synonyms for Jew and gentile respectively, so that, when he says "uncircumcision is nothing," he is, in fact, re-evaluating the previous way of life of most of his converts (and similarly with "circumcision" also his own life and that of other Jewish Christ-followers).[47]

Thus, Paul's deliberate widening of his comparisons to include the whole of life, and not just Jewish life, is both pastorally and theologically appropriate, but also ethically very essential, because it lays the same ethical demands on everyone, whatever their heritage and commitments. The strength of this call by Paul to re-evaluate the whole of life would be much weakened if he did not take himself and his own treasured heritage as his starting point.[48]

However, he himself and his relation to Judaism, though central, are by no means the final focus of his argument.[49] Paul and his values are in the end only examples on the way to arguing that he counts "all things" as loss, even σκύβαλα,[50] compared with being in Christ (whilst recognizing these words are part of Paul's rhetoric of comparison).[51] Thus, the apostle becomes an exemplar for all—whether of Jewish or gentile extraction—and their way of

47. See Douglas A. Campbell, "Unravelling Gal 3.11b," 20–32.

48. See Matera, *New Testament Theology,* 204–9. I am not persuaded, however, that "this dramatic reversal" in terms of values applies only to Paul's pre-conversion life— Paul's ongoing life as a self-effacing apostle is also exemplary; see 2 Cor 11:16–21.

49. If this were the case, then it would be legitimate to view Paul's gospel as essentially focused on works-righteousness; but though his stress against "boasting in the flesh" certainly includes such a prohibition, Paul's focus is not limited to such boasting in the flesh, as may have occurred in Judaism. He is concerned to oppose *all* boasting in all flesh, whether gentile or Jewish. The example of the Swiss reformer, Heinrich Bullinger, is relevant here. In keeping with his contemporaries, he sees the problem in Romans as a problem of humans boasting before God, but unlike them and many modern interpreters, he sees the warnings as addressed to gentiles as well as Jews. In a similar vein, Bullinger, in an independent approach, emphasized continuity between the Testaments and refused the law/gospel, works/faith dichotomy as the key to Paul. Bullinger's example is instructive in that it clearly demonstrates that to hold to the centrality of God's grace freely offered in Christ need not determine the exact formulation of our understanding of its operation. See my essay, "Built on Tradition, But Not Bound by Tradition," 166–70.

50. In declaring his previous life "rubbish" it should be recognized that Paul is resorting to *rhetorical exaggeration* to increase the power of his message. See similarly the argument of Rom 14:2, where πάντα cannot mean literally everything (Jewett, *Romans,* 837–41).

51. Paul's rhetoric intensifies from counting all things as ζημίαν, a commercial metaphor, to viewing these all as σκύβαλα, that is, valueless rubbish. See Sumney, *Philippians,* 78–79.

life, whether Jewish or gentile in pattern, has to be re-evaluated accordingly ("many live as enemies of the cross of Christ—they boast in their shame," Phil 3:18–19). Just as the comparison with the call of Christ effectively required all in Corinth, whether Jew or gentile, to abide in the state in which they received their call, so now, in Philippi, all have to re-evaluate their past and present lives in comparison with the surpassing value of knowing Christ, putting no confidence "in the flesh," whatever one's ethnic origin.

We have demonstrated above that Paul's comparison is not between being in Christ and being Jewish, but between being in Christ and *all other existence outside of Christ*. It might be argued, of course, that Judaism is included in the world outside of Christ. It is also true that Paul views the entire world both before and outside of Christ as being under the power of sin.[52] Yet, it is not Pauline thought to simply consider Judaism and the scriptural revelation as being part and parcel of a sinful world. Everything in Paul's view is re-evaluated by the coming of Christ, but this new valuation is not entirely negative in respect of Judaism, the law, and the covenants. The fact that the whole of life must be judged in the light of Christ does not mean that Judaism's contribution to the knowledge of God is simply or uncritically equated with that of gentile life; rather, both are equally subject to judgment, even if the outcome for each is not identical.[53]

For this reason we need a new paradigm in Pauline studies. The last half-century of scholarship has alerted us to the inherent inadequacies of presenting Paul as the hero of gentile emancipation from Judaism, or as a counter-cultural sectarian replacing everything in this world with a "new creation" that is culturally naked. We can put it this way: since the whole world is under the power of sin, God had to start afresh, from scratch as it were, in order to make all things new. But God is faithful to his own word and to those in Judaism who were faithful to God. As signified by the rainbow in the Noah narrative, God refuses to destroy all that God has made, but sends the Son to reclaim and restore what is rightfully his. For this reason, the careless use of such terms as annulment, termination of the

---

52. See Fitzmyer, *Romans*, 330–31.

53. The common reading of Rom 3:9–18 tends to view Paul as charging by means of Scripture that all, Jews and gentiles alike, are "under sin." But the verb προαιτιάομαι, in 3:9, need not be read as referring back to what Paul has just previously stated, since this renders the Scripture proof as somewhat superfluous. Paul is not summarizing a previous argument accusing all of being sinners, but introducing a new section of the argument that from a scriptural perspective shows that all, both Jews and gentiles, are now living in a time under Roman rule dominated by sin. It is in this sense that all are "under the power of sin" despite the difference between Jew and gentile. See Ehrensperger, "Reading Romans in the Face of the 'Other,'" 133–36. See also Thorsteinsson, *Paul's Interlocutor in Romans 2*, 235.

law, obliteration (of previous identities), or simply the easy assumption that Christianity *transcends* (read, is superior to) Judaism, is no longer acceptable. A more nuanced description of the Christ-event is urgently required if we are not to be guilty of an arrogance neither warranted nor permitted by the gospel of Christ. It is apparent that many Christian scholars, though recognizing that Christianity has deep roots in Judaism and yet differs from it because of the coming of Christ, do not adequately and consistently provide explanations how and why this is so.

It might be considered a viable option to regard Christianity as simultaneously appropriating and rejecting motifs of Judaism for its own self-understanding.[54] However, this particular approach is somewhat wooden and misses the deeper dimension of identity as a total understanding that somehow incorporates elements of both faiths, but in a coherent and properly integrated manner. Identity is not simply the combined totality of the number of elements in a particular group of people; it is something more pervasive and more distinct than the items that appear to comprise it or from which it is constituted. For this and other reasons, I have found that researching identity, rather than the various elements that taken together somehow combine to constitute identity, offers better insights into Paul's understanding of himself as an apostle and his own relation to his ancestral faith, especially as he sought to transform the life of his gentile converts.

Thus, this study is concerned with demonstrating that, in relation to circumcision/uncircumcision, the best paradigm for understanding Paul is transformative theology, not a displacement type of theology. Within this paradigm, Paul can compare degrees of whiteness, degrees of glory: in the ultimate value system of being in Christ, even the good and cherished things must take second place to following Christ. Nevertheless, being in second place is very different from being discarded or being declared worthless, or classed as "indifferents." They are *re*valued but not necessarily or uniformly *de*valued. Paul does compare what he has in the Messiah with what he has in Judaism, but what he (rhetorically) declares "rubbish" is only so in comparison to what he deems so much greater—not that the things themselves are refuse by their nature. Paul does say that both circumcision and uncircumcision are nothing (1 Cor 7:19; Gal 6:15), but what he means is not apparent in the mere repetition of his words out of context. Even if we translate Gal 6:15 "neither circumcision nor uncircumcision is anything,

---

54. See Sanders' concluding sentence in *Law and Jewish People*, 210. Sanders, by way of explanation and in response to criticism from Morna Hooker, states that whilst he sees a similar correspondence between Judaism and Christianity in relation to grace and requirement, he did not make the covenantal scheme central to Paul's thought since he finds that only aspects of it are present.

but a new creation is everything," this rendering does not stress obliteration of the past but a transformation of that which constituted the valued past. The significance of past values is changed and new value given to them in relation to the primary value, which is loyalty to Christ. This primary value is fundamental in Christian identity, but it cannot of itself entirely constitute that identity. "In Christ" identity does not displace local contextual identities but intertwines and interpenetrates them[55]—not in such a way as to create out of nothing a new identity, but in such a way as to begin, from the previous context and identity, a transformation of local contextual identities via the work of the Spirit in a dynamic, not merely internal, way.[56] Such transformation involves an ongoing evaluation and re-evaluation of all things in the light of Christ, not simply a giving up of those things no longer essential to the life of faith.

To relate this understanding of Paul to our contemporary scene, I suggest it should mean the following: from whatever background or tradition we may have come from, in whatever ethnic identity or social level we may stand, and whatever we value most in our ancestry and traditions, it must not be allowed to challenge our primary loyalty to Christ—this is what Paul would have us learn after 2,000 years. However marvelous our fleshly heritage, it is as nothing compared with what we have in Christ Jesus, and it must take second place to him. But Paul says also to us that having designated Christ as our primary value, our pearl of great price, we can then again take up our treasured inheritance, learn to appreciate it afresh, and cultivate it as something offered up as a sacrifice to Christ—now given back to us to use in a transformed manner in the contemporary world. This re-evaluation necessarily includes our identity as citizens of a particular country. Even this reality has to be offered up to God so that our patriotism can truly reflect the accounting system in Christ that Paul has taught us: our primary loyalty is to Christ. Cherishing the particularity of life goes hand in hand with the universal dimension of the gospel.[57]

---

55 See the recently completed PhD thesis of my student J. Brian Tucker, "*You Belong to Christ:*" *Paul and the Formation of Social Identity in 1 Corinthians 1–4* (University of Wales Lampeter, UK, 2009, now published by Pickwick Publications, 2010).

56. *Contra* Nguyen (*Christian Identity at Corinth,* 208), who views new creation as the essence of Christian identity a more appropriate form of identity in which to boast, in contrast to "the superficialities of one's identity" (such as status symbols like circumcision), and tends to stress the inner dimension of Christian identity via the transformative work of the Spirit.

57. This essay is also dedicated to those many people in Villanova who combined to make my wife and me so welcome, and to make our stay with them such a joyous and rewarding experience.

"I Rate All Things as Loss": Paul's Puzzling Accounting System

It was a great privilege for me to deliver this contribution in September 2008 as the opening address of the Villanova University celebration of the Jubilee Year of St. Paul, honoring Jerome Murphy-O'Connor and Joseph A. Fitzmyer, to whose contributions to biblical scholarship I am deeply indebted.

Bibliography

Aasgaard, Reinaar. *"My Beloved Brothers and Sisters!": Christian Siblingship in Paul.* London: T. & T. Clark, 2004.

Achtemeier, Paul. *Romans.* Interpretation Series. Atlanta: John Knox, 1985.

Adams, Edward. "First-Century Models for Paul's Churches: Selected Scholarly Developments since Meeks." In *After the First Urban Christians: The Social-Scientific Study of Pauline Christianity Twenty-Five Years Later,* edited by Todd D Still and David G. Horrell, 60–78. London: T. & T. Clark, 2009

Adams, Edward, and David G. Horrell, editors. *Christianity at Corinth: The Quest for the Pauline Church.* Louisville: Westminster John Knox, 2004.

Agamben, Giorgio. *The Time That Remains: A Commentary on the Letter to the Romans.* Stanford, CA: Stanford University Press, 2005.

Alexander, Philip. "'The Parting of the Ways' from the Perspective of Rabbinic Judaism." In *Jews and Christians: The Parting of the Ways A.D. 70 to 135,* edited by James D. G. Dunn, 1–25. Tübingen: Mohr Siebeck, 1992.

Anderson, Johnice C. et al., editors. *Pauline Conversations in Context: Essays in Honor of Calvin J. Roetzel.* Sheffield, UK: Sheffield Academic, 2002.

Anderson, R. Dean, Jr. *Ancient Rhetorical Theory and Paul.* Rev. ed. Leuven: Peeters, 1998.

Arendt, Hannah. *The Human Condition.* Chicago: University of Chicago Press, 1958.

Ascough, Richard. *Paul's Macedonian Associations: The Social Context of Philippians and 1 Thessalonians.* Tübingen: Mohr Siebeck, 2003.

Avemarie, Friedrich. "Erwählung und Vergeltung: Zur optionale Struktur rabbinischer Soteriologie." *NTS* 45 (1999) 108–26.

———. *Tora und Leben: Untersuchungen zur Heilsbedeutung der Tora in der frühen rabbinischen Literatur.* Tübingen: Mohr-Siebeck, 1996.

Bachmann, Michael, editor. *Antijudaism in Galatians?* Tranlated by Robert L. Brawley. Grand Rapids: Eerdmans, 2009.

———. *Lutherische und Neue Paulusperspektive.* WUNT 182. Tübingen: Mohr Siebeck, 2005.

Badenas, Robert. *Christ the End of the Law: Romans 10.4 in Pauline Perspective.* Sheffield, UK: JSOT, 1985.

Baird, William. *History of New Testament Research,* Vol. 1, *From Deism to Tübingen.* Minneapolis: Fortress, 1992.

Balch, David. *"Let Wives Be Submissive": The Domestic Code in 1 Peter.* SBLMS 26. Chico, CA: Scholars, 1981.

Bibliography

Bammel, Ernst. "Romans 13." In *Jesus and the Politics of His Day*, edited by Ernst Bammel and Charles F. D. Moule, 365–83. Cambridge: Cambridge University Press, 1984.

Banks, Robert. *Paul's Idea of Community*. Rev. ed. Peabody, MA: Hendrickson, 1994.

Barclay, John, M. G. "Do We Undermine the Law? A Study of Romans 14.1—15.6." In *Paul and the Mosaic Law*, edited by James D. G. Dunn, 287–308. Tübingen: Mohr, 1996.

———. *Jews in the Mediterranean Diaspora, From Alexander to Trajan (323 BCE–117 CE)*. Edinburgh: T. & T. Clark, 1996.

———. "Neither Jew Nor Greek: Multiculturalism and the New Perspective." In *Ethnicity and the Bible*, edited by Mark G. Brett, 171–96. Leiden: Brill, 1996.

———. "Paul's Story: Theology as Testimony." In *Narrative Dynamics in Paul: A Critical Assessment*, edited by Bruce W. Longenecker, 133–56. Louisville: Westminster John Knox, 2002.

Barrett, Charles K. *A Commentary on the Epistle to the Romans*. Black's New Testament Commentaries. London: Black, 1961.

———. *A Commentary on the Second Epistle to the Corinthians*. Harpers New Testament Commentaries. New York: Harper and Row, 1973.

Bartchy, Scott S. *Mallon Chresai: First-Century Slavery and the Interpretation of 1 Cor. 7:21*. Missoula, MT: Scholars, 1973.

———. "Paul Did not Teach 'Stay in Slavery': The Mistranslation of *klesis* in 1 Corinthians 7:20–21." Paper read at the SBL Annual Meeting, Boston, 2008.

———. "'When I'm Weak, I'm Strong': A Pauline Paradox in Cultural Context." In *Kontexte der Schrift Band II: Kultur, Politik, Religion. Sprache, Text Wolfgang Stegemann zum 60 Geburtstag*, edited by Christian Strecker, 49–60. Stuttgart: Kohlhammer, 2005.

Barth, Fredrik. *Rethinking Ethnicity: Arguments and Explorations*. London: Sage, 1997.

Barth, Karl. *Church Dogmatics 2.2: The Doctrine of God*. Edinburgh: T. & T. Clark, 1957.

———. *The Epistle to the Romans*. Translated by E. C. Hoskyns. Oxford: Oxford University Press, 1968.

———. *Kirchliche Dogmatik* 3.4. 4th ed. Zürich: Evangelischer Verlag, 1951.

———. *A Shorter Commentary on Romans*. London: SCM, 1959.

Barth, Marcus. *Ephesians*. Anchor Bible Commentary 34. New York: Doubleday, 1974.

———. "Jews and Gentiles: The Social Character of Justification in Paul". *JES* 5 (1968) 78–104.

———. "St. Paul, a Good Jew." *Horizons in Biblical Theology* 1 (1979) 7–45.

Barton, Stephen C. "Early Christianity and the Sociology of the Sect." In *The Open Book,* edited by Francis W. Watson, 140–62. London: SCM, 1993.

———. "Paul and the Limits of Tolerance." In *Tolerance and Intolerance in Early Judaism and Christianity*, edited by Graham N. Stanton and Guy G. Strousma, 121–34. Cambridge: Cambridge University Press, 1998.

Bartsch, Hans W. "Die antisemitischen Gegner des Paulus in Römerbrief." In *Antijudaismus in Neuen Testament?* edited by Werner Eckert et al., 27–43. Munich: Kaiser, 1969.

———. "The Concept of Faith in Paul's Letter to the Romans." *BR* 13 (1968) 41–53.

Bassler, Jouette M. "Divine Impartiality in Paul's Letter to the Romans." *NovT* 26 (1984) 43–58.

————, editor. *Pauline Theology.* Volume I: *Thessalonians, Philippians, Galatians, Philemon.* Minneapolis: Fortress, 1991.

————. "Paul's Theology: Whence and Whether?" In *Pauline Theology* Volume II, *1 and 2 Corinthians*, edited by David M. Hay, 3–17. Minneapolis: Fortress, 1993.

Battle, Michael J. *Reconciliation: The Ubunbtu Theology of Desmond Tutu.* Cleveland: Pilgrim, 1997.

Baur, Ferdinand C. "Die Christuspartei in der korinthischen Gemeinde, der Gegensatz des petrinischen und paulinischen Christenthums in der ältesten Kirche, der Apostel Petrus in Rom." *Tübingen Zeitschrift für Theologie* 5 (1831) 61–206. (Reprinted in F. C. Baur, *Historisch-kritische Untersuchungen zum Neuen Testament.* Ausgewählte Werke 1, 1–146. Stuttgart-Bad Cannstatt: Frommann, 1963.)

————. *The Church History of the First Three Centuries.* Translated by Allan Menzies. London: Williams and Norgate, 1878.

————. *Paul, His Life and Works.* Translated by A. Menzies. Edinburgh: Theological Translation Fund Library, 1876.

————. *Vorlesungen über neutestamentliche Theologie.* Edited by F. F. Baur. Leipzig: Fues, 1864.

Bauman-Martin, Betsy. "Women on the Edge: New Perspectives on Women in the Petrine Haustafel." *JBL* 123 (2004) 253–79.

Beale, Gregory. "The Old Testament Background of Reconciliation in 2 Corinthians 5–7 and its Bearing upon the Literary Problem of 2 Corinthians 6:14—17:1." *NTS* 35 (1989) 359–81.

————. "Reconciliation in 2 Corinthians 5–7." *NTS* 35 (1989) 550–81.

Beker, J. Christiaan. "The Faithfulness of God and the Priority of Israel in Paul's Letter to the Romans." In *Christians among Jews and Gentiles: Essays in Honor of Krister Stendahl on His Sixty-Fifth Birthday*, edited by George W. E. Nickelsburg and George W. MacRae, 10–16. Philadelphia: Fortress, 1986.

————. *Paul, the Apostle: The Triumph of God in Life and Thought.* Edinburgh: T. & T. Clark, 1980.

————. "Paul the Theologian: Major Motifs in Pauline Theology." *Interpretation* 43 (1989) 352–65.

————. "Recasting Pauline Theology: The Coherence-Contingency Scheme as Interpretive Model." In *Pauline Theology*, Vol. I, edited by Jouette M. Bassler, 15–24. Minneapolis: Fortress, 1991.

Berger, Peter, and Thomas Luckmann. *The Social Construction of Reality: A Treatise in the Sociology of Knowledge.* New York: Doubleday, 1966.

Best, Ernest. *A Critical and Exegetical Commentary on Ephesians.* ICC. Edinburgh: T. & T. Clark, 1998.

————. *Ephesians.* Sheffield, UK: Sheffield Academic, 1983.

Bjerkelund, Carl J. Παρακάλω, *Form, Funktion und Sinn der Parakalo-Sätze in den Paulinischen Briefen.* Bibliotheca theological norvegica 1. Oslo: Universiteitsforlaget, 1967.

Blanschke, Andreas. *Beschneidung :Zeugnisse der Bibel und verwandtes Texte.* Basel: Francke, 1998.

Blanton, Thomas R. "Paul's Covenantal Theology in 2 Corinthians 2:14—17:4." In *Paul and Judaism: Cross-currents in Pauline Exegesis and the Study of Jewish-Christian*

Bibliography

Relations, edited by Reimund Bieringer and Didier Pollefeyt, 61–71. London: T. & T. Clark, 2012.

Bockmuehl, Marcus N. A. *The Epistle to the Philippians*. BNTC. London: Black, 1997.

———. *Jewish Law in Gentile Churches: Halakhah and the Beginnings of Christian Public Ethics*. Grand Rapids: Baker Academic, 2003.

———. "The Noachide Commandments and New Testament Ethics: With Special Reference to Acts 15 and Pauline Halakah." *RB* 102 (1995) 72–101.

———. *Revelation and Mystery in Ancient Judaism and Pauline Christianity*. Grand Rapids: Eerdmans, 1990.

———. "Syrian Memories of Peter: Ignatius, Justin, and Serapion." In *The Image of the Judaeo-Christians in Ancient Jewish and Christian Literature*, edited by Peter J. Tomson and D. Lambers-Petry, 124–42. WUNT 158. Tübingen: Mohr Siebeck, 2003.

De Boer, Martinus C. *The Defeat of Death: Apocalyptic Eschatology in 1 Corinthians 15 and Romans 5*. JSNTSup 24. Sheffield, UK: Sheffield Academic, 1989.

———. "The Nazoreans: Living at the Boundary of Judaism and Christianity." In *Tolerance and Intolerance in Early Judaism and Christianity*, edited by Graham N. Stanton and G. G. Strousma, 239–63. Cambridge: Cambridge University Press, 1998.

De Boer, Martinus C., and Marion L. Soards, editors. *Paul and Jewish Apocalyptic Theology: Apocalyptic and the New Testament: Essays in Honor of J. Louis Martyn*. Sheffield, UK: JSOT, 1989.

Bornkamm, Günter. *Das Ende des Gesetzes: Paulusstudien*. Munich: Kaiser, 1952.

———. "The Letter to the Romans as Paul's Last Will and Testament." *Australian Biblical Review* (1963) 2–14. (German Translation "Der Römerbrief als Testament des Paulus." In *Geschichte und Glaube* 2. Gesammelte Aufsätze IV. München: Kaiser, 1971; now included in *The Romans Debate*, edited by Karl P. Donfried, 16–28. Peabody, MA: Hendrickson, 1991.)

———. "The Revelation of God's Wrath: Romans 1–3." In *Early Christian Experience*, 46–70. London: SCM, 1969.

Bourdieu, Pierre. *Pascalian Meditations*. Translated by R. Nice. Oxford: Blackwell, 2000.

Boyarin, Daniel. *Borderlines: The Partition of Judaeo-Christianity*. Philadelphia: University of Pennsylvania Press, 2004.

———. *Dying for God: Martyrdom and the Making of Christianity and Judaism*. Stanford, CA: Stanford University Press, 1999.

———. *A Radical Jew: Paul and the Politics of Identity*. Berkeley, CA: University of California Press, 1994.

Brändle, Rudolph, and Ekkehard W. Stegemann. "The Emergence of the First Christians in Rome in the Context of the Jewish Communities." In *Judaism and Christianity in First Century Rome*, edited by Karl P. Donfried and Peter Richardson, 117–27. Grand Rapids: Eerdmans 1998.

Brawley, Robert L. "Contextuality, Intertextuality, and the Hendiadic Relationship of Promise and Law in Galatians." *ZNW* 93 (2002) 99–119.

———. "Meta-Ethics and the Role of Works of Law in Galatians." In *Lutherische und Neue Paulusperspektive*, edited by Michael Bachmann, 135–59. WUNT 182. Tübingen: Mohr Siebeck, 2005.

Brett, Mark G. editor. *Ethnicity and the Bible*. Leiden: Brill, 1996.

Bibliography

————. "Israel's Indigenous Origins: Cultural Hybridity and the Formation of Israelite Ethnicity." *BibInt* 11 (2003) 400–12.

Breytenbach, Cilliers. *Versöhnung: Eine Studie in Paulinischer Soteriologie.* WMANT 60. Neukirchen-Vluyn: Neukirchener, 1989.

Brooke, George J. *The Dead Sea Scrolls and the New Testament.* Minneapolis: Fortress, 2005.

Brown, Raymond E. "Not Jewish Christianity and Gentile Christianity but Types of Jewish/Gentile Christianity." *CBQ* 45 (1983) 74–79.

Brown, Raymond E., and John P. Meier. *Antioch and Rome: New Testament Cradles of Catholic Christianity.* New York: Paulist, 1983.

Brummer, Vincent. "Philosophy, Theology and the Reading of Texts." *Religious Studies* 27 (1979) 451–62.

Bruns, Gerald L. "Midrash and Allegory: The Beginnings of Scriptural Interpretation." In *The Literary Guide to the Bible,* edited by Robert Alter and Frank R. Kermode, 634–35. Cambridge: Harvard University Press, 1987.

Buell, Denise K. *Why This New Race: Ethnic Reasoning in Early Christianity.* New York: Columbia University Press, 2005.

Bultmann, Rudolph. *The Theology of the New Testament.* 2 volumns. London: SCM, 1952–55.

Byron, John. *Recent Research on Slavery.* Sheffield, UK: Phoenix, 2008.

Calvert-Koyzis, Nancy. *Paul, Monotheism and the People of God: The Significance of Abraham Traditions for Early Judaism and Christianity.* London, New York: T. & T. Clark, 2004.

Campbell, Douglas A. "Apostolic Competition at Corinth." Review of M. Goulder, *Paul and the Competing Mission in Corinth. JBV* 23.2 (2002) 229–31.

————. *The Quest for Paul's Gospel: A Suggested Strategy.* London: T. & T. Clark, 2005.

————. "Unravelling Gal 3.11b." *NTS* 42 (1996) 20–32.

Campbell, Douglas A., et al., editors. *Gospel and Gender: A Trinitarian Engagement with Being Male and Female in Christ.* London: T. & T. Clark, 2003.

Campbell, William S. "The Addressees of Paul's Letter to the Romans: Assemblies of God in House Churches and Synagogues?" In *Between Gospel and Election: Explorations in the Interpretation of Romans 9–11,* edited by Florian Wilk and J. Ross Wagner, 171–95. Tübingen: Mohr Siebeck, 2010.

————. "All God's Beloved in Rome: Jewish Roots and Christian Identity." In *Celebrating Romans: A Template for Pauline Theology,* edited by Sheila McGinn, 67–82. Grand Rapids: Eerdmans, 2004.

————. "Built on Tradition But Not Bound by Tradition: Response to P. Opitz, 'Bullinger on Romans.'" In *Reformation Readings of Romans,* edited by Kathy Ehrensperger and R. Ward Holder, 148–70. Romans through History and Cultures Series 8. London: T. & T. Clark, 2008.

————. "The Church as Israel/People of God." In *Dictionary of the Later New Testament and its Developments,* edited by D. G. Reid, 204–19. Downers Grove, IL: InterVarsity, 1997.

————. "The Contribution of Traditions to Paul's Theology." In *Pauline Theology, Vol. II, 1 & 2 Corinthians,* edited by David M. Hay, 234–54. Minneapolis: Fortress, 1993.

————. "Covenantal Theology and Participation in Christ: Pauline Perspectives on Transformation." In *Paul and Judaism: Crosscurrents in Pauline Exegesis and the*

Bibliography

Study of Jewish-Christian Relations, edited by Reimund Bieringer and Didier Pollefeyt, 41–60. London: T. & T. Clark, 2012.

———. "Did Paul Advocate Separation from the Synagogue?" *SJT* 42 (1990) 457–67. (Also included in Campbell, *Paul's Gospel in an Intercultural Context, Jew and Gentile in the Letter to the Romans*, 122–33. Frankfurt: Lang, 1991.)

———. "Differentiation and Discrimination in Paul's Ethnic Discourse." Forthcoming in *Transformation* 2 (2013).

———. "Divergent Images of Paul and His Mission." In *Reading Israel in Romans: Legitimacy and Plausibility of Divergent Interpretations*, edited by Cristina Grenholm and Daniel Patte, 187–211. Romans through History and Cultures Series. Harrisburg, PA: Trinity, 2000.

———. "Ernst Käsemann on Romans: The Way Forward or the End of an Era." In *Modern Interpretations of Romans: Tracking Their Hermeneutical/Theological Trajectory*, edited by Daniel Patte and Cristina Grenholm, 161–86. London: T. & T. Clark, 2013.

———. "Gentile Identity and Transformation in Christ according to Paul." In *The Making of Christianity: Conflicts, Contacts, and Constructions: Essays in Honor of Bengt Holmberg*, edited by Samal Byrskog and Magnus Zetterholm, 22–55. Winona Lake, IN: Eisenbrauns 2012.

———. "The Interpretation of Paul: Beyond the New Perspective." Paper given at the British New Testament Conference, Manchester, 2001.

———. "'I Rate All Things as Loss': Paul's Puzzling Accounting System. Judaism as Loss or the Re-Evaluation of All Things in Christ." In *Celebrating Paul: Festschrift in Honor of Jerome Murphy O'Connor and Joseph A. Fitzmyer*, edited by Peter Spitaler, 39–61. The Catholic Biblical Quarterly Monograph Series 48. Washington, DC: Catholic Biblical Association, 2011.

———. "Israel." In *The Dictionary of Paul and His Letters*, edited by George F. Hawthorne, et al., 441–46. Downer's Grove, IL: InterVarsity, 1993.

———. "Martin Luther and Paul's Epistle to the Romans." In *The Bible as Book: The Reformation*, edited by Oliver O'Sullivan, 103–14. London: British Library, 2000.

———. *Paul and the Creation of Christian Identity*. London: T. & T. Clark, 2006.

———. "Paul's Application of Scripture to Contemporary Events." Paper given at the British New Testament Studies Seminar on the Use of the Old Testament in the New, Hawarden, UK, 1988.

———. "Perceptions of Compatibility between Christianity and Judaism in Pauline Interpretation." *BibInt* 13 (2005) 298–316. (Special Issue: Paul between Jews and Christians.)

———. "The Place of Romans ix-xi within the Structure and Thought of the Letter." In Studia Evangelica VII. Texte und Untersuchungen zur Geschichte der altchristlichen Literatur. Band 126, edited by Elisabeth A.Livingstone, 121–31. Berlin: Akademie-Verlag, 1982.

———. *The Purpose of Paul in the Letter to the Romans: A Survey of Romans I–XI with Particular Reference to Chapters IX–XI*. PhD, University of Edinburgh, 1972.

———. "'Remain as you were when called' and Paul's Stance on Slavery." *Journal of Beliefs and Values* 30 (2009) 205–7.

———. "Romans 3 as a Key to the Structure and Thought of the Letter." In *Paul's Gospel in an Intercultural Context, Jew and Gentile in the Letter to the Romans*, 25–42.

Frankfurt: Lang, 1991. (Also included in *The Romans Debate*, edited by Karl P. Donfried, 251–64. Peabody, MA: Hendrickson 1991.)

———. "The Rule of Faith in Romans 12:1—15:13: The Obligation of Humble Obedience as the Only Adequate Response to the Mercies of God." In *Pauline Theology Vol. III, Romans*, edited by David M. Hay and Elisabeth E. Johnson, 259–86. Minneapolis: Fortress, 1995.

———. "Unity and Diversity in the Church: Transformed Identities and the Peace of Christ in Ephesians." *Transformation* 25 (2008) 15–21.

———. "Why Did Paul Write Romans?" In *Paul's Gospel in an Intercultural Context: Jew and Gentile in the Letter to the Romans*, 14–24. Frankfurt: Lang, 1991.

Cappelleti, Sylvia. *The Jewish Community of Rome: From the Second Century BC to the Third Century CE*. Leiden: Brill, 2006.

Carroll, John T. et al. *Faith and History: Essays in Honor of Paul W. Meyer*. Atlanta: Scholars, 1990.

Carter, Warren. "John's Gospel and the Imperial Cult." Paper delivered at SBL Annual Meeting Washington, DC, 2006.

———. *The Roman Empire in the New Testament: An Essential Guide*. Nashville: Abingdon, 2006.

Cartlidge, D. R. "1 Cor. 7 as a Foundation for a Christian Sex Ethic." *JR* 55 (1975) 220–34.

Chae, Daniel J. S. *Paul as Apostle to the Gentiles*. Paternoster Monograph Series. Carlisle, UK: Paternoster, 1997.

Ciampa, Roy E. *The Presence and the Function of Scripture in Galatians 1 and 2*. WUNT 2/102. Tübingen: Mohr Siebeck, 1998.

Clarke, Andrew C. "Equality or Mutuality? Paul's Use of 'Brother' Language." In *The New Testament in Its First-Century Setting: Essays on Context and Background in Honour of B. W. Winter on His 65th Birthday*, edited by P. J. Williams, et al., 151–64. Grand Rapids: Eerdmans, 2004.

Clarke, Andrew D. *Serve the Community of the Church: Christians as Leaders and Ministers*. Grand Rapids: Eerdmans, 2000.

Claussen, Carsten. "Meeting, Community, Synagogue: Different Frameworks of Ancient Jewish Congregations in the Diaspora." In *The Ancient Synagogue from Its Origins to 200 CE*, edited by Birger Olssen and Magnus Zetterholm, 144–67. Stockholm: Almqvist & Wiksell, 2003.

Cohen, Shaye J. D. *The Beginnings of Jewishness: Boundaries, Varieties, Uncertainties*. Berkeley, CA: University of California Press, 1999.

———. "Crossing the Boundary and Becoming a Jew." *HTR* 1 (1989) 13–33.

———. "'Those Who Say They Are Jews and Are Not': How Do You Know a Jew in Antiquity When You See One?" In *Diasporas in Antiquity*, edited by Shaye J. D. Cohen and E. S. Frerichs, 1–45. Atlanta: Scholars, 1993.

Collins, John J. *Between Athens and Jerusalem: Jewish Identity in the Hellenistic Diaspora*. 2nd ed. Grand Rapids: Eerdmans, 2000.

Cornell, S., and D. Hartmann. *Ethnicity and Race: Making Identities in a Changing World*. Thousand Oaks, UK: Pine Forge, 1997.

Cosgrove, Charles. *Elusive Israel: The Puzzle of Election in Romans*. Louisville: Westminster John Knox, 1997.

———. "The Justification of the Other: An Interpretation of Romans 1:18—14:25." In *Society of Biblical Literature Seminar Papers*, edited by Eugene H. Lovering, 613–34. Atlanta: Scholars, 1992.

Cranfield, Charles E. B. *A Critical and Exegetical Commentary on The Epistle to the Romans*. 2 vols. Edinburgh: T. & T. Clark, 1975–79.

Crüsemann, Frank. *Kanon und Sozialgeschichte. Beiträge zum Alten Testament*. Gütersloh: Kaiser, 2003.

Cupitt, Don. "Identity Versus Globalization." In *The Future of Jewish-Christian Dialogue*, edited by Dan Cohn-Sherbok, 285–91. Lewiston, NY: Mellen, 1999.

Dabourne, Wendy. *Purpose and Cause in Pauline Exegesis: Romans 1.16—4.25 and a New Approach to the Letters*. SNTSMS 104. Cambridge: Cambridge University Press, 1999.

Dahl, Nils A. "The Atonement: An Adequate Reward for the Akedah? (Rom. 8:32)." In *Neotestamentica et Semitica*, edited by Earl E. Ellis and Max Wilcox, 15–29. Edinburgh: T. & T. Clark, 1969.

———. "The Doctrine of Justification and Its Implications." In *Studies in Paul: Theology for the Early Christian Mission*, 92–120. Minneapolis: Augsburg, 1977.

———. "The Future of Israel." In *Studies in Paul: Theology for the Early Christian Mission*, 137–58. Minneapolis: Augsburg, 1977.

———. "Gentiles, Christians, Israelites in the Epistle to the Ephesians." In *Christians among Jews and Greeks: Festschrift for Krister Stendahl*, edited by George W. E. Nicklesburg et al., 31–39. Philadelphia: Fortress, 1986.

———. "The Particularity of Paul's Letters as a Problem in the Ancient Church." In *Neotestamentica et Patristica:Eine Freundesgabe. O. Cullmann zu seinem 60. Geburtstag überreicht*, edited by W. C. van Unnik, 260–71. Suppl.NovT. 60. Leiden: Brill, 1962.

———. "Review of E. P. Sanders' *Paul and Palestinian Judaism*." *RSR* 4 (1978) 153–58.

———. "Review of Rudolf Bultmann, *Theologie des Neuen Testaments*." *Theologische Rundschau* 22 (1954) 21–40.

———. *Studies in Ephesians: Introductory Questions, Text and Editorial-Critical Issues, Interpretation of Texts and Themes*. Tübingen: Mohr Siebeck, 1990.

Das, Andrew A. *Solving the Romans Debate*. Minneapolis: Fortress, 2007.

Davies, Glen N. *Faith and Obedience in Romans: A Study in Romans 1–4*. JSNTSup. 39. Sheffield, UK: JSOT, 1990.

Davies, William D. *Jewish and Pauline Studies*. Philadelphia: Fortress, 1984.

———. "Paul and the New Exodus." In *The Quest for Context and Meaning: Studies in Biblical Intertextuality in Honour of James A. Sanders*, edited by Craig A. Evans and Shemaryahu Talmon, 443–63. Leiden: Brill, 1997.

———. "Paul and the People of Israel." *NTS* 24 (1977) 4–39.

———. *Paul and Rabbinic Judaism: Some Elements in Pauline Theology*. Fiftieth Anniversary Edition. Mifflintown, PA: Sigler, 1998.

———. "A Suggestion Concerning Romans 11:13–24." In *Jewish and Pauline Studies*, 153–63. Philadelphia: Fortress, 1985.

Dawson, John David. *Allegorical Readers and Cultural Revision in Ancient Alexandria*. Berkeley, CA: University of California Press, 1992.

———. *Christian Figural Reading and the Fashioning of Identity*. Berkeley, CA: University of California Press, 2002.

Bibliography

Day, John, editor. *Temple and Worship in Biblical Israel: Proceedings of the Oxford Old Testament Seminar*. London: T. & T. Clark, 2005.

Deming, Will. "Paul and Indifferent Things." In *Paul and the Greco-Roman World: A Handbook*, edited by Paul Sampley, 384–403. Harrisburg, PA: Trinity, 2003.

Derrida, Jacques. *Points: Interviews, 1974–1994*. Stanford, CA: Stanford University Press, 1995.

Dodd, Charles H. *The Epistle to the Romans*. London: Hodder & Stoughton, 1932.

———. *New Testament Studies*. New York: Scribner, 1954.

Donaldson, Terence L. "The Curse of the Law and the Inclusion of the Gentiles: Galatians 3.13–14." *NTS* 32 (1986) 94–112.

———. *Judaism and the Gentiles: Jewish Patterns of Universalism*. Waco, TX: Baylor University Press, 2007.

———. "Proselytes as Righteous Gentiles." *JSP* 7.3 (1990) 3–2.

———. *Paul and the Gentiles: Remapping the Apostle's Convictional World*. Minneapolis: Fortress, 1997.

Donfried Karl P. "False Presuppositions in the Study of Romans." In *The Romans Debate*, edited by Karl P. Donfried, 102–24. Peabody, MA: Hendrickson 1991.

———, editor. *The Romans Debate*. 2nd ed. Peabody, MA: Hendrickson, 1991.

Donfried, Karl P., and Peter Richardson, editors. *Judaism and Christianity in First Century Rome*. Grand Rapids: Eerdmans, 1998.

Duff, Paul B. "Glory in the Ministry of Death: Gentile Condemnation and Letters of Recommendation in 2 Cor. 3:6–8." *NovTest* 46 (2004) 313–37.

Dunn, James D. G. "The Formal and Theological Coherence of Romans." *The Romans Debate*, edited by Karl P. Donfried, 2nd ed., 245–50. Peabody, MA: Hendrickson, 1991.

———. "Judaizers." In *A Dictionary of Biblical Interpretation*, edited by R. J. Coggins and J. L. Houlden, 369–71. London: SCM, 1990.

———. "A Light to the Gentiles or The End of the Law: The Significance of the Damascus Road Christophany for Paul." In *Jesus, Paul and the Law: Studies in Mark and Galatians*, 89–107. London: SCPK, 1990.

———. "The New Perspective on Paul." In *The New Perspective on Paul: Collected Essays*, 89–110. Tübingen: Mohr Siebeck, 2005.

———. *The Partings of the Ways between Christianity and Judaism and Their Significance for the Character of Christianity*. Philadelphia: Trinity, 1991.

———. "Paul's Epistle to the Romans: An Analysis of Structure and Argument." In *Aufstieg und Niedergang der römischen Welt 11.25.4*, edited by Hildegaard Temporini, 2842–90. Berlin: de Gruyter 1987.

———. "The Relationship between Paul and Jerusalem according to Galatians 1 and 2." *NTS* 28 (1982) 461–78.

———. *Romans 1–8*. Word Bible Commentary 38A. Dallas: Word, 1988.

———. *Romans 9–16*. Word Bible Commentary 38B. Dallas: Word, 1988.

———. *The Theology of Paul, the Apostle*. Grand Rapids: Eerdmans, 1998.

———. "Who Did Paul Think He Was? A Study of Jewish-Christian Identity." *NTS* 45 (1999) 174–93.

Ehrensperger, Kathy. "'Be Imitators of Me as I am of Christ': A Hidden Discourse of Power and Domination in Paul?" *LTQ* 38 (2003) 241–61.

———. "Current Trends in Historical Jesus Research." In *Verdict on Jesus*, edited by Paul Badham, 239–58. London: SPCK, 2010.

———. "'Let everyone be convinced in his/her own mind': Derrida and the Deconstruction of Paulinism." In *SBLSP*, 53–73. Atlanta: Scholars, 2002.

———. "Levinas, the Jewish Philosopher meets Paul, the Jewish Apostle: Reading Romans in the Face of the Other." In *Reading Romans with Philosophers and Theologians*, edited by David Odell-Scott, 115–54. Romans through History and Cultures Series. London: T. & T. Clark, 2007.

———. *Paul and the Dynamics of Power: Communication and Interaction in the Early Christ-Movement*. London: T. & T. Clark, 2007.

———. *Paul at the Crossroads of Cultures: Theologising in the Space Between*. London: T. & T. Clark, 2013.

———. "Paulus und die Gnade. Zu Fragen von Macht, Dominanz und Ermächtigung." In *Kontexte der Schrift Bd. 1: Text, Ethik, Judentum und Christentum, Gesellschaft. Ekkehard W.Stegemann zum 60. Geburtstag*, edited by Gabriella Gelardini, 60–73. Stuttgart: Kohlhammer, 2005.

———. "Scriptural Reasoning—the Dynamic that Informed Paul's Theologizing." *IBS* 26.1 (2004) 32–52. (Also in JSR 5.2 2005 http://etext.lib.virginia.edu/journals/ssr.)

———. *That We May Be Mutually Encouraged: Feminism and the New Perspective in Pauline Studies*. London: T. & T. Clark, 2004.

Ehrensperger, Kathy, and J. Brian Tucker, editors. *Reading Paul in Context: Explorations in Identity Formation: Festschrift in Honour of Willam S. Campbell*. London: T. & T. Clark, 2010.

Eichholz, Georg. *Die Theologie des Paulus im Umriss*. Neukirchen-Vluyn: Neukirchener, 1977.

Eisenbaum, Pamela. "Is Paul the Father of Misogyny and Anti-Semitism?" *Crosscurrents* 50.4 (2000) 506–24.

———. "Paul as the New Abraham." In *Paul and Politics: Ekklesia, Israel, Imperium, Interpretation*, edited by Richard Horsley, 130–45. Harrisburg, PA: Trinity, 2000.

———. "Paul, Polemics and the Problem of Essentialism." *BibInt* 13 (2005) 236–37.

———. *Paul Was Not a Christian: The Original Message of a Misunderstood Paul*. New York: Harper/Collins, 2009.

Elliott, John H. *A Home for the Homeless: A Social-Scientific Criticism of 1 Peter*. Minneapolis: Fortress, 1990.

Elliott, Neil. *The Rhetoric of Romans: Argumentative Constraint and Strategy and Paul's Dialogue with Judaism*. Sheffield, UK: Sheffield Academic, 1990.

———. *Liberating Paul: The Justice of God and the Politics of the Apostle*. Sheffield, UK: Sheffield Academic, 1995.

———. "Paul and the Politics of the Empire." In *Paul and Politics: Ekklesia, Israel, Imperium, Interpretation: Essays in Honor of Krister Stendahl*, edited by Richard A. Horsley, 17–39. Harrisburg, PA: Trinity, 2000.

———. "The Patience of the Jews: Strategies of Resistance and Accommodation to Imperial Cultures." In *Pauline Conversations in Context: Essays in Honor of Calvin J. Roetzel*, edited by Janice C. Anderson and Claudia Setzer, 33–41. Sheffield, UK: Sheffield Academic, 2004.

———. "An American 'Myth of Innocence.'" *BibInt* 13 (2005) 239–49.

———. "Political Formation in the Letter to the Romans." Paper presented at the SBL Annual Meeting, Philadelphia, 2005.

———. *The Arrogance of Nations: Reading Romans in the Shadow of Empire*. Minneapolis: Fortress, 2008.

Bibliography

————. "Paul's Political Christology: Examples from Romans." In *Reading Paul in Context: Explorations in Identity Formation: Essays in Honour of William S. Campbell,* edited by Kathy Ehrensperger and J. Brian Tucker, 30–51. London: T. & T. Clark, 2010.

Engberg-Pedersen, Troels. "For the Jew First: The Coherence of Literary Structure and Thought in Romans in Conversation with James D. G. Dunn." Paper presented at the 1999 SNTS Annual Meeting in Pretoria.

————. *Paul and the Stoics.* Louisvillle: Westminster John Knox, 2000.

————. *Paul beyond the Judaism/Hellenism Divide.* Louisville: Westminster John Knox, 2001.

————, editor. *Paul in His Hellenistic Context.* Edinburgh: T. & T. Clark, 1994.

————. "The Relationship with Others: Similarities and Differences between Paul and Stoicism." *ZNW* 96 (2005) 35–60.

————. "Stoicism in Philippians." In *Paul in His Hellenistic Context,* edited by Troels Engberg-Pedersen, 256–90. T. & T. Clark: Edinburgh, 1994.

Epp, Eldon J. *Junia: The First Woman Apostle.* Minneapolis: Fortress, 2005.

Eskola, Timo. "Paul, Predestination, and Covenantal Nomism." *JST* 28 (1997) 390–412.

Esler, Philip F. "Ancient Oleiculture and Ethnic Differentiation: The Meaning of the Olive-Tree Metaphor in Romans 11." Paper presented at the Social-Scientific Criticism of the New Testament Section, SBL Annual Conference, Denver, 2001.

————. *Conflict and Identity in Romans: The Social Setting of Paul's Letter.* Minneapolis: Fortress, 2003.

————. *The First Christians in their Social Worlds: Social-Scientific Approaches to New Testament Interpretation.* London: Routledge, 1994.

————, editor. *Modelling Early Christianity: Social-Scientific Studies to the New Testament.* London: Routledge, 1995.

————. "Social Identity, Virtue Ethics and the Good Life: A New Approach to Romans 12:1—15:13." *BTB* 33 (2003) 51–63.

————. "Sodom Tradition in Romans 1:18–32." *BTB* 34 (2003) 2–16.

Faust, Eberhard. *Pax Christi et Pax Caesaris: Religionsgeschichtliche, traditionsgeschichtliche und sozialgeschichtliche Studien zum Epheserbrief.* Göttingen: Vandenhoeck & Ruprecht, 1993.

Feldman, Louis. *Josephus's Interpretation of the Bible.* Berkeley, CA: University of California Press, 1998.

Finney, Mark T. "Christ Crucified and the Inversion of Roman Imperial Ideology in 1 Corinthians." *BTB* 35 (2005) 20–33.

Fischer, Karl Martin. *Tendenz und Absicht des Epheserbriefes.* FRLANT 111. Göttingen: Vandenhoeck and Ruprecht, 1973.

Fisk, Bruce N. "Synagogue Influence and Scriptural Knowledge among the Christians at Rome." In *As It Is Written: Studying Paul's Use of Scripture,* edited by Stanley E. Porter and Christopher D. Stanley, 157–85. Atlanta: Society of Biblical Literature, 2008.

Fitzgerald, John T. "Paul and Paradigm Shifts: Reconciliation and Its Linkage Group." In *Paul beyond the Judaism/Hellenism Divide,* edited by Troels Engberg-Pedersen, 241–62. Louisville: Westminster John Knox, 2001.

Fitzmyer, Joseph A. *Paul and His Theology: A Brief Sketch,* 2nd ed. Englewood Cliffs, NJ: Prentice-Hall, 1989.

———. *Romans: A New Translation with Introduction and Commentary.* AB 33. New York: Doubleday, 1993.

Forsman, Rodger. "Double Agency and Identifying Reference to God." *Divine Action: Studies Inspired by the Philosophical Theology of Austin Farrer*, 123–42. Edinburgh: T. & T. Clark, 1990.

Fowl, Stephen. "Learning to Be a Gentile." In *Christology and Scripture: Interdisciplinary Perspectives*, edited by Andrew T. Lincoln and Angus Pattison, 22–40. London: T. & T. Clark, 2007.

———. "A Very Particular Universalism: Badiou and Paul." In *Paul, Philosophy, and Theopolitical Vision: Critical Engagements with Agamben, Badiou, Zizek and Others*, edited by Douglas Harink, 119–34. Eugene, OR: Cascade, 2010.

Fredriksen, Paula. "Augustine and Israel: *Interpretatio ad litteram*, Jews, and Judaism in Augustine's Theology of History." In *Engaging Augustine in Romans: Self, Context, and Theology in Interpretation*, edited by Daniel Patte and Eugene TeSelle, 91–110. Romans through History and Cultures Series. Harrisburg, PA: Trinity, 2002.

———. "Judaism, Circumcision of Gentiles, and Apocalyptic Hope: Another Look at Galatians 1 and 2." *JTS* 42 (1991) 532–64. (Now also in *The Galatians Debate*, edited by Mark D. Nanos, 235–60. Peabody, MA: Hendrickson, 2002.)

———. "Judaizing the Nations: The Ritual Demands of Paul's Gospel." *NTS* 56 (2010) 232–52.

———. "Paul, Purity, and the *Ekklesia* of the Gentiles." In *The Beginnings of Christianity*, edited by Jack Pastor and Menachem Mor, 205–17. Jerusalem: Yad Ben-Zvi, 1997.

———. "What 'Parting of the Ways? Jews, Gentiles and the Ancient Mediterranean City." In *The Ways That Never Parted*, edited by Annette H. Becker and A. Y. Reid, 35–63. Tübingen: Mohr Siebeck, 2003.

Friedrich, Johannes, Wolfgang Poehlman, and Peter Stuhlmacher. "Zur Historischen Situation und Intention von Röm. 13:1–7." *ZTK* 73 (1976) 131–66.

Fruchtenbaum, Arnold G. "A Danger of Throwing out the Baby with the Bathwater." In *How Jewish is Christianity?* edited by L. Goldberg and S. N. Gundry, 66–78. Grand Rapids: Zondervan, 2003.

Furnish, Victor. *2 Corinthians*. Anchor Bible. New York: Doubleday, 1984.

———. *Theology and Ethics in Paul*. Nashville: Abingdon, 1968.

Gäckle, Volker. *Die Starken und die Schwachen in Korinth und in Rom*. Tübingen: Mohr Siebeck, 2005.

Gager, John G. *Reinventing Paul*. Oxford: Oxford University Press, 2000.

———. "Social Description and Sociological Explanation in Early Christianity: A Review Essay." In *The Bible and Liberation: Political and Social Hermeneutics*, edited by Norman Gottwald, 428–40. New York: Orbis, 1983.

———. "Some Notes on Paul's Conversion." *NTS* 27 (1981) 697–704.

Gagnon, Robert. "Why the Weak at Rome Cannot Be Non-Christian Jews." *CBQ* 62 (2000) 54–82.

Garlington, Don B. "The New Perspective on Paul: An Appraisal Two Decades Later." *Criswell Theological Review*, N.S. 2.2 (2005) 17–38

———.*The Obedience of Faith: A Pauline Phrase in Historical Context*. WUNT 38. Tübingen: Mohr Siebeck, 1991.

Gaston, Lloyd. "Faith in Romans 12 in the Light of the Common Life of the Roman Church." In *Common Life in the Early Church: Essays Honoring Graydon F. Snyder*, edited by Julian V. Hill, 258–64. Harrisburg, PA: Trinity, 1998.

————. *Paul and the Torah.* Vancouver, BC: University of British Columbia, 1987.

————. "Retrospect." In *Anti-Judaism in Early Christianity, Vol. 2, Separation and Polemic,* edited by Stephen G. Wilson, 163–74. Waterloo, ON: Wilfred Laurier University Press, 1986.

————. "Romans in Context: The Conversation Revisited." In *Pauline Conversations in Context: Essays in Honor of Calvin J. Roetzel,* edited by Janice C. Anderson and Claudia Setzer, 125–43. Sheffield, UK: Sheffield Academic, 2002.

Gathercole, Simon J. "The Petrine and Pauline *Sola fide* in Galatians 2." In *Lutherische und Neue Paulusperspektive,* edited by Michael Bachmann, 309–27. WUNT 182. Tübingen: Mohr Siebeck, 2005.

Gaventa, Beverly R. *From Darkness to Light.* Philadelphia: Fortress, 1986.

————. *Our Mother Saint Paul.* Louisville: Westminster John Knox, 2007.

————. "The Singularity of the Gospel: A Reading of Galatians." In *Pauline Theology* Vol. 1, edited by David M. Hay, 147–59. Minneapolis: Fortress, 1991.

Georgi, Dieter. "The Early Church: Internal Jewish Migration or New Religion." *HTR* 88.1 (1995) 35–68.

————. "God Turned Upside Down." In *Paul and Empire Religion and Power in Roman Imperial Society,* edited by Richard A. Horsley, 148–57. Harrisburg, PA: Trinity, 1997.

————. *Remembering the Poor: The History of Paul's Collection for Jerusalem.* Nashville: Abingdon, 1992.

————. *Theocracy in Paul's Praxis and Theology.* Minneapolis: Fortress, 1991.

Gerhardsson, Birger. *Memory and Manuscript: Oral Tradition and Written Transmission in Rabbinic Judaism and Early Christianity.* Lund: CWK Gleerup, 1961.

Gombis, Timothy G. "Ephesians 2 as a Narrative of Divine Warfare." *JSNT* 26 (2004) 403–18.

Goodman, Martin. "Who Was a Jew?" The Yarnton Trust Lecture, published as a booklet. Oxford: The Oxford Centre for Postgraduate Hebrew Studies, 1994.

Goppelt, Leonhard. *Jesus, Paul and Judaism: An Introduction to New Testament Theology.* New York: Nelson, 1964.

Gorday, Peter. *Principles of Patristic Exegesis: Romans 9–11 in Origen, John Chrysostum and Augustine.* New York: Mellen, 1983.

Gorman, Michael. *Cruciformity: Paul's Narrative Spirituality of the Cross.* Grand Rapids: Eerdmans, 2001.

Goulder, Michael. *Paul and the Competing Mission in Corinth.* Peabody, MA: Hendrickson, 2001.

Grenholm, Cristina, and Daniel Patte, editors. *Reading Israel in Romans: Legitimacy and Plausibility of Divergent Interpretations.* Romans through History and Cultures Series. Harrisburg, PA: Trinity, 2000.

Grieb, A. Katherine. "Paul's Theological Preoccupation in Romans 9–11." In *Between Gospel and Election: Explorations in the Interpretation of Romans 9–11,* edited by Florian Wilk and J. Ross Wagner, 301–400. Tübingen: Mohr Siebeck, 2010.

Griffiths, Paul J. "The Cross as the Fulcrum of Politics: Expropriating Agamben on Paul." In *Paul, Philosophy, and Theopolitical Vision: Critical Engagements with Agamben, Badiou, Zizek, and Others,* edited by Douglas Harink, 179–87. Eugene OR: Cascade, 2010.

Gruen, Erich S. *Diaspora: Jews amidst Greeks and Romans.* Cambridge: Harvard University Press, 2003.

Bibliography

————. *Heritage and Hellenism: The Reinvention of Jewish Tradition.* Berkeley, CA: University of California Press, 1998.

Gundry, Robert H. "Grace, Works and Staying Saved in Paul." *Bib* 66 (1985) 1–38.

Gundry-Volf, Judith. "Beyond Difference? Paul's Vision of a New Humanity in Galatians 3:28." In *Gospel and Gender: A Trinitarian Engagement with Being Male and Female in Christ,* edited by Douglas A. Campbell, 8–36. London: T. & T. Clark, 2003.

————. "'The One' and 'the Two', Jews, Gentiles, and the Church in Ephesians." Paper read at the SBL Annual Conference, Nashville, 2000.

Haacker, Klaus. "Der Römerbrief als Friedensmemorandum." *NTS* 36 (1990) 25–41.

————. *The Theology of Paul's Letter to the Romans.* Cambridge: Cambridge University Press, 2003.

Hall, Jonathan M. *Ethnic Identity in Greek Antiquity.* Berkeley, CA: University of California Press, 1997.

Hansen, Gary N. "Door and Passageway: Calvin's use of Romans as Theological and Hermeneutical Guide." In *Reformation Readings of Romans,* edited by Kathy Ehrensperger and R. Ward Holder, 77–94. Romans through History and Cultures Series. London: T. & T. Clark 2008.

Hanson, Anthony T. *The Living Utterances of God: The New Testament Exegesis of the Old.* London: Darton, Longman and Todd, 1983.

————. *Studies in Paul's Technique and Theology.* London: SPCK, 1974.

Hanson, G. Walter. *Abraham in Galatians: Epistolary and Rhetorical Contexts.* Sheffield, UK: Sheffield Academic, 1989.

Hare, Richard M. *Essays in Philosophical Method.* London: Macmillan, 1971.

Harink, Douglas. *Paul among the Postliberals: Pauline Theology beyond Christendom and Modernity.* Grand Rapids: Brazos, 2003.

————. "Paul and Israel: An Apocalyptic Reading." Paper delivered at the Pauline Soteriological Group at the SBL Annual Meeting, Philadelphia, 2005.

————. editor. *Paul, Philosophy, and Theopolitical Vision: Critical Engagements with Agamben, Badiou, Zizek, and Others.* Eugene OR: Cascade, 2010.

Harnack Adolf von. *Die Mission und Ausbreitung des Christentums in den ersten drei Jahrhunderten.* 4th ed. Leipzig: Hinrichs, 1924.

Harrill, J. Albert. *The Manumission of Slaves in Early Christianity.* Tübingen: Mohr Siebeck, 1995.

Harvey, Anthony E. "Forty Strokes Save One: Social Aspects of Judaizing and Apostasy." In *Alternative Approaches to New Testament Study,* edited by Anthony E. Harvey, 79–96. London: SPCK, 1985.

Hay, David M. editor. *Pauline Theology, Vol. II: 1 & 2 Corinthians.* Minneapolis: Fortress, 1993.

Hay, David M., and Elisabeth E. Johnson, editors. *Pauline Theology, Vol. III: Romans.* Minneapolis: Fortress, 1995.

Hays, Richard. "Crucified with Christ: A Synthesis of the Theology of 1 and 2 Thessalonians, Philemon, Philippians and Galatians." In *Pauline Theology, Vol.1,* edited by David M. Hay, 227–46. Minneapolis: Fortress, 1995.

————. *Echoes of Scripture in the Letters of Paul.* New Haven: Yale University Press, 1989.

Bibliography

————. "The Role of Scripture in Paul's Ethics." In *Theology and Ethics in Paul and His Interpreters: Essays in Honour of Victor Paul Furnish*, edited by Eugene H. Lovering and Jerry L. Sumney, 30–48. Nashville: Abingdon, 1996.

Heckel, Ulrich. "Das Bild der Heiden und die Identität der Christen bei Paulus." In *Die Heiden: Juden, Christen, und das Problem des Fremden*, edited by Reinhold Feldmeier and Ulrich Heckel, 269–96. Tübingen: Mohr Siebeck, 1994.

Heemstra, Marius. *The Fiscus Judaicus and the Parting of the Ways*. Tübingen, Mohr Siebeck, 2010.

Hellholm David, et al., editors. *Mighty Minorities? Minorities in Early Christianity— Positions and Strategies*. Oslo: Skandinavian University Press, 1995.

Heschel, Susannah. *Abraham Geiger and the Jewish Jesus*. Chicago: University of Chicago Press, 1998.

Hock, Ronald F. *The Social Context of Paul's Ministry*. Philadelphia: Fortress, 1980.

Hodge, Caroline J. *If Sons, Then Heirs: A Study of Kinship and Ethnicity in the Letters of Paul*. Oxford: Oxford University Press, 2007.

Holl, Karl. "Der Kirchenbegriff des Paulus in seinem Verhaltnis zu dem der Urgemeinde." In *Aufsätze zur Kirchengeschichte* II, edited by Holl, Karl, 44–67. Tübingen: Mohr, 1928.

Holmberg, Bengt. "Identity as a Textual Phenomenon." In *Exploring Christian Identity: Understanding the First Hindred Years of Christian Identity*, edited by Bengt Holmberg et al., 1–32. Tübingen: Mohr/Siebeck, 2008.

————. "Jewish versus Christian Identity in the Church." *RB* 105-3 (1998) 397–425.

————. "The Methods of Historical Reconstruction in the Scholarly 'Recovery' of Corinthian Christianity." In *Christianity at Corinth: The Quest for the Pauline Church*, edited by Edward Adams and David Horrell, 255–71. Louisville: Westminster, John Knox, 2004.

————. *Paul and Power: The Structure of Power in the Primitive Church as Reflected in the Pauline Epistles*. Philadelphia: Fortress, 1980.

Holmberg, Bengt et al., editors. *Exploring Christian Identity*. Tübingen: Mohr Siebeck, 2008.

Hooker, Morna D. *Continuity and Discontinuity: Early Christianity in Its Jewish Setting*. London: Epworth, 1986.

————. "'Heirs of Abraham': The Gentiles' Role in Israel's Story—A Response to Bruce W. Longenecker." In *Narrative Dynamics in Paul: A Critical Assessment*, edited by Bruce W. Longenecker, 85–96. Louisville: Westminster John Knox, 2002.

————. "Paul and Paulinism." In *Paul and Paulinism: Essays in Honour of C. K. Barrett*, edited by Morna D. Hooker and Stephen D. Wilson, 102–14. London: SPCK, 1982.

Hooker, Morna D., and Stephen D. Wilson, editors. *Paul and Paulinism: Essays in Honour of C. K. Barrett*. London: SPCK, 1982.

Horbury, William. "The Depiction of the Judaeo-Christians in the Toledot Yeshu." In *The Image of the Judaeo-Christians in Ancient Jewish and Christian Literature*, edited by Peter J. Tomson and Doris Lambers-Petry, 280–86. WUNT 158. Tübingen: Mohr Siebeck, 2003.

————. *Jews and Christians in Contact and Controversy*. Edinburgh: T. & T. Clark, 1998.

Horn, Ferdinand W. "Juden und Heiden. Aspekte der Verhältnisbestimmung in den paulinischen Briefen. Ein Gespräch mit Krister Stendahl." In *Lutherische und Neue Paulusperspektive*, edited by Michael Bachmann, 17–39. Tübingen: Mohr Siebeck, 2005.

Bibliography

Horowitz, D. L. *Ethnic Groups in Conflict*. Berkeley, CA: University of California Press, 1985.

Horrell, David G. "From Ἀδέλφοι to οἶκος θεοῦ: Social Transformation in Pauline Christianity." *JBL* 120 (2001) 293–311.

———. "'No Longer Jew or Greek' Paul's Corporate Christology and the Construction of Christianity." In *Christology, Controversy and Community: New Testament Essays in Honour of David R. Catchpole*, edited by David G. Horrell and Christopher M. Tuckett, 320–44. Leiden: Brill, 2000.

———. "Paul's Narratives or Narrative Substructure? The Significance of Paul's Story." In *Narrative Dynamics in Paul: A Critical Assessment*, edited by Bruce W. Longenecker, 157–71. Louisville: Westminster John Knox, 2002.

———. *Solidarity and Difference: A Contemporary Reading of Paul's Ethics*. London: T. & T. Clark, 2005.

Horsley, Richard A. "1 Corinthians: A Case Study of Paul's Assembly as an Alternative Society." In *Christianity at Corinth: The Quest for the Pauline Church*, edited by *Edward* Adams and David G. Horrell, 227–37. Louisville: Westminster John Knox, 2004.

———, editor. *Paul and Empire: Religion and Power in Roman Imperial Society*. Harrisburg, PA: Trinity, 1997.

———, editor. *Paul and Politics: Ekklesia, Israel, Imperium, Interpretation. Essays in Honour of Krister Stendahl*. Harrisburg, PA: Trinity, 2000.

———. "Rhetoric and Empire—and 1 Corinthians." In *Paul and Politics: Ekklesia, Israel, Imperium, Interpretation*, edited by Richard A. Horsley, 72–102. Harrisburg, PA: Trinity, 2000.

Hubbard, Moyer V. *New Creation in Paul's Letters and Thought*. SNTSMS 119. Cambridge: Cambridge University Press, 2002.

Hultgren, Arland J. *Paul's Letter to the Romans: A Commentary*. Grand Rapids: Eerdmans, 2011.

Hutchinson, John, and A. D. Smith, editors. *Ethnicity*. Oxford: Oxford University Press, 1996.

Jenkins, Richard. *Rethinking Ethnicity: Arguments and Explorations*. London: Sage, 1997.

———. *Social Identity*. London: Routledge, 1996.

Jervell, Jacob. "The Letter to Jerusalem." In *The Romans Debate*, edited by Karl Donfried, 53–64. Peabody, MA: Hendrickson, 1991.

———. "Mighty Minority." *ST* 34 (1980) 13–38.

Jewett, Robert. *Christian Tolerance: Paul's Message to the Modern Church*. Philadelphia: Westminster, 1982.

———. "Following the Argument of Romans." In *The Romans Debate*, 2nd ed, edited by Karl P. Donfried, 265–77. Peabody, MA: Hendrickson, 1991.

———. "The Law and the Co-Existence of Jews and Gentiles in Romans." *Interpretation* 39 (1985) 341–56.

———. *Letter to Pilgrims. A Commentary on the Epistle to the Hebrews*. New York: Pilgrim, 1981.

———. "Paul, Phoebe and the Spanish Mission." In *The Social World of Formative Christianity and Judaism: Essays in Tribute to Howard Clark Kee*, edited by Jacob Neusner et al., 142–61. Philadelphia: Fortress, 1988.

———. *Paul's Anthropological Terms: A Study of their Use in Conflict Settings*. Leiden: Brill, 1971.

Bibliography

————. "Romans as an Ambassadorial Letter." *Interpretation* 36 (1982) 5–20.

————. *Romans: A Commentary*. Hermeneia. Minneapolis: Fortress, 2007.

————. "Tenement Churches and Communal Meals in the Early Church: The Implications of a Form-Critical Analysis of 2 Thessalonians 3:10." *BR* 38 (1993) 23–42.

Johnson, E. Elisabeth. *The Function of Apocalyptic and Wisdom Traditions in Romans 9–11*. SBLDS. Atlanta: Scholars, 1989.

Johnson, E. Elisabeth, and David Hay, editors. *Pauline Theology, Vol. IV: Looking Back, Pressing On*. Atlanta: Scholars, 1997.

Judge, Edwin A. "St Paul and Classical Society." *JAC* (1972) 19–36.

————. "The Roman Base of Paul's Mission." *TynBul* 56 (2005) 103–17.

Judge, Edwin A., and G. S. R. Thomas. "The Origin of the Church at Rome: A New Solution." *Reformed Theological Review* 25.3 (1966) 81–94.

Kahl, Brigitte. *Galatians Re-Imagined: Reading with the Eyes of the Vanquished*. Minneapolis: Fortress, 2010.

————. "Gender Trouble in Galatia: Paul and the Rethinking of Difference." In *Is There a Future for Feminist Theology?* edited by Deborah F. Sawyer & Diane M. Collier, 57–73. Sheffield, UK: Sheffield Academic, 1999.

Karris, Robert J. "The Occasion of Romans: A Response to Professor Donfried." In *The Romans Debate*, 2nd ed., edited by Karl P. Donfried, 165–84 and 125–27. Peabody, MA: Hendrickson, 1991.

Käsemann, Ernst. *Commentary on Romans*. London: SCM, 1980.

————. "The Faith of Abraham in Romans 4." In *Perspectives on Paul*, 79–101. London: SCM, 1971.

————. "Justification and Salvation History in the Epistle to the Romans." In *New Testament Questions for Today*, 60–78. London: SCM, 1969.

————. *New Testament Questions of Today*. London: SCM, 1969.

————. "On the Subject of Primitive Christian Apocalyptic." In *New Testament Questions for Today*, 108–37. London: SCM, 1969.

————. "Paul and Israel." In *New Testament Questions for Today*, 183–87. London: SCM, 1969.

————. *Perspectives on Paul*. London: SCM, 1971.

————. "The Righteousness of God in Paul." *New Testament Questions for Today*, 168–82. London: SCM, 1969.

Kaylor, R. David. *Paul's Covenant Community: Jew and Gentile in Romans*. Atlanta: John Knox, 1988.

Keck, Leander. "The Poor among the Saints in the New Testament." *ZNW* 56 (1965) 100–129.

————. *Romans*. Abingdon New Testament Commentaries. Nashville: Abingdon, 2005.

————. "What Makes Romans Tick?" In *Pauline Theology, Vol. III: Romans*, edited by David Hay, 3–29. Minneapolis: Fortress, 1995.

Kee, Howard C. *Knowing the Truth: A Sociological Approach to New Testament Interpretation*. Philadelphia: Fortress, 1989.

Kee Howard C., and L. H. Cohick. "Defining the First-Century CE Synagogue: Progress and Problems." In *Evolution of the Synagogue: Progress and Problems*, 11–23. Harrisburg, PA: Trinity, 2000.

Bibliography

Keesmaat, Sylvia C. *Paul and His Story: (Re)Interpreting the Exodus Tradition.* Sheffield, UK: JSOT, 1999.

Kelley, Shawn. *Racializing Jesus: Race, Ideology and the Formation of Modern Biblical Scholarship.* London: Routledge, 2002.

Kertelge, Karl. *Rechtfertigung bei Paulus.* Münster: Aschendorff, 1967.

Kettunen, Markku. *Der Abfassungszweck des Römerbriefes.* Annales Academiae Scientiarum Fennicae. Helsinki: Suomalainen Tiedeakemia, 1979.

Kim, Seyoon. *The Origin of Paul's Gospel.* WUNT 2/4. Tübingen: Mohr Siebeck, 1981.

Kim, Yung Suk. *Christ's Body in Corinth: The Politics of a Metaphor.* Minneapolis: Fortress, 2008.

Kittredge, Cynthia Briggs. *Community and Authority: The Rhetoric of Obedience in the Pauline Tradition.* Harrisburg, PA: Trinity, 1998.

Klein, Günter. "Römer 4 und die Idee der Heilsgeschichte." *Evangelische Theologie* 23 (1963) 424–47 (Also in *Rekonstruktion und Interpretation,* 145–79. München: Kaiser, 1969.)

Kloppenborg, John S., and Stephen G. Wilson editors. *Voluntary Associations in the Graeco-Roman World.* London: Routledge, 1996.

Knox, John. *The Epistle to the Romans.* The Interpreter's Bible. Nashville: Abingdon, 1951.

Koester, Helmut. *Introduction to the New Testament,* Vol. 2. Philadelphia: Fortress, 1982.

Kraftchick, Stephen J. "Death's Parsing: Experience as a Mode of Theology in Paul." In *Pauline Conversations in Context: Essays in Honour of Calvin J. Roetzel,* edited by Janice C. Anderson and Claudia Setzer, 144–66. Sheffield, UK: Sheffield Academic, 2002.

Krauss, Wolfgang. "Gottes Gerechtigkeit und Gottes Volk. Oekumenisch—ekklesiologische Aspekte der New Perspective on Paul." In *Lutherische und Neue Paulusperspektive,* edited by Michael Bachmann, 329–48. Tübingen: Mohr Siebeck, 2005.

Kreitzer, Larry J. "The Messianic Man of Peace as Temple Builder: Solomonic Imagery in Ephesians 2:13–22." In *Temple and Worship in Biblical Israel: Proceedings of the Oxford Old Testament Seminar,* edited by John Day, 484–512. London: T. & T. Clark, 2005.

Krentz Edgar. "On Tracking the Elusive Center: On Integrating Paul's Theology." Seminar Paper presented at SBL, New Orleans, 1990.

Kümmel, Werner G. *The New Testament: The History of Its Problems.* Nashville: Abingdon, 1972.

LaGrande, James. "Proliferation of the 'Gentile' in the New Revised Standard Version." *BR* 41 (1996) 77–87.

Lambrecht, Jan. "Reconcile Yourselves . . . A Reading of 2 Corinthians 5:11–21." In *Studies in 2 Corinthians,* edited by Reimund Bieringer and Jan Lambrecht, 263–68. Leuven: Leuven University Press, 1994.

Lampe, Peter. *From Paul to Valentinus: Christians at Rome in the First Two Centuries.* Translated by M. Steinhauser. London: T. & T. Clark 2003.

Lane, William L. "Social Perspectives on Roman Christianity during the Formative Years from Nero to Nerva." In *Judaism and Christianity in First Century Rome,* edited by Karl P. Donfried and Peter Richardson, 196–244. Grand Rapids: Eerdmans 1998.

Langton, Daniel R. "Modern Jewish Identity and the Apostle Paul: Pauline Studies as an Intra-Jewish Ideological Battleground." *JSNT* 28 (2005) 217–58.

———. "The Myth of the 'Traditional View of Paul' and the Role of the Apostle in Modern Jewish-Christian Polemics." *JSNT* 28 (2005) 69–104.

Lee, Jae W. "Justification of Difference in Galatians." Paper presented at the SBL Annual Meeting Philadelphia, 2005.

———. "Paul and Reconciliation in Romans: From a Korean Post-Colonial Perspective." Paper presented at the SBL Annual Meeting, New Orleans, 2009.

Leenhardt, Franz J. *The Epistle to the Romans.* London: Lutterworth, 1961.

Leonhardt-Balzer, Jutta. "Jewish Worship and Universal Identity in Philo of Alexandria." In *Jewish Identity in the Greco-Roman World,* edited by Jörg Frey, et al., 29–54. Leiden: Brill, 2007.

Levinas, Emmanuel. *Totality and Infinity: An Essay on Exteriority.* Translated by A. Lingis. Pittsburgh, PA: Duquesne University Press, 1969.

Levine, Lee L. *The Ancient Synagogue: The First Thousand Years.* 2nd ed. New Haven, CT: Yale University Press, 2005.

———. "The First Century C.E. Synagogue in Historical Perspective." In *The Ancient Synagogue from its Origins until 200 CE,* edited by Birger Olsson and Magnus Zetterholm, 1–24. Stockholm: Almqvist & Wiksell, 2003.

Lieu, Judith M. "The Attraction of Women in/to Early Judaism and Christianity: Gender and the Politics of Conversion." *JSNT* 72 (1998) 5–22.

———. *Image and Reality: The Jews in the World of the Christians in the Second Century.* Edinburgh: T. & T. Clark, 1996.

———. "'Impregnable Ramparts and Walls of Iron': Boundary and Identity in Early 'Judaism' and 'Christianity.'" *NTS* 48 (2002) 297–313.

———. *Neither Jew Nor Greek: Constructing Early Christianity.* London: T. & T. Clark, 2002.

Lim, Kar Y. *The Sufferings of Christ Are Abundant in US (2 Corinthians 1:5): A Narrative Dynamics Investigation of Paul's Sufferings in 2 Corinthians.* London: T. & T. Clark, 2009.

Lim, Timothy H., editor. *The Dead Sea Scrolls in Their Historical Context.* Edinburgh: T. & T. Clark, 2000.

Lincoln, Andrew T. "The Church and Israel in Ephesians 2." *CBQ* 49 (1987) 601–27.

———. *Ephesians.* Word Biblical Commentary. Dallas: Word, 1990.

———. *Paradise Now and Not Yet.* Cambridge: Cambridge University Press, 1981.

Lindsay, Dennis R. *Josephus and Faith: Pistis and Pisteuein as Faith Terminology in the Writings of Flavius Josephus and the New Testament.* Leiden: Brill, 1993.

———. "The Roots and Development of the '*pist*' Word Group as Faith Terminology." *JSNT* 49 (1993) 103–18.

Lodge, John G. *Romans 9–11: A Reader-Response Analysis.* Atlanta: Scholars, 1996.

Lofland, John, and Rodney Stark. "Becoming a World-Savior: A Theory of Conversion to a Deviant Perspective." *American Sociological Review* 30 (1965) 862–75.

Longenecker, Bruce, editor. *Narrative Dynamics in Paul: A Critical Assessment.* Louisville: Westminster/John Knox, 2002.

Longenecker, Richard N. *Introducing Romans: Critical Issues in Paul's Most Famous Letter.* Grand Rapids: Eerdmans, 2011.

Lopez, Davina. *Apostle to the Conquered: Reimagining Paul's Mission.* Minneapolis: Fortress, 2008.

Lüdemann, Gerd. *Opposition to Paul in Jewish Christianity.* Minneapolis: Fortress, 1989.

————. *Paul, Apostle to the Gentiles: Studies in Chronology.* Philadelphia: Fortress, 1982.

MacDonald, Margaret Y. "The Politics of Identity in Ephesians." *JSNT* 26 (2005) 419–44.

————., Osiek, Carolyn, *A Woman's Place: House Churches in Earliest Christianity.* Minneapolis: Fortress 2006.

Magda, K. *Paul's Territoriality and Mission Strategy.* Tübingen: Mohr Siebeck, 2009.

Magonet, Jonathan. "The Biblical Roots of Jewish Identity: Exploring the Relativity of Exegesis." *JSOT* 54 (1992) 3–24.

Malherbe, Abraham. *Social Aspects of Early Christianity.* Baton Rouge, LA: Louisiana State University Press 1977.

Malina, Bruce. "Social-scientific Methods in Historical Jesus Research." In *Jesus and the Gospels,* edited by Wolfgang Stegemann et al., 3–26. Minneapolis: Fortress, 2002.

Manson, Thomas W. "Paul's Letter to the Romans and Others." *BJRL* 31 (1948) 224–40.

Marcus, Joel. "The Circumcision and Uncircumcision in Rome." *NTS* 35 (1989) 67–81.

————. "'Under the Law': The Background of a Pauline Expression." *CBQ* 63 (2001) 72–83.

Martin, Dale B. "Paul and the Judaism/Hellenism Dichotomy: Toward a Social History of the Question." In *Paul beyond the Judaism/Hellenism Divide,* edited by Engberg-Pedersen Troels, 29–62. Louisville: Westminster John Knox, 2001.

————. *Slavery as Salvation.* New Haven: Yale University Press, 1990.

Martin, Ralph P. *2 Corinthians.* Word Biblical Commentary. Waco, TX: Word, 1986.

————. *Reconciliation: A Study of Paul's Theology.* Atlanta: John Knox, 1981.

————. "Reconciliation in 2 Corinthians." *NTS* 35 (1989) 550–81.

Martin, Troy W. "Apostasy to Paganism: The Rhetorical Stasis of the Galatian Controversy." In *The Galatians Debate,* edited by Mark D. Nanos, 73–94. Peabody, MA: Hendrickson, 2002.

————. "The Covenant of Circumcision (Genesis 17:9–14) and the Situational Antithesis in Galatians 3:28." *JBL* 122 (2003) 111–25.

Martyn, J. Louis. "Apocalyptic Antinomies in Paul's Letter to the Galatians." *NTS* 31 (1985) 410–24.

————. "Events in Galatia: Modified Covenantal Nomism versus God's Invasion of the Cosmos in the Singular Gospel: A Response to J. D. G. Dunn and B. R. Gaventa." In *Pauline Theology, Vol I,* edited by Jouette M. Bassler, 160–79. Minneapolis: Fortress, 1991.

————. *Galatians: A New Translation with Introduction and Commentary.* New York: Doubleday, 1997.

————. "Listening to Paul and John on the Subject of Gospel and Scripture." *WW* 12 (1992) 61–81.

————. *Theological Issues in the Letters of Paul.* Nashville: Abingdon, 1997.

Marxsen, Willy. *Introduction to the New Testament.* Oxford: Blackwell, 1968.

Matera, Frank J. *New Testament Theology: Exploring Diversity and Unity.* Louisville: Westminster John Knox, 2007.

Matlock, R. Barry. *Unveiling the Apocalyptic Paul: Paul's Interpreters and the Rhetoric of Criticism.* Sheffield, UK: Sheffield Academic, 1996.

McGinn, Sheila E., editor. *Celebrating Romans: Template for Pauline Theology. Essays in Honor of Robert Jewett.* Grand Rapids: Eerdmans, 2004.

———. "Feminists and Paul in Romans 8:18–23: Toward a Theology of Creation." In *Gender, Tradition and Romans: Shared Ground, Uncertain Borders,* edited by Cristina Grenholm and Daniel Patte, 21–38. London: T. & T. Clark, 2005.

Meeks, Wayne A. "Breaking Away: Three New Testament Pictures of Christianity's Separation from the Jewish Communities." In *To See Ourselves as Others See Us: Christians, Jews and Others in Late Antiquity,* edited by Jacob Neusner and E. S. Frerichs, 93–115. Chico, CA: Scholars, 1985.

———. *Christ is the Question.* Louisville: Westminster John Knox, 2006.

———. "The Circle of Reference in Pauline Morality." In *Greeks, Romans, Christians: Essays in Honour of Abraham Malherbe,* edited by David Balch et al., 305–15. Minneapolis: Fortress, 1998.

———. *The First Urban Christians: The Social World of the Apostle Paul.* New Haven: Yale University Press, 1983.

———. "Judaism, Hellenism, and the Birth of Christianity." In *Paul beyond the Judaism/Hellenism Divide,* edited by Troels Engberg Pedersen, 17–28. Louisville: Westminster John Knox, 2001.

———. "Judgment and the Brother: Romans 14:1—15:13." In *Tradition and Interpretation in the New Testament: Essays in Honor of E. Earle Ellis,* edited by Gerald F. Hawthorne and Otto Betz, 290–300. Grand Rapids: Eerdmans, 1987.

———. "On Trusting an Unpredictable God: A Hermeneutical Meditation on Romans 9–11." In *Faith and History: Essays in Honor of Paul W. Meyer,* edited by J. T. Carroll et al., 105–24. Atlanta: Scholars, 1990.

———. *The Origins of Christian Morality: The First Two Centuries.* New Haven: Yale University Press, 1993.

Meeks, Wayne A., and Robert L. Wilken. *Jews and Christians in Antioch: In the First Four Centuries of the Common Era.* Missoula, MT: Scholars, 1978.

Megahey, Alan. *The Irish Protestant Churches in the Twentieth Century.* London: Macmillan, 2000.

Mendes-Flohr, Paul. *German Jews: A Dual Identity.* New Haven: Yale University Press, 1999.

Meyer, Ben F. "The World Mission and the Emergent Realisation of Christian Identity." In *Critical Realism and the New Testament,* edited by Allison Park, 173–94. Princeton Theological Monograph Series 17. Philadelphia: Pickwick, 1989.

Meyer, Paul. "The Justification of God: Response to C. H. Cosgrove." Paper read at the SBL Pauline Theology Group.

———. "Pauline Theology: Some Thoughts for a Pause in its Pursuit." *SBLSP* edited by Eugene H. Lovering Jr., 688–703. Atlanta: Scholars, 1995.

Michel, Otto. *Der Brief an die Römer: Kritisch exegetischer Kommentar über das Neue Testament.* Göttingen: Vandenhoeck & Ruprecht, 1976.

Minear, Paul S. *The Obedience of Faith: The Purpose of Paul in the Letter to the Romans.* London: SCM, 1971.

Mitchell, Margaret. *The Heavenly Trumpet: John Chrysostom and the Art of Pauline Interpretation.* Tübingen: Mohr Siebeck, 2000.

Mitternacht, Dieter. "Current Views on the Synagogue of Ostia Antica and the Jews of Rome and Ostia." In *The Ancient Synagogue: From its Origins until 200 C.E.,* edited by Olsson Birger and Magnus Zetterholm, 521–71. Stockholm: Almqvist & Wiksell, 2003.

———. "Foolish Galatians? A Recipient-Oriented Assessment of Paul's Letter to the Galatians." In *The Galatians Debate: Contemporary Issues in Rhetorical and Historical Interpretation,* edited by Mark D. Nanos, 408–33. Peabody, MA: Hendrickson, 2002.

Moo, Douglas. *The Epistle to the Romans.* Grand Rapids: Eerdmans, 1996.

Moore, George F. "Christian Writers on Judaism." *HTR* 14 (1921) 197–254.

Muddiman, John. *The Epistle to the Ephesians.* New York: Continuum, 2001.

Munck, Johannes. *Christ and Israel: An Interpretation of Romans 9–11.* Philadelphia: Fortress, 1967.

———. *Paul and the Salvation of Mankind.* London: SCM, 1959.

Murphy-O'Connor, Jerome. *Paul: A Critical Life.* Oxford: Clarendon, 1996.

———. *Paul: His Story.* Oxford: Oxford University Press, 2004.

Mustakallio, Antti. "The Very First Audiences of Paul's Letters: The Implications of End Greetings." In *The Nordic Paul: Finnish Approaches to Pauline Theology,* edited by Lars Aejmelaeus and Antti Mustakallio, 227–37. London: T. & T. Clark, 2008.

Nagata, J. A. *The Reflowering of Malaysian Islam: Modern Religious Radicals and Their Roots.* Vancouver, BC: University of British Columbia Press, 1984.

———. "What is a Malay? Situational Selection of Ethnic Identity in a Plural Society." *American Ethnologist* 1 (1974) 331–50.

Nanos, Mark D., editor. *The Galatians Debate: Contemporary Issues in Rhetorical and Historical Interpretation.* Peabody, MA: Hendrickson, 2002.

———. "How Inter-Christian Approaches to Paul's Rhetoric Can Perpetuate Negative Evaluations of Jewishness—Although Proposing to Avoid that Outcome." *Bib.Int.,* 13 (2005) 255–69.

———. "The Inter- and Intra-Jewish Political Context of Paul's Letter to the Galatians." In *Paul and Politics: Ekklesia, Israel, Imperium, Interpretation,* edited by Richard A. Horsley, 146–59. Harrisburg, PA: Trinity, 2000. (Also in *The Galatians Debate: Contemporary Issues in Rhetorical and Historical Interpretation,* edited by Mark D. Nanos, 396–407. Peabody, MA: Hendrickson, 2002.)

———. "Introduction." In *The Galatians Debate: Contemporary Issues in Rhetorical and Historical Interpretation,* edited by Mark D. Nanos, xi–xli. Peabody, MA: Hendrickson, 2002.

———. *The Irony of Galatians: Paul's Letter in First-Century Context.* Minneapolis: Fortress, 2002.

———. "The Jewish Context of the Gentile Audience Addressed in Paul's Letter to the Romans." *CBQ* 61 (1999) 283–304.

———. *The Mystery of Romans: The Jewish Context of Paul's Letter to the Romans.* Minneapolis: Fortress, 1996.

———. "Paul's Reversal of Jews Calling Gentiles 'Dogs' (Philippians 3:2): 1600 Years of an Ideological Tale Wagging an Exegetical Dog?" *Bib.Int.* 17 (2008) 448–82.

———. "What Was at Stake in Peter's 'Eating with Gentiles' at Antioch?" In *The Galatians Debate: Contemporary Issues in Rhetorical and Historical Interpretation,* 282–318. Peabody, MA: Hendrickson, 2002.

Nguyen, Henry. *Christian Identity at Corinth: A Comparative Study of 2 Corinthians, Epictetus and Valerius Maximus.* WUNT 243. Tübingen: Mohr Siebeck, 2008.

Nickelsburg, George W. *Ancient Judaism and Christian Origins: Diversity, Continuity and Transformation.* Minneapolis: Fortress, 2003.

Nickelsburg, George W. E., and George W. MacRae, editors. *Christians among Jews and Gentiles: Essays in Honor of Krister Stendahl on His Sixty-fifth Birthday.* Philadelphia: Fortress, 1986.

Niebuhr, Karl W. *Heidenapostel aus Israel: Die Jüdische Identität des Paulus nach ihrer Darstellung in seinen Briefen.* Tübingen: Mohr Siebeck, 1992.

Nineham, David. *The Use and Abuse of the Bible.* London: SPCK, 1976.

Noack, Bengt. "Current and Backwater in the Epistle to the Romans." *Studia Theologica* 19 (1965) 155–65.

Nobs, Alanna. "'Beloved Brothers' in the New Testament and Early Christian World." In *The New Testament in Its First Century Setting: Essays on Context and Background in Honour of B. W. Winter on His 65th Birthday,* edited by Andrew D. Clarke et al., 143–50. Grand Rapids: Eerdmans, 2004.

Olson, Dennis T. *Deuteronomy and the Death of Moses: A Theological Reading.* Minneapolis: Fortress, 1994.

Olsson, Birger, and Magnus Zetterholm, editors. *The Ancient Synagogue: From Its Origins until 200 C.E.* Stockholm: Almqvist & Wiksell, 2003.

Olsson, Birger. "The Origins of the Synagogue: An Evaluation." In *The Ancient Synagogue: From Its Origins until 200 C.E.,* edited by Birger Olsson and Magnus Zetterholm, 132–38. Stockholm: Almqvist & Wiksell, 2003.

Opitz, Peter. "Bullinger on Romans." In *Reformation Readings of Romans,* edited by Kathy Ehrensperger and R. Ward Holder, 148–65. London: T. & T. Clark, 2007.

Ortlund, Dane C. *Zeal without Knowledge: The Concept of Zeal in Romans 10, Galatians 1, and Philippians 3.* London: T. & T. Clark 2013.

Osiek, Carolyn. "The Oral World of the First Christians at Rome." Paper read at the SNTS Annual Meeting, Chicago, 1993.

O'Sullivan, Oliver, editor. *The Bible as Book: The Reformation.* London: British Library, 2000.

Painter, John. "James and Peter: Models of Leadership and Mission." In *The Missions of James, Peter, and Paul: Tensions in Early Christianity,* edited by Bruce Chilton and Craig Evans, 143–209. Leiden: Brill, 2005.

Park, Eung Chun. *Either Jew or Gentile: Paul's Unfolding Theology of Inclusivity.* Louisville: Westminster John Knox, 2003.

Parkes, James. *The Conflict of the Church and the Synagogue: A Study in the Origins of Antisemitism.* 4th reprint. New York: Atheneum, 1979.

Patte, Daniel. *Early Jewish Hermeneutics in Palestine.* SBLDS 22. Missoula, MT: Scholars, 1975.

———. *Paul's Faith and the Power of the Gospel: A Structural Introduction to the Pauline Letters.* Philadelphia: Fortress, 1983.

Patte, Daniel, and Cristina Grenholm, editors. *Modern Interpretations of Romans: Tracking Their Hermeneutical/Theological Trajectory.* Romans through History and Cultures Series 10. London: T. & T. Clark, 2013.

Patte, Daniel, and Eugene TeSelle, editors. *Engaging Augustine in Romans: Self, Context, and Theology in Interpretation.* Romans through History and Cultures Series. Harrisburg, PA: Trinity, 2003

Pauck, Wilhelm. *Luther: Lectures on Romans.* Library of Christian Classics 15. London: SCM, 1961.

Peerbolte, Lietaert J. L. *Paul the Missionary.* Leuven: Peeters, 2003.

Bibliography

Perkins, Pheme. *Ephesians*. Abingdon New Testament Commentaries. Nashville: Abingdon, 1997.

Plietzsch, Susanne. *Kontexte der Freiheit:Konzepte der Befreiung bei Paulus und im rabbinischen Judentum*. Stuttgart: Kohlhammer, 2005.

Plummer, Alfred. *2 Corinthians*. ICC. Edinburgh: T. & T. Clark, 1951.

Porter, Stanley E. "The Argument of Romans 5: Can a Rhetorical Question Make a Difference?" *JBL* 110 (1991) 655–77.

Quine, Van Orman Willard. *From a Logical Point of View*. Cambridge: Harvard University Press, 1961.

Rader, William. *The Church and Racial Hostility: A History of the Interpretation of Ephesians 2:11–22*. Tübingen: Mohr Siebeck, 1978.

Räisänen, Heikki. *Die paulinische Literatur und Theologie*. Aarhus: Forlaget Aros, 1980.

———. *Paul and the Law*. WUNT. Tübingen: Mohr Siebeck, 1983.

———. *Beyond New Testament Theology*. London: SCM, 1990.

———. "Paul's Conversion and the Development of His View of the Law." *NTS* 33 (1987) 404–19.

———. "Paul, God, and Israel: Romans 9–11 in Recent Research." In *The Social World of Formative Christianity and Judaism: Essays in Tribute to Howard Clark Kee*, edited by Jacob Neusner et al., 178–206. Philadelphia: Fortress, 1988.

Rajak, Tessa. "The Jewish Community and its Boundaries." In *The Jews among Pagans and Christians in the Roman Empire*, edited by Judith Lieu et al., 9–28. London: Routledge, 1992.

Rambo, Louis R. *Understanding Religious Conversion*. New Haven: Yale University Press, 1993.

Rauer, Maximilian. *Die "Schwachen" in Korinth und Rom nach den Paulusbriefen*. BT 120. Freiburg: Herder, 1923.

Reasoner, Mark. "Potentes and Inferiores in the Roman Church." Paper read in the SBL annual meeting, San Francisco, 1992.

———. *The Strong and the Weak in Romans 14:1—15:13 in Context*. Cambridge: Cambridge University Press, 1999.

Reckwitz, Andreas. "Der Identitätdiskurs: Zur Bedeutung einer sozialwissenschaftlichen Semantik: Kollektive Identitäten und kulturelle Innovationen." In *Ethnologische, soziologische und historische Studien*, edited by Werner Rammert et al., 21–38. Leipzig: Leipziger Universitätsverlag, 2001.

Reed, David. "Rethinking John's Social Setting: Hidden Transcript, Anti-language, and the Negotiation of the Empire." *BTB* 36 (2006) 93–106.

Richardson, Peter. "An Architectural Case for Synagogue as Associations." In *The Ancient Synagogue: From its Origins until 200 C.E.*, edited by Olsson Birger and Magnus Zetterholm, 90–117. Stockholm: Almqvist & Wiksell, 2003.

Riesner, Rainer. *Paul's Early Period: Chronology, Mission Strategy, Theology*. Grand Rapids: Eerdmans 1998.

Robinson, Donald W. B. "The Priesthood of Paul in the Gospel of Hope." In *Reconciliation and Hope: Essays Presented to Leon Morris on his 60th Birthday*, edited by Robert Banks, 231–45. Exeter, UK: Paternoster, 1974.

Rock, Ian E. "Another Reason for Romans: A Pastoral Response to Augustan Imperial Theology: Paul's Use of the Song of Moses in Romans 9–11 and 14–15." In *Reading Paul in Context: Explorations in Identity Formation, Festschrift in Honour*

Bibliography

of Willam S Campbell, edited by Kathy Ehrensperger and J. Brian Tucker, 74–89. London: T. & T. Clark, 2010.

————. "Paul's Letter to the Romans and Roman Imperialism." PhD Dissertation submitted to the University of Wales, Lampeter, UK, 2004.

————. *Paul's Letter to the Romans and Roman Imperialism: An Ideological Analysis of the Exordium (Romans 1:1–17)*. Eugene, OR: Pickwick, 2012.

Roetzel, Calvin. "The Grammar of Election in Four Pauline Letters." In *Pauline Theology, Vol. II: 1 and 2 Corinthians*, edited by David M. Hay, 211–33. Minneapolis: Fortress 2003.

————. *The Letters of Paul: Conversations in Context*. Louisville: Westminster John Knox, 1990.

————. *Paul, the Man and the Myth*. Minneapolis: Fortress, 1998.

Rohrbaugh, Richard L. "Ethnocentricism and Historical Questions about Jesus." In *Jesus and the Gospels*, edited by Wolfgang Stegemann et al., 27–44. Minneapolis: Fortress, 2002.

————. editor. *The Social Sciences and the New Testament Interpretation*. Peabody, MA: Hendrickson, 1996.

Rosner, Brian. *Scripture and Ethics: A Study of 1 Corinthians 5–7*. Leiden: Brill, 1994.

Rowland, Christopher. *Christian Origins: An Account of the Setting and Character of the Most Important Messianic Sect of Judaism*. 2nd ed. London: Pilgrim, 2002.

————. *The Open Heaven: A Study of Apocalyptic in Judaism and Early Christianity*. 1983. Reprint. Eugene, OR: Wipf and Stock, 2002.

Runesson, Anders. "Inventing Christian Identity." In *Exploring Early Christian Identity*, edited by Bengt Holmberg, 59–92. WUNT 226. Tübingen: Mohr Siebeck, 2008.

————. "Persian Imperial Politics, the Beginnings of Public Torah Reading and the Origins of the Synagogue." In *The Ancient Synagogue: From its Origins until 200 C.E.,* edited by Olsson Birger and Magnus Zetterholm, 63–89. Stockholm: Almqvist & Wiksell, 2003.

Rutgers, Leonard V. *The Hidden Heritage of Diaspora Judaism*. Leuven: Peeters, 1998.

————. "Rome's Policy towards the Jews." In *Judaism and Christianity in First-Century Rome*, edited by Karl P. Donfried and Peter Richardson, 93–116. Grand Rapids: Eerdmans, 1998.

Sabin, Marie N. "Reading Mark 4 as Midrash." *JSNT* 45 (1992) 3–26.

Sacks, Jonathan. *The Dignity of Difference: How to Avoid the Clash of Civilizations*. London, New York: Continuum, 2002.

Sampley, J. Paul, editor. *Paul in the Greco-Roman World: A Handbook*. Harrisburg, PA: Trinity, 2003.

————. "The Weak and the Strong: Paul's Careful and Crafty Rhetorical Strategy in Romans 14:1—15:13." In *The Social World of the First Urban Christians: Studies on Honour of Wayne A. Meeks,* edited by White L. Michael and O. Larry Yarbrough, 40–52. Minneapolis: Fortress, 1994.

Sanders, E. P. "Patterns of Religion in Paul and Rabbinic Judaism: A Holistic Method of Comparison." *HTR* 66 (1973) 455–78.

————. *Paul and Palestinian Judaism: A Comparison of Patterns of Religion*. Philadelphia: Fortress, 1977.

————. *Paul, the Law, and the Jewish People*. Philadelphia: Fortress, 1983.

Sanders, Jack T. *Schismatics, Sectarians, Dissidents, Deviants: The First One Hundred Years of Jewish-Christian Relations*. Valley Forge, PA: Trinity, 1993.

Bibliography

Schäfer, Peter. *Judeophobia: Attitudes Toward the Jews in the Ancient World*. Cambridge: Harvard University Press, 1997.

Schaller, Bernd. "Christus, der Diener der Beschneidung . . . auf ihn werden die Völker hoffen. Zu Charakter und Funktion der Schriftzitate in Röm. 15:7–13." In *Das Gesetz im Frühen Judentum und im Neuen Testament. Festschrift für Christoph Burchard zum 75 Geburtstag*, edited by Dieter Sänger und Matthias Konradt, 261–85. Fribourg: Vandenhoeck & Ruprecht, 2006.

Schelke, Karl H. *Paulus, Lehrer der Väter: Die altkirchliche Auslegung von Römer 1–11*. Düsseldorf: Patmos, 1956.

Schiffmann, Lawrence H. *Who Was a Jew? Rabbinic and Halakhic Perspectives on the Jewish-Christian Schism*. Hoboken, NJ: Ktav, 1985.

Schlatter, Adolf. *Romans: The Righteousness of God*. Translated by Siegfried S. Schatzmann. Peabody, MA: Hendrickson, 1995.

Schmithals, Walter. "The Corpus Paulinum and Gnosis." In *The New Testament and Gnosis*, edited by A. Logan and Alexander Wedderburn, 107–24. Edinburgh: T. & T. Clark, 1983.

———. *The Office of an Apostle*. Translated by John E. Steely. Nashville: Abingdon, 1973.

———. *Paul and the Gnostics*. Translated by J. Steely. Nashville: Abingdon, 1972.

Schuele, Andreas. "Theology as Witness: Gerhard von Rad's Contribution to the Study of Old Testament Theology." *Int* 62 (2008) 256–67.

Schütz, John H. *Paul and the Anatomy of Apostolic Authority*. 1975. Reprint. Louisville: Westminster John Knox, 2007.

Schwartz, Seth. *Imperialism and Jewish Society, 200 BC to 640 CE*. Princeton: Princeton University Press, 2001.

Schweitzer, Albert. *Die Mystik des Apostels Paulus*. 1930. Reprint. Tübingen: Mohr, 1981.

———. *Paul and His Interpreters: A Critical History*. New York: Macmillan, 1951.

Scott, James M. *Paul and the Nations: The Old Testament and Jewish Background of Paul's Mission to the Nations with Special Reference to the Destination of Galatians*. WUNT 84. Tübingen: Mohr Siebeck, 1995.

Scroggs, Robin. "Paul as Rhetorician: Two Homilies in Romans 1–11." In *Jews, Greeks and Barbarians: Religious Cultures in Late Antiquity: Essays in Honour of W. D. Davies*, edited by Robert Hamerton-Kelly and Robin Scroggs, 271–98. Leiden: Brill, 1976.

Segal, Alan F. *Paul the Convert: The Apostolate and Apostasy of Saul the Pharisee*. New Haven: Yale University Press, 1990.

———. "Paul's Experience and Romans 9–11." In *The Princeton Seminary Bulletin*, Supplementary Issue, No. 1: The Church and Israel: Romans 9–11 (1995) 56–70.

Shkul, Minna. "Religious Identity and the Power of Naming." Paper presented at the Pauline Epistles Section, SBL/AAR Annual Meeting, Philadelphia, 2005.

Siker, John S. *Disinheriting the Jews: Abraham in Early Christian Controversy*. Louisville: Westminster John Knox, 1991.

Slingerland, Dixon H. *Claudian Policymaking and the Early Imperial Repression of Judaism at Rome*. Atlanta: Scholars, 1997.

Smallwood, E. Mary. *The Jews under Roman Rule*. Leiden: Brill, 1981.

Smith, J. A. *The Marks of an Apostle: Deconstruction, Philippians, and Problematizing Pauline Theology*. Atlanta: Society of Biblical Literature, 2005.

Bibliography

Soderlund, Sven K., and N. T. Wright, editors. *Romans and the People of God: Essays in Honor of Gordon D. Fee*. Grand Rapids: Eerdmans, 1999.

Soulen, R. Kendall. *The God of Israel and Christian Theology*. Minneapolis: Fortress, 1996.

Spilsbury, Paul. *The Image of the Jew in Flavius Josephus' Paraphrase of the Bible*. Texte und Studien zum AntikenJudentum, 69. Tübingen: Mohr Siebeck, 1998.

Standhartinger, Angela. "'Join in imitating me' (Philippians 3:17): Towards an Interpretation of Philippians 3." *NTS* 54 (2008) 417–35.

Stanley, Christopher D. *Arguing with Scripture: The Rhetoric of Quotations in the Letters of Paul*. London: T. & T. Clark, 2003.

———. *Paul and the Language of Scripture: Citation Technique in Pauline Epistles and Contemporary Literature*. Cambridge: Cambridge University Press, 1992.

———. "Paul the Ethnic Hybrid? Postcolonial Perspectives on Paul's Ethnic Categorizations." In *The Colonized Apostle: Paul through Post-colonial Eyes*, edited by Christopher D. Stanley, 110–26. Minneapolis: Fortress, 2011.

Stanton, Graham N., and G. G. Strousma, editors. *Tolerance and Intolerance in Early Judaism and Christianity*. Cambridge: Cambridge University Press, 1998.

Stark, Rodney. *The Rise of Christianity: A Sociologist Reconsiders History*. Princeton: Princeton University Press, 1996.

Stegemann, Ekkehard W. "The Contextual Ethics of Jesus." In *The Social Setting of Jesus and the Gospels*, edited by Stegemann Wolfgang et al., 45–61. Minneapolis: Fortress, 2002.

———. *The Jesus Movement: A Social History of Its First Century*. Edinburgh: T. & T. Clark, 1999.

———. *Paulus und die Welt: Aufsätze*. Edited by Christina Tuor and Peter Wick. Zürich: Theologischer Verlag, 2005.

———. "Reconciliation and Pauline Eschatology in Romans." Paper read at the Romans through History and Cultures Group, SBL Annual Meeting, New Orleans, 2009.

———. "Wird εὐαγγέλιον bei Paulus auch als nomen actionis gebraucht?" In *Der Römerbrief: Brennpunkte der Rezeption, Aufsätze*, edited by Christina Tuor and Peter Wick, 141–67. Zürich: Theologischer Verlag, 2012.

Stegemann, Wolfgang et al., editors. *The Social Setting of Jesus and the Gospels*. Minneapolis: Fortress, 2002.

Stendahl, Krister. *Final Account: Paul's Letter to the Romans*. Minneapolis: Fortress, 1995.

———. "In No Other Name, Christian Witness and the Jewish People." *The Report of a Consultation Held under the Auspices of the Lutheran World Federation*, edited by A. Sovik, Oslo, August 1975. Geneva: Lutheran World Federation, 1976.

———. *Paul among Jews and Gentiles and Other Essays*. Philadelphia: Fortress, 1976.

Stowers, Stanley K. *The Diatribe and Paul's Letter to the Romans*. SBLDS 57. Chico, CA: Scholars, 1981.

———. "Ἐκ πίστεως and διὰ τῆς πίστεως in Rom 3:30." *JBL* 108 (1989) 665–74.

———. "Paul's Dialogue with a Fellow-Jew in Romans 3:1–9." *CBQ* 46 (1984) 707–22.

———. *A Rereading of Romans: Justice, Jews and Gentiles*. New Haven: Yale University Press, 1994.

Strecker, Christian. "Fides-Pistis-Glaube: Kontexte und Konturen der 'Annahme' bei Paulus." In *Lutherische und Neue Paulusperserpektive*, edited by Michael Bachmann, 32–41. Tübingen: Mohr Siebeck, 2005.

Bibliography

Stuhlmacher, Peter. "Der Abfassungszweck des Römerbriefes." *ZNW* 77 (1986) 180–93.

———. "The Theme of Romans." *Australian Biblical Review* 361 (1988) 31–44.

Sturm, Richard E. "Defining the Word 'Apocalyptic': A Problem in Biblical Criticism." In *Apocalyptic and the New Testament: Essays in Honor of J. Louis Martyn*, edited by Joel Marcus and Marion L. Soards, 17–47. Sheffield, UK: Sheffield Academic Press, 1989.

Sumney, Jerry L. *Identifying Paul's Opponents*. Sheffield, UK: Sheffield Academic, 1990.

———. *Philippians: A Greek Student's Intermediate Reader*. Peabody, MA: Hendrickson, 2007.

———. *"Servants of Satan," "False Brothers," and Other Opponents of Paul*. Sheffield, UK: Sheffield Academic, 1999.

Talbert, Charles H. "Paul, Judaism, and the Revisionists." *CBQ* 63 (2001) 1–22.

Tanner, Kathryn. *Theories of Culture: A New Agenda for Theology*. Minneapolis: Fortress, 1997.

Taubes, Jacob. *The Political Theology of Paul*. Translated by D. Hollander. Stanford, CA: Stanford University Press, 2004.

Taylor, Miriam S. *Antijudaism and Early Christianity: A Critique of the Scholarly Consensus*. Leiden: Brill, 1995.

Taylor, Nicholas H. *Paul, Antioch, and Jerusalem: A Study in Relationships in Early Judaism and Christianity*. JSNTSS 66. Sheffield, UK: Sheffield Academic, 1992.

———. "The Social Nature of Conversion in the Early Christian World." In *Modelling Early Christianity: Social-Scientific Studies of the New Testament in Its Context*, edited by Philip F. Esler, 128–36. London: Routledge, 1995.

Taylor, Nicholas T., and Charles A. Wanamaker. "The Construction of Christian Identity." Paper presented at the SNTS Annual Meeting in Pretoria, 1999.

Tajfel, Henri. "Social Categorization, Social Identity and Social Comparison." In *Differentiation between Social Groups: Studies in the Social Psychology of Intergroup Relations*, edited by Henri Tajfel, 61–76. London: Academic, 1978.

Tellbe, Mikael. *Paul between Synagogue and State: Christians, Jews and Civic Authorities in 1 Thessalonians, Romans, and Philippians*. Stockholm: Almquist & Wiksell, 2001.

Theissen, Gerd. *Social Reality and the Early Christians: Theology, Ethics, and the World of the New Testament*. Translated by M. Kohl. Minneapolis: Fortress, 1992.

———. *The Social Setting of Pauline Christianity: Essays on Corinth*. Philadelphia: Fortress, 1982.

Thielman, Frank. "Unexpected Mercy: Echoes of a Biblical Motif in Romans 9–11." *SJT* 47 (1994) 169–81.

Thiselton, Anthony C. *1 Corinthians: A Shorter Exegetical and Pastoral Commentary*. Grand Rapids: Eerdmans, 2006.

———. *The First Epistle to the Corinthians*. NIGTC. Grand Rapids: Eerdmans, 2000.

Thomas Owen C. "Recent Thought on Divine Agency." In *Studies Inspired by the Philosophical Theology of Austin Farrer*, edited by Brian Hebblethwaite and Edward H. Henderson, 35–50. Edinburgh: T. & T. Clark, 2000.

Thompson, Michael. *Clothed with Christ: The Example and Teaching of Jesus in Romans 12.1—15.13*. Sheffield, UK: Sheffield Academic, 1991.

Thorsteinsson, Runar M. *Paul's Interlocutor in Romans 2: Function and Identity in the Context of Ancient Epistleography*. Stockholm: Almqvist & Wiksell, 2003.

Bibliography

Tomson, Peter J. *Paul and the Jewish Law: Halakha in the Letters of the Apostle to the Gentiles.* Minneapolis : Fortress, 1990.

————. "Paul's Jewish Background in View of His Law-Teaching in 1 Corinthians 7." In *Paul and the Mosaic Law: The Third Durham-Tübingen Research Symposium on Earliest Christianity and Judaism,* edited by James D. G. Dunn, 251–70. Tübingen: Mohr Siebeck, 1996.

Tomson, Peter J., and Doris L. Lambers-Petry, editors. *The Image of the Judeo-Christians in Ancient Jewish and Christian Literature.* WUNT 158. Tübingen: Mohr Siebeck, 2001.

Travisano, Richard V. "Alternation and Conversion as Qualitatively Different Transformations." In *Social Psychology through Symbolic Interaction,* edited by G. P. Stone and H. A. Fabedrman, 594–606. Waltham, MA: Ginn-Blaisdell, 1970.

Trebilco, Paul. *Early Christians in Ephesus from Paul to Ignatius.* Tübingen: Mohr Siebeck, 2004.

Tucker, J. Brian. *"Remain in Your Calling": Paul and the Continuation of Social Identities in 1 Corinthians.* Eugene, OR: Pickwick, 2011.

————. *"You Belong to Christ": Paul and the Formation of Social Identity in 1 Corinthians 1–4.* Eugene, OR: Pickwick, 2010.

Tutu, Desmond. *No Future without Forgiveness.* London: Rider, 1999.

Tyson, Joseph B. *Luke, Judaism and the Scholars: Critical Approaches to Luke-Acts.* Columbia, SC: University of South Carolina Press, 1999.

Volf, Miroslav. "Exclusion and Embrace: Theological Reflections in the Wake of Ethnic Cleansing." *Journal of Ecumenical Studies* 29 (1992) 230–48.

————. *Exclusion and Embrace. A Theological Exploration of Identity, Otherness and Reconciliation.* Nashville :Abingdon, 1996.

————. "Forgiveness, Reconciliation and Justice: A Theological Contribution to a More Peaceful Environment." *Millenium: Journal of International Sudies* 29 (2000) 861–77.

Wagner, J. Ross. *Heralds of Good News: Isaiah and Paul "In Concert" in the Letter to the Romans.* Leiden: Brill, 2002.

Walters, James C. *Ethnic Issues in Paul's Letter to the Romans: Changing Self Definitions in Earliest Roman Christianity.* Valley Forge, PA: Trinity, 1993.

————. "The Impact of the Romans on Jewish-Christian Relations." In *Judaism and Christianity in First-Century Rome,* edited by Karl P. Donfried and Peter Richardson, 175–95. Grand Rapids: Eerdmans, 1998.

Wan, Sze-kar. "Collection for the Saints as an Anticolonial Act: Implications of Paul's Ethnic Reconstruction." In *Paul and Politics: Ekklesia, Israel, Imperium, Interpretation. Essays in Honour of Krister Stendahl,* edited by Richard A. Horsley, 191–215. Harrisburg, PA: Trinity, 2000.

Watson, Francis W. *Paul, Judaism and the Gentiles. A Sociological Approach.* SNTSMS 56. Cambridge: Cambridge University Press, 1986.

————. "The Scope of Hermeneutics." In *The Cambridge Companion to Christian Doctrine,* edited by Colin Gunton, 65–80. Cambridge: Cambridge University Press, 1997.

Watt, J. "Language Pragmatism in a Multilingual Religious Community." In *The Ancient Synagogue from its Origins until 200 CE,* edited by Birger Olsson and Magnus Zetterholm, 277–97. Stockholm: Almqvist & Wiksell, 2003.

Bibliography

Weber, Ferdinand. *Jüdische Theologie auf Grund des Talmud und verwandter Schriften.* 2nd ed. Leipzig: Dörffling & Franke, 1897.

Weber, Max. *Economy and Society: An Outline of Interpretative Sociology.* Vol. 1. Edited by G. Roth and C. Wittich. New York: Bedminster, 1968.

Wedderburn, Alexander G. M. *The Reasons for Romans.* Edinburgh: T. & T. Clark, 1988.

Westerholm, Stephen. *Israel's Law and the Church's Faith: Paul and His Recent Interpreters.* Grand Rapids: Eerdmans, 1988.

White, L. Michael, and O. Larry Yarbrough, editors. *The Social World of the First Urban Christians: Studies in Honor of Wayne A. Meeks.* Minneapolis: Fortress, 1994.

Wick, Peter. *Die Urchristlichen Gottesdienste: Entstehung und Entwicklung im Rahmen der Frühjüdischen Tempel-, Synagogen- und Haus-Frömmigkeit.* Stuttgart: Kohlhammer, 2002.

Wiefel, Walter. "The Jewish Community of Ancient Rome and the Origins of Christianity." In *The Romans Debate,* edited by Karl P. Donfried, 2nd ed., 75–99. Peabody, MA: Hendrickson, 1991.

Wilckens, Ulrich. *Der Brief an die Römer.* 3 vols. Neukirchen Vluyn: Neukirchener, 1978, 1980, 1982.

Williams, Peter J. et al., editors. *The New Testament in Its First Century Setting: Essays on Context and Background in Honour of B. W. Winter on His 65th Birthday.* Grand Rapids: Eerdmans, 2004.

Wilson, Bryan. *Religious Sects: A Sociological Study.* London: Weidenfeld and Nicholson, 1970.

Wilson, Stephen G., editor. *Anti-Judaism in Early Christianity,* vol 2: *Separation and Polemic.* Waterloo, ON: Wilfred Laurier University Press, 1986.

———. "Gentile Judaizers." *NTS* 38 (1992) 605–16.

———. *Related Strangers: Jews and Christians 70–170 CE.* Minneapolis: Fortress, 1996.

Wolff, Christian. "True Apostolic Knowledge of Christ: Exegetical Reflections on 2 Cor. 5:14ff." In *Paul and Jesus: Collected Essays,* edited by Alexander J. M. Wedderburn, 81–98. JSNTS 37. Sheffield, UK: Sheffield Academic, 1989.

Wright, N. T. *The New Testament and the People of God.* London: SPCK, 1992.

———. "Paul's Gospel and Caesar's Empire." In *Paul and Politics: Ekklesia, Israel, Imperium, Interpretation: Essays in Honour of Krister Stendahl,* edited by Richard A. Horsley, 160–83. Harrisburg, PA: Trinity, 2000.

———. "Romans and the Theology of Paul." In *Pauline Theology, Vol. 3: Romans,* edited by David M. Hay and E. Elisabeth Johnson, 30–67. Minneapolis: Fortress, 1995.

Wyschogrod, Michael. *Abraham's Promise: Judaism and Jewish-Christian Relations.* Edited by R. Kendall Soulen. Grand Rapids: Eerdmans, 2004.

Yee Tet-Lim, N. *Jews, Gentiles, and Ethnic Reconciliation: Paul's Jewish Identity and Ephesians.* SNTSMS 130. Cambridge: Cambridge University Press, 2005.

Young, Iris M. "The Ideal of Community and the Politics of Difference." In *Feminism/Postmodernism,* edited by Linda Nicholson, 300–23. New York: Routledge, 1990.

———. *Justice and the Politics of Difference.* Princeton: Princeton University Press, 1990.

Zetterholm, Magnus. *The Formation of Christianity at Antioch: A Social-Scientific Approach to the Separation between Judaism and Christianity.* London: Routledge, 2002.

———. "Jews, Christians and Gentiles: Rethinking the Categorisation within the Early Jesus Movement." In *Reading Paul in Context: Explorations in Identity Formation.*

Bibliography

Essays in Honour of William S. Campbell, edited by J. Brian Tucker and Kathy Ehrensperger, 242–54. London: T. & T. Clark, 2010.

Ziesler, John. *Paul's Letter to the Romans.* London: SCM, 1989.

Zoccali, Christopher. *Whom God Has Called: The Relationship of the Church and Israel, 1920 to the Present.* Eugene, OR: Pickwick, 2010.

Scriptural Passages

Modern Authors